RESEARCH HANDBOOK ON ECONOMIC MODELS OF LAW

RESEARCH HANDBOOKS IN LAW AND ECONOMICS

Series Editors: Richard A. Posner, *Judge, United States Court of Appeals for the Seventh Circuit and Senior Lecturer, University of Chicago Law School, USA* and Francesco Parisi, *Oppenheimer Wolff and Donnelly Professor of Law, University of Minnesota, USA and Professor of Economics, University of Bologna, Italy*

Edited by highly distinguished scholars, the landmark reference works in this series offer advanced treatments of specific topics that reflect the state-of-the-art of research in law and economics, while also expanding the law and economics debate. Each volume's accessible yet sophisticated contributions from top international researchers make it an indispensable resource for students and scholars alike.

Titles in this series include:

Research Handbook on Economic Models of Law

Edited by

Thomas J. Miceli

University of Connecticut, USA

Matthew J. Baker

Hunter College, CUNY, USA

RESEARCH HANDBOOKS IN LAW AND ECONOMICS

Edward Elgar
Cheltenham, UK • Northampton, MA, USA

Published by
Edward Elgar Publishing Limited
The Lypiatts
15 Lansdown Road
Cheltenham
Glos GL50 2JA
UK

Edward Elgar Publishing, Inc.
William Pratt House
9 Dewey Court
Northampton
Massachusetts 01060
USA

A catalogue record for this book
is available from the British Library

Library of Congress Control Number: 2013946838

This book is available electronically in the ElgarOnline.com
Law Subject Collection, E-ISBN 978 1 78100 015 1

ISBN 978 1 78100 014 4 (cased)

Typeset by Servis Filmsetting Ltd, Stockport, Cheshire
Printed and bound in Great Britain by T.J. International Ltd, Padstow

Contents

Contributors

Luca Anderlini, Professor of Economics, Georgetown University, USA.

Matthew J. Baker, Associate Professor of Economics, Hunter College and The Graduate Center, CUNY, USA.

Florian Baumann, Professor of Economics, Düsseldorf Institute for Competition Economics, Germany.

Jef De Mot, Postdoctoral Researcher, Center for Advanced Studies in Law and Economics, University of Ghent, Belgium.

Ben Depoorter, Professor of Law and Roger E. Traynor Research Chair, University of California, Hastings, USA.

Dhammika Dharmapala, Professor of Law, University of Illinois College of Law, USA.

Winand Emons, Professor of Economics, Universität Bern, Switzerland.

Leonardo Felli, Professor of Economics, London School of Economics, UK.

Claude Fluet, Professor of Economics, Université du Quebec à Montréal, Canada.

Tim Friehe, Professor of Law and Economics, University of Bonn, Germany.

Nuno Garoupa, Professor of Law and H. Ross and Helen Workman Research Scholar, University of Illinois College of Law, USA.

Zachary Grossman, Professor of Economics, University of California, Santa Barbara, USA.

Sergei Izmalkov, Professor of Economics, The New Economic School, Moscow, Russia.

Claudia M. Landeo, Professor of Economics, University of Alberta, Canada.

Richard McAdams, Bernard D. Meltzer Professor of Law, University of Chicago Law School, USA.

Thomas J. Miceli, Professor of Economics, University of Connecticut, USA.

Maxim Nikitin, Professor of Economics, International College of Economics and Finance, State University—The Higher School of Economics, Moscow, Russia.

Jonathan Pincus, Visiting Professor of Economics, University of Adelaide, Australia.

Andrew Postlewaite, Professor of Economics, University of Pennsylvania, USA.

Rebecca Rabon, M.A. Candidate, Department of Economics, University of Connecticut, USA.

Giovanni B. Ramello, Professor of Economics, Università del Piemonte Orientale Amedeo Avogadro, Italy.

Kathleen Segerson, Philip E. Austin Alumni Distinguished Professor of Economics, University of Connecticut, USA.

Perry Shapiro, Professor of Economics Emeritus, University of California, Santa Barbara, USA.

Tsvetan Tsvetanov, Postdoctoral Associate, School of Forestry and Environmental Studies, Yale University, USA.

Thomas S. Ulen, Swanlund Chair Emeritus, University of Illinois, and Professor Emeritus of Law, University of Illinois College of Law, USA.

Niklas J. Westelius, Professor of Economics, Hunter College and The Graduate Center, CUNY, USA.

Abraham L. Wickelgren, Bernard J. Ward Professor of Law, University of Texas, Austin, USA.

Introduction
Thomas J. Miceli and Matthew J. Baker

Economic analysis differs from other approaches to the study of law most notably in its use of formal models to describe human behavior, and in particular, how people will respond to different legal rules. The usefulness of models is that they allow the analyst to focus on answering a specific question with respect to the particular rule under scrutiny, and to derive a clear understanding of what its effects will be, much as a controlled laboratory experiment allows a researcher to isolate a specific physical or chemical effect. Of course, there is a necessary sacrifice of realism when undertaking a modeling exercise of this sort, but the hope is that those factors that are excluded from the model are peripheral to the question at hand, and so can be safely ignored, at least as a first approximation. The most important challenge in developing a 'good' economic model, of law or any social phenomenon, is therefore the decision of what factors to exclude. This is the role of the model's assumptions, and as any economist knows, debates about the quality of a model, and the validity of its conclusions, generally center on the appropriateness of its assumptions. Once the assumptions are accepted, the results usually follow logically from the structure of the model.

One of the most important (and controversial) assumptions underlying virtually all economic models of law is that individuals behave in a rational manner, meaning that they pursue their self-interests, however those interests are defined in the model. Rationality does not mean that individuals are perfectly informed about the consequences of their actions – this would be an untenable assumption in most legal or economic settings – but rather that they do the best they can in the presence of whatever constraints they face, whether those constraints take the form of limited resources, information, or knowledge. Some critics of the economic approach to law doubt that people behave in this way outside of the market arena, and so they question the insights that an economic model based on rationality can yield about how people respond to law. But the economic approach views legal rules as acting *like market prices* to guide peoples' behavior in certain, hopefully desirable, ways. As one illustration, consider that the widely accepted notion of using harsher criminal laws to deter anti-social behavior reflects a decidedly economic perspective.

The history of the economic analysis of law dates back at least to the criminal law theories of Bentham and Beccaria, which reflected the view that threatened legal sanctions can be used to discourage socially undesirable conduct. Surprisingly, this view of law as creating incentives for behavior seems not to have been resurrected again until the 1960s with the work of Coase (1960), Calabresi (1961), and Becker (1968), among others.[1] Much of this early work (excepting, of course, Becker) was, by today's standards, rather informal in that it did not employ mathematical models. Still, the insights it offered set that stage for the next generation of formal economic analysis.

Ironically, the first use of mathematics to model law was apparently by a judge, Learned Hand, in the well-known tort case of *U.S. v. Carroll Towing*.[2] In that case, Judge Hand put forth his famous 'Hand rule' for determining negligence, which says that an injurer should be found negligent if $B<PL$, where B is the burden (or cost) of care sufficient to eliminate the risk of an accident, P is the probability of an accident if no care is taken, and L is the loss from the accident. This simple formula, when properly interpreted in its marginal form (Posner, 1972), turns out to give exactly the right answer regarding when care is efficient.[3] This was formally demonstrated by Brown (1973), whose 'model of precaution' has become the standard framework for examining the efficiency of various liability rules.[4]

One of the most important insights that emerged from Brown's formalization is that a negligence rule can simultaneously induce both injurers and victims to invest in efficient precaution. Establishing this result, which provides an economic justification for the predominance of negligence law throughout the twentieth century (and beyond), likely would not have been possible without formal modeling because it required the derivation of a Nash equilibrium in a two person, non-cooperative game setting. Cooter (1985) went on to show that the insights from the model of precaution can be extended beyond tort law to illuminate doctrines in contracts and property as well. Thus, the simple approach first employed by Judge Hand to decide a specific case in tort law has been used by economists to develop a coherent framework for understanding large areas of the common law, thereby illustrating the unifying power of economic models.

This unity extends to criminal law as well, as illustrated by Becker's (1968) formalization of the ideas of Bentham and Beccaria. After all, criminal law, like tort law, is primarily about preventing unwanted harm, and to that end Becker interpreted criminal sanctions, whether in the form of fines or prison, as functioning like liability to attach a 'price' to harmful behavior. In particular, if H is the harm caused by a criminal act, then optimal deterrence requires that the expected sanction, PS, be set equal to

H (or *PS*=*H*), where *P* is the probability that the offender is caught and convicted, and *S* is the sanction. One of the central insights arising from this perspective is that it does not matter whether the harm is intentionally or accidentally imposed; as long as the sanction (or liability) is appropriately set, the would-be criminal (injurer) will optimally refrain from the harmful act. (In this sense, there is no obvious theoretical reason to separate criminal and tort law, an insight that has spawned a large literature – see, for example, Friedman (2000, Chapter 18).) Nor does it matter if the sanction is imposed with certainty; as long as it is appropriately scaled to reflect uncertain enforcement – that is, as long as the *expected sanction* is properly set – it will have the desired effect on behavior. (In particular, the optimal sanction is given by *S*=*H*/*P*.) Of course, the modern economic theory of crime has extended this analysis in many ways (see, for example, Polinsky and Shavell, 2007), but the basic insights follow from this simple formulation.

Most recent exercises in economic modeling of law have been to apply more rigorous methods such as game theory to better understand the role of strategic behavior and the impact of imperfect and asymmetric information (see Baird, Gertner, and Picker (1994)). Many of the chapters in this volume reflect that effort. Another emerging area of research is the application of insights from behavioral economics to law (Sunstein, 2000). This is still a developing area, the fruits of which have yet to be fully harvested, but the two chapters in this volume that take this perspective (Segerson and Tsvetanov; Landeo, Nitkin, and Izmalkov) suggest that many new insights may be learned from it.

The chapters in this volume, which were specially commissioned from leading law-and-economics scholars working at the cutting edge of research, display a wide range of both topics and methodologies. As editors, we made no special efforts to achieve this breadth – it was a natural consequence of the current state of the field. This reflects the continuing vitality of the economic approach to law and suggests that, although the field has reached a level of maturity after more than five decades, there is still much to be done. Our hope is that this volume provides inspiration for the next generation of theorists.

OVERVIEW OF THE BOOK

The variety of topics and methods, while welcome, posed something of a challenge in terms of organizing the chapters. We considered classifying the papers by subject matter, by methodology, by modeling technique used, or by a combination of those things. Table I.1 presents the results of

Table I.1 Papers and topics in the volume

Authors	Title (abbreviated)	Property	Tort	Contract	Procedure	Crime	Information	Decision-Making
		Traditional Classification					Microeconomic Model Content:	
Grossman, Pincus, and Shapiro	Land assemblage: efficiency and equity	X						
Garoupa and Ulen	Activity levels in tort liability and regulation		X					
Miceli, Rabon, and Segerson	Liability vs regulation for product-related risks		X				X	X
Segerson and Tsvetanov	Regulation vs liability: a behavioral perspective		X				X	X
Baumann and Friehe	Strict liability when victims choose asset value		X					
Landeo, Nikitin, and Izmalkov	Incentives for care, litigation and tort reform		X		X		X	X
De Mot and Depoorter	Tort standards and legal expenditures		X		X			
De Mot	Litigation success functions				X			
Emons and Fluet	The optimal amount of distorted testimony				X		X	

Author	Title						
Dharmapala, Garoupa, and McAdams	Do exclusionary rules convict the innocent?			X		X	
Dharmapala and Miceli	Search, seizure, and false (?) arrest				X	X	X
Baker and Westelius	Crime, expectations, and the deterrence hypothesis				X	X	X
Anderlini, Felli, and Postlewaite	Active courts and menu contracts		X			X	
Wickelgren	Affirmative action with historical discrimination			X		X	
Ramello	The multi-layered action of trademark	X				X	

some of these classification experiments. The table first indicates how each paper in the volume relates to traditional subject areas in law: property, torts, contracts, procedure, and crime. From the breakdown in the table, it is apparent that all branches of law and economics are well-represented in the volume.

Table I.1 also includes information about the methodology proposed in the paper. The column marked 'Information' records whether or not there is a significant informational aspect to the paper (i.e., hidden information about type or action), while the column heading marked 'Decision-making' indicates whether the paper contains some extension or modification of the usual assumption that decision-makers act rationally. Beginning in the 1970s, and culminating with the 2001 Nobel Prize awarded to George Akerlof, Michael Spence, and Joseph Stiglitz, the modeling and analysis of asymmetric information has become a fundamental component of nearly all fields of study in economics. A parallel development has been concerned with models of decision-making and the implications of the rationality axiom (reflected by the 2002 Nobel Prize awarded to Daniel Kahneman and Vernon Smith). The 'information' and 'decision-making' columns in Table I.1 indicate that these new and important aspects of economic analysis have come to occupy prominent places in the economic analysis of the law as well.

Summary of Individual Chapters

The first chapter by Grossman, Pincus, and Shapiro examines the problem of land assembly for the purposes of undertaking a large-scale redevelopment project. The common practice in such cases is for the government to use its eminent domain power to facilitate the acquisition as part of a private-public partnership. The drawbacks of this approach, however, are twofold: first, there is no guarantee that the transfer of land will be efficient, and second, owners may receive less than their true valuation since compensation is generally tied to the market value of acquired properties. Both problems stem from the lack of a market test for individual transfers, coupled with the inability of government to observe owners' true valuations. This chapter examines two alternative auction-based mechanisms aimed at overcoming the failings associated with this common practice. While both achieve the objective of inducing owners to truthfully reveal their valuations (i.e., both are incentive compatible), neither is capable of simultaneously achieving efficiency and full compensation (fairness): one guarantees full compensation but forgoes some efficient projects, while the other guarantees efficiency but sacrifices fairness. The authors compare the proposed mechanisms with the common practice (eminent domain with market value compensation) using a modified Kaldor-Hicks welfare criterion adapted to account for fairness concerns.

The chapter by Garoupa and Ulen is the first of several on tort (accident) law. It examines the relationship between so-called 'activity levels' and tort law. Standard economic models of accidents dating back to Shavell (1980) have distinguished between care and activity as alternative determinants of accident risk, where 'care' typically describes those actions that reduce the risk of a given venture, while 'activity' describes how intensively one engages in that venture. In the case of driving, for example, how fast one drives is a measure of care, and how many miles one drives is a measure of activity, where accident risk is assumed to be monotonic in both (decreasing in care and increasing in activity). One of the authors' key points, however, is that accident risk is not necessarily monotonically increasing in activity, as when learning or other sources of non-convexity are present. A second point is that the distinction between care and activity is not always clear, and often amounts to simply defining care as those things that are included as part of negligence law and activity levels as those things that are not included, a definition that borders on tautology. A better definition is that care involves those actions that are verifiable by the court, while activity involves those actions that are not verifiable. Still, the authors argue that when activity levels are important determinants of accident risk, courts will often develop the ability to measure them for purposes of establishing due standards of behavior. And when courts cannot do this efficiently, the activity in question may be better controlled by regulation rather than tort law, anyway.

The next two chapters pick up on this theme of choosing between tort liability and safety regulation as alternative means for controlling risk. The chapter by Miceli, Rabon, and Segerson extends Shavell's (1984) seminal analysis of this choice by comparing liability and regulation in the context of product-related accidents when consumers possibly misperceive the risk of an accident. When consumers all suffer the same expected harm, liability is preferred to regulation because under liability, consumers are fully compensated and so misperceptions do not distort consumer purchase decisions, which are therefore efficient (given that the product price accurately signals risk). Under regulation, in contrast, consumers bear their own damages and so over- or underconsume the product based on their misperceptions. When consumers vary in their susceptibility to harm, however, liability is no longer efficient because it does not induce consumers to self-select in their purchase decisions. Thus, there is a trade-off between liability and regulation: specifically, regulation is preferred when consumers perceive risk fairly accurately, and liability is preferred when consumers substantially misperceive risk.

Segerson and Tsvetanov also compare liability and regulation for controlling risk, but their focus is on how insights from the emerging field of behavioral economics can inform the choice when injurers make care decisions that are inter-temporal (i.e., there is a time lag between the care choice and the realization of damages). This setting is especially important for many environmental risks such as hazardous waste disposal or toxic discharges where harm can arise years or decades after the risk first emerged. The specific behavioral issue that the authors consider is the 'temptation' people often display to indulge immediate opportunities for gratification at the expense of long-term consequences. In the context of accident avoidance, for example, this might lead some injurers to forgo current care choices that would otherwise result in socially desirable accident avoidance. They show that even if injurers expect to be held fully responsible for all future damages under strict liability, they will underinvest in care as a result of temptation. Regulation might be superior in this context because, by setting a standard that injurers must meet, it eliminates the temptation for injurers to choose sub-optimal care. An important contribution of this chapter is to highlight how insights from behavioral economics can inform debates in the field of law and economics, often overturning conventional wisdom derived from traditional (neo-classical) models.

The chapter by Baumann and Friehe examines the efficiency of strict liability when victims can choose the value of the asset at risk of being damaged. When victims vary in their valuation of the asset and expect to be fully compensated for the value of that asset in the event of an accident, they will make inefficient purchase decisions because they will not take account of the full social cost of the asset (which includes the possibility that it will be lost). In contrast, a rule that sets damages equal to the average of asset values (so-called damage averaging) will induce efficient victim decision-making while still giving injurers efficient incentives for accident avoidance. In other words, it induces efficient decisions by both injurers and victims. A potential problem with this scheme, however, is that it 'overcompensates' low-damage victims, and therefore may induce some victims to participate in the activity who should refrain from doing so from a social standpoint. The chapter describes the damage scheme that prevents this excessive entry, and shows that it may be second best.

The chapter by Landeo, Nikitin, and Izmalkov uses behavioral economics to study tort litigation, but their focus is how 'self-serving bias' – the belief by litigants that the court will favor their position – influences litigation and incentives for care. Although there is considerable experimental evidence for such a bias, little theoretical work exists on this issue, save the early 'differing perceptions' models of pre-trial bargaining by Landes (1971) and Gould (1973), which attributed trials to the existence of 'mutual optimism' by plaintiffs and defendants about the outcome of a trial. This chapter develops a sophisticated model of pretrial bargaining in the presence of asymmetric information and self-serving bias, thereby offering a hybrid of the differing perceptions and asymmetric information models of trials. In this context, the authors study the effects of tort reform policies aimed at capping non-economic damages and show that the purported benefits of those caps may not be realized in environments with biased litigants.

De Mot and Depoorter also develop a model of litigation in the context of tort law, but they use a traditional game-theoretic model to compare the costs of litigation under various forms of the negligence rule. Conventional wisdom holds that simple negligence is cheaper to litigate than comparative negligence because it involves fewer factual issues for the court to investigate (i.e., it need only consider the care of one party, not both). The current chapter shows that when litigation expenditures are endogenous, this may not be the case. In fact, the model compares simple, contributory, and comparative negligence, and derives the conditions under which each involves lower total litigation expenditures. The conclusions depend on specific elements of the case at hand, thus precluding general claims about costs under the various rules.

The results in the preceding chapter relied on the use of a particular 'success function' that determined the probability of victory at trial by a plaintiff or a defendant, based on their litigation efforts and other parameters. The chapter by De Mot studies in detail the characteristics of this function, called the 'ratio form' because it models the probability of each party's success as depending on the ratio of that party's expenditure to the total expenditure of the two parties (plaintiff and defendant). This is a popular formulation that has been widely used to study the economics of conflict (see, for example, Garfinkel and Skaperdas (2007)). The current chapter discusses the implications of this form for the outcome of litigation in particular, including a comparison of adversarial and inquisitorial systems. It also offers some empirical evidence in support of its predictions, and points out weaknesses.

The chapter by Emons and Fluet continues the analysis of the litigation process by examining the desirability of allowing parties to a legal dispute to present evidence to a judge regarding the value of the item in dispute (e.g., the magnitude of damages one party owes to the other). Testimony is costly and parties can misrepresent evidence in their favor, though it costs more to present erroneous evidence. The judge wishes to minimize a weighted sum of error and evidence costs, and decides whether to hear from one, both, or neither of the parties. (If he/she chooses one, he/she picks the more reliable one.) The results of the model characterize the judge's optimal strategy under two scenarios: when he/she can commit to an adjudication rule, and when he/she cannot commit. (The reason that he/she may not be able to commit is that the true value of the disputed variable can be inferred with certainty ex post from the parties' evidence.) When the judge can commit, all three scenarios may be optimal, depending on parameter values. When the judge cannot commit, it is more likely that he/she will hear from both or neither party.

The chapter by Dharmapala, Garoupa, and McAdams turns to criminal litigation and examines the impact of exclusionary rules in criminal cases. In particular, it asks whether these rules benefit guilty defendants, as is commonly assumed, or if their impact is more complex. For example, might the jury not infer the existence of excluded evidence that would be detrimental to the defendant, and hence implicitly lower the standard of proof for conviction? Such a response would harm truly innocent defendants by increasing their chances of being convicted. An even more sophisticated jury, however, would take account of the motives of prosecutors, who, if self-interested, might try to take advantage of the lower implicit standard of proof and bring indictments against innocent defendants who otherwise would not have been charged. A rational jury would anticipate this and would raise the standard of proof accordingly. Overall, the analysis in this paper shows that the impact of an exclusionary rule on trial outcomes is complex and therefore is not easily generalizable.

Dharmapala and Miceli continue in this vein by examining Fourth Amendment prohibitions on unreasonable searches and seizures in criminal investigations. The Supreme Court has interpreted this to require that police obtain a warrant prior to search and that illegally seized evidence be excluded from trial. A consensus has developed in the law and economics literature, however, that tort liability for police officers would be a superior means of deterring unreasonable searches. The authors argue that this conclusion depends on the assumption of truth-seeking police, and develop a game-theoretic model to compare the two remedies when some police officers ('bad' types) are willing to plant evidence in order to obtain convictions, while other police ('good' types) are not (where an officer's type is private information). They characterize the perfect Bayesian equilibria of the asymmetric-information game between the police and a court that seeks to minimize error costs in deciding whether to convict or acquit suspects. In this framework, they show that the exclusionary rule with a warrant requirement leads to superior outcomes (relative to tort liability) in terms of the truth-finding function of courts, because the warrant requirement can reduce the scope for 'bad' types of police to plant evidence.

The chapter by Baker and Westelius continues on the theme of criminal law, but turns to the actual commission decision by the criminal. The paper specifically re-examines the deterrence hypothesis, first developed in Becker (1968), that criminals are rational economic agents who respond to costs and benefits of committing crime. The authors extend the simple Becker model to account for the effect of future and past conditions on current criminal behavior. For example, because past crimes reduce an agent's job market prospects, current offenders will be more prone to commit crimes in the future, all else equal. Ultimately, the model predicts that current crime rates depend both on past crime and the expectation of future crime, as well as on enforcement variables. Using this model, the authors develop a novel procedure for estimating the effect of enforcement policies on crime rates and show that once expectations are accounted for, elasticities of crime with respect to enforcement variables are larger than have been previously estimated.

The chapter by Anderlini, Felli, and Postlewaite turns to contract law by examining a contractual environment in which two parties may profit from trading a good whose value is potentially increased by ex ante investment by the buyer prior to trade. The buyer, however, has private information about his type, which affects the value of trading different varieties of the good in question. The analysis incorporates litigation over disputes by showing that an 'active court,' defined to be one that can void certain contracts, can improve on welfare by eliminating an inefficient pooling equilibrium. The paper goes on to consider a situation in which the informed party (the buyer) can offer so-called 'menu contracts.' In this richer setting, the authors show that active courts can still improve on welfare by again eliminating inefficient pooling equilibria.

The next chapter, by Wickelgren, focuses on employment law. It specifically examines the desirability of affirmative action policies based on the rationale of correcting for past discrimination. Assuming that job success depends on ability and schooling and that ability is inherited from one's parents, victims of past discrimination who achieve equal educational achievement will on average be more able because they have had to overcome discrimination. Thus, it is rational for employers to favor minorities with equal (or even slightly lower) education because they will have higher average ability. In this sense, voluntary affirmative action is efficiency enhancing. Coercive affirmative action is possibly justified if voluntary affirmative action does not eliminate racial differences quickly enough. This might be true if education and ability are complements in job performance, because then there is a potential future benefit from creating a higher correlation between ability and class (income). The offsetting cost is a current-period misallocation of jobs.

The final chapter, by Ramello, considers the economics of trademark law, which falls under the broad heading of intellectual property law. The chapter begins with a discussion of the traditional economic functions of trademark – namely, to provide consumers with signals about product quality in the presence of asymmetric information, thereby mitigating the 'lemons' problem – but then goes on to discuss its role in creating product 'brands,' which can allow firms to differentiate their products from competitors and thereby generate market power. Ramello relies on insights from the field of semiotics, or the study of 'signs,' to explain specifically how branding occurs in the market through the conveyance of meaning from producers to consumers. He concludes that the efficiency-enhancing function of trademarks under the traditional theory has been supplanted by firm efforts to use product identity as a way to create differentiated products and brand loyalty. The resulting market power and barriers to entry are not necessarily conducive to efficiency, suggesting a more complex perspective on the economic functions of trademark. This chapter, along with the one by Garoupa and Ulen, show that rigorous theorizing can still be done without the need of a formal (mathematical) model.

NOTES

1. See Posner (2005) for a discussion of the early history of law and economics.
2. 159 F.2d 169 (2d. Cir., 1947).
3. The case involved a barge that broke free from its moorings and collided with another ship, causing the barge to sink. The question at hand was whether the barge owner's failure to post an attendant to make sure it was properly moored constituted negligence. Since the care choice here was dichotomous (attendant or no attendant), the proper application of the Hand rule is as a cost-benefit comparison of the two options.
4. See, for example, Shavell (1987) and Landes and Posner (1987).

REFERENCES

Baird, Douglas, Robert Gertner and Randal Picker (1994) *Game Theory and the Law*, Cambridge, MA: Harvard Univ. Press.
Becker, Gary (1968) 'The Economics of Crime and Punishment,' 76 *Journal of Political Economy* 169–217.
Brown, John (1973) 'Toward an Economic Theory of Liability,' 2 *Journal of Legal Studies* 323–49.
Calabresi, Guido (1961) 'Some Thoughts on Risk Distribution and the Law of Torts,' 70 *Yale Law Journal* 499–553.
Coase, Ronald (1960) 'The Problem of Social Cost,' 3 *Journal of Law and Economics* 1–44.
Cooter, Robert (1985) 'Unity in Tort, Contract, and Property: The Model of Precaution,' 73 *California Law Review* 1–51.
Friedman, David (2000) *Law's Order: What Economics Has to Do with Law and Why it Matters*, Princeton: Princeton Univ. Press.
Garfinkel, Michelle and Stergios Skaperdas (2007) 'Economics of Conflict: An Overview,'

in *Handbook of Defence Economics*, Todd Sandler and Keith Hartley, eds., Amsterdam: North-Holland, vol. 2, 741–74.

Gould, John (1973) 'The Economics of Legal Conflicts,' 2 *Journal of Legal Studies* 279–300.

Landes, William (1971) 'An Economic Analysis of the Courts,' 14 *Journal of Law and Economics* 61–107.

Landes, William and Richard Posner (1987) *The Economic Structure of Tort Law*, Cambridge, MA: Harvard Univ. Press.

Polinsky, A. Mitchell and Steven Shavell (2007) 'The Theory of Public Law Enforcement,' in *Handbook of Law and Economics*, A. Mitchell Polinsky and Steven Shavell, eds., Amsterdam: North-Holland, vol. 1, 403–54.

Posner, Richard (2005) 'The Law and Economics Movement: From Bentham to Becker,' in *The Origins of Law and Economics*, F. Parisi and C. Rowley, eds., Cheltenham, UK: Edward Elgar, 328–49.

Posner, Richard (1972) 'A Theory of Negligence,' 1 *Journal of Legal Studies* 29–96.

Shavell, Steven (1987) *Economic Analysis of Accident Law*, Cambridge, MA: Harvard Univ. Press.

Shavell, Steven (1984) 'A Model of the Optimal Use of Liability and Safety Regulation,' 15 *Rand Journal of Economics* 271–80.

Shavell, Steven (1980) 'Strict Liability versus Negligence,' *Journal of Legal Studies* 9: 1–25.

Sunstein, Cass, ed. (2000) *Behavioral Law and Economics*, Cambridge: Cambridge Univ. Press.

1. Land assemblage: efficiency and equity in public-private projects

Zachary Grossman, Jonathan Pincus, and Perry Shapiro

INTRODUCTION

Because the market frequently fails to efficiently allocate parcels that are complementary in value, eminent domain is often used to assemble large land parcels from many individually-owned contiguous parcels in a public-private partnership for redevelopment. While the process can be contentious, particularly if the property is taken to be given to private developers, efficiency of land use alone might justify a community interest in facilitating the transition of ownership. The common practice, while it is expeditious, suffers from two potential failings. The first is a matter of efficiency. The evaluation of existing holding by market value may undervalue its current use by a considerable amount. Without a market test, the newer use created by the redevelopment assemblage is not guaranteed to be more valuable than what it replaces. The second is a matter of fairness. It is common practice for communities to pay landowners the market value of their property when it is taken. Even if the use of the assembled properties is efficient, current market value can be considerably smaller than the owners' personal value. In this way redevelopment using eminent domain assemblage can be inequitable. The root of the efficiency-equity problem stems from the inability to know personal value.

In what follows we provide background on the assembly problem and discuss why and how eminent domain has been used to overcome market failures. We will examine as alternatives to the current practice two direct mechanisms, each of which provides owners with the incentive to reveal their personal valuation for their property. While this information allows one to accurately assess efficiency and determine adequate compensation, in order to maintain these incentives there must in all cases be a tradeoff between efficiency and equity. We compare the three processes using a common metric with an explicit cost for unfair outcomes.

BACKGROUND

The present configuration and ownership of land parcels are the result of historical processes, beginning with the official subdivisions and surveys. Large plots of land are subdivided and sold to individual owners and the smaller plots are sold and resold through time. The structure of holdings may have been efficient a century or more ago, but today there are more efficient and profitable holdings that require assembling many contiguous individual holdings into larger plots. The mom and pop merchants of an earlier time give way to more efficient larger retailers that require large acreages for efficient operation. Minutely subdivided low-rise commercial properties may later be more efficiently deployed in larger and more extensive commercial or mixed development. Properties with single family residences in the inner suburbs may now be better dedicated to a higher density use that requires more land than any one lot provides. Moreover, substantial areas of cities may have so deteriorated that large scale redevelopment is desirable.

The process of assembling land is done by the private sector[1] often with long and drawn out expensive bargaining. Individual property owners must be approached with offers and each has an incentive to extract as much as possible from the assembler. Specialists in large scale private assemblages try to maintain as much secrecy as possible to improve their bargaining strength. Existing landowners, if they get wind of the attempted assembly have an incentive to hold out to improve their own bargaining strength for the most profitable exchange. The process is long with large transaction costs. The costs can be so large that they discourage what would otherwise be efficiency-increasing redevelopment.

When contemplating a development project that requires large scale assemblages, private firms will not account for the spillover benefits to the community. New, more modern facilities can produce more employment, larger tax revenues, less blight, among other positive community-wide consequences. If the public benefits are added to the private profits opportunities, and a project that would not justify the assemblage transaction cost would be economically justified, particularly if the transaction costs can be reduced by the community using its eminent domain power. The possibility of joint benefits is used to justify public-private cooperative arrangements for redevelopment. Poletown (Detroit) and Kelo (New London) are two of the most familiar cases.

In the 1980s Detroit found itself on the brink of losing one of its major employers. General Motors could not find sufficient land to build a new Cadillac assembly plant. Faced with the prospect of the economic loss, the city used its eminent domain power to acquire the needed acreage and turned it over to GM at favorable terms. In the process it displaced many long-term residents with compensation equal to the market value of their property.

New London, Connecticut, faced a dilemma similar to Detroit's. The loss of its shipbuilding industry, a dominant part of its economic base, meant job losses and smaller tax revenues to support community services. The city undertook a redevelopment effort and used eminent domain condemnation to assemble a large block of land to be turned over to private firms (most notably Pfizer Pharmaceuticals) for development. As in Detroit, displaced landowners were paid market value for their property.

There is an intense debate, judicial, academic and popular, about whether or not governmental assemblage of land to be handed to private businesses constitutes the 'public use' for which the Constitution grants eminent domain powers.[2] On the face of it this kind of cooperation between a community and a private firm is a dubious public use. But, there is more to the public-private cooperation. Considerable planning precedes a redevelopment project. Some of the expertise resides in the public sector, but much depends on the specialized knowledge of profit oriented private individuals and firms. No matter how well planned, large scale developments are risky investments. Most academic examinations of the eminent domain issue ignore inevitable planning costs and risk.

Analyses of the taking problem often treat the outcome of the underlying project as a certainty. It is common that redevelopment projects are undertaken by publicly subsidized private developers. The developers are offered assembled properties at very low prices in exchange for producing a land use outcome that is in the public interest, as with Poletown and Kelo. These might be examples of political cronyism but it is also reasonable to think that these are examples of efficient ways to share the planning costs and spread the risk of lower than expected returns from the proposed projects. The disadvantage of the procedure followed is that there is no way of knowing whether or not the ownership transfers were efficient.

The rationale for assembling land, by public agencies or private individuals, is that the assembled plot is more valuable than the collective sum of the unassembled individual properties.[3] The fundamental difference between private and public assemblies is that the former provides *prima facie* evidence that the transformation of property boundaries is an efficient one – at least it survived a market test: a buyer was willing to pay at least as much for all the individual property claims as the pre-existing owners were willing to accept. It is not as obvious that a public assemblage, aided by the coercive threat of eminent domain condemnation, can survive the simple efficiency test. Excessive transaction costs are often cited as justification for the use of eminent domain condemnation.

The absence of a market test is not proof that the assemblage is inefficient. For a multitude of public welfare reasons, the property realignment done by a public agency can be efficient. Consequential increases in tax revenues and employment opportunities can reduce a city's welfare roles and allow it to upgrade its services for the benefit of the large fraction of its citizens.[4] Perhaps the inefficiency of public assemblages is not the problem; rather the problem is that a small and focused group, namely the collection of residents whose life is disrupted by the forced relocation, bears a disproportionate burden. For the private assembly, it is reasonable to assume that the disruptive costs are covered when a purchase offer is accepted.

Private assemblies are done with as much secrecy as possible. The assemblers are aware that individual property owners will extract as much of the purchase profit as possible.[5] If the seller knows that an assembly is in progress, negotiations can be lengthy and costly. Irrespective of how much of potential surplus is captured by the buyers or sellers, the negotiations towards agreement by many parties can be very costly. Some advocate the limited use of eminent domain for private assembler to reduce these transactions costs.[6]

Private assemblers are not yet armed with the threat of eminent domain condemnation; indeed it is doubtful that they ever will be.[7] However, partnerships between developers and public agencies, under the name of redevelopment, are common. The redevelopment partnerships may be legitimate ways to reduce transaction costs and share development risks, but they smack of cozy dealing between city hall and special private interests. Even if all is on the up-and-up, a public-private cooperative arrangement does not have the advantage of a market test for the efficacy of its project.

The public assemblage of privately held property for redevelopment by private firms is bedeviled by a number of problems. One of them has to do with the efficiency of the outcome: the most profitable among all possible uses, we will call projects, of the assembled land must be identified and the profit it generates must exceed the value of the land at its existing use. If either of these tests is failed the community is not as well off as it could be, indeed it could even be worse off than it would have been had there had been no assemblage. The second problem relates to fairness of the process. Even if a community's well-being is enhanced by an assemblage and subsequent redevelopment, some of it citizens may suffer significant, uncompensated losses. Existing landowners are forced to cede their property for an amount that may be far smaller than their own personal value, their reservation price.[8] This doesn't seem to be fair. While most economic analysis focuses on efficiency, for the general public, fairness is a more salient issue. Sandra Day O'Connor's dissent in the Kelo decision illustrates how important is the perceived heavy-handed inequity of public assemblage:

> Petitioner Wilhelmina Dery, for example, lives in a house on Walbach Street
> that has been in her family for over 100 years. She was born in the house in
> 1918; her husband, petitioner Charles Dery, moved into the house when they
> married in 1946. Their son lives next door with his family in the house he
> received as a wedding gift, and joins his parents in this suit.[9]

The image of citizens forced from their property was a strong motivator
for this dissent and, most probably, the thing that motivated the subsequent public outcry.

There is a simultaneous solution to the efficiency-fairness twins. All
that needs to be known is the truth about the developer (those who are
the potential recipients of the assembled property) values and individual
property owners' (those whose properties are to be assembled) values.
With this information in hand, no project need be considered unless it
is the most profitable and no redevelopment condemnation would take
place unless the most profitable value exceeds the sum of individual owner
values. But, of course neither set of values is observable as they exist either
in the private business plans or in the minds (and hearts) of individual land
owners.

The problem is clear, figure out a way, design a process, to get folks
to reveal privately-known individual values and use those to make sure
that the assemblage is successful if, and only if, it is efficient and if, and
only if, it is fair. What we will find out is that there is no such mechanism.
Perfection isn't possible in the world, so we will need to compromise and
examine the consequences of non-ideal mechanisms. In what follows
we will examine three less-than-perfect mechanisms and then suggest a
way to rank them consistent with community preferences. Number 1 is
the current practice (CP) (perhaps somewhat idealized as well) of using
market values, both to determine the assemblage costs and owner compensation; 2, labeled Strong Pareto (SP), is an auction-based design that
insures an entirely fair outcome, but efficiency cannot be guaranteed; and
3, a variant of the Vickery Clark Groves (VCG) mechanism, guarantees an
efficient outcome, but sacrifices fairness.

We begin with the illustrative example of Garden City whose problem
typifies that encountered in many redevelopment efforts. Following this
the ideal properties of the mechanism are presented. The CP, SP and VCG
are described and then, for a vivid explanation, applied to Garden City
assemblage. CP, in spite of its obvious shortcomings, has the advantage
of being a widely accepted common practice whose implementation is
well understood. SP ensures that outcomes are entirely fair and that there
should be no objection to its use on that account and no compulsion is
involved. Indeed existing landowners would voluntarily agree to participate in the process. Efficient outcomes are ensured with VCG, but they are

achieved at the cost of fairness – it is unlikely that existing landowners would voluntarily choose to participate. Both SP and VCG suffer from a lack of familiarity that may mitigate against their use as a substitute for CP.

GARDEN CITY: A STORY

Garden City is facing severe financial difficulties: its major employer has moved away and its tax base is insufficient to maintain adequate public services. In GC there are three contiguous plots of land, each one acre, owned by three different people, Able, Baker and Charlie. The plots are identical and each has a market value of $1000. Able values his property for $1000 – he is indifferent to retaining ownership or selling the property at the market price. Baker values his property for $2000: if offered that amount, or more, she would cede ownership. Since the market value is less than her personal value, she will not sell. Charlie is the least likely to sell as his personal value is $3000. The true (social) value of the three acres in their current use is $6000, the sum of individual values, while the market value is $3000. The information is summarized in Table 1.1.

The mayor of Garden City has announced the city's interest in promoting development and its willingness to cooperate with developers in an attempt to improve its tax base. Three developers indicate interest in using the three contiguous ABC acres. Each of them must have the assembled three acres; anything less has no value. Xenos builders can use the three acres for a shopping center for which possible land acquisition is worth $4000; Yardley Corp anticipates an industrial park for which the land value is $9000; and Zenith Living envisions an apartment complex for which the land value is $12,000.

Given this configuration of values, it is clear what is the social optimum. Zenith Living acquires the assembled property, pays at least $6000 and the proceeds of the sale distributed to A, B and C who are paid at least $1000, $2000 and $3000 respectively. Is there a mechanism that will always pick the most valuable options and ensure that every landowner is fully compensated?

There is no problem if the individual values, both landowners' and

Table 1.1

Landowner Value	A	B	C	Sum
Personal	$1000	$2000	$3000	$6000
Market	$1000	$1000	$1000	$3000

developers', are known (if not common knowledge, at least known by the planner). But these are not known, they exist in the minds of the individual. How might the planner learn the values. How about asking? Consider the following: 'I have an upper limit to how much I will pay you for your land, tell me your lower limit for acceptance and if that number is smaller than my upper limit I will pay you an amount that is half way between your number and mine.' What is the most likely response?

What about Abel? He will think: 'anything greater than $1000 is great, so if the planner's number is $1001 and I truthfully reveal my value then I will get $1000.50, but if I announce a larger number, say $1000.50 then I will get $1000.75. If I think there is a good chance that the planner's reservation price is higher than my value, I will announce an untruthful value'. Similarly for the potential buyers. Ask Zenith what is the maximum you are willing to pay for the assemblage and by similar reasoning, it will give a figure smaller than its true reservation price.

The lesson of this fable is that, with no further structure, individuals will not reveal their true underlying values.[10] It is a problem that vexes all non-market transactions. We propose to examine three alternative mechanisms to deal with this problem: Common Practice (CP) in which market values alone inform the ultimate decision about both project desirability and landowner compensation; Strong Pareto (SP) in which an auction is incorporated combined with a method for inducing true revelation of landowner values, and Vickery Clark Groves (VCG), in which truthful revelation is induced by the introduction of a tax for certain revelations. The three mechanisms are illustrated with the Garden City example and measured against a set of criteria that will describe a perfect mechanism.

A PERFECT MECHANISM

Searching for a perfect mechanism for assembling private property for redevelopment would naturally lead us to apply certain criteria. The list that follows begins with efficiency and then lists others that assure that the implementation depends only on what is observable, is self-financing, and is fully respectful of private property rights. Here is the list:

1. *Efficient*: Land is assembled and then employed in alternative use if and only if the alternative use chosen is the most profitable among all possible uses and that it exceeds the sum of individual values for the existing property rights configuration.
2. *Private Knowledge*: The working of the mechanism does not depend upon knowledge of people's private valuations and/or beliefs.

3. *Incentive Compatible*: It is the best interest of all participants to announce their true value irrespective of what anyone else announces, i.e., truthful revelation of value is a dominant strategy.
4. *Full Respect for Property*: Individuals will receive no less than their stated value in exchange for their property.[11]
5. *Balanced Budget*: The amount paid out must not exceed the amount collected.[12]

COMMON PRACTICE

Even though there are difficulties determining agents' true value, there remains a need to go forward with a public policy. When there is a per-ceived public purpose to be served, the government may rightfully acquire property. Traditionally governments invoke their eminent domain powers to condemn property in order to assemble large, individually-owned parcels for some public purpose, for example, building roads, economic development and slum clearance. Let's examine how that works for Garden City.

First the city will undertake a benefit cost study, and using the usual market-based measure will conclude that the cost of the project is $3000, irrespective of what it ends up paying the landowners (for the usual theory, market value, is the 'true' opportunity cost). The city searches for potential developers and in the search it finds Zenith Living. Clearly a transfer of use for A, B and C to Z is an efficient choice. Z's value is larger than the market value so the development award is given to it. A, B and C are reimbursed the market value of their property (with revenues taken from community-wide taxation or, perhaps from a sale to Zenith for some amount, no greater than $12,000). By the usual (Kaldor-Hicks) criterion, this is the end of the story – a clear gain in efficiency by converting land from one use to another. But there is more going on here than just a simple transfer of land from one use to a more efficient one – B and C are forced to cede their property for less than its personal value. These two are made to bear a disproportionate cost[13] for the efficiency improvement: While some of the 'true' costs are spread among the citizens of Garden City (if the purchase is tax-financed) B and C are assessed an additional $1000 and $2000 respectively.

The foregoing illustrates one problem with the traditional policy instrument: even if the choice is efficient its distributional consequence is unfortunate. And this is the most optimistic outcome. Things can be worse. Suppose in its search the best development opportunity the city dis-covers is Xenos, the developer of shopping centers. A $4000 value exceeds the market value of existing use. Applying its benefit cost logic, it chooses eminent domain condemnation with market value compensation and then awards the property to X. There remains the distribution loss, but, in addition, because the true values are not known, the city's decision is inefficient. The city has converted $6000 worth of land use into $4000 worth.

Finally, we can reasonably envision the city finding Yardley Corp's industrial park the highest value alternative. In this case there is a transfer to a higher value use, but not the highest. The efficiency loss in this case is the difference between the Yardley $9000 value and Zenith $12,000. Additionally the landowners are made to suffer less than full compensation for their displacement.

These scenarios of common practice highlight its potential shortcoming: individuals are made to surrender their land for a price smaller than its personal value. Absent information about true landowner value and/or true and complete development value, inefficient choices are likely.

STRONG PARETO[14]

There is an alternative that will ensure that no landowner will be made to suffer a loss because of the assemblage, and a transfer of the assembled property to a developer will happen only if it is efficient. Garden City announces there will be an auction for the assembled properties. The rules of the auction are that the assembled property will be sold to the highest bidder for a price equal to the next highest bid, with one caveat: the second highest price must be at least as large as a pre-set, and secret, reserve amount. This is an implementation of a well-known Vickery auction that induces all potential buyers to bid the highest price they are willing to pay. For example Z will be the highest bidder and he will own the assemblage if the reserve is no larger than $9000, the amount that Y will bid. It is apparent that the reserve value plays an important part in this story. Ideally, it would be set at $6000, the aggregate value of the property for the current landowners. But it is impossible to know individual values accurately, they are known only to each landowner. Therefore every landowner is required to announce the lowest acceptable price, r_i, for his property.

Prior to announcing r_i every landowner is told he will get a share, α_i ($\Sigma \alpha_i = 1$), of the buyer payment, if the auction is successful (if for instance the auction results in a sale, landowner i will be paid $\alpha_i$$9000). The auction reserve, R, is to be the largest of the ratio $\frac{r_i}{\alpha_i}$. With this scheme, landowners are induced to reveal their true reservation price. If a landowner does that, he will receive no less than his reservation price if the auction is successful, and he may receive more if the sales price is larger than $\frac{r_i}{\alpha_i}$. If he announces a number less than his value, he opens up the possibility of being less than fully compensated, and if he announces a number larger than personal value, there is a risk of missing a profitable (surplus-generating) sale because the second bid is lower than the reserve but large enough to generate a payment that exceeds i's personal value.

To clarify the use of the auction, consider the example. Any reserve no greater than $9000 will result in an efficient transfer from the current landowners to Zenith, its most valuable user. Suppose that the shares happen to be in the same proportion as the values (this would be a pure accident because the value is known only to the landowner and not to those allocating the shares): $\alpha_A = 1/6$, $\alpha_B = 1/3$ and $\alpha_C = 1/2$. In this case all ratios, $\frac{r_i}{\alpha_i}$ equal $6000. There would be a sale and the $9000 would be divided $1500 for A, $3000 for B and $4500 for C – every landowner received more than personal value, all are improved by the sale. Suppose, however, the shares happen to come out the mirror image of proportional: $\alpha_A = 1/2$, $\alpha_B = 1/3$ and $\alpha_C = 1/6$. It remains in the best interest of every landowner to truthfully state personal value, but the $\frac{r_i}{\alpha_i}$ ratio is $2000 for A, $6000 for B and $18,000 for C. The auction reserve is $18,000, the largest of the individual ones. The result is that there is no sale even though there is a more efficient use of the property. This illustrates the shortcoming of the SP mechanism: it can result in a failure of efficient transfers if the shares are allocated improperly.

While SP is not a perfect mechanism, it does not infallibly conclude with the most efficient outcome, it has particular attributes that make a desirable choice. It satisfies four of the five criteria for a perfect land assembly mechanism:

- It is incentive-compatible. It provides landowners and potential buyers no incentive to misrepresent their private valuation of their land and the assembled parcels, respectively. Thus, it not only provides an economic answer to the legal puzzle of what is 'just compensation' for property taken, but it also provides an appropriate test of the efficiency of the project in question.
- It requires no subsidization.
- It fully protects the rights of all property owners, ensuring that displaced owners are not made worse-off if their property is taken.
- It has low informational requirements: its application and functioning does not require knowledge of the actual distribution of valuations or participants' subjective beliefs about those distributions.

However, SP has an unfortunate side as well. It is fully protective of private property rights, but it does that at the cost of assured efficiency. In fact, in some cases the efficiency costs can be quite large, as illustrated in the previous Garden City example: even though there is a project, Zenith, for which the welfare gains ($6000 in this case) are significant, its success is thwarted by an unfortunate distribution of share.

The good news for SP is that it is fair: no owner is forced to cede property unwillingly. Furthermore, a successful auction always results in an efficient change. But, employing SP can lead to the rejection of welfare increasing projects. It seems, then, that sacrificing potential efficiency gains is the cost of equity. However, there is no way to ensure perfect equity that is less likely to reject the most efficiency improving projects. This 'second best' conclusion, proved in Grossman, Pincus and Shapiro (2010), states

Proposition (Second Best):   Any assemblage mechanism that fulfills properties 2 – 5, can be no more efficient that SP.

For simplicity and clarity of exposition of the proof, we ignore the buyer side and assume that the most efficient project has been identified and the highest auction bid is known. An informal sketch is offered here to give the flavor of the proof in five steps.

1)   Incentive compatibility, whatever are the beliefs of the landowners, requires that the shares are independent of the announced value.
2)   Any mechanism that assures a balanced budget and full respect for property rights must approve efficient sales, and each person's share of W, the approved price, must at least match the individual value.
3)   If a mechanism accepts an offer W', efficiency requires that it accept a higher offer $W > W'$. Thus the efficient mechanism will have a reserve price, R, that is at least as high as the sum of individual values.
4)   Given the share distribution, α_i, the lower the reserve, R, the higher the probability of sale.
5)   The SP reserve, $\max\{\frac{r_i}{\alpha_i}\}$, is the smallest that ensures full compensation (Full Respect for Property).

This completes the proof of the Second Best proposition because the higher the probability of a successful auction (given that the most efficient alternative use is selected) the more efficient is the mechanism.

The Garden City parable shows that SP fails the efficiency tests sometimes, therefore

Corollary (Impossibility):   There is no perfect mechanism (one that satisfies 1–5).

VICKERY CLARK GROVES (VCG) MECHANISM

Whether or not SP achieves an efficient transfer strongly depends on the share assignments. With our insistence on a mechanism that does not require prior knowledge of values or beliefs, there is no way to guarantee a share distribution that does not lead to an inefficient outcome. Other mechanisms have been proposed that induce efficient outcomes, but, from the SP corollary, all of these must violate at least one of the desired restrictions. Among the closest alternatives[15] to SP is the straightforward concordance mechanism of Kominers and Weyl (2010). It is based on the well known Vickery Clark Groves mechanism that penalizes a landowner whose value revelation affects the welfare of everyone else in the community. A simplified version of this is given here.

To make sure that the symbols are understood: v_i and r_i are, respectively, landowner i's true and announced values; W is the highest bid, that, for simplicity of exposition, is assumed to be the value of the most efficient alternative use of the assembled properties and α_i is i's share of the auction revenue if it is successful (i will receive $\alpha_i W$).

The problem with the SP mechanism is that it does not invariably result in the success of welfare-increasing projects. An unfortunate distribution of auction shares can result in an inefficient auction reserve that is so high that it rejects projects with the potential of making all better off. In the Garden City case when C is allocated a 1/6 share, C's truthful announcement results in no sale. Given the share allocation, that is best for C, but it represents a loss on landowners A and B. The amount of the loss is, in a sense, an externality imposed by C on his neighbors. The VCG mechanism assesses a tax on C equal to the amount lost by A and B.

The VCG mechanism works as an auction with reserve R equal to the sum of individual announcements ($R = \sum_i r_i$): the auction is successful if $W \geq R$ and unsuccessful otherwise. If landowner announcements are truthful, $r_i = v_i$, a project is successful if and only if it is efficient. To ensure that truthfulness, a tax is imposed on any responder whose announced value imposes a cost on the other landowners, as does C when his share is 1/6.

Without C's deal-killing announcement, A and B would have had five-sixths of $9000, the efficient bid, to split between them ($4500 for A and $3000 for B with the stated pre-assigned shares). With this split A's revealed profit would have been $3500 ($4500 – $1000) and B's would have been $1000 ($3000 – $1000). C will impose a $4500 externality by truthfully revealing his value and be made to pay a penalty (tax) of that amount. C is faced with two bad choices: 1) a truthful announcement, $r_C = v_C = \$3000$, results in a $6000 reserve, a successful sale and the surrender of a $3000 valued property for a compensation of $1000; or 2) an announcement of a value sufficient to block the sale, say $r_C = \$10,000$ and pay a tax of $4500. Truthful revelation costs \$2000 compared with a \$4500 bill for lying. In this case truth telling is the best of a bad deal.

In the VCG story C is pivotal – it is C's revelation that determines the success or failure of the efficiency improving transaction. This is specified as a simultaneous move game, so no landowner knows whether or not he is pivotal. Here is a simple version of the individual decision calculus.

To start define $R_i = \Sigma_{j \neq i} r_j$, the VCG reserve less landowner i's announcement. Landowner i does not know the value of R_i when he makes his announcement, nor does he know the outstanding offer, W, but neither need be known because i's announcement decision does not depend on either. If i is pivotal in that his announcement is transaction blocking he will pay a penalty of $(1 - \alpha_i) W - R_i$ and he will retain his property. His net benefit from blocking is $v_i - \alpha_i W$, the personal value less the amount he would have received from a successful sale.

VCG mechanism focuses on the pivotal individual. Every landowner is potentially pivotal, so each must consider the consequences of being the marginal individual, the one that makes a difference in one of two ways: (1) without his announcement the auction would be successful $((1 - \alpha_i) W > R_i)$ and i's truthfulness $(r_i = v_i)$ spoils the sale $(R_i + v_i > W)$, or (2) without his announcement the auction would be unsuccessful $((1 - \alpha_i) W < R_i)$ and i's truthfulness induces the sale $(R_i + v_i > W)$. For (1) truthfulness is in i's best interest if the value of retaining his property less the penalty is greater than the compensation for surrendering ownership $(v_i - [(1 - \alpha_i) W - R_i] > \alpha_i W)$. But case (1) is based on the condition that $R_i + v_i > W$ that ensures that this is the case. i will make a similar analysis for case (2) to conclude that if pivotal, irrespective of which way, it is best to announce the true personal value, and if not pivotal truthfulness will be fine as well.

There is much to recommend the VCG mechanism. It assures that each landowner truthfully reveals their reservation prices and, since the reserve is the sum of these revelations, efficiency is assured as well. However, as an example of the SP corollary, VCG cannot be a perfect mechanism. Indeed, by entering the VCG environment, a landowner may be penalized for preserving his property or may lose his property without adequate compensation.

AN EFFICIENCY EQUITY METRIC

The SP corollary illustrates the basic principle of economics. It can be summarized by the old maxim 'you can't make an omelet without cracking eggs.' Perfection is compromised by the reality of what must be given up. This is most clearly spelled out in *The Calculus of Consent*. In the famous work on social choice, Buchanan and Tullock (1962) first confront the vexing problem of welfare economics. Pareto superior policy choices, namely, those that make some citizens better off without harming any others, are the gold standard of public policy. However, they are rarely available to governments. Most policy choices will have benefits for some and impose costs on others. The problem is to find the balance between community and private interests. A decision mechanism that requires unanimous approval by all citizens will result in only universal welfare improving choices. But achieving unanimity can be excessively costly: there is the valuable time spent on making a decision and, more to the point, there is a cost of opportunities not taken because they are damaging to some. Economists use the 'Kaldor-Hicks' expedient of claiming an efficient choice is one for which the total benefits, no matter how they are distributed, exceed the total costs. Policy choices, if they are mutually exclusive, are ranked only by the impersonal measure. This is a legitimate way to make choices among imperfect alternatives, but it is our contention that this misses one of the most important aspects of community choices.

Kaldor-Hicks may be fine in the confines of an economics workshop, it does not play well on the street. Most citizens realize that not all public policies are personally helpful, and some may cause some harm. Nonetheless if the personal costs are perceived as too high, the harmed will protest (bring law suits, lobby with their elected representatives). Costly litigation, political action or civil disobedience are potential consequences of ignoring distributional outcomes. Even if we keep the problem off the streets, there are legitimate ethical and moral concerns about imposing unfair (inequitable) government decision related costs on a subset of citizens. However, since true unanimous consensus is an infeasible alternative for complex public choices, it is necessary to have some criterion, other than unanimity, on which to base those choices. What we propose is a extension of Kaldor-Hicks that allows negative consequences to be weighted appropriately by recognizing a dollar of personal loss to one citizen, particularly at the hands of the government, may not be ethically offset by a dollar gain for another.

The measure we label EE, for Efficiency-Equity, adds a penalty for community-choice caused loss to the Kaldor-Hicks calculation of net benefits. Suppose a policy option, if taken, results in net gains for individuals of ΔV_i. Using the K-H criterion, the policy is efficient, and should be chosen if $\sum_{i=1}^{n} \Delta V_i > 0$. An increase in social value, so calculated, justifies the policy choice, even if some (perhaps even most) of the $\Delta V_i's$ are negative. One only need consider a case in which one citizen enjoys an enormous reward and all the rest suffer significant losses to understand how poorly is Kaldor-Hicks adapted to real world policy or how poorly it can conform to natural ethical norms of fairness. What we propose is a measure that recognizes a social price, β, for policy-imposed losses on individual citizens. Suppose, for simplicity, that citizens 1 through m gain (or do not lose) from the policy ($\Delta V_i \geq 0, i = 1 \cdots m$) and the remaining suffer losses ($\Delta V_j < 0, j = m + 1 \cdots n$). The ethically adjusted Kaldor-Hicks measure is

$$EE = \sum_{i=1}^{m} \Delta V_i + \beta \sum_{j=m+1}^{n} \Delta V_i$$

The value of β reflects what is considered the social cost of imposed losses. Suppose, for instance, the policy is the forced sale of land for public use. There are some who would stick by the strict KH criterion (Kaplow and Shavell (2002) for instance) and assert that efficiency is the only relevant factor; for them β = 1. There are others who think that no violation of private property is ever justified; for that group β is infinite.

EE CALCULATIONS

In order to understand how the EE can focus the choice between the three assemblage processes, apply it to the Garden City problem. Unsurprisingly, the choice depends on community concern for fairness. In what follows, EE is calculated for the CP, SP and VCG processes as they would be implemented.

Common Practice

CP is subject to three sorts of errors: the first is under valuing the opportunity cost of the project; the second is the failure to identify the most valuable redevelopment project; and the third is under-compensating displaced owners. The first error is unavoidable: the true cost of the Garden City redevelopment is $6000, the sum of the individual values and the estimated cost is $3000, the market value of the properties. Because costs are under valued, the city is apt to choose an inferior project for its redevelopment: even though there is a $12,000 potential project, it may end up approving the $4000 one because it compares favorably with the $3000 cost.

Suppose the GC redevelopment agency is sufficiently skillful that it is most likely to choose the most profitable project, but there is some chance that it will be missed. Characterize this by assuming that there is a one-half probability that Zenith, with its $12,000 value will be chosen, a one-third probability of choosing Yardley and $9000 and a one-sixth probability that Xenos and $4000 will be chosen. Notice that each of these exceed the market value cost. The net community gain (the project value less the true cost of $6000) is $6000 for Z, $3000 for Y and -$2000 for X. With market value compensation A will be exactly compensated and B and C will suffer losses of $1000 and $2000 respectively. The expected value of EE is

$$EE = \frac{1}{2}\$6,000 + \frac{1}{3}\$3,000 - \frac{1}{6}\$2,000 - \beta\$3,000 = \$3,766 - \beta\$3,000$$

Strong Pareto

Fairness is assured with SP, so its expected value is unaffected by the inequity aversion parameter β, however, efficiency is not. If the SP auction is successful, the most favorable project, Z, will always be selected, so the inefficiency does not arise from making the wrong redevelopment choice. Rather it arises because the auction may result in a rejection of the best offer; one, in the case of Garden City, is clearly superior to the status quo. The outcome depends on the selection of the distributional parameters α_i. There are many ways these can be chosen, but for illustrative purposes we only arbitrarily choose three. These are listed in Table 1.2. Furthermore we assume that I, II and III are equally probable.

With distribution I and II the auction reserve is $6000 and $9000 respectively. In both cases project Z, with a $6000 gain in value, is successful. However with share distribution III the reserve is $18,000 and the profitable redevelopment opportunity is lost. Thus the expected value of EE is

$$EE = \frac{2}{3}\$6000 = \$4,000$$

Table 1.2

	χ		
	I	II	III
A	1/6	1/3	1/2
B	1/3	1/3	1/3
C	1/2	1/3	1/6
Prob	1/3	1/3	1/3

For this simplistic example SP dominates CP irrespective of community fairness concerns. This is so because inefficient redevelopment projects are never selected with SP; the competitive auction process, rather than bureaucratic selection, ensures this. The probabilities of project choice are arbitrarily selected for the example; a redevelopment agency with more acumen than portrayed here might do much better. However, even if the agency was well enough informed to always select Z the EE for it would be $EE = \$6000 - \beta\$3000$. In this case, if the community would need to undervalue the landowner losses relative to the community gains, $\beta < 2/3$ for CP to be preferred to SP.

Vickery Clark Groves

Let the potential share distributions be the ones given above. With VCG the most efficient project, Z, is always chosen. Since the individuals are induced to truly reveal values, and the sum of these is smaller than the value of Z, none will be required to pay a tax. Furthermore, with distributions I and II neither A nor B nor C will receive less than full value. With distribution III, A and B will be compensated fully at least, but C surrenders a property he values at $3000 for $2000, his distributional share. Thus the EE for VCG is

$$EE = \$6000 - \frac{1}{3}\beta\$1000$$

In this example, irrespective of fairness concern, VCG dominates CP, even if the community chooses the best among alternative private projects. However, the ranking of SP and VCG depends on how important are concerns for equity. For β values less than 6 VCG dominates SP but for larger values the ranking is reversed.

CONCLUSION

Historical process of establishing land ownership leaves a legacy of antiquated holdings. Because of a community's interest in protecting its economic base, it may engage, in partnership with private developers, to assemble individually-owned properties into larger, economically more valuable plots. The common practice is for the community to use eminent domain to condemn property, compensate the owners the market value of their property, and then make the land available for large scale private development. The common practice suffers from three potential failings. The first is that market value is an imperfect measure of community cost if individual owners place a higher value on their property than does the market. The second is that the community may not choose the most efficient private developer to use the assembled property. The third is that the outcome can be inequitable: unless compensation to owners is at least as large as their individual value, the process may enrich the community but place an unfair burden on a few property owners. These failures can be solved if only individual values are known, but, of course they are not.

Two auction-based direct mechanisms are proposed as alternatives to the common practice. Both solve the value revelation: both buyers and sellers are induced to truthfully reveal individual values. One, SP, does so by ensuring every landowner receives, at least, individual value as compensation. The other, VCG, uses a tax, commensurate with an externality that a particular value response imposes on other landowners. SP solves the equity problem: a landowner is never forced to cede ownership without compensation that is at least as large as personal value. Furthermore, a successful project is more valuable than any other and more valuable than the sum of current owner value. Its shortcoming is that in order to ensure equity, some alternative uses, more profitable than current use, are rejected. Success in an SP process is sufficient, but not necessary for efficiency. The VCG mechanism ensures that the outcome, whether it is a new development on the assembled property or maintenance of the status quo, is efficient. It achieves this by sacrificing the equity guarantee.

The choice of the three examples highlights the equity-efficiency trade-offs. The presented EE metric focuses on the inevitable comparison. Whatever method is preferred depends on how much the community values equity. The EE index allows community fairness concerns to be expressed as one number, β, the community inequity price.

NOTES

1. See, for example, Hellman (2004).
2. The question of what constitutes 'public use' is a difficult one. The complexities of this issue, with much clear thinking, are found in Merrill (1986).
3. The inefficient distribution of ownership rights has received a good deal of interest; it is often labeled the problem of the anticommons. The first use of this term that we know of is in Michelman (1967). An extensive and thorough analysis from a legal perspective is in Heller (1998). Buchanan and Yoon (2000) appear to be the first to present a formal economic analysis of the issue. The analysis is advanced and refined by Parisi, Schultz and Depoorter (2006).
4. See John Lindsey forward to Alpern and Durst (1997).
5. See the story of the Citibank assembly in Hellman (2004) op.cit.
6. Alpern and Durst op. cit.
7. However, a precedent exists in the compulsory private acquisition of minority stock holders.

8. So called because it is the minimum price at which they would voluntarily sell their property.
9. *Kelo v. New London* (04-108), 545 U.S. 469 495 (2005).
10. This is the conclusion of Samuelson's (1954) famous articles on Pure Public Goods.
11. We do not require that the received amount be at least as great as the true reservation value because it is up to the landowner to state what that is. Since the true value is unknowable and unverifiable this seems a reasonable notion of respect for property.
12. In Grossman, Pincus, and Shapiro (2010) this condition is relaxed to include all self-finance projects, i.e., all for which the amount collected from the buyer is no less than the amount paid in compensation to the landowners.
13. Richard Epstein (1985).
14. Strong Pareto resembles the method suggested by Becker, DeGroot and Marschak (1964).
15. There are other promising suggestions for dealing with the assembly issue. Plassmann and Tideman (2010) propose a self reporting scheme in which insurance contracts based on the probability of a taking induce the truth. Miceli and Segerson (2007) suggest direct bargaining between landowners and potential buyers. The threat of eminent domain condemnation induces a quick and successful conclusion to the negotiation.

REFERENCES

Alpern, A., S. Durst (1997), *New York's Architectural Holdouts*, Dover: New York.
Becker, G.M., M.H. DeGroot and J. Marschak (1964), Measuring utility by a single-response sequential method, *Behavioral Science*, 9(3), 226–32.
Buchanan, J.M. and G. Tullock (1962), *The Calculus of Consent*, University of Michigan Press: Ann Arbor.
Buchanan, J.M. and Y.J. Yoon (2000), Symmetric tragedies, commons and anticommons, *Journal of Law and Economics*, 43, 1–13.
Epstein, R.A. (1985), *Private Property and the Power of Eminent Domain*. Harvard University Press: Cambridge, MA.
Grossman, Z.J, J. Pincus and P. Shapiro (2010), A second-best mechanism for land assembly. Working Paper. Santa Barbara: Department of Economics, University of California, Santa Barbara. http://www.escholarship.org/ux/item/1dn8g6vk.
Heller, M. (1998), The tragedy of the anti-commons: property in transition from Marx to market, *Harvard Law Review*, 111: 621–88.
Hellman, P. (2004), *Shaping the Skyline: The World According to Real Estate Visionary Julien Studley*, Wiley: Hoboken.
Kaplow, L. and S. Shavell (2002), *Fairness versus Welfare*, Harvard University Press: Cambridge, MA.
Kelo v. New London (04-108), 545 U.S. 469 495 (2005).
Kominers, S.D. and G. Weyl (2010), Concordance among holdouts, Mimeo.
Merrill, T. (1986), The economics of public use. *Cornell Law Review* 72L, 61–116.
Miceli, T.J. and K. Segerson (2007), A bargaining model of holdouts and takings, *American Law and Economics Review* 9(1), 1–30.
Michelman, F.H. (1967), Property, utility and fairness: comments on the ethical foundations of 'just compensation law', *Harvard Law Review* 80(6), 1165–258.
Parisi, F., Schulz, N. and B. Depoorter (2006), Duality in property, commons and anticommons, Int. Rev. Law Econ., 25, 578–91.
Plassman, F. and T.N. Tideman (2010), Providing incentives for efficient land assembly, mimeo.
Samuelson, P.A. (1954), The pure theory of public expenditures, *Review of Economics and Statistics* 36(4), 387–89.

2. The economics of activity levels in tort liability and regulation
Nuno Garoupa[1,2] and Thomas S. Ulen[3]

I. INTRODUCTION

More than 25 years ago, when law and economics was just beginning and its analyses were still at an attention-grabbing but incomplete stage, there was a vigorous scholarly search for the efficiency and equitable differences between negligence and strict liability. The accepted doctrinal distinction between the standards was reasonably clear, but those differences did not map clearly onto efficiency and equity differences. For a period of years, Richard Posner, in his field-defining text, asserted that the central principle for tort law generally, and negligence particularly, was to identify and assign liability to the 'least-cost avoider' so as to create an incentive for future, potential tortfeasors and victims to investigate their comparative precaution costs and for whichever of them had the lower avoidance costs to take care.[4] Strict liability was much more straightforward – an instance of almost absolute liability for the injurer, who was presumed to be, always, the 'least-cost avoider.'

Of course, in the intervening 30 or 40 years much but not all of this early analysis has changed. There are, as we will see, some fundamental problems with the earlier views. Nonetheless, those earlier views have had a remarkably strong staying power. The 'least-cost avoider' as the touchstone for assigning liability under negligence and as the central explanatory variable for distinguishing strict liability from negligence has remained very strong.

In one of the early issues of the *Journal of Legal Studies*, the economist John Prather Brown laid out an economic theory of tort liability that was so far ahead of the field that it took almost 20 years for its full import to become evident to those learned in the field.[5] One of us found that it was not until the fourth edition of the text that he felt as if that text had accurately articulated the economic theory of tort liability, including providing a reasonably coherent account of the efficiency differences between negligence and strict liability.[6]

Some contend that the field of law and economics has become one of the dominant methods of looking at legal issues. While this might not be true of all fields in law or equally true among all fields, this is certainly the case in tort law. The focus there has shifted from concentration on doing justice in compensating victims of unintentional wrongs to consideration of the ability of exposure to tort liability to induce socially optimal precaution-taking designed to minimize the social costs of accidents. And the understanding of the roles to be played by negligence – indeed, by the different forms of negligence – strict liability, administrative agency regulation, and other regulatory tools in minimizing the social costs of accidents is reasonably complete and widely accepted.[7] One of the now-conventional conclusions of that literature is that there is a significant difference between the negligence and strict liability standards in at least one important respect – that having to do with 'activity levels.'[8] That settled interpretation has also made its way into justifications given for deciding an important case.[9]

The economic theory of the 'activity level effect' and its relationship to the efficiency analysis of tort liability standards was first articulated by Steve Shavell and Mitch Polinsky in 1980 in two independent, yet related articles.[10] The thrust of their argument is that there are circumstances in which the likelihood of an accident's occurring or of harm's being inflicted is a direct function of the volume or amount of the underlying activity in which the potential wrongdoer engages, regardless of other precautionary activity. Consider, to use one of Shavell's examples, a commercial restaurant. The proprietor is mindful of potential liability to his customers for injuries that they might suffer at his eatery – for example, about the possibility that his patrons may be subject to food poisoning from a meal eaten at his place of business. Conventional analysis – both economic and doctrinal – would suggest that the fear of liability would motivate the owner to take reasonable care in preparing food and serving customers.[11] If the restaurant owner's behavior were to be judged according to a negligence standard and if compliance with that standard were determined according to economic principles, then the owner should be held liable for his customers' losses only if he failed to take all cost-justified precautions. This would, for example, induce him to compare the cost of such actions as further cleaning or sterilizing of utensils, surfaces, and food with the anticipated benefits of those actions and to take them only if it were the case that the costs (direct and opportunity) of further cleaning were less than the anticipated benefits. The anticipated benefits of further care are roughly, in this calculus, the reduction in the probability of an accident's occurring times the anticipated accident losses that would be avoided. Both economic and doctrinal analyses expect that the law can – either through *ex ante* safety standards or *ex post* adjudication of liability – define socially efficient standards on the relevant aspects of operating a commercial restaurant.

The insight of Polinsky and Shavell was to suggest that the regulatory regime or exposure to negligence liability might not be enough to minimize the social costs of some activities, such as the number of meals served to restaurant customers. The potential inadequacy of those means of inducing socially optimal care lies in their not defining duties of care over a missing element: the probability that an injury's occurring (or of accident losses increasing) might rise – independently of all other factors – with the quantity of the underlying activity in which the potential tortfeasor is engaged. Suppose that the probability of inflicting food poisoning on one's customers rises with the number of meals served, independently of whatever other safety precautions the restaurant may be taking. The intuition of the contention is that if one does not engage in the underlying activity at all – if, that is, one serves *no* restaurant meals at all, then the probability of an accident's occurring is zero, and that once one starts serving meals, the likelihood of injury simply must rise and keeps rising as one serves additional meals. Because the focus is on the underlying activity and not on the precaution levels taken, this has come to be called the 'activity level effect.'

The importance of Shavell's and Polinsky's observation for the theory of the efficiency of tort liability standards is that for those instances in which there is an activity level effect, strict liability may be superior to negligence. This is because, under strict liability, the wrongdoer cannot avoid liability (by, for example, complying with a legal duty of care); the best that he can do is simply to minimize expected liability costs. As a result, the potential wrongdoer has an incentive to take into account *every* action or failure to act that can reduce those expected costs – not just those for which a duty of care exists or might exist. So, if reducing the level of the underlying activity (by staying open for business for a limited number of hours, limiting seatings per evening, expanding the bar area and reducing the restaurant area, and so on) reduces the expected liability costs, then the wrongdoer subject to strict liability has an incentive to do so.

In contrast, the same wrongdoer, if subject to negligence liability, would have an incentive to take the activity-level effect into account only if the law had established a legal duty of care with respect to that activity. If not, then the wrongdoer subject to negligence will ignore that effect.[12] The implication is that negligence typically does *not* impose duties of care on activity levels. And, indeed, it might be difficult for the fault standard to do so. How could it restrict the number of customers served in a restaurant in a given time period? Presumably, establishing standards on activity levels through private causes of action would be extremely difficult, if not impossible. It might just be possible to take this effect into account – if it is, in fact, present – through licensure regulation that specified opening hours, maximum floor space area, and other indirect means of keeping the number of meals served to a predetermined level.

In a recent article, Aaron Edlin and Pinar Karaca-Mandic have found some evidence of an activity-level effect like that envisioned by Polinsky and Shavell.[13] The authors note that simply by getting onto the road, each driver increases the likelihood of an accident with other drivers. Almost no driver, however, takes this externality into account in deciding whether and how much to drive. As a result, increasing one's miles-driven imposes an uncompensated external cost – an increase in expected accident losses – on other drivers. Edlin and Karaca-Mandic seek to estimate the value of this externality so as to show how far from the social optimum we are (with respect to automobile driving) and what might be done about that situation.

They recognize that the accident externality must be greater, all other things equal, in jurisdictions where the density of cars is greater. So, in North Dakota, where congestion is minimal, they estimate the annual value of the externality to be $10 per driver, while in California, the value ranges between $1,725 and $3,239. Clearly, in densely populated states these externalities can be substantial, and, as a result, the fact that these externalities are not being internalized could lead to far too much driving and, therefore, far too many and too severe accidents. Nationwide, the authors estimate that the value of this accident externality may run to more than $200 billion per year.

The question then is, 'How do we induce drivers to internalize this accident externality?' Edlin and Karaca-Mandic suggest a gasoline tax (not, interestingly, a change in tort liability standards or licensure regulation). But that (and like solutions) are not ideal in that they apply equally to good and bad drivers. Moreover, there is no stomach among politicians for these taxes. One might take account of that fact by having a separate tax on accident-insurance premiums, hoping that experience rating would have adjusted those premiums to reflect the quality of the insuree's driving.

Our point in this article is to question whether the activity-level effect is an independent reason for preferring strict liability to negligence and whether there might not be more texture to this issue than the literature has heretofore recognized. We make three central arguments: one about an implicit assumption regarding the activity-level effect (and some other definitional issues), and two about the appropriate legal means of taking the effect into account and creating incentives for socially optimal precaution.

The first central argument questions the implicit assumption of the activity-level effect literature – namely, that there is a monotonically increasing relationship between the probability of an accident's occurring and the quantity of the underlying risky activity. That assumes, we believe, a special and not a general relationship. For example, it could be that the relationship between activities and the likelihood of harm is nonmonotonic – that the probability of an accident's occurring initially rises as the activity rises from zero, reaches a peak, and then declines as the activity level continues to increase. There is some intuition to buttress such a relationship: As the potential wrongdoer begins his or her activity (assuming she is new to it), it is likely to be the case that she is not particularly adept at it. So, no matter how much care she may take, she is still likely to make mistakes. Consider, for illustrative purposes, a new driver. When first learning to drive, the likelihood of an accident is, generally, higher than it is likely to be later. It could be that that probability falls continuously as the experience of the driver increases. But in keeping with our intuition, let us imagine that it rises from zero to some peak (which may occur years after the young person begins driving) and then continuously falls as the driver acquires more experience (and, perhaps, increasing incentives to take care).[14]

If this more complicated, nonlinear pattern holds between activity levels and the likelihood of harm, then the problem of adequately taking the activity-level effect into account in choosing among liability standards or other regulatory devices becomes far more complicated. For instance, strict liability might deal with *any* pattern of activity-level effect – in that that standard creates an incentive for the potential tortfeasor to discover the relationship between activity levels and the possibility of harm, whatever that relationship may be.

But there are costs to leaving a complex relationship like that imagined above to strict liability. One is that there are adjustment costs to the potential tortfeasor of trying to imagine where he or she is on the 'activity level'– 'probability of accident' curve. Mistakes seem inevitable, particularly in light of the predictable cognitive errors, such as overoptimism about our own abilities, from which we all suffer.

Consider the following situation. Cab drivers are presumably more experienced drivers and therefore strict liability will be cheaper for them than for inexperienced drivers. Hence inexperienced drivers should ride in cabs rather than in their own cars, hence reducing the likelihood of accidents and the social cost of car accidents. However, this reasoning ignores an important long-run effect. If only experienced drivers drive, once the current pool is dead, there are no experienced drivers since no learning took place. Clearly imposing strict liability in this example raises other concerns – namely, the possible effects on learning and the stock of experienced drivers.

Another cost of relying on strict liability to deal with a nonmonotonic activity-level effect is that the underlying accident may be bilateral, not unilateral. If both parties experience similar activity-level effects, then one should be led to believe that she is strictly liable while the other, that there is no liability. But that misdirection seems unlikely to be practicable.

As we will see, considerations of a nonmonotonic relationship between activity levels and the likelihood of harm may argue for an alternative to the tort liability system as a method of regulating the social costs of these accidents – as Edlin and Karaca-Mandic implied.

There is also the possibility that the relationship is monotonic but negative (rather than positive as conventionally assumed by the economic literature) between activity levels and expected harm. For example, many of the activities taken by medical doctors (preventive medicine) could reduce the possibility of an accident later in surgery. Our chapter does not focus on these cases since the consequences in terms of designing tort liability regimes are largely unsurprising.

The second central argument that we make in criticism of the standard understanding of the activity-level effect is to question the contention that some form of negligence cannot induce efficient precaution when the effect is present. We make two separate criticisms of the conventional understanding.

First, we raise further questions (independent of those we previewed above) about the meaning of the activity-level effect. Some examples that have appeared in the literature (or that one might imagine) seem to deal with doing too much of an activity within a given time period more than with ignoring a difficult-to-detect causal relationship that extends over time. Return to the example of the restaurateur and the possibility of harm to his patrons. The common understanding of the activity-level effect seems to contemplate that the more months or years that a restaurant is in business, the greater the likelihood that someone who dines there will be injured. That is, independent of the precautionary actions that are being taken on a day-to-day basis, this understanding imagines that the more customers that the restaurant has served cumulatively over a long time period, the more likely it is that an accident will occur.[15] But there is another sense in which common discussion seems to mean a problematic relationship between the quantity of the underlying activity and the risk or extent of harm – namely, that if too much of the activity is done within a given (short) time period, the probability and severity of harm may be heightened. So, imagine that a driver of ordinary skill has been driving for 36 hours continuously, without sleep. Surely, the probability and severity of harm have increased significantly because of his having done more than a normal amount of driving within that time span. And just as surely, prevailing notions of negligence can and do adequately evaluate that lack of precaution and thereby send appropriate signals to potential tortfeasors on how much of the underlying risky activity to engage in during a given time period.

Second, even if we were to adopt the standard understanding of the activity-level effect (as described in the preceding paragraph), we believe that the negligence standard is perfectly capable of incorporating the activity-level effect as a duty with which potential wrongdoers must comply or face liability. Just as the strict liability standard creates incentives for potential tortfeasors to take into account *any* source of harm, so the negligence standard creates an incentive for plaintiff's counsel to find all sources of negligence, regardless of whether they are currently defined in law, and to check to see if the defendant took all cost-justified precaution.[16] That being the case and assuming that the defendant knew that any victim of his would have an incentive to discover anything that he might do to reduce the probability and severity of an accident – including taking the activity-level effect into account – the prudent potential tortfeasor will take all cost-justified and cost-justifiable precaution.

The third central argument is to question whether tort liability is the most appropriate regulatory tool for inducing parties to take socially optimal precaution where there are activity-level effects. As we saw in the Edlin–Karaca-Mandic 'accident externality of driving' example, there are circumstances in which safety regulations or carefully levied taxes are a far more effective method of achieving optimality than are changes in the *ex post* liability regime.

II.   PREVIOUS LITERATURE

An overview of the literature on activity levels since the original Polinsky–Shavell arguments of the early 1980s shows us that the analysis has evolved essentially in four different, albeit complementary, directions – namely: (i) defining activity levels; (ii) assessing the implications for tort law of *exogenously* defined activity levels (namely, tort law failures); (iii) establishing the legal implications of *endogenously* defined activity levels and (iv) applications.

A.   The Definition of Activity Level

The distinction between care and activity levels is by no means uncontroversial. Shavell's original definition is that the only substantive difference between care and activity levels is that negligence rules do not incorporate the activity level.[17] Therefore, all actions that are included in negligence rules are part of care whereas all actions that are excluded from negligence rules are part of activity. The definition was somehow anticipated by Peter Diamond who nevertheless already pointed out that the distinction between care and activity level is to a certain extent artificial and, we would add, essentially didactic.[18] This approach has been largely followed by the main textbooks and pedagogical surveys in the field.[19] Nevertheless, many authors have recognized that a distinction based on inclusion *versus* exclusion in the negligence standard is misleading and generates serious practical drawbacks, not least because it assumes some mechanism independent of tort law to partition the set of all possible actions into two mutually exclusive subsets.[20] Furthermore, other notions in tort law, such as avoidable *versus* unavoidable accidents, verifiable *versus* unverifiable measures, or reasonableness *versus* unreasonableness of particular activities, make a direct application of the original definition uneasy in many situations. For example, the extent to which all verifiable activities are considered 'care' and all unverifiable activities are perceived as 'activity' is hardly true. At the same time, under some circumstances activity-level could satisfy the criteria of reasonableness, but in many others it will not.

A common example is the number of miles an individual drives (the activity level) and the level of care she takes in her driving (the precaution or care level). However, it has been pointed out that the use of the rear-view mirror is a typical precautionary measure and still usually not taken into account to determine negligence. The exclusion of the use of the rear-view mirror from the care level has essentially to do with verifiability, but it can hardly be regarded as an 'activity level.'[21]

Other related illustrative examples are in relation to truck drivers and pilots. The likelihood of an accident increases with the number of hours of driving and piloting. Therefore, industry bylaws usually impose quantitative limitations for all providers. However, not only are these limitations not individually tailored (different drivers and pilots might have different needs), but *ex post* verifiability is usually costly (if possible at all). The inclusion of the number of hours of sleep or rest as an element of the care level in a tort liability action might impose very high costs on the industry.

Another example comes from a recent scholarly debate on medical negligence.[22] Suppose an obstetrician has to make a decision whether to deliver a baby by vaginal or Cesarean birth, both with unavoidable risks of harm. If we see the delivery of a baby as the activity level, the immediate problem is that the obstetrician cannot not deliver the baby. Hence, even if strictly liable, the obstetrician cannot make a choice concerning the activity level.

We can say that although most legal economists refer to activity-level as a standard concept in tort law, its application is far more problematic than anticipated. Definitional issues are important because they are at the heart of the argument for strict liability when activity levels matter.

B.   The Consequences of Activity Level for Tort Law

A substantive part of the literature is about the consequences for tort law and the design of negligence rules from taking an *exogenous* approach to activity levels, that is, what is included and what is excluded from due care is taken as given. The problem is framed as a trade-off between providing the appropriate incentives to invest in precautionary measures (in bilateral accidents, the negligence rules are superior to strict liability since the former assigns liability between injurer and victim) and the adequate reduction of activity (strict liability is better than negligence since the former penalizes the injurer more than the latter).[23]

Consider the example of a car driver and a pedestrian in a typical situation of bilateral precaution. Imposing strict liability on the car driver provides insurance for the pedestrian, thereby reducing incentives for him as a potential victim to take care (a phenomenon called 'moral hazard' in the economic literature). A negligence rule, however, would apportion liability in such a way that both sides have adequate incentives to take care.

Suppose now an activity-level effect by the car driver is very relevant as a potential cause of the accident. A negligence rule does not provide the incentive to choose an activity-level efficiently because there is no activity-level standard above which the car driver is not liable. Knowing this, a rational car driver will increase care to the negligence standard to avoid liability but will not reduce her activity level to the appropriate level. The claim is that the same rational car driver will do that if subject to strict liability because there the probability and magnitude of accidental harm are relevant. The activity level reduces the probability and magnitude of accidental harm, which is relevant under strict liability, but it does not change compliance with the standard, which is relevant under negligence. When the activity level on the injurer's side is more important to the outcome than care by the victim, then strict liability is the most efficient liability regime. This simple trade-off gets more complicated when an activity level on the victim's side is also determinant, or other dimensions are accounted for, such as litigation costs, liability insurance, and the imperfect determination of causation.

Other scholars have expanded the economic model to account for the process by which actions are included and excluded – that is, they recognize and model an *endogenous* mechanism to address the nature and scope of negligence standards. The *endogenous* definitions have looked at different explanations, including repetition of certain risky activities and the development of appropriate rules,[24] information concerning causation and the determination of negligence (for example, abnormal activities[25]), and a cost-benefit analysis of the benefit from improving incentives and the administrative cost of more complex tort liability (by extending the set of care).[26] Take the example of the use of the rear-view mirror in driving. One could contemplate the possibility of including it in the negligence standard. That might improve incentives for careful driving. However, the cost of assessing the appropriate use of the rear-view mirror in actual accidents would be quite expensive. Therefore, we might just prefer to leave the use of the rear-view mirror out of the negligence standard (thereby including it in the category of activity level) although sacrificing incentives.

C. Applications

Several applications of how the dichotomy between care and activity levels applies in specific contexts of the law have been developed, for example, in relation to IPOs,[27] with respect to oil pollution damage,[28] nuclear accidents,[29] and products liability,[30] considering medical malpractice liability[31] and other forms of liability,[32] discussing discrimination,[33] framing cigarette regulation,[34] assessing cross-border torts,[35] or even from a more historical perspective.[36]

III. NONCONVEXITIES

One of the implicit assumptions of the activity-level literature (on which the reason for penalizing the activity is based) is that there is a positive monotonic relationship between the probability of an accident or the harm caused by the accident and the risky activity. That presupposes, in our view, a special relationship with very important consequences. In fact, unless the relationship is indeed positive and monotonic, looking for the liability regimes that penalize the activity more effectively is a serious mistake. Consider again the example provided in Section I. The probability of an accident's occurring initially rises as the activity rises from zero, reaches a peak, and then declines as the activity level continues to increase. Depending on where the efficiency level of the activity is (below or above the peak), we might want to increase or decrease the activity. Suppose we want to increase (in order to reduce the probability of harm) whereas we adopt a liability regime that further penalizes the activity.[37] Then, the potential injurer reduces the activity (hence increasing the probability of harm). Suppose the relevant dimension of an activity is learning (how to drive, how to fly, how to perform professional duties as a medical doctor or as a lawyer). The efficient liability system should encourage more activity until learning reduces the possibility of mistakes, not less, even if for a period of time the probability of harm increases.

Not only learning-by-doing might justify the existence of a peak function rather than a monotonic relationship. Production technology could be another reason. Suppose a potential injurer manufactures certain specific goods. It could be that certain technologies that actually reduce the likelihood of harm are only available or operationally justifiable when the injurer engages in high levels of activity. In other words, for certain industries, it could be that by being larger, companies can reduce the probability or the level of harm.

A third possible reason for a nonmonotonic relationship has to do with imperfections of the market for insurance and government intervention. Consider a situation in which a company might create an environmental accident. If it is a large company and the environmental accident is of substantial costs, the state might be willing to provide certain civil protection activities that effectively reduce the harm of the accident (it could be simply because a large company can lobby the government for such complementary activities). For a small company, the state might not be willing to provide such complementary activities (for example, a small company has a more limited ability to influence the government).

A similar reasoning applies to insurance. Once the level of activity is reasonably high and thus the probability of an accident is significant, an insurance company might require the adoption of certain technologies or operational norms that effectively reduce the likelihood of accident or the level of harm. Another example is provided by the observation that in many regulatory fields only the larger firms are actually exposed to control of activity levels.

Consider another important but different case. Suppose the probability of harm is zero as long as the level of activity is zero. However, once the level of activity starts rising from zero, the probability of harm jumps to a reasonably high value. Technically, we have a discontinuity when the level of activity is very close to zero. Here the relationship is monotonic but with a discontinuity. But rather than being a mere technical curiosity, it is of the utmost importance for certain activities. As already mentioned in Section II, consider the decision faced by an obstetrician (or by many other medical specialists). Once they participate in delivering a baby (or many types of surgery), the probability of harm is reasonably high immediately. These are called "participation activities."[38] Another example of a participation activity is the decision whether to drive. For participation activities, the relevant dimension is not quantitative but qualitative (whether to participate). Penalizing participation might create serious negative externalities (for example, nobody wants to deliver babies (who, obviously, have to be delivered), or nobody wants to drive when driving is important for productive economic activity). In fact, if the activity is mandatory to the performance of certain services or the provision of certain goods, then it should not be an issue for determining liability.

A third category of nonconvexities is created by the interaction of activity levels produced by multiple agents. The obvious example relates to activity levels that are imperfect strategic substitutes so that when a potential injurer increases a certain activity level, another potential injurer or even the victim reduces their own activity level in a disproportional way. Consider the following situation: An environmental accident takes place if the level of pollution goes above some critical value. Suppose competing companies might respond to a reduction in production by one of them with a disproportional increase in their production for low levels of production and with a decrease in their production for high levels of production. Although for the first company there is a reduction of activity level, the probability of an accident might have gone up under certain circumstances or might have gone down under a different set of circumstances. Summing up, the interaction between activity levels can generate important nonconvexities.

One could simply argue that nonconvexities are only serious if there are few actors. After all, what matters is at the aggregate level, and in the presence of large numbers, nonconvexities tend to disappear as they are averaged-out (that is the standard argument in the general equilibrium literature in economics). Furthermore, since most markets with few actors are regulated, one way or another, nonconvexities are not very relevant for tort liability.

However, it seems to us that the argument is unconvincing in two ways. First, regulation should do its best to resolve nonconvexities, and yet it is not clear that that is what happens through regulation in industries with few players (although we do believe that nonconvexities should be primarily addressed by regulation and not tort liability).

Second, even if markets have many actors, costs of care and activity-level effects are not necessarily sufficiently heterogeneous to eliminate nonconvexities at the aggregate level. As a result, aggregation could be more complicated than simply averaging-out. Depending on how heterogeneity distributes costs (that is, the variance of costs), nonconvexities might prevail for certain ranges of levels of activity. An obvious example is participation activities. Potential candidates to become obstetricians have different skill levels and, thus, different costs, but the nonconvexity still exists because it is plausible that we do not have huge variances over participation costs.

It is important to note why our argument on nonconvexities is qualitatively different from the standard argument about externalities. The externality argument in liability introduces another dimension into the problem that we have not considered. That problem has to do with the nonmarket value of certain activities. The point has been raised by Robert Cooter and Ariel Porat.[39] Certain activities might increase the probability of an accident but at the same time might have a positive or negative externality upon the potential victims. Consider the case of a broken leg. The same leg could have been broken during a difficult chirurgic intervention that saved the patient's life, or could have resulted from a reckless driver who hurt a pedestrian, or could be the unintended outcome of the behavior by a group of drunken individuals at a bar. The harm is the same – a broken leg. However, the activity that produced the harm is substantively different in all three instances. Driving per se has no external effect on the pedestrian; a chirurgic intervention has a positive externality on the patient; and a fight between drunk people has a negative externality on anyone else in the bar. These different external effects justify a different treatment of activity levels. Strict liability might well not be the appropriate tort regime for activities that cause positive externalities. In fact, increasing an activity that causes positive externalities even if it also increases the probability of harm might be appropriate. However, this dimension of the problem is independent of nonconvexities.

Once nonconvexities are recognized as a significant problem, we argue that it becomes very complex and costly to develop a tort system that addresses adequate incentives for preventive activities for all parties plus takes care of activity-level effects. We therefore argue that regulation plays an important role in internalizing nonconvexities. We could conceivably develop a subset of activity levels for which nonconvexities are quite important and have these activities regulated; we could have another subset of activity levels for which nonconvexities are really not a significant issue and have them solved by the tort system. We would argue that to a certain extent that is what the law currently does.

Appropriate regulation of nonconvexities could require caps as well as minimum activity requirements. It seems to us that if it is difficult for courts to impose caps on activity levels in general, it is certainly much more complex to have courts imposing minimum activity requirements. Regulation seems to be superior to tort liability when minimum activity requirements are needed.[40]

IV.   WHAT CONSTITUTES AN ACTIVITY LEVEL

As we have discussed in Section II, what constitutes an activity level is not as simple as it might appear from the more pedagogical literature. It is true that the simplest approach with a wide categorization (an activity level is everything that courts find difficult to observe or all relevant dimensions that are not included in the standard) is useful to start a discussion, but we need to move to a more sophisticated and narrow interpretation if a deep understanding of the law is the goal. Clearly, standards are usually based on reasonable indicators whereas relevant dimensions that usually do not have good indicators could be regarded as what legal economists define as an activity-level effect. For example, although maintenance of certain relevant physical capital is part of the activity level of a company, there are usually reasonable indicators of that maintenance, and, therefore, it can be included in a standard of care. Another example, the number of flying hours of a plane or of a particular pilot, is easily calculated, and although those hours are an activity level, they are typically relevant for negligence determination.

As we have observed in previous examples, there are nevertheless several activities with reasonable indicators that still are excluded from the negligence standard and end up in the category of activity level. The most immediate example is the number of miles driven by an injurer in a car accident. We believe that nonconvexities could be the reason for why the negligence standard does not include them. Looking at the number of miles driven by an injurer, the court would have to balance the positive learning effect against the negative physical and psychological effects on a driver (exhaustion).

We do not exclude externalities as another possible explanation for why activities with indicators are excluded from the negligence standard in the vein of Cooter and Porat. It is possible that the inclusion of miles driven on the negligence standard would reduce the private expected benefit of driving with serious consequences in economic productivity. Looking at the number of babies an obstetrician has delivered to determine negligence would undoubtedly generate a negative externality that could affect the survival of the species. Taking production as a measure of care could eventually lead to the collapse of certain markets due to potential product liability issues, which certainly hurts consumers.

The conventional wisdom seems to indicate that the activities with reasonable indicators are better managed by the tort system *ex post* whereas the activities without indicators are better addressed by *ex ante* regulation or even by criminal law (in the case of prohibitions).[41] This raises the question of who is in a better position to gather information in order to achieve the efficient rate of accidents. As we have seen in Section II, at the end of the day, the issue is to compare the administrative cost of addressing activity levels with the cost of relying on the tort system and thus failing to internalize the activity levels. However, it seems to us that this approach is essentially static, neglecting that the creation of indicators is dynamic and responds to incentives to a certain extent. This naturally raises the question of who should provide the incentive for the parties to generate such indicators, in particular whether courts are well-positioned to require this and to evaluate those indicators.

Our argument is that if a certain activity level plays a very substantial role in determining the probability or the harm of an accident, courts will develop the necessary incentives to create reasonable indicators of that activity level. At some point, that standard will be included in the relevant standard. In other words, we do not believe that a relevant activity level is systematically and continuously ignored by the courts. We argue that standards are dynamic and respond to relevant activity levels.

Clearly the role of the courts is not immune to the presence of regulation. Indeed, if regulation took care efficiently of activity levels, not only the tort system should be unproblematic in this respect, but there would be no pressure to adjust standards. That is, it may well be that regulation and the tort liability system are complementary in the sense that regulation tends to deal with activity-level effects while the tort liability system deals with care levels. So, regulation specifies licensure requirements for drivers (as well as some other aspects of safety) – thereby addressing the principal activity-level effect – and leaves to negligence law the determination of such care levels as maintenance of the lighting and signaling abilities of the car. Precisely because regulation is imperfect and cannot effectively address all of the concerns with respect to activity levels, courts may feel the need to provide incentives to generate indicators and improve standards. One way to provide incentives to generate indicators is to move to strict liability. This makes a certain activity more costly, hence providing an incentive to generate relevant indicators that can push the tort regime back to negligence.

The imperfections of regulations and the dynamic role of the courts also helps us to understand significant comparative institutional differences. If it were all about assigning activity levels to regulation or correcting them by strict liability, we would find similar solutions across countries. After all, traffic accidents, environmental accidents, and medial malpractice cannot be perceived to be technologically so different between the United States and Europe to justify the observed differences. In civil law, strict liability is narrowly used and only for activities that are particularly risky and activities to which assessing the injurer's fault is particularly difficult.[42] In fact, activity levels in areas such as environmental liability, product liability, consumer policy, and public health are traditionally allocated to state regulation rather than liability. For example, considerations about activity levels in torts have been absent to the point that it is considered a major drawback of the principles of European tort law.[43]

Once we recognize the role of courts, then some of these differences are less puzzling. If courts enjoy reasonable discretion to produce incentives to generate indicators or adjust negligence standards, regulation is less required. However, if courts are very constrained, then activity levels should be mainly internalized by regulation. We are prepared to argue that this stylized picture fits broadly with the notion that courts in civil law enjoy less discretion than in common law.

V.   CONCLUSION

In this chapter, we make three central arguments. The first important argument questions the implicit assumption of the activity-level effect literature that there is a monotonically increasing relationship between the probability of an accident's occurring and the quantity of the underlying risky activity.

The second significant observation is that, even if we were to adopt the standard understanding of the activity-level effect, we believe that the negligence standard is perfectly capable of incorporating that effect as a duty with which potential wrongdoers must comply or face liability.

The third argument questions whether tort liability is the most appropriate regulatory tool for inducing parties to take socially optimal precaution where there are activity-level effects.

In an ideal world, activity levels should be included in the negligence standard. The traditional explanation is that they are not included because it is infeasible to do so, that it is too costly to verify them, or that eventually there are other legal restrictions (such as data protection that impedes certain activity levels to be measured or used for negligence standards). Our argument is that if an activity level is really relevant for reducing the probability or harm of an accident, then dynamically or evolutionarily we expect the development of the necessary technology to make the inclusion of such activity level in the standard feasible at some affordable cost. Still, quite importantly, if the nature and scope of harm caused by an accident changes over time, it might be that such an activity level is not consistently and systematically important, hence it never gets to be included in the standard.

The next question is, given that the activity level will be included in the standard at some point, who should do it, the courts or the regulator? We have argued, from the positive perspective, that if regulators do not do it, courts will do at some point in some form of 'regulation of activity levels by litigation.'

From a normative perspective, we have indicated that regulation is likely to be better equipped to expand standards in order to achieve inclusion of activity levels since this usually requires some technology development. Regulators seem to have better specific knowledge and more information (since only a small fraction of cases are litigated) to achieve that goal. However, it is possible that the creation of measurability of activity levels is better done by regulators while the specific enforcement of such measurability of activity levels is more adequately done by courts.

NOTES

1. The authors are extremely grateful to Robert Cooter, Giuseppe Dari-Mattiacci, Kevin Davis, Christoph Engel, Andrew Guzman, Fernando Gomez-Pomar, Gillian Hadfield, Henry Hansmann, Gerard Hertig, Lewis Kornhauser, Francesco Parisi, Ariel Porat, Susan Rose-Ackerman, Daniel Rubinfeld, Joanna Shepherd, Urs Schweizer, Avraham Tabbach, and Katrina Wyman for their valuable comments on a previous preliminary version of the paper presented at the 2007 CLEF meeting, New York, the 2007 MLEA meeting, Minneapolis, the 2008 ALEA meetings, New York, and at Bonn University. Research assistantship by Amber Evans, Sofia Amaral Garcia, and Guilherme Vilaça is duly acknowledged. The usual disclaimers apply.
2. Professor of Law, University of Illinois College of Law. ngaroupa@illinois.edu.
3. Swanlund Chair Emeritus, University of Illinois at Urbana-Champaign, and Professor Emeritus of Law, University of Illinois College of Law, t-ulen@illinois.edu.
4. See Posner (1972a, 1972b). For later developments in the field of the economics of tort liability, see Landes and Posner (1987) and Shavell (1987).
5. See Brown (1973). Indeed, our experience is that even today only those who work professionally in law and economics are fully conversant with Brown's economic theory of tort liability and the extensions that have been made to the model in the intervening forty years.
6. See Cooter and Ulen (2011).
7. We summarize that literature in Section II below.
8. The central difference, as we will see in Section II below, is that between unilateral and bilateral precaution. Broadly speaking, strict liability is the more efficient standard under unilateral precaution, and negligence, under bilateral precaution.
9. See the reasons given by Richard Posner for resolving a dispute about accident losses in *Indiana Harbor Belt Railroad Co. v. American Cyanamid Co.*, 916 F.2d 1174 (7th Cir. 1990). See also Sykes (2007).
10. See Shavell (1980, 1987 and 2004) and Polinsky (1980).
11. The early economic analysis might also focus on the restaurant's being the 'least cost avoider' for minimizing the accident losses from this sort of injury.
12. This is not, of course, strictly true. We shall return to a discussion of this possibility in Section II below.
13. See Edlin and Karaca-Mandic (2006).
14. Of course, it could be the case that at a much later age the driver's probability of inflicting harm increases again. We do not contend that this is the actual pattern. Our point, rather, is that there is likely to be a complicated relationship between activity levels and likelihood of harm, not the simple pattern imagined in the literature.
15. Put somewhat technically, this understanding imagines that if x is a vector of precautionary activities, then there is the expected accident losses facing a potential tortfeasor for whom this is the case are $P(x, l_t)A(x, l_t)$, where l_t indicates the volume of activity,

indexed by time. The sense is that while the probability and severity of an accident decline with respect to $\mathbf{x}$, they increase with respect to l_t.

16. Suppose that there are n factors that can have an influence on the probability of an accident so that the expected cost of an accident is given by $P(x_1, x_2, \ldots, x_{n-1}, x_n) A(x_1, x_2, \ldots, x_{n-1}, x_n)$. If legal duties are defined over only, say, 10 of those factors, then we might partition the expected accident losses as follows, with the bars over the x's indicating that those are factors for which legal duties have been defined and those factors to the right of the vertical bar representing factors for which no legal duty has been defined: $P(\bar{x}_1, \bar{x}_2, \bar{x}_3, \ldots, \bar{x}_{10} | x_{11}, \ldots, x_n) A(\bar{x}_1, \bar{x}_2, \bar{x}_3, \ldots, \bar{x}_{10} | x_{11}, \ldots, x_n)$. The key for a dynamic theory of negligence is to explain how factors move from the right of the vertical line to the left.

17. See Shavell (1980, 1987).
18. See Diamond (1974).
19. See Cooter and Ulen (2011) as well as Landes and Posner (1987), Miceli (1997, 2004), Moorhouse, Morriss and Whaples (1998), and Shavell (2004).
20. See, among others, Latin (1987), Donohue (1989), Grady (1988, 1994) and Gilles (1992).
21. A point already noted by Shavell (1987).
22. See Cooter and Porat (2006) as well as Hylton (2006).
23. For example, Ordover (1978), Landes and Posner (1981), Grady (1983, 1998), Arlen (1990), Hylton (1991, 1996, 2006), Goldberg (1994), Demougin and Fluet (1999), Meese (2001), Fluet (2002), Nell (2003), Parisi and Fon (2004), Schlanger (2005), Kim (2006), Shepherd (2008), Tabbach (2008).
24. See Gilles (1992).
25. See King (1996).
26. See Dari-Mattiacci (2005).
27. See Sher (2006).
28. See Faure and Hui (2006).
29. See Trebilcock and Winter (1997).
30. See Bonney (1985) and Ben-Shahar (1998).
31. See Vandall (1984) and Arlen and MacLeod (2003).
32. See Johnston (1987), Hanson and Logue (1990), Verkerke (1995), Croley (1996) and Keating (2001).
33. See Wax (1999).
34. Hanson and Logue (1998).
35. See Michaels (2006).
36. See Ross (2006).
37. We are concerned with exogenous nonconvexities – that is, nonconvexities created by the activity-level technology, and by the law. There are endogenous convexities created by the law: for example, those related to the judgment-proof problem. High levels of activity might consume so much capital that companies have not enough resources to pay for the harm they caused. Hence as the activity level increases, the expected harm borne by the company goes down. Notice however that it is a reduction of the expected harm borne by the company and not the expected harm borne by society. See the discussion in Dari-Mattiacci and De Geest (2006).
38. See Cooter and Porat (2006).
39. See Cooter and Porat (2006).
40. See Gilo and Guttel (2009) and responses by Abraham (2009), Epstein (2009), Grady (2009) as well as Gilo and Guttel (2010).
41. See, among others, Shavell (1984a, 1984b), Kolstad, Ulen and Johnson (1990), and Schmitz (2000).
42. See Zweigert and Kötz (1998).
43. See van den Bergh and Visscher (2006), making the point that strict liability is too narrow and does not take into account the goals of prevention more generally.

REFERENCES

Abraham, Kenneth (2009) 'Insufficient Analysis of Insufficient Activity,' 108 *Michigan Law Review* 24.

Arlen, Jennifer (1990) 'Reconsidering Efficient Tort Rules for Personal Injury: The Case of Single Activity Accidents,' 32 *William and Mary Law Review* 41.

Arlen, Jennifer and Bentley MacLeod (2003) 'Malpractice Liability for Physicians and Managed Care Associations,' 78 *N.Y.U. Law Review* 1929.

Ben-Shahar, Omri (1998) 'Should Products Liability Be Based on Hindsight?' 14 *Journal of Law, Econ., and Organization* 325.

Bonney, Paul (1985) 'Manufacturers' Strict Liability for Handgun Injuries: An Economic Analysis,' 73 *Georgia Law Journal* 1437.

Brown, John (1973) 'Toward an Economic Theory of Liability,' 2 *Journal of Legal Studies* 323.

Cooter, Robert and Ariel Porat (2006) 'Liability Externality and Mandatory Choices: Should Doctors Pay Less?' 1 *Journal of Tort Law* (Article 2).

Cooter, Robert and Thomas Ulen (2011) *Law and Economics*, 6th Edition, Boston: Addison-Wesley.

Croley, Steven (1996) 'Vicarious Liability in Tort: On the Sources and Limits of Employee Reasonableness,' 69 *Southern Calif. Law Rev.* 1705.

Dari-Mattiacci, Giuseppe (2005) 'On the Optimal Scope of Negligence,' 1 *Review of Law and Economics* 331.

Dari-Mattiacci, G. and G. De Geest (2006) 'When Will Judgment Proof Injurers Take Too Much Precaution?' *International Review of Law and Economics* 26: 336–54.

Demougin, Dominique and Claude Fluet (1999) 'Further Justifications for the Negligence Rule,' 19 *Int'l Review of Law and Econ* 33.

Diamond, Peter (1974) 'Single Activity Accidents,' 3 *Journal of Legal Studies* 107.

Donahue, John (1989) 'The Law and Economics of Tort Law: The Profound Revolution,' 102 *Harvard Law Review* 1047.

Edlin, Aaron and Pinar Karaca-Mandic (2006) 'The Accident Externality from Driving,' 114 *Journal of Political Economy* 931.

Epstein, Richard (2009) 'Response: Activity Levels Under the Hand Formula,' 108 *Michigan Law Review* 37.

Faure, Michael and Wang Hui (2006) 'Economic Analysis of Compensation for Oil Pollution Damage,' 37 *Journal of Maritime Law and Commerce* 179.

Fluet, Claude (2002) 'Liability Insurance and Moral Hazard under Strict Liability and Negligence Rules,' 12 *Revue de Economie Politique* 845.

Gilles, Stephen (1992) 'Rule-Based Negligence and the Regulation of Activity Levels,' 21 *Journal of Legal Studies* 319.

Gilo, David and Ehud Guttel (2009) 'Negligence and Insufficient Activity: The Missing Paradigm in Torts,' 108 *Michigan Law Review* 277.

Goldberg, Victor (1994) 'Litigation Costs under Strict Liability and Negligence,' 16 *Research in Law and Economics* 1.

Grady, Mark (2009) 'Response: Another Theory of Insufficient Activity Levels,' 108 *Michigan Law Review* 30.

Grady, Mark (1994) '*Res Ipsa Loquitur* and Compliance Error,' 142 *Univ. of Pennsylvania Law Rev.* 887.

Grady, Mark (1988) 'Why Are People Negligent?: Technology, Nondurable Precautions, and the Medical Malpractice Explosion,' 82 *Northwestern Univ. Law Rev.* 293.

Grady, Mark (1983) 'A New Positive Economic Theory of Negligence,' 92 *Yale Law Review* 799.

Hanson, Jon and Kyle Logue (1998) The Costs of Cigarettes: The Economic Case for Ex Post Incentive-based Regulation, *Yale Law Journal*, 107: 1163–361.

Hanson, Jon and Kyle Logue (1990) 'The First-Party Insurance Externality: An Economic Justification for Enterprise Liability,' 76 *Cornell Law Review* 129.

Hylton, Keith (2006) 'Liability and Externalities: A Comment on Cooter and Porat,' 1 *Journal of Tort Law* (article 3).

Hylton, Keith (1996) 'A Missing Markets Theory of Tort Law,' 90 *Northwestern Univ. Law Rev.* 977.

Hylton, Keith (1991) 'Litigation Costs and the Economic Theory of Tort Law,' 46 *Univ. of Miami Law Rev.* 111.

Johnston, Jason (1987) 'Punitive Liability: A New Paradigm of Efficiency in Tort Law,' 87 *Columbia Law Review* 1385.

Keating, Gregory (2001) 'The Theory of Enterprise Liability and Common Law Strict Liability,' 54 *Vanderbilt Law Review* 1285.

Kim, Jeong-Yoo (2006) 'Strict Liability versus Negligence When the Injurer's Activity Involves Positive Externalities,' 22 *European Journal of Law and Econ.* 95.

King, Joseph (1996) 'A Goals-Oriented Approach to Strict Liability for Abnormally Dangerous Activities,' 48 *Baylor Law Review* 341.

Kolstad, Charles, Thomas Ulen, and Gary Johnson (1990) 'Ex Post Liability for Harm versus Ex Ante Safety Regulation: Substitutes or Complements?' 80 *American Economic Review* 888.

Landes, William and Richard Posner (1987) *The Economic Structure of Tort Law*, Cambridge, MA: Harvard Univ. Press.

Landes, William and Richard Posner (1981) 'The Positive Economic Theory of Tort Law,' 15 *Georgia Law Review* 851.

Latin, Howard (1987) 'Activity Levels, Due Care, and Selective Realism in Economic Analysis of Tort Law,' 39 *Rutgers Law Review* 487.

Meese, Alan (2001) 'The Externality of Victim Care,' 68 *Univ. of Chicago Law Rev.* 1201.

Miceli, Thomas (2004) *The Economic Approach to Law*, Stanford, CA: Stanford Univ. Press.

Miceli, Thomas (1997) *Economics of the Law: Torts, Contracts, Property, Litigation*, New York: Oxford Univ. Press.

Michaels, Ralf (2006) 'Two Economists, Three Opinions? Economic Models for Private International Law – Cross Border Torts as an Example,' in J. Basedow and T. Kono, eds., *An Economic Analysis of Private International Law*, Mohr Siebeck.

Moorhouse, John, Andrew Morriss and Robert Whaples (1998) 'Law and Economics and Tort Law: A Survey of Scholarly Opinion,' 62 *Alabama Law Review* 667.

Nell, Martin (2003) 'The Design of Liability Rules for Highly Risky Activities – Is Strict Liability Superior When Risk Allocations Matter?' 23 *Int'l Review of Law and Economics* 31.

Ordover, Janusz (1978) 'Costly Litigation in a Model of Single Activity Accidents,' 7 *Journal of Legal Studies* 243.

Parisi, Francesco and Vincy Fon (2004) 'Comparative Causation,' 6 *American Law and Economics Rev.* 345.

Polinsky, A. Mitchell (1980) 'Strict Liability versus Negligence in a Market Setting,' 70 *American Economic Review* 363.

Posner, Richard (1972a) *Economic Analysis of Law*, Boston: Little-Brown.

Posner, Richard (1972b) 'A Theory of Negligence' 1 *Journal of Legal Studies* 29.

Ross, Jeremy (2006) 'An Economic Analysis of Aquilian Liability,' 14 *Tulane Journal of Int'l and Comparative Law* 521.

Schlanger, Margo (2005) 'Second Best Damage Action Deterrence,' 55 *DePaul Law Review* 517.

Schmitz, P. W. (2000) 'On the Joint Use of Liability and Safety Regulation,' 20 *Int'l Review of Law and Economics* 371.

Shavell, Steven (2004) *Foundations of Economic Analysis of Law*, Cambridge, MA: Belknap Press.

Shavell, Steven (1987) *Economic Analysis of Accident Law*, Cambridge, MA: Harvard Univ. Press.

Shavell, Steven (1984a) 'Liability for Harm versus Regulation of Safety,' 13 *Journal of Legal Studies* 357.

Shavell, Steven (1984b) 'A Model of the Optimal Use of Safety Regulation,' 15 *Rand Journal of Economics* 271.

Shavell, Steven (1980) 'Strict Liability versus Negligence,' 9 *Journal of Legal Studies* 1.

Shepherd, Joanna (2008) 'Tort Reforms' Winners and Losers: The Competing Effects of Care and Activity Levels,' 55 *UCLA Law Review* 905.

Sher, Noam (2006) 'Negligence versus Strict Liability: The Case of Underwriter Liability in IPOs,' 4 *DePaul Business and Comm. Law Journal* 451.

Sykes, A. (2007) 'Strict Liability Versus Negligence in *Indiana Harbor*,' Stanford Law and Economics, Olin Working Paper No. 332.

Tabbach, Avraham (2008) 'Causation, Discontinuity and Incentives to Choose Levels of Care and Activity Under the Negligence Rules,' 4 *Review of Law and Economics* 45.

Trebilcock, Michael and Ralph Winter (1997) 'The Economics of Nuclear Accidents Law,' 17 *International Review of Law and Econ.* 215.

Vandall, Frank (1984) 'Applying Strict Liability to Professions: Economic and Legal Analysis,' 59 *Indiana Law Journal* 25.

Van den Bergh, Roger and Louis Visscher (2006) 'The Principles of European Tort Law: The Right Path to Harmonization?' German Working Papers in Law and Economics, Article 8.

Verkerke, J. Hoult (1995) 'Notice Liability in Employment Discrimination Law,' 81 *Virginia Law Review* 273.

Wax, Amy (1999) 'Discrimination as an Accident,' 74 *Indiana Law Journal* 1129.

Zweigert, Konrad and Hein Koetz (1998) *An Introduction to Comparative Law*, 3rd Edition, Oxford: Oxford University Press.

3. Liability versus regulation for product-related risks

Thomas J. Miceli, Rebecca Rabon, and Kathleen Segerson

1. INTRODUCTION

Liability and safety regulation represent alternative mechanisms for controlling the risks that often arise from otherwise socially beneficial activities. Liability represents a private response whereby the victim of an accident brings suit for monetary damages against the responsible party, while regulation is a publicly imposed and enforced standard of conduct or safety that potential injurers must adhere to under threat of legal sanction. Historically, product-related harm was largely controlled by market forces under the doctrine of *caveat emptor*, or buyer beware, but the twentieth century witnessed a trend toward increasing producer liability, culminating with the establishment of strict producer liability in the 1960s (Cooter and Ulen, 1988, pp. 421–436). Government regulation of product safety, as distinct from tort liability, did not emerge until the 1970s, but has since become an important means, along with the liability system, for controlling product risk (Viscusi, Harrington, and Vernon, 2005, Chapter 22).

Shavell (1984) has examined the optimal choice between these two modes of controlling risk in the context of a standard model of accidents between strangers (i.e., parties not in a contractual relationship). His analysis showed that neither approach generally produces the socially optimal level of risk-reduction. The drawback of regulation is that it sets a single standard that applies to all accident settings, given the inability of the regulator to observe victim-specific harm. Thus, care is not individualized under the optimal regulatory standard. Liability, in contrast, allows individualization of care under the assumption that injurers can observe and respond to individual victim types, but its effect on accident prevention is diluted because some injurers may escape suit or not have sufficient assets to pay damages. Thus, depending on the situation, either approach may be optimal, and in some cases it may be desirable to combine the two methods.

This chapter examines the choice between liability and safety regulation for controlling the risk of accidents involving products; that is, accidents in which the injurer and victim have a pre-existing contractual relationship.[1] In this context, the trade-off between the two modes of risk control is different. This is true, first of all, because firms cannot individualize care (product safety) under either approach, given that, like the regulator, they cannot observe or respond to individual consumer susceptibility to harm. In other words, firms produce a single, standardized product for all consumers, and as a result, the individualization of care that ideally occurs under a liability rule in Shavell's model is not possible for product-related accidents. Even if all victims file suit and injurers can fully cover their losses, regulation will be at least as good as liability in establishing optimal product safety, all else equal.

A second difference between accidents involving strangers and product-related accidents is that in the latter case, consumers can observe the level of product safety before purchase.[2] As a result, they can decide whether or not to buy the product in the first place based on its consumption benefit relative to its risk. This decision provides a second avenue, not present in the accidents-between-strangers model, along which accidental harm can be reduced. This consideration is especially important when consumers vary in their susceptibility to harm – as in the case of food allergies, drug side effects, or their ability to use an inherently dangerous product (like a chain saw) correctly – because consumers can self-select in their purchase decisions, with those who are especially prone to harm (ideally) refraining from buying the product.

Note that a crucial factor in inducing this sort of self-selection is that consumers must expect to bear their own harm. For this reason, strict liability will not be able to achieve efficient sorting because it fully compensates victims for their losses, whereas regulation, because it leaves consumers to bear their own damages, will. This feature of regulation gives it an advantage over liability for product-related accidents, but exploiting that advantage requires that consumers correctly assess the risk of harm. If consumers misperceive risk, either over- or underestimating it, then they will buy too little or too much of the product (respectively) under a regulatory standard, even if that standard is optimally chosen. Liability, in contrast, is not hindered by consumer misperceptions precisely because victims do not bear their own damages. Instead, the firm, which is assumed to assess risk correctly, sets the price of the product to signal the average risk among purchasers, thereby mitigating the over- or underconsumption problem. The principal conclusion of this chapter is that, based on these competing factors (i.e., the absence of sorting under liability and the misperception of risk under regulation), regulation of product safety is preferred when consumers perceive risks fairly accurately, and producer liability for product accidents is preferred when they significantly misperceive risks.

The remainder of the chapter is organized as follows. Section 2 sets up the model. Section 3 then compares liability and regulation when consumers all suffer the same harm. In this benchmark case, we show that liability is at least as good as regulation for controlling product risk, and is strictly preferred when consumers misperceive risk. Section 4 turns to the case where consumers vary in their susceptibility to harm and examines the trade-off between the two modes of risk control, as described above. Finally, Section 5 concludes.

2.   THE MODEL

Consider a product the consumption of which creates the risk of harm. Let $\pi(x)$ be the true probability of an accident per unit of the product, where x is the manufacturer's dollar investment in product safety, or care (per unit), and $\pi'<0$, $\pi''>0$. Thus, as usual, product risk is decreasing at a decreasing rate in the firm's investment in safety.[3] To account for misperceptions, let $\lambda\pi(x)$ be the consumer's perceived risk, where $\lambda \leq 1$ is an index of the degree of the misperceptions (Polinsky and Rogerson, 1983; Spence, 1977). For simplicity, we focus on the case of consumer underestimation of risk, though the main results would also hold for overestimation. We assume, however, that firms correctly assess risk.

Let a be the gross value of a unit of the product to the consumer (i.e., the value of the product if it were risk-free), and let h be the harm from an accident. Thus, the net expected value of a unit of the product is $a-\pi(x)h$. In the general model below, we will assume that consumers differ in both a and h. As a benchmark, however, we will consider a simpler version in which all consumers have a common h (or at least have the same expected h prior to purchase) and only vary in their gross valuation, a. Let $G(a)$ be the distribution function of a, with the associated density $g(a)$. Consumers have private information about their own a, though firms and regulators know the distribution. In this initial version of the model, firms and regulators are assumed to know the common h of consumers. Finally, let c be the (fixed) production cost per unit, exclusive of safety features. The total unit cost of production is therefore $c + x$. Throughout, we will assume that consumers buy at most one unit of the product.

3.   CONSUMERS SUFFER THE SAME HARM

As noted, we first examine a model where all consumers expect to suffer the same harm from a product-related accident. We begin by deriving the efficient outcome, and then compare the actual outcome under strict liability and an optimally chosen safety standard.

3.1 The Social Optimum

First consider the efficient consumption decision, given x, which we assume consumers can observe prior to purchase. It is efficient for a consumer of type a to purchase the product if and only if

$$a - \pi(x)h \geq c + x,$$

or if and only if

$$a \geq c + x + \pi(x)h \equiv \hat{a}. \tag{3.1}$$

Given efficient purchase, the optimal level of safety maximizes social welfare, which equals net consumption benefits for those consumers who purchase the product:

$$W = \int_{\hat{a}}^{\infty} (a - c - x - \pi(x)h)g(a)\,da. \tag{3.2}$$

The resulting first-order condition for x is

$$1 + \pi'(x)h = 0, \tag{3.3}$$

which, as usual, equates the marginal cost and marginal benefit of safety per unit. Let x^* denote the resulting level of safety, and let W^* denote the maximized value of (3.2).

3.2 Strict Liability

Under a rule of strict liability, the consumer expects to be fully compensated for any damages after the fact, and so purchases a unit of the product if and only if $a \geq P$, where P is the price. The expected profit of a representative firm is equal to

$$\Pi = \int_{P}^{\infty} (P - c - x - \pi(x)h)g(a)\,da. \tag{3.4}$$

To avoid introducing market power issues,[4] we assume that the firm is competitive and takes P as given. Thus, its only decision is over x. Note that maximizing (3.4) yields the same condition as (3.3), so the firm invests in efficient safety, x^*. Assuming zero profit, we obtain the price

$$P = c + x^* + \pi(x^*)h. \tag{3.5}$$

Substituting this into the consumer's purchase criterion yields (3.1), so consumption of the product is also efficient. Thus, strict liability yields the socially optimal (first-best) outcome.[5]

3.3   Regulation

Now consider a regulatory standard that sets the required level of safety at x_s. Since consumers bear their own risk in this case, the purchase decision is based on

$$a \geq P + \lambda\pi(x_s)h \equiv a_s(\lambda), \tag{3.6}$$

where, recall, $\lambda\pi(x_s)$ is the perceived risk, with $\lambda \leq 1$. Assuming that the firm complies with the regulatory standard, its profit is

$$\Pi = \int_{a_s(x)}^{\infty} (P - c - x_s)g(a)da. \tag{3.7}$$

Thus, by meeting the standard, the firm avoids liability or any other legal sanction.[6] Zero profit implies that $P = c + x_s$, which, from (3.6), yields

$$a_s(\lambda) = c + x_s + \lambda\pi(x_s)h. \tag{3.8}$$

Consumers therefore make efficient purchase decisions if $\lambda = 1$, but they will overconsume the product if $\lambda < 1$, given x_s.

The safety standard is chosen to maximize welfare, which is given by

$$W_s = \int_{a_s(\lambda)}^{\infty} (a - c - x - \pi(x)h)g(a)da. \tag{3.9}$$

The first-order condition defining x_s, after re-arranging, is

$$1 + \pi'(x)h = \frac{(1 - \lambda)\pi(x)hg(a_s(\lambda))(\partial a_s/\partial x)}{1 - G(a_s(\lambda))}, \tag{3.10}$$

where, from (3.8), $\partial a_s/\partial x = 1 + \lambda\pi'h$. Realized social welfare, denoted $W_s^*(\lambda)$, is given by (3.9) evaluated at $x_s(\lambda)$. Note that when $\lambda = 1$, the right-hand side is zero and $x_s(1) = x^*$, the efficient level of safety. Thus, when consumers correctly perceive risk, the regulatory standard approach, like strict liability, achieves the socially optimal outcome.

When $\lambda < 1$, however, x_s will deviate from x^*. Starting from x^*, as λ falls below 1, $1 + \lambda\pi'h > 0$, and the right-hand side of (3.10) becomes positive. Thus, $1 + \pi'h > 0$ at the optimum, which implies that $x_s > x^*$, or the stringency of the standard is increased above the efficient level. Intuitively, when consumers underestimate risk, they will overconsume the product according to (3.8) (i.e., a_s will be too low). The regulator will optimally respond by increasing the required level of product safety above the first-best level. The resulting outcome is therefore second-best. In contrast, the outcome under strict liability is not affected by consumer perceptions, so it must be more efficient than the regulatory standard in this case.

The results of this section can be summarized as follows:

Proposition 1: Suppose that all consumers expect to suffer the same harm from a product-related accident. Then (a) when consumers correctly perceive product risk, both strict liability and an optimally chosen safety standard achieve the first-best outcome; (b) when consumers underestimate risk, strict liability continues to achieve the first-best outcome, but the outcome under the safety standard is second-best. Thus, strict liability is more efficient than the safety standard.

This result implies that liability is at least as good as regulation for controlling product risk when consumers suffer the same harm. The advantage of liability is that it avoids the problem of consumer misperceptions because accident victims are fully compensated. Instead, the price of the product accurately signals risk to consumers. When consumers vary in their susceptibility to risk, however, the price can only signal average risk, so liability will no longer be able to achieve the first-best outcome. In that case, the choice between liability and regulation (which is also unable to achieve the first-best) becomes ambiguous, as the next section shows.

4. CONSUMERS VARY IN THEIR HARM

Suppose that consumers vary in the amount of harm they expect to suffer from a product-related accident. Consumers know their own h prior to purchase, but firms cannot observe individual h's.[7] However, firms know the distribution function of h, $F(h)$, and the associated density, $f(h)$. As above, we first derive the social optimum, and then compare liability and regulation.

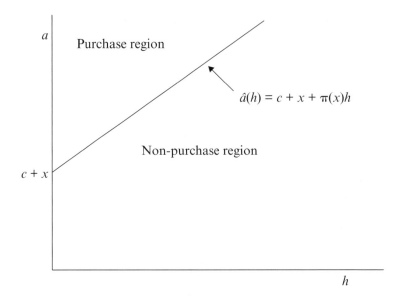

Figure 3.1   Efficient purchase region when consumers vary in both a *and* h

4.1   The Social Optimum

Efficient purchase continues to be defined by the inequality

$$a \geq c + x + \pi(x)h = \hat{a}(h), \tag{3.11}$$

but now, because consumers vary in two dimensions, this condition defines an efficient-purchase *region* in (a, h) space, as shown in Figure 3.1, where the positively sloped line is the locus of points defined by (3.11) written as an equality. Note that it is efficient for consumers with high a and/or low h to purchase the product.

Given this purchase region, the efficient level of product safety maximizes the following welfare function:

$$W = \int_0^\infty \int_{\hat{a}(h)}^\infty (a - c - x - \pi(x)h) g(a) f(h) \, da \, dh. \tag{3.12}$$

The resulting first-order condition is

$$\int_0^\infty \int_{\hat{a}(h)}^\infty (1 + \pi'(x)h) g(a) f(h) \, da \, dh = 0. \tag{3.13}$$

Let x^{**} denote the socially optimal level of safety as defined by (3.13), and let W^{**} denote the maximized value of (3.12). Note that this optimum is not first-best in the sense that a single level of safety is set for all consumers, regardless of their individual susceptibility to harm (i.e., x is not conditioned on h). The chosen level is tailored, however, to the average harm of those consumers who actually purchase the product (as defined by (3.11)), rather than to the average harm in the population as a whole. In other words, for each a, consumers with relatively high h refrain from purchase, and as a result, the level of product safety defined by (3.13) is lower than would be chosen based on the overall average harm.

4.2 Strict Liability

Now consider the outcome under strict liability. As above, consumers expect to be fully compensated for any harm and so will purchase the product if and only if $a \geq P$, where P is the price. Thus, only variation in a matters for consumers since the price cannot be individualized to reflect consumer-specific risk. As a result, in contrast to the model with a single level of harm, the first-best outcome will not generally be attainable under strict liability.

The profit of a representative firm in this case is given by

$$\Pi = \int_0^\infty \int_P^\infty (P - c - x - \pi(x)h)g(a)f(h)\,da\,dh.$$
$$= [1 - G(P)](P - c - x - \pi(x)E(h)). \tag{3.14}$$

The profit maximizing safety level, denoted x_L, therefore solves the first-order condition

$$1 + \pi'E(h) = 0. \tag{3.15}$$

Thus, the firm chooses safety based on the average harm in the *population as a whole*. This reflects the absence of self-selection by consumers based on their individual susceptibility to risk. As a consequence, the firm chooses a higher level of safety than is implied by (3.13) (i.e., $x_L > x^{**}$), given that the population of actual consumers includes some high-risk types who would be deterred from purchase in the socially optimal outcome. Self-selection based on individual consumer harm is not possible under strict liability because there is a single price,

$$P = c + x_L + \pi(x_L)E(h), \tag{3.16}$$

which reflects the average risk among consumers.

Given (3.16), realized social welfare under a liability regime is given by

$$W_L = \int_0^{\infty} \int_P^{\infty} (a - c - x_L - \pi(x_L)h)g(a)f(h)\,dadh.$$

$$= \int_P^{\infty} (a - c - x_L - \pi(x_L)E(h))g(a)\,da. \tag{3.17}$$

Note that x_L, the firm's profit-maximizing safety level, also maximizes (3.17); that is, x_L coincides with the level of safety that a planner would choose to maximize (3.17). This is true because a planner, like the firm, would not be able to individualize product safety based on differences in consumer susceptibility to harm.

4.3   Regulation

Consider next the outcome under a regulatory standard, where $\lambda\pi(x)$ is again the risk of an accident as perceived by consumers when they bear their own damages.[8] The purchase region in this case is defined by the inequality

$$a \geq P + \lambda\pi(x_s)h \equiv a_s(\lambda,h), \tag{3.18}$$

which, unlike the case under strict liability, depends on both a and h (given $\lambda > 0$). The expected profit of the representative firm is given by

$$\Pi = \int_0^{\infty} \int_{a_s(\lambda,h)}^{\infty} (P - c - x_s)g(a)f(h)\,dadh. \tag{3.19}$$

where x_s is the regulated level of product safety. As above, zero profit implies that $P = c + x_s$, in which case

$$a_s(\lambda,h) = c + x_S + \lambda\pi(x_s)h. \tag{3.20}$$

The purchase region therefore coincides with the efficient region if and only if consumers perceive risk accurately (i.e., if and only if $\lambda = 1$).

The optimal safety standard is chosen to maximize welfare subject to the purchase region defined by (3.18):

$$W_s = \int_0^{\infty} \int_{a_s(\lambda,h)}^{\infty} (a - c - x - \pi(x)h)g(a)f(h)\,dadh. \tag{3.21}$$

The resulting first-order condition defining x_s is

$$\int_0^\infty \int_{a_s(\lambda,h)}^\infty (1 + \pi'(x)h)g(a)f(h)\,dh = \int_0^\infty (1 - \lambda)\pi(x)hg(a_s)\frac{\partial a_s}{\partial x}f(h)\,dh, \tag{3.22}$$

where, from (3.18), $\partial a_s/\partial x = 1 + \lambda\pi'h$. Realized welfare, $W_s^*(\lambda)$ is given by (3.21) evaluated at $x_s(\lambda)$. When consumers perceive risk correctly ($\lambda = 1$), the right-hand side is zero and (3.22) coincides with the condition for efficient safety in (3.13); that is, $x_s(1) = x^{**}$. Also, the consumption region in (3.18) coincides with the efficient region in (3.11). Together, these results establish:

Proposition 2:   Suppose consumers differ in the harm they would suffer from a product-related accident. Then if consumers correctly perceive the risk of an accident (i.e., if $\lambda = 1$), the regulatory approach achieves the socially optimal outcome, whereas strict liability does not. Thus, regulation dominates liability.

When $\lambda < 1$, however, optimal safety deviates from the social optimum for the same reason described in the previous section. In that case, the comparison between liability and regulation is ambiguous because neither achieves the socially optimal outcome. In comparing the two, however, we can prove the following result:

Proposition 3:   Suppose consumers differ in the harm they suffer from a product-related accident, and they may misperceive risk. Then there exists a threshold value of λ, $\lambda_T \in (0,1)$, such that strict liability dominates when $\lambda < \lambda_T$ and the safety standard dominates when $\lambda > \lambda_T$.

Proof: First define $\widetilde{W}_s(\lambda)$ to be realized welfare under the optimal regulatory standard, but with the purchase region defined by the average rather than the actual harm in the population, i.e.,

$$\widetilde{W}_s(\lambda) = \int_{\tilde{a}(\lambda)}^\infty (a - c - \tilde{x}_s - \pi(\tilde{x}_s)E(h))g(a)\,da, \tag{3.23}$$

where $\tilde{a}(\lambda) \equiv c + \tilde{x}_s + \lambda\pi(\tilde{x}_s)E(h)$, and $\tilde{x}_s$ is the level of product safety that maximizes (3.23). Note that when $\lambda = 0$, $\widetilde{W}_s(0) = W_s^*(0)$ with $\tilde{x}_s(0) = x_s(0)$, and when $\lambda = 1$, $\widetilde{W}_s(1) = W_L$, with $\tilde{x}_s(1) = x_L$. (The latter equality is true because when $\lambda = 1$, $\tilde{a}(1) = P$ as defined in (3.16).) Now, differentiating (23) with respect to λ, and invoking the Envelope Theorem, we obtain

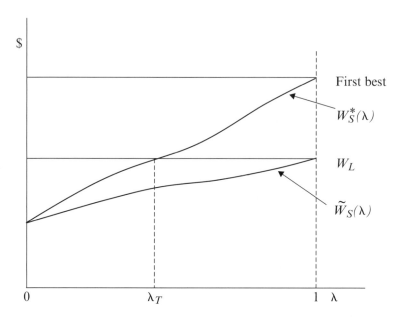

Figure 3.2   Comparison of strict liability and regulation for different values of λ

$$\frac{\partial \widetilde{W}_s}{\partial \lambda} = \int_0^\infty (\pi(\tilde{x}_s)h - \lambda\pi(\tilde{x}_s)E(h))g(\bar{a})f(h)\,dh\,\frac{\partial \bar{a}}{\partial \lambda}$$

$$= \pi(\tilde{x}_v)E(h)(1-\lambda)g(\bar{a})\pi(\tilde{x}_v)E(h). \qquad (3.24)$$

which is positive given $0 < \lambda < 1$. Thus, $\widetilde{W}_s(\lambda)$ coincides with welfare under the optimal standard at $\lambda = 0$, then rises with λ until it equals welfare under strict liability at $\lambda = 1$. Differentiating the optimized value of (3.21) also shows that $\partial W_s^*(\lambda)/\partial\lambda > 0$. Now, since $W_s^*(1)$ coincides with the social optimum, and $\widetilde{W}_s(0) = W_s^*(0) < W_L$, it must be the case that $W_s^*(\lambda)$ cuts W_L from below at a single point $\lambda_T \in (0,1)$.

This result is shown graphically in Figure 3.2. Intuitively, when consumers perceive risk fairly accurately (i.e., when λ is near 1), the safety standard is preferred over liability because it requires consumers to bear their own harm and thereby induces them to self-select in their purchase decisions. The closer perceptions are to the true risk, the closer this outcome will approach the social optimum. When consumers substantially underestimate risk, however, liability is preferred. Although no self-selection can occur in this case, the price at least signals the average risk among consumers and thus mitigates the problem of overconsumption.

4.4 Discussion of the Results

It is worth comparing the results here to those in Shavell (1984). Recall that in his model, the advantage of liability was that it allowed individualization of safety according to variation in victim types. This advantage is not possible in the context of product-related accidents because firms, like regulators, cannot tailor product safety to individual consumers. Further, under a liability regime those consumers who are especially susceptible to harm have no incentive to refrain from purchasing the product because they expect to be fully compensated for their damages. In contrast, regulation encourages some sorting based on risk because consumers expect to bear their own damages and thus self-select in their consumption decisions. This advantage of regulation is offset, however, to the extent that consumers misperceive risk, an issue that is not present under liability precisely because consumers are fully compensated for their damages. If the misperception problem is severe, liability will therefore be preferred over regulation because the price of the product will at least accurately signal average risk.

Having shown that neither liability nor regulation generally achieves the socially optimal outcome for product-related accidents when consumers vary in their susceptibility to harm, the question arises as to whether there might be a gain from using the two approaches simultaneously. Shavell (1984) showed that there was such a gain in his model of accidents between strangers, but that turns out not to be the case here. The reason is that the inefficiency in Shavell's model concerned the extent to which injurers had an incentive to tailor their care choices to the circumstances of individual victims. In that context, he was able to show that the joint use of liability and regulation allowed a better such tailoring of care. That gain is not available in the current model because care (safety) is not individualized under either approach. The principal inefficiency here is instead over the extent to which consumers are induced to self-select in their purchase decisions based on their individual harm, and combining the two approaches cannot improve matters in this regard.

To see why not, suppose first that $\lambda < \lambda_T$, which implies that, according to Proposition 3, liability is preferred to regulation. Imposing a regulatory standard of x_s on top of the threat of liability will only change the behavior of firms if $x_s > x_L$ (assuming that the standard must be met), but since x_L is the same level of care that a planner would choose to maximize welfare under a liability regime, there would be no social gain from imposing a higher standard, given the behavior of consumers. As for consumers, since they are fully compensated under the liability system, their behavior is not sensitive to the level of risk (except as signaled indirectly by the price of the product). More particularly, the social benefit of a standard as noted above – the fact that consumers bear their own damages and so self-select – is not available when consumers are simultaneously compensated by the liability system.

Now suppose that $\lambda > \lambda_T$, which implies that regulation is preferred. The effect on consumer behavior of adding liability would be to remove any incentive for them to self-select because they would now be compensated for their losses. As a result, the gains from sorting would be lost. In effect, the outcome would become identical to that under liability alone, which is inferior to regulation for the case being considered.

The preceding argument shows that joint use of liability and regulation appears to offer no advantages over the sole use of the preferred mode of risk control for product accidents. Two important qualifications might alter this conclusion. First, we have ignored imperfections in the liability system of the sort emphasized by Shavell – specifically, litigation costs and judgment-proofness on the part of firms – both of which would impede its ability to induce firms to choose optimal product safety. That might leave room for the use of a safety standard in conjunction with liability under some circumstances. Second, if regulators acted on behalf of certain political interests rather than pursuing social welfare, the added threat of liability might be socially advantageous under the assumption that judges are less influenced by political interests than regulators.

5.   CONCLUSION

This chapter has compared liability and safety regulation for controlling risks arising from dangerous products. The principal conclusions, which are summarized in Table 3.1, are as follows. First, when consumers expect

Table 3.1   Summary of results

		Consumer perceptions of risk:	
		Accurate	Inaccurate
Consumer harm:	Same	Regulation and liability equally efficient	Liability preferred over regulation
	Varies	Regulation preferred over liability	Liability preferred if $\lambda < \lambda_T$; regulation preferred if $\lambda > \lambda_T$

to suffer the same harm from product risk and perceive the risk of harm accurately, then liability and regulation are equally capable of achieving the socially optimal outcome in terms of both product safety (care) and consumption. Second, when consumers suffer the same harm but misperceive risk, then liability is preferred over regulation. Both approaches are capable of achieving optimal product safety, but because regulation leaves consumers to bear their own risk, they will tend to overconsume the product (assuming underestimation of risk). In contrast, because consumers expect to be fully compensated for their damages under liability, perceptions do not matter, but the product price accurately signals risk, thereby inducing efficient consumption.

Third, when consumers vary in their susceptibility to harm but perceive risk correctly, regulation dominates liability. In this case, full compensation of consumers under a liability regime prevents them from engaging in optimal self-selection in their purchase decisions, whereas regulation induces efficient sorting because consumers bear their own damages. Finally, when consumers vary in their harm and misperceive risk, the comparison between the two approaches is ambiguous, with liability being preferred when consumers significantly misperceive risk, and regulation being preferred when they perceive risks fairly accurately.

An issue not considered in this chapter but which is often discussed in the context of products liability is insurance against product risk.[9] If consumers are risk averse, then it is efficient for them to be insured against the risk from product-related accidents. However, it should be clear from the arguments in this chapter that full insurance against product risk, whether provided by the liability system or by the private insurance market, will not be compatible with efficient sorting by consumer types.

NOTES

1. Previous models of products liability include Epple and Raviv (1978), Polinsky and Rogerson (1983), Landes and Posner (1985), Marino (1988), Daughety and Reinganum (1995), Hay and Spier (2005), and Spier (2011). For recent surveys, see Polinsky and Shavell (2010) and Daughety and Reinganum (forthcoming).
2. We therefore focus on goods whose safety features are readily observable – so-called inspection goods.
3. For simplicity, the model does not allow for victim care, interpreted, for example, as proper use of the product. As discussed, consumers can only affect risk by their decision of whether or not to purchase the product. These assumptions seem reasonable for the case of food and drugs.
4. For models of products liability where firms have market power, see Epple and Raviv (1978), Polinsky and Rogerson (1983), and Marino (1988).
5. Because we are focusing on a different trade-off from that in Shavell (1984), we assume

a perfectly functioning liability system and no possibility of judgment-proofness on the part of the firm.

6. If the standard is administered by a regulatory agency like the FDA, the firm must comply under penalty of sanction. Note that a negligence standard administered by a court would have the same effect on the firm's profit, (assuming that the firm finds it optimal to comply) and on consumer behavior. Thus, for purposes of this chapter, there is no difference between a regulatory (publicly-imposed) standard and a negligence (court-imposed) standard.

7. None of the previous models of products liability (see citations in footnote 1 above) allows consumers to differ in harm in a known way *prior* to purchase.

8. Although consumers know their own susceptibility to harm from an accident, they still may underestimate the likelihood of such an accident. In other words, their misperceptions only apply to the $\pi(x)$ function.

9. See, for example, Viscusi (1991, pp. 75–7) and Shavell (2004, Chapter 11).

REFERENCES

Cooter, R. and T. Ulen, *Law and Economics*, (Glenview, IL: Scott, Foresman and Co. 1988).

Daughety, A. and J. Reinganum, Economic Analysis of Products Liability: Theory, in *Research Handbook on the Economics of Torts* (Jennifer Arlen ed., Edward Elgar, forthcoming).

Daughety, A. and J. Reinganum, Product Safety: Liability, R&D and Signaling, 85 *American Economic Review* 1187–206 (1995).

Epple, D. and A. Raviv, Product Safety: Liability Rules, Market Structure, and Imperfect Information, 68 *American Economic Review* 80–95 (1978).

Hay, B. and K. Spier, Manufacturer Liability for Harms Caused by Consumers, 95 *American Economic Review* 1700–711 (2005).

Landes, W. and R. Posner, A Positive Economic Theory of Products Liability, 14 *Journal of Legal Studies* 535–67 (1985).

Marino, A., Monopoly Liability and Regulation, 54 *Southern Economic Journal* 913–27 (1988).

Polinsky, A.M. and W. Rogerson, Products Liability, Consumer Misperceptions, and Market Power, 14 *Rand Journal of Economics* 581–89 (1983).

Polinsky, A.M. and S. Shavell, The Uneasy Case for Product Liability, 123 *Harvard Law Review* 1437–92 (2010).

Shavell, S., *Foundations of Economic Analysis of Law*, (Cambridge, MA: Belknap Press 2004).

Shavell, S., A Model of the Optimal Use of Liability and Safety Regulation, 15 *Rand Journal of Economics* 271–80 (1984).

Spence, A.M., Consumer Misperceptions, Product Failure, and Producer Liability, 44 *Review of Economic Studies* 561–72 (1977).

Spier, K., Product Safety, Buy-Backs, and the Post-Sale Duty to Warn, 27 *Journal of Law, Economics and Organization* 515–29 (2011).

Viscusi, W.K., *Reforming Products Liability*. (Cambridge, MA: Harvard Univ. Press 1991).

Viscusi, W.K., J. Harrington and J. Vernon, *Economics of Regulation and Antitrust*, (4th ed. Cambridge, MA: MIT Press 2005).

4. Regulation versus liability: a behavioral economics perspective

Kathleen Segerson and Tsvetan Tsvetanov

1. INTRODUCTION

Much of the field of law and economics focuses on the design and evaluation of alternative ways of reducing accident risks. In the context of environmental or safety risks, two alternative approaches are regulation and legal liability for damages. Regulations are designed to control directly decisions that affect either the probability of an accident or the damages that would result if an accident were to occur. They are invoked 'ex ante,' i.e., before an accident occurs. In contrast, liability is invoked 'ex post,' i.e., after an accident occurs, but anticipation of the imposition of liability can create incentives for changes in behavior that reduce accident risks. In practice, a combination of the two is often used.[1] For example, in the U.S. the risks associated with hazardous waste disposal are controlled both through the regulation of disposal-related activities under the Resource Conservation and Recovery Act (RCRA)[2] and through the imposition of legal liability under the Comprehensive Environmental Response, Compensation, and Liability Act (CERCLA).[3]

There is a large literature within the field of law and economics comparing the welfare effects of reducing environmental or safety risks through regulation versus liability. This dates back to the early work by Shavell (1984a, 1984b). It identifies potential tradeoffs in the use of liability versus regulation (see, for example, Shavell 1993). These tradeoffs relate, among other things,[4] to the degree of heterogeneity among injurers and the likelihood that an injurer would be able to escape a suit or payment under liability. *Ceteris paribus*, more heterogeneity tends to favor liability since regulations cannot typically be tailored to individual injurer circumstances or characteristics. In contrast, a reduction in the probability that the injurer would ultimately be held liable tends to favor the regulatory approach, since the incentive effects of liability will be reduced if the likelihood that the injurer would actually pay full compensation is reduced. Among the factors that affect the likelihood that an injurer would be held fully liable are the incentives to bring suit, the injurer's wealth, and the lag time between the injurer's care decision and the realization of any resulting damages.

As with nearly all of the law and economics literature, the existing analyses comparing regulation and liability are based on a neoclassical model of injurer care, i.e., injurers are assumed to choose the care level that minimizes their expected total costs, including any liability-related costs. However, the emerging field of behavioral economics has highlighted the need to incorporate into economic models other behavioral assumptions (see, e.g., Fudenberg 2006, Pesendorfer 2006, DellaVigna 2009).[5] A key insight from behavioral economics is that individuals may not make intertemporal decisions in the rational way assumed in neoclassical models. For example, when making intertemporal choices, rather than exponential discounting, a number of authors have suggested that individuals employ hyperbolic or quasi-hyperbolic discounting to weight current and future costs and benefits (e.g., Loewenstein and Prelec 1992, Laibson 1997). For finite decision problems, these weights can be viewed as representing preference structures under which individuals face temptation and always give into it (Gul and Pesendorfer 2004, Lipman and Pesendorfer 2013). Gul and Pesendorfer (2001, 2004) present a more general model of temptation that allows for the possibility that individuals will resist temptation (albeit at a cost). These alternative behavioral assumptions can have important implications for how individuals make decisions in the current period when those decisions have implications for the future.

The purpose of this chapter is to explore the implications of incorporating some of the insights from behavioral economics into the evaluation of regulation versus liability as alternative means of reducing accident risks in the context where care decisions are intertemporal, i.e., there is a lag time between the injurer's care decision and the realization of damages. This context is relevant to many environmental risks. For example, it can take years for the disposal or storage of hazardous substances to result in (realized) contamination of soil and water, or for exposure to hazardous chemicals to lead to discernible health effects for exposed parties. This implies a lag between the time the care decision is made and the time that liability might be imposed. Thus, the injurer's care decision involves an intertemporal tradeoff that could be influenced by the behavioral factors noted above.

We focus here on one particular factor, namely, temptation.[6] People may face temptation in a variety of decision contexts. For instance, the existing evidence shows that individuals experience self-control problems due to their tendency to pursue immediate gratification (Magen and Gross 2007). Examples include consumption of 'vice' products (e.g., cigarettes, unhealthy food) (Wertenbroch 1998), aversion to medical checkups (Trope and Fishbach 2000), and difficulties in resisting school parties (Zhang *et al.* 2010). Similarly, one might argue that injurers would be 'tempted' by the lower costs associated with 'low care' decisions when weighing current and future costs and benefits. This notion of temptation is consistent with the recognition that consumers may exhibit 'price consciousness' arising from their focus on low product prices (Lichtenstein *et al.* 1993, Esteban *et al.* 2007). While some people may overcome this temptation and in the process incur a self-control cost, there are others who succumb to it and make decisions that could be *ex-ante* inefficient.

A key behavioral implication of temptation is that consumers can benefit from restrictions on their choices so as to avoid the temptation that short-term gains create in some contexts. There is an extensive literature demonstrating that people often have a preference for commitment (see, for example, Bryan *et al.* 2010 and Fishbach and Converse 2010 for surveys of this literature). Furthermore, Tsvetanov and Segerson (2013a, 2013b) show that, if consumers face temptation when making decisions about energy-using durable goods, energy efficiency standards (a form of regulation that restricts consumer choices) can play a potentially important role in promoting efficient purchase decisions. As pointed out by Loewenstein and O'Donoghue (2006) and McAdams (2011), law can also play an important role in preventing individuals from succumbing to temptation by increasing the costs of vice behavior.

In this chapter, we present a model of regulation vs. liability that incorporates temptation, using the general framework for modeling temptation that was originally developed by Gul and Pesendorfer (2001, 2004).[7] The model incorporates two key features that have been well recognized as influencing the welfare ranking of the two policy approaches in neoclassical models, namely, heterogeneity across injurers and a lag time between the care decision and the realization of damages (intertemporal choice). It is designed so that, in the absence of temptation, strict liability always yields efficient care choices. However, using the model, we show that, if injurers are tempted by short run low costs, the welfare impacts of the two policy approaches and hence their welfare ranking can change. More specifically, we show that, in contrast to the result under neoclassical choice, even if the injurer would be fully liable for all damages that occur (i.e., the probability of a successful suit with full compensation is one), a strict liability rule will not yield efficient care choices when injurers face temptation. Moreover, we show that, depending on the source of heterogeneity, a regulatory approach might or might not yield efficient care choices. However, even when regulation does not ensure efficiency, it can still dominate a strict liability rule when temptation is sufficiently strong. This suggests that non-neoclassical behavior may be an important consideration when choosing between alternative means of reducing accident risks with long lag times.

The chapter is organized as follows. In the next section, we present an overview of the basic temptation model developed by Gul and Pesendorfer (2001, 2004) and an adaptation of the model to the context of injurer care decisions. In Sections 3–5, we use the model to characterize the first-best outcome as well as the outcomes under a strict liability rule and regulation, under three alternative sources of injurer heterogeneity: income, temptation (self-control costs), and cost of care. Section 6 concludes.

2.   MODEL

2.1   General Model of Temptation and Self-Control

Gul and Pesendorfer (2001, 2004) set up an axiomatic framework to represent time-consistent preferences over choice sets in the presence of temptation. In this framework, agent preferences over sets can be represented by a function W defined as follows: the agent weakly prefers set S_1 over set S_2 if and only if $W(S_1) \geq W(S_2)$, where

$$W(S) = \max_{z \in S}\{u(z) + v(z)\} - \max_{z \in S}v(z), \qquad (4.1)$$

for some functions u and v.[8]

Let a and b be two possible options in a given choice set, with b being the tempting alternative. Then, function u, called the agent's 'commitment utility,' represents her ranking over singleton sets containing only one possible choice option and hence no temptation. The preference ranking $\{a\} \geq \{b\}$ is therefore represented by $u(a) \geq u(b)$. On the other hand, function v is the agent's 'temptation utility,' where $v(b) \geq v(a)$. When S consists of a single option, e.g., $S = \{a\}$, then $w(S) = u(a)$. However, once we add a tempting option to the choice set, i.e., $S = \{a,b\}$, then $W(S)$ depends on whether or not the individual will give into temptation. When presented with the choice set $\{a,b\}$, the agent chooses the option z^* that maximizes $u(z) + v(z)$. If $z^* = b$, the agent gives in to temptation and $W(S) = u(b)$. If $z^* = a$, she exercises self-control and resists temptation, but in doing so incurs a 'self-control cost' given by $v(b) - v(a) \geq 0$. In this case, $W(S) = u(a) - [v(b) - v(a)]$.

While the above model is static, the Gul and Pesendorfer model can also be set in a multi-period framework. Assume that, when the agent chooses z in period t, she only faces temptation in the current period and receives a future payoff Ω_{t+1} conditional on her choice of z. We can then specify the dynamic version of (4.1) as follows:

$$W_t(S_t) = \max_{z_t \in S_t} \{ u_t(z_t) + v_t(z_t) + \delta\Omega_{t+1}(z_t) \} - \max_{z_t \in S_t} v_t(z_t), \ t \geq 1. \ (4.2)$$

In this setting, $u_t + \delta\Omega_{t+1}$ represents the present discounted value of the 'commitment utility' of the period t choice, and v_t is the 'temptation utility' in period t.[9]

2.2   A Model of Injurer Care Choice under Temptation

In this section we adopt the above model to the context where an injurer makes a care decision that influences the probably of third-party damages in the future. More specifically, we consider an injurer with income $y - v$ who chooses between two levels of care: high (H) and low (L). Let x_i represent expenditure on care under the two alternatives $i = H, L$. Investing in greater care is more costly, i.e., $x_H > x_L$, but is associated with a lower probability of future accidents, i.e., $p(x_H) < p(x_L)$. Hence, the injurer's decision involves an intertemporal tradeoff between immediate payoffs, given by her net wealth after investing in care, i.e., $y - x$, and expected future costs $p(x)C$, where C represents future costs borne by the injurer if an accident occurs. Under a regulatory approach, these costs would be zero, while under strict liability they would equal the liability payment, which, in the absence of wealth constraints, would be set equal to the damages from the accident. As discussed by Gul and Pesendorfer (2004), Miao (2008), and Tsvetanov and Segerson (2013a), in contexts where a tradeoff exists between short-term and long-term payoffs, individuals can find immediate rewards tempting. Therefore, when presented with a choice set $\{H, L\}$, an injurer may be tempted by L due to its lower upfront costs.

We adapt the Gul and Pesendorfer model to this context by defining ϕ_i, where $i \in \{H, L\}$, as follows:

$$\phi_i \equiv u_i + v_i + \delta EC_i, \tag{4.3}$$

where u_i is the initial payoff (i.e., net wealth $y - x_i$) and $\delta EC_i = \delta p(x_i)C$ denotes discounted expected future costs. We follow Gul and Pesendorfer (2004) and Miao (2008) and specify the temptation utility as $v_i = \lambda u_i$. Thus, $\lambda \geq 0$ can be interpreted as a parameter representing the extent to which the injurer is tempted by the low care level. Given this, (4.3) becomes:

$$\phi_i \equiv (1+\lambda)(y - x_i) - \delta p(x_i)C. \tag{4.4}$$

Therefore, when faced with a choice set $\{H, L\}$, the injurer chooses $i \in \{H, L\}$ to maximize (4.4). Note that, if $\lambda = 0$, i.e., for an individual with no self-control problem, this model reduces to a standard accident model where the individual chooses care to minimize expected discounted total costs given by $x + \delta p(x) C$.

Next, we characterize the injurer's preferences across different choice sets, which are represented by the function $W(S)$. Adapting (4.2) to our framework and maintaining our previous functional form assumptions, we obtain $W(S)$ for an individual faced with the set $S = \{H, L\}$:

$$W(S) = \max_{i \in S} \{(1 + \lambda)(y - x_i) - \delta p(x_i) C\} - \lambda \max_{i \in S}(y - x_i)$$

$$= \max_{i \in S} \{y - (1 + \lambda)x_i - \delta p(x_i) C\} + \lambda x_L. \tag{4.5}$$

The maximized utility of an injurer faced with a choice set $S = \{H, L\}$ is therefore given by:[10]

$$W(S) = \begin{cases} \omega_L = y - x_L - \delta p(x_L) C & \text{if } \phi_L > \phi_H \\ \omega_H = y - x_H - \delta p(x_H) C - \lambda(x_H - x_L) & \text{if } \phi_L \leq \phi_H. \end{cases} \tag{4.6}$$

The first line in (4.6) corresponds to the outcome when the injurer 'gives in to temptation.' The second line corresponds to the outcome when she 'resists temptation' and incurs a self-control cost equal to $\lambda(x_H - x_L)$.

In the following discussion, we consider three sources of heterogeneity across agents. We first focus on the case where all individuals incur the same care costs, but differ either in their income levels or in the degree of temptation they experience. We then consider an alternative case, in which agents are identical in their income and temptation levels, but vary in their care costs. The results imply that the source of heterogeneity plays an important role in determining the welfare ranking of regulation and strict liability in our context.

3.   HETEROGENEOUS INCOME

Suppose that all injurers have the same care and self-control costs, but differ in their income y. In particular, let y be distributed over the range $[\underline{y}, \bar{y}]$ with distribution g and let Y denote the mean income in the population of injurers. In what follows, we show that under this scenario (i) the socially optimal care level is the same for all injurers, (ii) a strict liability rule does not achieve the socially optimal outcome in the presence of temptation, and (iii) the optimal care level can be implemented through a (uniform) regulatory approach.

3.1   Social Optimum

The first-best outcome is equivalent to assuming that a planner dictates the most efficient care choice for each injurer, implying that injurers do not experience temptation. Let D denote the damages from an accident. The efficient choice for an injurer with income y is then defined as $i \in \{H,L\}$ that maximizes this injurer's commitment utility when expected damages are accounted for:

$$\phi_i = y - x_i - \delta p(x_i)D. \tag{4.7}$$

Note that the socially optimal choice $i \in \{H,L\}$ is independent of y and will therefore be the same for all injurers. We assume that high care is the socially optimal choice for all injurers, i.e., $x_H + \delta p(x_H)D < x_L + \delta p(x_L)D$.[11] In this case, first-best social welfare is given by:

$$SW^* = \int_{\underline{y}}^{\bar{y}} [y - x_H - \delta p(x_H)D]g(y)dy = Y - x_H - \delta p(x_H)D. \tag{4.8}$$

Note that self-control costs are absent from the first-best social welfare, since individuals are not confronted with temptation in this case.

3.2   Strict Liability

We examine the welfare implications of a strict liability rule mandating that injurers pay compensation equal to D if an accident occurs. Note that, under this policy, injurers are still faced with the choice set $S = \{H, L\}$ and experience temptation due to the lower upfront costs of choosing low care. Thus, each injurer chooses $i \in S$ to maximize:

$$\phi_i \equiv (1 + \lambda)(y - x_i) - \delta p(x_i)D. \tag{4.9}$$

The choice of care is independent of income and is therefore the same for all injurers. However, that choice depends on the magnitude of λ. Define λ_y through $\phi_H = \phi_L$, i.e., $\lambda_y = \frac{\delta D[p(x_L) - p(x_H)]}{x_H - x_L} - 1$. Clearly, $\frac{d}{d\lambda}(\phi_H - \phi_L) < 0$, implying that $\phi_H \geq \phi_L$ for $\lambda \leq \lambda_y$. Then, if $\lambda \leq \lambda_y$, strict liability yields the following social welfare:

$$SW_L = \int_{\underline{y}}^{\bar{y}} [y - x_H - \delta p(x_H)D - \lambda(x_H - x_L)]g(y)dy$$

$$= Y - x_H - \delta p(x_H)D - \lambda(x_H - x_L). \tag{4.10}$$

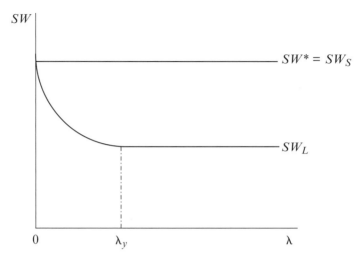

Figure 4.1   Policy ranking with heterogeneous income

Note that strict liability yields the first-best outcome at $\lambda = 0$, as predicted by the standard neoclassical model. However, when $\lambda > 0$ and temptation is present, although all injurers make the optimal care choice, there are welfare losses relative to the first-best outcome due to self-control costs.[12] Therefore, $SW_L < SW^*$ for all $\lambda \in (0, \lambda_y]$, as shown in Figure 4.1.

On the other hand, if $\lambda > \lambda_y$, $\phi_H < \phi_L$ and all injurers choose L under strict liability, which is a suboptimal choice of care level. No self-control costs are incurred, and the SW_L curve is horizontal at values of λ above λ_y, as shown in Figure 4.1. Social welfare in this case is given by:

$$SW_L = \int_{\underline{y}}^{\bar{y}} [y - x_L - \delta p(x_L)D]g(y)dy = Y - x_L - \delta p(x_L)D. \quad (4.11)$$

The above results are summarized in the following proposition.

Proposition 1:   When individuals vary only by income levels, strict liability is not a first-best policy in the presence of temptation, i.e., if $\lambda > 0$.

The intuition is simply that, if temptation is sufficiently strong, all injurers give in to temptation and choose a care level that is inefficiently low; alternatively, if temptation is present but is relatively low, all injurers resist the temptation to 'cut corners' up front, but in doing so, incur self-control costs that would not exist under a first-best outcome.

3.3   Regulation

Consider instead a regulatory standard, which mandates that all injurers choose a care level at least as high as H. This effectively eliminates L as a choice option, implying that each injurer faces a singleton choice set $S' = \{H\}$. Therefore, the utility of an injurer with income y in this case is:

$$W(S') = y - x_H. \tag{4.12}$$

No self-control costs are present, since the tempting option L has been removed from the choice set. Social welfare under this policy is given by:

$$SW_s = \int_{\underline{y}}^{\bar{y}} [y - x_H - \delta p(x_H)D]g(y)dy = Y - x_H - \delta p(x_H)D = SW^*. \tag{4.13}$$

Hence, by 'forcing' all injurers to choose H and eliminating self-control costs, the regulatory standard achieves the first-best outcome. Note that this result holds regardless of the value of λ, implying that the standard is first-best in this setting even in the absence of temptation.

Proposition 2:   When injurers vary only by income levels, the socially optimal outcome can be obtained through a regulatory standard.

The following is a direct result of Propositions 1 and 2.

Corollary 1:   When injurers vary only by their income levels, a uniform regulation dominates strict liability in terms of social welfare in the presence of temptation, i.e., when $\lambda > 0$.

4.   HETEROGENEOUS TEMPTATION

In this section, we explore the case in which injurers vary in the degree of temptation they experience. Hence, we assume that λ is individual-specific, while all other parameters (including income) are the same for the entire population. We let λ be distributed over a given range $[0, \lambda^{max}]$ with distribution h and evaluate the outcomes under strict liability and regulation. Our results are very similar to the ones obtained in Section 3, suggesting that, even under heterogeneous temptation or self-control costs, a regulatory standard dominates strict liability in the presence of temptation.

4.1   Social Optimum

The efficient outcome is characterized as in the previous section. Note that, since no temptation is experienced under the first-best outcome, the socially optimal choice of care is the same for all agents. Again, assuming that high care is the efficient choice for all injurers, SW^* is given by:

$$SW^* = \int_0^{\lambda^{max}} [y - x_H - \delta p(x_H)D] h(\lambda)d\lambda = y - x_H - \delta p(x_H)D. \qquad (4.14)$$

4.2   Strict Liability

The strict liability rule is set as in Section 3.2, under which injurers are responsible for the full damage D if an accident occurs. Hence, an injurer with a given λ chooses $i \in S$ to maximize:

$$\phi_i \equiv (1 + \lambda)(y - x_i) - \delta p(x_i)D. \qquad (4.15)$$

Note that, unlike in the case of heterogeneous income, here all injurers do not make the same care decision. Rather, the individual choice of i depends on the magnitude of λ for that injurer. Nonetheless, the same cutoff value λ_y as in Section 3.2 gives the degree of temptation at which $\phi_H = \phi_L$. Now, all injurers with $\lambda \leq \lambda_y$ choose H, while all remaining injurers choose L. Thus, unlike in the case of heterogeneous income, heterogeneous temptation induces a sorting of injurers by their temptation parameter. Recall that an individual who overcomes temptation and chooses H will incur a self-control cost given by $\lambda(x_H - x_L)$. Therefore, the social welfare under this policy is given by:

$$SW_L = \int_0^{\lambda_y} [y - x_H - \delta p(x_H)D - \lambda(x_H - x_L)]h(\lambda)d\lambda$$

$$+ \int_{\lambda_y}^{\lambda^{max}} [y - x_L - \delta p(x_L)D]h(\lambda)d\lambda. \qquad (4.16)$$

A comparison between (4.14) and (4.16) reveals that social welfare under strict liability differs from the first-best social welfare in two ways. First, injurers who choose the efficient level of care, i.e., individuals with low temptation represented by $\lambda \in [0,\lambda_y]$, incur welfare losses due to self-control costs, which are not present under the first-best outcome. Second, high-temptation injurers, i.e., injurers with $\lambda > \lambda_y$, choose an inefficient level of care by 'giving in to' temptation. As a result, $SW_L < SW^*$, as stated in the following proposition.

Proposition 3: With heterogeneity in temptation across injurers, a strict liability rule does not yield a first-best, i.e., $SW_L < SW^*$.

4.3 Regulation

Similar to Section 3.3, a regulatory standard forces all injurers to invest in the efficient level of care, which by assumption is H. In addition, the standard eliminates the tempting option from injurers' choice sets. Therefore, each injurer's utility under the standard is still given by (4.12), regardless of that individual's λ, and social welfare becomes

$$SW_S = \int_0^{\lambda^{max}} [y - x_H - \delta p(x_H) D] h(\lambda) d\lambda = y - x_H - \delta p(x_H) D = SW^*. \quad (4.17)$$

Clearly, $SW_S = SW^*$ even in the absence of temptation. The welfare impacts of a regulatory standard under this scenario can therefore be summarized as follows:

Proposition 4: When injurers vary only in their temptation parameter, a regulatory standard is a first-best policy.

Corollary 2 follows immediately.

Corollary 2: In the presence of temptation, if injurers vary only in their temptation parameters, a regulation dominates strict liability in terms of social welfare.

5. HETEROGENEOUS CARE COSTS

In this section, we assume that y and λ are the same for all injurers, whereas care costs vary across individuals. Suppose θ is an individual-specific characteristic affecting the costs of care and let θ be continuously distributed over the range $[\underline{\theta}, \overline{\theta}]$ with distribution f. Thus, an injurer with type θ incurs a cost of θx_i when investing in i. Note that we still assume that the probability of an accident, conditional on a choice of i, is the same across individuals. So, ϕ_i for an injurer with a given θ becomes:

$$\phi_i \equiv (1 + \lambda)(y - \theta x_i) - \delta p(x_i) C, \quad (4.18)$$

while (4.6) is now:

$$W(S) = \begin{cases} \omega_L = y - \theta x_L - \delta p(x_L)C & \text{if } \phi_L > \phi_H \\ \omega_H = y - \theta x_H - \delta p(x_H)C - \theta\lambda(x_H - x_L) & \text{if } \phi_L \le \phi_H \end{cases} \quad (4.19)$$

5.1 Social Optimum

The efficient choice for a type θ injurer is again defined as $i \in \{H,L\}$ that maximizes this agent's commitment utility when expected damages are accounted for:

$$\phi_i \equiv y - \theta x_i - \delta p(x_i)D. \quad (4.20)$$

Let θ^* denote the type of an individual for whom net social benefits given in (4.20) are the same under H and L. Setting $\phi_H = \phi_L$ in (4.20) yields $\theta^* = \frac{\delta D[p(x_L) - p(x_H)]}{x_H - x_L}$. We assume the parameter values in the model are such that $\theta^* \in (\underline{\theta}, \bar{\theta})$. Unlike in the previous cases of income and temptation heterogeneity, here the socially optimal care choice varies across injurers. It is easy to show the following result:

Proposition 5:   It is socially optimal for injurers with $\theta > \theta^*$ to choose the low level of care, while choosing the high care level is the efficient choice for all individuals with $\theta \le \theta^*$.

Proof: Note that $\frac{d\phi_H}{d\theta}(\theta^*) = -x_H < 0$ and $\frac{d\phi_H}{d\theta}(\theta^*) = -x_H < -x_L = \frac{d\phi_L}{d\theta}(\theta^*)$. Thus, if $\theta > \theta^*$, an injurer with this θ will choose L, while the opposite holds true for $\theta \le \theta^*$.

Social welfare under the first-best outcome is therefore given by:

$$SW^* = \int_{\underline{\theta}}^{\theta^*} [y - \theta x_H - \delta p(x_H)D]f(\theta)d\theta +$$

$$\int_{\theta^*}^{\bar{\theta}} [y - \theta x_L - \delta p(x_L)D]f(\theta)d\theta. \quad (4.21)$$

5.2 Strict Liability

Under strict liability, each injurer chooses $i \in S$ to maximize:

$$\phi_i \equiv (1 + \lambda)(y - \theta x_i) - \delta p(x_i)D. \quad (4.22)$$

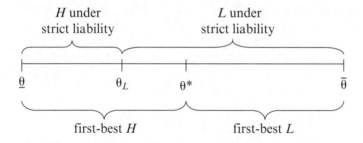

Figure 4.2   Care choice for $\lambda > 0$ with heterogeneous care costs

We define the cutoff value θ_L as corresponding to the individual for whom $\phi_H = \phi_L$ under strict liability. Thus, $\theta_L = \frac{\delta D[p(x_L) - p(x_H)]}{(1 + \lambda)(x_H - x_L)} = \frac{\theta^*}{1 + \lambda}$, which implies that $\theta_L < \theta^*$ if $\lambda > 0$. Applying Proposition 5 to this context, we find that all injurers with $\theta \in (\theta_L, \bar{\theta}]$ choose L under the strict liability rule, while all injurers with $\theta \in [\underline{\theta}, \theta_L]$ choose H. Hence, as in the case of heterogeneous temptation, strict liability results in underinvestment in care when injurers face (uniform) temptation and varying care costs. As shown in Figure 4.2, injurers with $\theta \in (\theta_L, \theta^*]$ choose L under strict liability, although the efficient choice for them is H.

Clearly, $\frac{d\theta_L}{d\lambda} < 0$. We define $\bar{\lambda} \equiv \frac{\theta^* - \underline{\theta}}{\underline{\theta}}$, so that $\theta_L(\bar{\lambda}) = \underline{\theta}$. Hence, $\bar{\lambda}$ represents the degree of temptation, beyond which no one chooses H. For $\lambda < \bar{\lambda}$, social welfare under strict liability is given by:

$$SW_L = \int_{\underline{\theta}}^{\theta_L} [y - \theta x_H - \delta p(x_H) D - \theta\lambda(x_H - x_L)]f(\theta)\, d\theta \;+$$

$$\int_{\theta_L}^{\bar{\theta}} [y - \theta x_L - \delta p(x_L) D]f(\theta)\, d\theta. \qquad (4.23)$$

Note that, for $\lambda > 0$, SW_L differs from SW^* in two ways: (i) inefficiently low investment in care by some injurers (i.e., $\theta_L < \theta^*$); and (ii) welfare losses due to self-control costs.

Furthermore, if $\lambda \geq \bar{\lambda}$, then strict liability results in all injurers giving into temptation and choosing L. In this case, (4.23) becomes:

$$SW_L = \int_{\underline{\theta}}^{\bar{\theta}} [y - \theta x_L - \delta p(x_L) D]f(\theta)\, d\theta. \qquad (4.24)$$

Since none of the agents choose H, no self-control costs are incurred, but SW_L still differs from SW^* due to the suboptimally low investment in care.

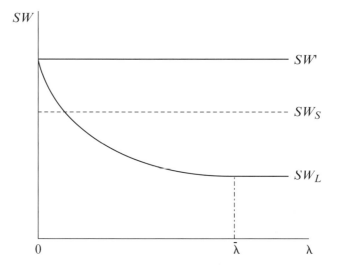

Figure 4.3   Example of policy ranking with heterogeneous care costs

Therefore, strict liability results in an inefficient outcome for any $\lambda > 0$, as shown in Figure 4.3.

The following proposition summarizes the welfare impacts of strict liability with regards to the social optimum:

Proposition 6:   In the presence of temptation, i.e., for $\lambda > 0$, strict liability does not achieve the first best, i.e., $SW_L < SW^*$.

5.3   Regulation

A regulatory standard eliminates L and results in the following social welfare:

$$SW_S = \int_{\underline{\theta}}^{\bar{\theta}} [y - \theta x_H - \delta p(x_H) D] f(\theta) d\theta. \tag{4.25}$$

Note that, as before, no temptation is present and self-control costs are eliminated. However, in the presence of heterogeneous care costs, this policy also creates a distortion by 'forcing' all injurers to choose H, whereas, for high cost injurers, i.e., injurers with $\theta > \theta^*$, L is the efficient choice. Due to this distortion, regulation cannot achieve the social optimum.

Proposition 7:   With heterogeneous care costs, a regulatory standard does not achieve the first best, i.e., $SW_S < SW^*$.

While neither strict liability nor regulation are first-best in this case, we are also interested in the relative welfare ranking between these policies. Note that, for $\lambda = 0$, strict liability achieves the first-best outcome and therefore dominates the standard. Note also that social welfare under the standard is unaffected by temptation. On the other hand, as temptation increases, the welfare losses under strict liability due to underinvestment in L and self-control costs also increase, as long as $\lambda < \bar{\lambda}$. Once temptation becomes too strong (i.e., $\lambda \geq \bar{\lambda}$), all agents choose the low level of care, no self-control costs are incurred, and any subsequent increase in the degree of temptation no longer affects SW_L. Since $SW_S - SW_L$ is monotonic in λ over the range $[0,\bar{\lambda}]$, it is possible for the standard to dominate strict liability for high enough values of λ, as long as $SW_S > SW_L$ at $\lambda = \bar{\lambda}$.

Proposition 8: With heterogeneous care costs, a regulatory standard can dominate strict liability for sufficiently strong temptation.

Proof: First, note that SW_S does not depend on λ. Similarly, $\frac{dSW_L}{d\lambda}=0$ for $\lambda \geq \bar{\lambda}$. On the other hand, for $\lambda \in (0,\bar{\lambda})$, $\frac{dSW_L}{d\lambda} = \{[y-\theta_L x_H - \delta p(x_H)D - \theta_L\lambda(x_H-x_L)] - [y-\theta_L x_L - \delta p(x_L)\,D]\}f(\theta_L)\frac{d\theta_L}{d\lambda} - \int_\theta^{\theta_L}\theta(x_H-x_L)]f(\theta)\,d\theta = -\int_\theta^{\theta_L}\theta(x_H-x_L)]f(\theta)\,d\theta < 0$, after using the fact that $\phi_H = \phi_L$ at θ_L to eliminate the first term in the expression. Therefore, if the model parameters are such that $SW_S > SW_L$ at $\lambda = \bar{\lambda}$, then there exists a $\tilde{\lambda} \in (0,\bar{\lambda})$, such that $SW_S > SW_L$ for all $\lambda \geq \tilde{\lambda}$.

Figure 4.3 depicts the policy rankings for different values of λ for the case where $SW_S > SW_L$ at $\lambda = \bar{\lambda}$. Note that, since self-control costs are absent under the first best or with a standard in place, the SW^* and SW_S curves are horizontal. Furthermore, SW^* always lies above SW_S, as regulation is never first-best. On the other hand, strict liability is first-best for $\lambda = 0$, but not when temptation is present, i.e., $SW_L < SW^*$ for $\lambda > 0$. Finally, for $\lambda \geq \bar{\lambda}$, social welfare under strict liability no longer varies with λ and the SW_S curve becomes horizontal.

Proposition 8 implies a potential tradeoff between liability and regulation in the presence of temptation and heterogeneous care costs. Strict liability has the advantage of allowing care decisions that can vary with care costs. However, under strict liability temptation can lead to under-investment in care and/or self-control costs. On the other hand, while a uniform regulation does not allow care choices that reflect differing care costs, it eliminates temptation and the associated under-investment and/or self-control costs. Hence, the stronger the temptation, the more likely it is that a regulatory standard dominates strict liability, *ceteris paribus*.

6.   CONCLUSION

Previous comparisons of regulation and liability as alternative ways to reduce accident risks have been based on models that assume injurers choose care levels simply to minimize expected total costs. These standard models show that, if the probability of a successful suit with full compensation is one, then a strict liability rule will induce efficient care choices by injurers. In this context, absent administrative costs and information asymmetries, regulation is typically viewed as an inferior alternative because of injurer heterogeneity. We show that these conclusions no longer hold if injurers face temptation to 'cut corners' and choose low care levels in the short run, even if they do not give in to that temptation. As shown by Tsvetanov and Segerson (2013a, 2013b) in the context of energy efficiency standards, in the presence of temptation policies that regulate or restrict choices can serve as welfare-improving commitment devices. Here, regulations that restrict injurer care choices (i.e., require 'high care') can eliminate the temptation for injurers to make decisions that would actually result in them imposing higher expected total costs on themselves. Thus, if injurers face temptation, the choice between reducing risks through regulation or liability should consider this factor. *Ceteris paribus*, a high degree of temptation tends to favor regulation over liability.

Beyond contributing to the literature on regulation vs. liability, this chapter also demonstrates how insights from behavioral economics can be used in the study of law and economics. More specifically, it shows how standard law and economics models can be modified to incorporate non-neoclassical behavior and how consideration of this broader set of preference structures can affect standard conclusions regarding the welfare impacts and rankings of alternative legal rules.

NOTES

1.   For theoretical discussions of the joint use of regulation and liability, see, for example, Kolstad *et al.* (1990) and Schmitz (2000).
2.   See http://www.epa.gov/lawsregs/laws/rcra.html for a summary of RCRA.
3.   See http://www.epa.gov/superfund/policy/cercla.htm for an overview of CERCLA.
4.   Other considerations include the frequency of accidents, which affects the administrative costs of implementing the two approaches, and whether regulators or private parties have better information about risks and associated costs.
5.   For discussions of the increasing influence of behavioral economics on the study of law, see, for example, Sunstein (2000), Jolls *et al.* (1998), Prentice (2003), and Hayden and Ellis (2007).
6.   See Tsvetanov and Segerson (2013a) for a detailed justification for focusing on temptation when evaluating alternative environmental policy approaches.
7.   One advantage of this model is that it embodies time-consistent preferences, which

allows for standard welfare analysis of alternative policies. See Tsvetanov and Segerson (2013a) for a related discussion.

8. See Gul and Pesendorfer (2001) for a list of assumptions on these functions.
9. Note that this setup is specific to our context. See Gul and Pesendorfer (2004) for more general setup and applications of this dynamic framework.
10. By convention, we assume that injurers who are indifferent choose H.
11. Clearly, $x_H + \delta p(x_H)D \geq x_L + \delta p(x_L)D$ is not an interesting case, as it implies that it is optimal for all injurers to invest in low care.
12. We follow Gul and Pesendorfer (2004) and treat self-control costs as real costs that are included in the social welfare. See Tsvetanov and Segerson (2013a) for a more detailed discussion.

REFERENCES

Bryan, Gharad, Dean Karlan, and Scott Nelson (2010). "Commitment Devices." *Annual Review of Economics*, 2(1): 671–698.

DellaVigna, Stefano (2009). "Psychology and Economics: Evidence from the Field." *Journal of Economic Literature*, 47(2): 315–372.

Esteban, Susanna, Eiichi Miyagawa, and Matthew Shum (2007). "Nonlinear Pricing with Self-Control Preferences." *Journal of Economic Theory*, 135(1): 306–338.

Fishbach, Ayelet, and Benjamin Converse (2010). "Walking the Line between Goals and Temptations: Asymmetric Effects of Counteractive Control." In Hassin, Ran, Kevin Ochsner, and Yaacov Trope (eds.): *Self-Control in Society, Mind, and Brain*. Oxford University Press: 389–407.

Fudenberg, Drew (2006). "Advancing Beyond Advances in Behavioral Economics." *Journal of Economic Literature*, 44(3): 694–711.

Gul, Faruk, and Wolfgang Pesendorfer (2001). "Temptation and Self-Control." *Econometrica*, 69(6): 1403–1435.

Gul, Faruk, and Wolfgang Pesendorfer (2004). "Self-Control, Revealed Preference and Consumption Choice." *Review of Economic Dynamics*, 7(6): 243–264.

Hayden, Grant and Stephen Ellis (2007). "Law and Economics and Behavioral Economics." *University of Kansas Law Review*, 55: 629–675.

Jolls, Christine, Cass Sunstein, and Richard Thaler (1998). "A Behavioral Approach to Law and Economics." *Stanford Law Review*, 50(5): 1471–1550.

Kolstad, Charles, Thomas Ulen, and Gary Johnson (1990). "Ex Post Liability vs. Ex Ante Safety Regulation: Substitutes or Complements?" *American Economic Review*, 80(4): 888–901.

Laibson, David (1997). "Golden Eggs and Hyperbolic Discounting." *The Quarterly Journal of Economics*, 112(2): 443–477.

Lichtenstein, Donald, Nancy Ridgway, and Richard Netemeyer (1993). "Price Perceptions and Consumer Shopping Behavior: A Field Study." *Journal of Marketing Research*, 30(2): 234–245.

Lipman, Barton, and Wolfgang Pesendorfer (2013). 'Temptation.' In Acemoglu, Daron, Manuel Arellano, and Eddie Dekel (eds.): *Advances in Economics and Econometrics: Tenth World Congress, Volume 1*. Cambridge: Cambridge University Press, 243–88.

Loewenstein, George and Drazen Prelec (1992). "Anomalies in Intertemporal Choice: Evidence and an Interpretation." *The Quarterly Journal of Economics*, 107(2): 573–597.

Loewenstein, George and Ted O'Donoghue (2006). "'We Can Do This the Easy Way or the Hard Way': Negative Emotions, Self-Regulation, and the Law." *University of Chicago Law Review*, 73(1): 183–206.

Magen, Eran, and James Gross (2007). "Harnessing the Need for Immediate Gratification: Cognitive Reconstrual Modulates the Reward Value of Temptations." *Emotion*, 7(2): 415–428.

McAdams, Richard (2011). "Present Bias and Criminal Law." *University of Illinois Law Review*, 5: 1607–1631.

Miao, Jianjun (2008). "Option Exercise with Temptation." *Economic Theory*, 34(3): 473–501.

Pesendorfer, Wolfgang (2006). "Behavioral Economics Comes of Age: A Review Essay on Advances in Behavioral Economics." *Journal of Economic Literature*, 44(3): 712–721.

Prentice, Robert (2003). "Chicago Man, K-T Man, and the Future of Behavioral Law and Economics." *Vanderbilt Law Review*, 56(6): 1663–1777.

Schmitz, Patrick (2000). "On the Joint Use of Liability and Safety Regulation." *International Review of Law and Economics*, 20(3): 371–382.

Shavell, Steven (1984a). "Liability for Harm versus Regulation of Safety." *Journal of Legal Studies*, 13(2): 357–374.

Shavell, Steven (1984b). "A Model of the Optimal Use of Liability and Safety Regulation." *RAND Journal of Economics*, 15(2): 271–280.

Shavell, Steven (1993). "The Optimal Structure of Law Enforcement." *Journal of Law and Economics*, 36(1): 255–287.

Sunstein, Cass R. (2000). *Behavioral Law and Economics*. Cambridge, UK: Cambridge University Press.

Trope, Yaacov, and Ayelet Fishbach (2000). "Counteractive Self-Control in Overcoming Temptation." *Journal of Personality and Social Psychology*, 79(4): 493–506.

Tsvetanov, Tsvetan and Kathleen Segerson (2013a). "Re-Evaluating the Role of Energy Efficiency Standards: A Behavioral Economics Approach." *Journal of Environmental Economics and Management* 66(2):347–62.

Tsvetanov, Tsvetan and Kathleen Segerson (2013b). "Temptation as a Factor behind the Energy-Efficiency Gap: Some Empirical Evidence." *Working Paper, University of Connecticut.*

Wertenbroch, Klaus (1998). "Consumption Self-Control by Rationing Purchase Quantities of Virtue and Vice." *Marketing Science*, 17(4): 317–337.

Zhang, Ying, Szu-chi Huang, and Susan Broniarczyk (2010). "Counteractive Construal in Consumer Goal Pursuit." *Journal of Consumer Research*, 37(1): 129–142.

5. Strict liability when victims choose the value of the asset at risk
Florian Baumann and Tim Friehe

1   INTRODUCTION

From an economic perspective, tort law serves to promote optimal behavioral incentives for potential injurers and victims. Incentives are to a large extent shaped by the level of compensation (i.e., damages) in the event of an accident. Consequently, the *proper* damages awards are a critical ingredient of efficient tort liability systems (Visscher 2009). In the system we focus on in this chapter, strict liability, standard economic prescriptions predict that incentives will be optimal when the injurer is obliged to compensate the victim for harm caused, thereby internalizing the full expected social costs resulting from the injurer's behavior. However, when there are different potential levels of harm which cannot be discriminated by the injurer *ex ante*, then efficient care incentives result when average damages payments for accidents are equal to the level of average harm incurred by the accidents (Kaplow and Shavell 1996). This requirement permits a certain flexibility in how this equivalence is established; the reimbursement of actual harm for each accident or a fixed reimbursement equal to the average harm incurred in accidents are just two of the possible options (Arlen 2000).

If we seek to ensure the equivalence between average damages payments and average harm, the freedom to choose the precise level of compensation in a given case may be restricted when victim incentives are taken into account, as this chapter will demonstrate. Potential victims can influence expected accident costs in a number of ways: They may take precautions and/or select their level of the activity that can result in harm (see, e.g., Shavell 2004). However, it is also the victims who decide the value of the asset that could be damaged or destroyed in an accident. This concept of how victims can affect expected harm was first taken up by Baumann and Friehe (2009). The present contribution builds on this article by offering an important extension of their analysis.

The victim's decision regarding the value of the asset at risk in an accident is influenced by the scheme of damages. To be more precise, a potential victim's expected costs associated with the asset at risk consist of the cost of the good at the time of its original purchase and the additional expense required to replace the good after its loss in an accident. The replacement costs for the victim are determined by the difference between the actual price of the asset and the level of compensation received from the injurer. When deciding on the asset value, potential victims will compare additional total expenses for a more expensive variant of the good with the utility gain therefrom. In this comparison, damages that increase with the value of the asset imply lower additional total expenses than flat damages that are independent of the actual harm incurred. From a social perspective, when selecting the asset value, potential victims should take into account the full marginal costs, which necessarily include the higher accident losses when a more expensive variant of the good is chosen; this internalization can be achieved by a flat damages scheme. When this flat scheme is based on the average expected harm in an accident, it is possible to simultaneously induce optimal incentives for injurers. This is one of the main results presented in Baumann and Friehe (2009).

As an illustration of this result, consider the choice of which car to drive. Each buyer selects a level of equipment, quality, and comfort, where the different features are reflected in the price of the car. At the same time, the buyer should be aware that the value of the car can be lost or reduced in an accident, and that replacement or repair could be necessary as a result. When individuals are fully compensated for the actual value of the car lost in an accident, they will not take into account the increase in the (socially relevant) replacement costs associated with their purchase of a somewhat more expensive car, but will instead buy cars that are too expensive from an efficiency perspective.

The discussion thus far suggests that damages averaging in combination with strict liability is an efficient arrangement in a world in which injurers decide their level of care and victims determine the asset value placed at risk. However, a counter-argument could be raised: With damages equal to average expected harm, individuals who consume small asset values of the good could possibly receive compensation far in excess of the actual level of harm incurred by an accident. While overcompensation is not per se problematic in terms of efficiency (since it constitutes a transfer between individuals), it may cause inefficiencies when it entices individuals to participate in the activity who would not do so if the level of harm were accurately compensated. Such suboptimal participation could make damages averaging unsatisfactory as a policy choice. In this contribution, we extend the analysis of Baumann and Friehe (2009) in order to take this possible objection to damages averaging into account. As we will see, a deviation from damages averaging is indeed called for; however, this does not question the practice of overcompensation for low and undercompensation for high asset values.

This chapter analyzes damages schemes (such as damages averaging) in which victims make decisions at the intensive and extensive margins; some related research on the subject can be found in the literature. For example, the analysis of (non-)participation constraints is important for many areas of economics in which optimal payment schedules are derived, such as optimal labor contracts (see Wang and Weiss, 1998) and group organization (see Berglöf et al. 2012), among other applications. Rather than *switching* agents on or off, Finsinger (1991) considers the introduction of new activities as a consequence of which the appropriate care expected from potential victims changes under the liability rule to strict liability with a defense of contributory negligence. With regard to damages schemes, there is a large literature competently surveyed by Visscher (2009). For example, Kaplow and Shavell (1996) use a unilateral-care model with heterogeneous victim harm levels and assume that the assessment of harm is costly. Since an injurer's care incentives are unaffected by the court's choice between accurate and average harm when injurers do not know precise harm *ex ante*, Kaplow and Shavell argue that courts should use average harm to save on administrative costs. The present analysis, in contrast, is primarily concerned with victims' behavioral incentives. This also sets our study apart from Dari-Mattiacci and de Geest (2005), who examine the compensation of average harm in the context of potentially judgment-proof injurers. The literature on *exposure suits* similarly addresses average harm measures, as the actual realization of harm has not yet occurred (see, e.g., Miceli and Segerson 2005). The real-world use of an average as a compensation measure can be found in class-action suits. Given different individual levels of harm, this practice (*inter alia*) can influence who initiates a class-action suit (see Marceau and Mongrain 2003) and the composition with respect to the damage levels of claimants in the class action (see Che 1996).

The outline of this chapter is as follows: After providing a description of the main components of the model in Section 2.1, we first analyze the scenario in which potential injurers choose care while victims remain passive (i.e., asset values are given exogenously) in Section 2.2. This sets the stage for the extended analysis in Section 2.3, in which potential injurers choose care *and* potential victims choose the asset value at risk, thereby narrowing the options for efficient damages schemes. Finally, the participation constraint will be investigated in Section 2.4, in which we illustrate our findings with numerical examples. The chapter ends with a brief conclusion in Section 3.

2   THE MODEL

2.1   Description

Throughout the following analysis, we always consider two sets of individuals: potential injurers and potential victims. Each group consists of an equal (large) number of people that is normalized to unity. For the group of potential injurers, we assume that each individual is characterized by the same cost of care function, which is linear.[1] Potential victims differ in the utility they obtain from the value of the asset at risk in the event of an accident caused by an injurer. More precisely, potential victims can be classified according to their type θ, with $\underline{\theta}$ and $\bar{\theta}$ representing the lower and upper limit, respectively, which determines the value they place on the object at risk. The cumulative distribution function for the type parameter θ is denoted by $F(\theta)$. In our analysis, we will consider both a discrete and a continuous distribution of victim types. Injurers exert care, which reduces the probability of an accident at a diminishing rate, where $p(x)$ is the probability of an accident, x the level of care taken by an insurer, and $p'(x) < 0 < p''(x)$. Throughout this chapter, we assume that a victim's type cannot be observed by a third party in the event of an accident, but that the value of the asset lost in the accident can be assessed. Therefore, in a setting of strict liability, the compensation received by the victim in the event of an accident, denoted by D, can only depend on the observed value of the asset, $D = D(l)$. Finally, the injurer cannot anticipate *ex ante* which type of victim will require compensation in the event of an accident.

We assume that the utility function of potential victims can be represented by a quasi-linear function of the form

$$U^V(l,\theta) = u(l,\theta) - l - p(x)(l - D(l)), \qquad (5.1)$$

where $\partial u/\partial l, \partial u/\partial \theta > 0 > \partial^2 u/\partial l^2$. This signifies that an object with a value of l will be immediately replaced in the event of an accident. Furthermore, the utility function implies that victims in our set-up are risk-neutral with respect to monetary terms. Assuming risk-neutrality, an injurer's expected utility is

$$U^I(x) = -x - p(x)E(D(l)), \qquad (5.2)$$

where $E(.)$ denotes the expectations operator. As is standard in the literature on the economic analysis of law, we assume social welfare to be described by the sum of the utilities of the individual members of society (see, e.g., Shavell 2004).

2.2   Optimal Damages Given Exogenous Values of the Asset at Risk

In this section, we start by considering the textbook case of exogenous heterogeneity in the values of the objects placed at risk. We begin with a discrete distribution of victim types: A victim may be either of type $\theta = H$ (i.e., will suffer a high level of harm in the event of an accident) or of type $\theta = L$, $H > L$, with the proportion of type-H individuals represented by q, $0 < q < 1$. The value of the asset at risk is $l(H)$ for the former group, and $l(L)$ for the latter. The only decision taken in this set-up is the decision made by potential injurers regarding their level of care.

The social welfare function can be described by

$$SW = q[u(l(H),H) - (1 + p(x))l(H)] + (1 - q)[u(l(L),L)$$

$$- (1 + p(x))l(L)] - x, \tag{5.3}$$

where damages payments cancel out, as they are assumed to represent pure transfers between individuals. The first-best care level x is determined by

$$\frac{dSW}{dx} = -p'(x)[ql(H) + (1 - q)l(L)] - 1 = -p'(x)E(l) - 1 = 0. \tag{5.4}$$

In other words, the marginal gain from higher care in the form of a reduction in expected accident costs should equal the marginal costs of care, which amount to one.

The representative injurer chooses the level of care in order to maximize utility, as described in (5.2). The corresponding first-order condition is given by

$$\frac{dU^I(x)}{dx} = -1 - p'(x)E(D(l)) = 0. \tag{5.5}$$

The privately optimal level of care equates the marginal care costs (equal to one) and the reduction in expected damages payments. It is easily established that the privately optimal level of care coincides with the socially optimal level when the expected damages $E(D(l))$ are equal to the expected harm $E(l)$.

The equivalence of expected damages and expected harm can be established in several ways. Indeed, any combination of damages payments that fulfills $qD(l(H)) + (1 - q)D(l(L)) = ql(H) + (1 - q)l(L)$ induces the first-best outcome. Economic intuition for this result can be provided by reference to the fact that the injurer takes into account the social marginal benefit from an increase in care when expected damages are equal to expected harm. For the purposes of our investigation, note that the condition of expected liability equal to expected harm is fulfilled both for accurate damage assessment, $D(l(\theta)) = l(\theta)$, and for damages averaging, $D(l(H)) = D(l(L)) = (ql(H) + (1 - q)l(L))$; this latter will play a prominent role in the subsequent analysis.

The result transfers to the setting in which victim types are continuously distributed, $\theta \in [\underline{\theta}, \bar{\theta}]$. It still holds that socially optimal care equates marginal costs of care and the marginal gain in reduced expected harm, and that the injurer equates marginal costs of care with the marginal reduction in expected damages. Again, a first-best allocation is achieved as long as the expected value of the asset destroyed in an accident equals expected damages, which allows the use of accurate damage assessment, damages averaging, or any other damages function guaranteeing $E(D(l)) = E(l)$.

Result 1:   When the values of the assets at risk are exogenous, a first-best allocation can be achieved by any damages function that ensures that expected damages equal expected harm. This encompasses damages functions with damages individually determined by the harm in each accident as well as those with damages set equal to average harm.

2.3   Optimal Damages When Victims Choose the Value of the Asset at Risk

Following Baumann and Friehe (2009), we now allow potential victims to choose the value of the asset at risk. As in the previous section, we start by considering the case of two victim types before commenting on the setting featuring a continuum of victim types.

The social welfare function is again given by (5.3); the only difference here is that $l(H)$ and $l(L)$ are now choice variables. The first-order conditions for maximizing social welfare are thus given by

$$\frac{\partial SW}{\partial l(H)} = q\left(\frac{\partial u(l(H),H)}{\partial l(H)} - (1 + p(x))\right) = 0 \qquad (5.6)$$

$$\frac{\partial SW}{\partial l(L)} = (1 - q)\left(\frac{\partial u(l(L),L)}{\partial l(L)} - (1 + p(x))\right) = 0 \qquad (5.7)$$

$$\frac{\partial SW}{\partial x} = -p'(x)[ql(H) + (1 - q)l(L)] - 1 = -p'(x)E(l) - 1 = 0. \qquad (5.8)$$

The first two conditions establish that the marginal utility of a higher value of the asset at risk should equal marginal costs, which consist of the cost of the initial purchase and any expected replacement costs. The final condition, (5.8), is essentially the same as the condition in the case in which asset values were exogenously given, see (5.4).

Moving from the solution of the social planner to the outcome in which individuals make decentralized decisions, we assume that injurers choose care for given asset values (determined by victims), and that each individual victim takes the care level determined by injurers as given when selecting the asset value. The conditions that guide individual behavior result from maximization of (5.1) and (5.2):

$$\frac{\partial U^V(l(H),H)}{\partial l(H)} = \frac{\partial u(l(H),H)}{\partial l(H)} - (1 + p(x)) + p(x)D'(l(H)) = 0 \quad (5.9)$$

$$\frac{\partial U^V(l(L),L)}{\partial l(L)} = \frac{\partial u(l(L),L)}{\partial l(L)} - (1 + p(x)) + p(x)D'(l(L)) = 0 \quad (5.10)$$

$$\frac{\partial U^I(x)}{\partial x} = -p'(x)[qD(l(H))+(1-q)D(l(L))]-1 = -p'(x)E(D(l))-1 = 0. \quad (5.11)$$

A comparison of the set of equations (5.6) to (5.8) and of (5.9) to (5.11) yields the conclusion that: (i) setting expected damages equal to expected harm induces the injurer to choose the socially optimal response to the (given) decisions of potential victims; and (ii) designing the damages function $D(l)$ to be flat (at least) in the neighborhood of the points of the socially optimal consumption levels may produce socially optimal values for the assets placed at risk. In other words, the condition regarding the optimal level of expected damages carries over to a setting in which potential victims choose the value of the asset at risk. The additional requirement of a locally flat damages function is new; it results from the importance of confronting potential victims with the total social costs at the margin that result from their purchases. Each potential victim should take into account the full marginal costs of an increase in the value of the asset at risk, which, from a social perspective, includes not only the initial acquisition costs but also the expected replacement costs. A damages function that requires the level of compensation to be equal to the actual value of the asset lost in an accident clearly violates this precondition. The damages rule "compensation = harm" actually implies that potential victims impose a negative externality on potential injurers when they decide to buy a more expensive variety of the asset at risk, resulting in excessively high asset value selections.

The above analysis establishes that when potential victims can decide on the value of the asset at risk, the rule equating damages to actual assessed harm does not result in a first-best allocation. However, the discrete scenario with two types of potential victims still permits considerable leeway in determining the actual damages levels. Thus far, it has been established that the damages function must be flat at the first-best values of the asset values for the two victim types, and that damages must be equal to average harm in expectation. However, obeying these conditions for setting damages is not sufficient to guarantee the first-best outcome, as we must also ensure that each type of potential victim chooses the appropriate asset value, i.e., no potential victim should have an incentive to imitate the behavior of another victim type. The corresponding incentive compatibility conditions are given by

$$U^V(l^*(H),H) = u(l^*(H),H) - l^*(H) - p(x)(l^*(H) - D(l^*(H)))$$

$$\geq U^V(l^*(L),H) = u(l^*(L),H) - l^*(L) - p(x)(l^*(L) - D(l^*(L)))$$
(5.12)

for victim type H, and

$$U^V(l^*(L),L) = u(l^*(L),L) - l^*(L) - p(x)(l^*(L) - D(l^*(L)))$$

$$\geq U^V(l^*(H),L) = u(l^*(H),L) - l^*(H) - p(x)(l^*(H) - D(l^*(H)))$$
(5.13)

for victim type L. It must be preferable for victim type θ to choose $l^*(\theta)$, where socially optimal levels are denoted by asterisks.

As described above, injurers will select first-best care when the two damages levels are additionally linked by the condition

$$qD(l^*(H)) + (1 - q)D(l^*(L)) = ql^*(H) + (1 - q)l^*(L), \quad (5.14)$$

which can be rearranged to represent $D(l^*(H))$ as a function of $D(l^*(L))$, $l^*(H)$, and $l^*(L)$. Using this expression in (5.12) and (5.13) enables us to derive upper and lower limits for the damages paid to victims of type L:

$$D(l^*(L)) \leq \frac{q}{p}\left[u(l^*(H),H) - u(l^*(L),H) - l^*(H) + l^*(L)\frac{q+p}{q}\right]:$$

$$= D^{max}(l^*(L)) \tag{5.15}$$

and

$$D(l^*(L)) \geq \frac{q}{p}\left[u(l^*(H),L) - u(l^*(L),L) - l^*(H) + l^*(L)\frac{q+p}{q}\right]:$$

$$= D^{min}(l^*(L)). \tag{5.16}$$

This demonstrates that the choice of the level of damages is restricted in comparison to the setting with exogenously given asset values. Notably, setting the level of compensation equal to the level of average harm complies with all constraints described above, as there is no incentive to mimic the other victim type when there is no difference in compensation. Furthermore, a damages function of

$$D(l) = \begin{cases} l^*(L), & l < l^*(H) \\ l^*(H), & l \geq l^*(H) \end{cases} \tag{5.17}$$

would also be effective, since each victim type's utility level $u(l,\theta) - l$ is higher when they choose the asset value *appropriate* to the respective victim type. However, note that this is not the same as a damages function that requires damages to be equal to the harm caused in each individual accident, and that the result is also due to the current constraint limiting the number of victim types to two.

Again, we would like to explore how these results extend to the case featuring a continuum of victim types. The generalized requirements impose $D'(l^*(\theta)) = 0$ for every victim type and $E(D(l)) = E(l)$ with respect to the injurer. However, with a continuum of victim types, the incentive compatibility constraints reduce to a single value for each victim type, i.e., the compensation for expected harm in any accident. Damages averaging turns out to be the only damages function that ensures that the decentralized outcome coincides with the first-best allocation. This is the basic result presented by Baumann and Friehe (2009).

Result 2:   When the values of the asset at risk are determined by victims, a first-best allocation requires that the damages function: (i) is locally flat for the asset values actually chosen; (ii) ensures that no victim type mimics another; and (iii) results in expected damages equal to expected harm. These requirements are fulfilled by a damages function that sets damages equal to average (or expected) harm in accidents.

Result 3:   When the values of the assets at risk are determined by victims and there is a continuum of victim types, a first-best allocation can only be achieved by a damages function that demands for each single accident a compensatory payment equal to average (or expected) harm.

2.4   Optimal Damages Function when Victims Choose the Value of the Asset at Risk and Whether or Not To Participate

Our search for the optimal damages function has thus far relied on the (implicit) assumption that all potential victims would indeed take part in the activity, i.e., would purchase an asset that might be lost in an accident. Based on this assumption, we focused on the victims' incentive compatibility constraint, while abstracting from constraints on their participation. However, the following objection to our scenario could be raised: Setting the level of compensation equal to the level of average harm might induce some individuals who should not take part in the activity from an efficiency standpoint to become active; such individuals would buy a fairly cheap variant of the asset in hope of winning the relatively higher damages award in the event of an accident. This would imply that damages averaging cannot achieve a first-best outcome because it distorts the (non-) participation constraint.

In this section, we generalize the previously presented analysis by explicitly taking into account the participation constraint of potential victims. We establish how the optimal damages function must be adjusted in order to prevent individuals from buying the asset who should not do so. In order to be able to present the results and economic intuition in an easily accessible form, we assume an exogenous accident probability p. However, by requiring that expected damages must be equal to expected harm, we retain the rule that has demonstrated to be optimal with respect to injurer incentives in the discussion so far.[2]

2.4.1   Three potential victim types

We return to the model with two victim types used above, now introducing a third type indexed by N. For the utility function of individuals of type N, it holds that

$$u(l,N) - l < u(0,N) \tag{5.18}$$

for every value $l > 0$, which implies that

$$\frac{\partial u(l,N)}{\partial l} < 1. \tag{5.19}$$

These individuals should not participate in the activity from a social welfare point of view, even if the accident probability were equal to zero.

The social welfare function that takes into account the fact that individuals of type N do not participate in the activity and that the accident probability is exogenous is given by

$$SW = q[u(l(H),H) - (1+p)l(H)] + (1-q)[u(l(L),L) - (1+p)l(L)].$$
(5.20)

The maximization of (5.20) gives rise to the familiar first-order conditions:

$$\frac{\partial SW}{\partial l(H)} = \frac{\partial u(l(H),H)}{\partial l(H)} - (1+p) = 0$$
(5.21)

$$\frac{\partial SW}{\partial l(L)} = \frac{\partial u(l(L),L)}{\partial l(L)} - (1+p) = 0;$$
(5.22)

these conditions require that marginal utility and the marginal social costs of an increase in the asset value be equal for each active victim type. In contrast, in the decentralized equilibrium, asset values chosen by type L and H individuals are again determined according to (5.9) and (5.10) for an exogenous value of the accident probability p.

The social planner who seeks to align decentralized choices with the socially optimal behavior through the implementation of a damages scheme must ensure that: (i) type N individuals do not participate (i.e., do not consume a positive value of the asset l); (ii) expected damages are equal to expected harm in the event of an accident; and (iii) type H and L individuals choose the asset levels that maximize (5.20) subject to these constraints. The conditions that require expected damages to be equal to expected harm and type H and L individuals to choose appropriate asset values result in limits on the level of compensation for the low asset value $l(L)$ as described in (5.15) and (5.16). In addition, to ensure non-participation by type N individuals, it must hold that

$$(1-p)u(l(L),N) + pu(0,N) - l(L) + pD(l(L)) \le u(0,N) \quad (5.23)$$

The above equation ensures that individuals of type N will never find it optimal to participate even at the low asset value $l(L)$, acknowledging of the fact that these individuals would not replace the asset value in the event of an accident. Rearranging the terms in (5.23), we obtain a second upper bound for the damages $D(l(L))$ amounting to

$$D(l(L)) \le \frac{1}{p}[l(L) - (1-p)(u(l(L),N) - u(0,N))] := D^{max,2}(l(L)).$$
(5.24)

The extent to which the consideration of participation decisions restricts the planner's freedom to set the optimal damages scheme will be dependent on the circumstances. For this reason, we will first explore the setting that permits victims of types L and H to choose their first-best value, while the planner sets the level of compensation equal to the level of average harm. In the next step, we will consider circumstances that permit victims of types L and H to choose their first-best value, incentivized by a damages scheme that does not set the level of compensation equal to the level of average harm. Finally, we analyze the scenario in which the asset values of victims of types L and H must deviate from their first-best levels in order to fulfill all conditions.

In our quest to describe the optimal damages function, we start by deriving limit values for the case in which damages averaging fulfills all constraints when active victim types choose their first-best consumption levels. In this case, the incentive compatibility constraints for victims of type L and H are fulfilled, but it must be verified whether the non-participation constraints for type N individuals holds as well. The use of damages averaging, resulting in asset values of $l^*(H)$ and $l^*(L)$ for the respective potential victim types, is feasible as long as

$$D^{max,2}(l^*(L)) = \frac{1}{p}[l^*(L) - (1 - p)(u(l^*(L),N) - u(0,N))]$$

$$\geq ql^*(H) + (1 - q)l^*(L). \tag{5.25}$$

For $q = 0$, condition (5.25) is fulfilled due to (5.18). An increase in the proportion of type-H individuals, i.e., a higher value of q, leads to an increase in average expected harm, while the maximum damages award intended to prevent the participation of type-N individuals remains the same. Consequently, for a high enough proportion of type-H individuals, the non-participation constraint may become binding and damages averaging no longer be an option.

When the condition (5.25) is not fulfilled, it may nevertheless be possible to support an outcome in which victims of types L and H choose their first-best asset values by a modification of the damages scheme. As previously established, the first-best asset values for type H and L individuals can also be induced by a piecewise flat damages function that awards a lower payment to individuals consuming $l^*(L)$ in comparison to individuals choosing $l^*(H)$. More specifically, a first-best allocation may be obtained using a one-step damages function. The requirements that type-L victims do not mimic type-H victims, and that type-N individuals do not participate will be fulfilled, according to (5.16) and (5.24), when

$$D^{max,2}(l^*(L)) \geq D^{min}(l^*(L)), \tag{5.26}$$

since this creates a range for $D(l^*(L))$ that ensures the desired choices. The condition (5.26) may be rearranged to obtain

$$(1 - p)[u(0,N) - u(l^*(L),N) + l^*(L)]$$

$$\geq q[l^*(L) - l^*(H) + u(l^*(H),L) - u(l^*(L),L)]:=qB. \quad (5.27)$$

Whereas the left-hand side of (5.27) is positive according to (5.18) and is independent of the proportion of type-H victims given by q, the term on the right-hand side depends on q but cannot be signed unambiguously. It follows from the definition of first-best asset values that $u(l^*(H),L) - u(l^*(L)) - (1 + p)(l^*(H) - l^*(L)) < 0$. However, this ensures $B < 0$ only for sufficiently small levels of the accident probability p. For very high levels of p, the term B may be positive, ruling out the possibility that (5.27) will hold for a sufficiently high proportion of potential victims of type H. In this latter case, a first-best allocation can no longer be obtained; we will now turn to the conditions that describe the second-best solution.

Applying both the participation constraint and the self-selection constraint for type-L victims, the planner's optimization problem can be stated as

$$SW = q[u(l(H), H) - (1 + p)l(H)] + (1 - q)[u(l(L), L) - (1 + p)l(L)]$$

$$+ \lambda\{(1 - p)[l(L) + u(0, N) - u(l(L), N)] - q[l(L) - l(H) + u(l(H), L)$$

$$- u(l(L), L)]\}, \quad (5.28)$$

where λ represents the Lagrange multiplier and the constraint (cf. (5.27)) results from a combination of the binding incentive compatibility constraint, the non-participation constraint, and the requirement that expected damages equal expected harm. With respect to the Lagrange multiplier, it can be noted that $\lambda > 0$ will hold in equilibrium.[3]

The social planner assigns the asset values $l(L)$ and $l(H)$, which results in the following first-order conditions:

$$\frac{\partial SW}{\partial l(H)} = q\left[\frac{\partial u(l(H),H)}{\partial l(H)} - (1 + p)\right] + \lambda q\left[1 - \frac{\partial u(l(H),L)}{\partial l(H)}\right] = 0 \quad (5.29)$$

and

$$\frac{\partial SW}{\partial l(L)} = (1 - q)\left[\frac{\partial u(l(L),L)}{\partial l(L)} - (1 + p)\right] - \lambda q\left[1 - \frac{\partial u(l(L),L)}{\partial l(L)}\right]$$

$$+ \ \lambda(1 \ - \ p)\left[1 \ - \ \frac{\partial u(l(L),N)}{\partial l(L)}\right] = 0. \tag{5.30}$$

It is obvious that both of the second-best asset values, $l(H)$ and $l(L)$, deviate from their first-best counterparts, $l^*(H)$ and $l^*(L)$. That is, the decision regarding the asset value made by type-L individuals is distorted in order to prevent type-N individuals from participating. However, in the next step, we see that this requires a distortion in the purchase decision made by type-H individuals, because type-L individuals would otherwise be incentivized to mimic type-H behavior. From (5.31) in combination with (5.19), we find that the asset value assigned to type-L individuals is necessarily greater than the corresponding first-best value $l^*(L)$, as the derivative of the objective function would still be positive when evaluated at $l(L) = l^*(L)$. The economic intuition for this result is that a higher value of $l(L)$ makes mimicking a less attractive option for type-N individuals, due to the fact that the increase in the associated expense is not compensated by the increase in the valuation of type-N victims. As a consequence, the non-participation condition excluding individuals of type N can be satisfied more easily. In order to induce type-L individuals to indeed choose this higher value, the damages function must be increasing in the asset value for $l(L)$, $D'(l(L)) > 0$ (see (5.10)). In contrast, for the deviation in the asset-value decision made by type-H individuals, no unambiguous statement can be made. The second-best asset value $l(H)$ is higher (lower) than the first-best value $l^*(H)$ when $\frac{\partial u(l(H),L)}{\partial l(H)} < (>)1$ holds. Without further information on the utility function and the parameters of the model, it cannot be determined which outcome will result. However, the larger the difference between potential victim types in the marginal utility resulting from a higher asset value, the more likely it is that the extra utility from mimicking will be so low that the asset value of type-H individuals will be distorted upwards. In this case, type-L individuals would not gain much in utility by selecting the inflated asset value of type-H individuals while bearing the high costs of mimicking. Because it is not possible to unambiguously determine the deviation in the asset value $l(H)$ from its first-best counterpart, we are also unable to state the slope of the damages function at $l(H)$. The derivative $D'(l(H))$ will be positive (negative) when $l(H) > (<)l^*(H)$.

Overall, we have shown for the scenario with a binding non-participation constraint that the optimal damages function is no longer flat, but increasing for low asset values. We summarize this finding in Result 4; a numerical illustration is provided in the next subsection to allow a better understanding of our conclusions.

Result 4: When the values of the asset at risk are determined by victims and a non-participation constraint holds, a first-best allocation can no longer be achieved. The second-best allocation requires a damages function that is no longer flat, but increasing for low asset values.

2.4.2 A numerical example

In this section, we provide a numerical example of the scenario in which three types of individuals can purchase the asset at risk of being lost in an accident. This illustration is intended to facilitate understanding of the findings from the previous section.

In our example, an individual's utility function takes the form

$$U(l, \theta) = \theta l - \frac{l^2}{2} - (1 + p)l + pD(l), \qquad (5.31)$$

where we allow three different realizations of θ: $H = 2$, $L = 7/4$, and $N = 9/10$. Consequently, for an accident probability lower than 3/4, the first-best allocation is described by asset values of $l^*(H) = 1 - p$, $l^*(L) = 3/4 - p$, and $l^*(N) = 0$.

In order to induce the first-best solution, it must hold that the damages associated with an asset value of $l^*(L)$ must not exceed the critical value $D^{max,2}(l^*(L))$ established in (5.24). In our example, this upper limit is given by

$$D^{max,2}(l^*(L)) = \frac{1}{80p}(3 - 4p)[17 + 3p + 10p^2]. \qquad (5.32)$$

Consequently, damages averaging will yield the first-best allocation as long as

$$D^{max,2}(l^*(L)) \geq ql^*(H) + (1 - q)l^*(L) = \frac{1}{4}(3 + q - 4p). \qquad (5.33)$$

When condition (5.33) is not fulfilled, it might still be possible to achieve a first-best allocation by using a one-step damages function that is flat at the two asset levels $l^*(L)$ and $l^*(H)$. We must ensure that this damages function does not violate the incentive compatibility constraint for an individual of type L (i.e., that it does not distort incentives to choose $l^*(L)$ instead of $l^*(H)$); the damages $D(l^*(L))$ should not be lower than the minimum damages defined in (5.16). In our example, this is feasible as long as

$$D^{max,2}(l^*(L)) \geq D^{min}(l^*(L)) = \frac{3}{4} - p + \frac{q}{4} - \frac{q}{32p}. \qquad (5.34)$$

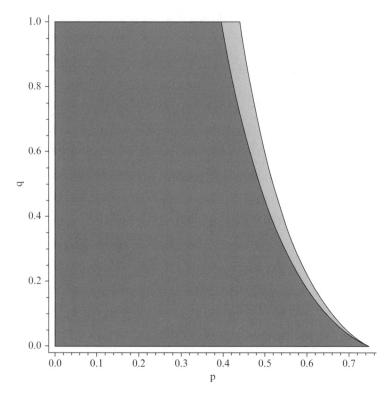

Figure 5.1   Feasibility of first-best solution

Figure 5.1 illustrates the results obtained thus far. The dark area indicates combinations of $q \in (0, 1)$ and $p \in (0, 3/4)$ for which damages averaging can be applied in order to achieve a first-best solution. With an increase in the proportion of type-H individuals, the level of compensation (fixed at the level of average harm) increases, which results in damages averaging violating the non-participation constraint for type-N individuals when p is high. Likewise, an increase in the accident probability p makes a damages award more likely and thereby may also lead to violation of the non-participation constraint. The adjoining grey area indicates parameter combinations for q and p in which it still holds that a first-best allocation can be achieved by applying a one-step damages function. The damages awarded to type-L individuals would then be lower than average harm. An increase in q or p would lower the minimum damages award that could be granted to type-L individuals while still satisfying the self-selection constraint. This gives rise to the unshaded area in which a first-best allocation can no longer be obtained.

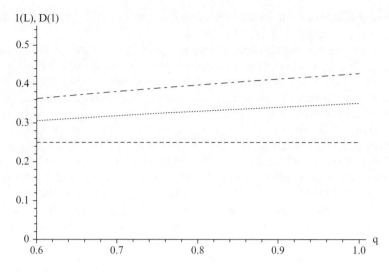

Figure 5.2   Second-best solution for l(L)

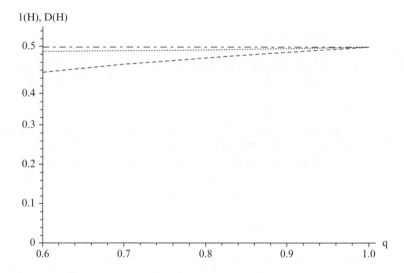

Figure 5.3   Second-best solution for l(H)

To illustrate the resulting second-best asset values and the corresponding damages payments, we set the accident probability to $p = 1/2$. In this case, the first-best asset values are $l^*(L) = 1/4$ and $l^*(H) = 1/2$, but a first-best solution cannot be obtained for $q > 3/5$. Figures 5.2 and 5.3 depict the second-best asset values in comparison to the first-best values and the resulting damages $D(l(L))$ and $D(l(H))$ for $3/5 < q < 1$.

In Figure 5.2, we can see an example of what was established more generally above. The second-best asset value for individuals of type L, the curve in the middle, is above its first-best value, indicated by the straight lower line. In order to prevent type-N individuals from participating, the asset value is increased; these individuals are now deterred by the higher expenses. The damages paid to a type-L individual, the upper curve, still imply overcompensation, as would be the case with damages averaging. In our example, the distortion in the asset value for type-H individuals turns out to be a downward adjustment in comparison to the first-best value (see Figure 5.3). The first-best asset value is shown by the straight upper line; the second-best value is depicted by the curve in the middle, which is somewhat lower. Corresponding to the overcompensation of type-L individuals, type-H individuals remain undercompensated in the event of an accident, with the lower curve describing the damages award. Only for q approaching one – that is, when only type-H individuals participate in the activity – will damages awards fully compensate these individuals.

2.4.3   Continuum of potential victim types

In this final step, we solve for the optimal damages function when there is a continuum of individuals potentially who might purchase the asset. Individuals are distributed in the interval $[\underline{\theta}, \overline{\theta}] = [L, H]$ according to a uniform distribution with density function $f(\theta)$ and the corresponding cumulative distribution function $F(\theta)$. In addition, there are again some individuals for whom $\theta = N < L$ who should not participate in the activity. The analysis will generalize the findings presented thus far; the economic intuition closely follows the explanation of the discrete version of the model. In the following section, we present the results of a numerical example. The mathematics behind the example are relegated to the appendix.

To illustrate the optimal damages function for the scenario in which there is a continuum of potential victim types, we apply the utility function according to (5.31) and the following parameter values:

$$L = \frac{7}{4}, \ H = \frac{15}{4}, \ N = \frac{9}{10}, \ p = \frac{1}{2},$$

which imply $f(\theta) = 1/2$. In a first-best allocation, the asset value would increase linearly with the type parameter θ, starting at $l^*(L) = 1/4$ and with a maximum value of $l^*(H) = 9/4$. Average harm in an accident

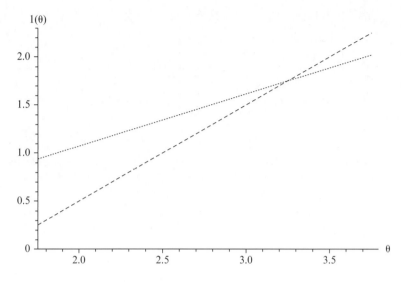

Figure 5.4   Second-best versus first-best values for l(θ)

implied by this allocation amounts to $E(l) = 5/4$. However, given the first-best asset values, the maximum damages award for type-L individuals that still guarantees the non-participation of type-N individuals is given by $D^{max,2}(l*(L)) = 9/80$, which is lower than the average harm. Consequently, both the non-participation constraint and the self-selection constraint for type-L individuals are binding, indicating that only a second-best allocation is attainable.

Figures 5.4 and 5.5 illustrate the results. In Figure 5.4, the resulting second-best values for the assets are compared to their first-best counterparts. As in the discrete version of the model, the asset values for low values of the preference parameter θ are distorted upwards in order to deter mimicking by type-N individuals; mimicking becomes more expensive and therefore less attractive. The function displaying the second-best asset values exhibits a flatter slope than the corresponding function for the first-best values, and the second-best values fall short of their first-best counterparts for high realizations of the preference parameter, which is in line with the results illustrated in the discrete scenario.

Figure 5.5 displays the damages function that induces the second-best asset values and compensates for average expected harm. The damages function is necessarily increasing for low values of the preference parameter θ, since individuals must be incentivized to buy more expensive assets than they would in the first-best allocation scenario. As individuals with a high realization of the preference parameter are meant to consume lower

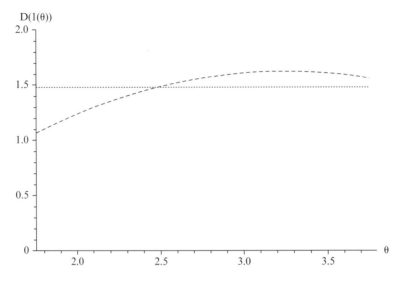

Figure 5.5   Second-best damages $D(l(\theta))$

asset values than in a first-best situation, the damages function is decreasing in its upper part. In comparison to a situation with flat damages corresponding to average expected harm, compensation is lower for small realizations of θ and higher for large realizations, but still implies overcompensation for low asset values and undercompensation for high asset values.

3   CONCLUSION

The determination of the level of compensation is critical for a liability system's incentive effects. The baseline level of compensation in most jurisdictions is the accurate level of harm (see, e.g., Shavell 2004). The objective of fully compensating the victim of an accident is consistent with the objective of inducing efficient care in a standard unilateral-care setting that is – inter alia – characterized by exogenous levels of harm. The present contribution considers the possibility that the asset value that is exposed to risk is a choice variable of the potential victim, who takes into account the full expected price of the asset at the time of purchase when strict liability applies. The expected price is determined in part by the damages scheme, given that the victim's replacement costs following an accident are equal to the difference between the price of the asset and the level of compensation received from the injurer.

In this more general framework, social optimality also requires that potential victims choose efficient asset values, which imposes additional conditions on the levels of compensation applied. It results that granting damages that are equal to the average expected harm induces socially optimal purchase decisions by potential victims. The important characteristic of the optimal damages scheme is that the compensation does not lower the buyer's marginal costs below the level of social marginal costs, a requirement that implies that the level of compensation is (at least locally) non-increasing in the asset value.

Using damages averaging may correct for distortions at the so-called *intensive* margin, but may at the same time introduce distortions at the *extensive* margin. In other words, the prospect of obtaining compensation equal to the average of all possible harm levels may tempt individuals to participate in the activity (by purchasing a very low-valued asset) who should refrain from it from an efficiency standpoint. We establish that attempts to ensure both that active potential victims choose appropriate asset values (values that are not unduly inflated or deflated due to the consequences of the damages scheme) and that certain individuals remain inactive (despite the promise of overcompensation in the event of an accident) may prevent the attainment of the first-best allocation. However, our results indicate that overcompensation for low asset values and under-compensation for high asset values, a feature of damages averaging, might also be a characteristic of the second-best damages function.

APPENDIX

The Case of a Continuum of Individuals and a Binding Non-participation Constraint

The optimization problem can be understood as follows: The social planner determines the asset values for each type in $[\underline{\theta},\bar{\theta}]$, subject to the self-selection constraint, the non-participation constraint for individuals of type N, and the requirement that average damages equal average harm. Given the asset values, the optimal damages function that induces this allocation can be derived.

The self-selection constraint requires that

$$U^V(l(\theta),\theta) = \theta l(\theta) - \frac{l(\theta)^2}{2} - (1 + p)l(\theta) + pD(l(\theta))$$

$$\geq U^V(l(\theta'),\theta) = \theta l(\theta') - \frac{l(\theta')^2}{2} - (1 + p)l(\theta') + pD(l(\theta')).$$

(5A.1)

Since individuals choose their asset values, application of the envelope theorem yields

$$\frac{dU^V(l(\theta),\theta)}{d\theta} = l(\theta). \qquad (5A.2)$$

The second constraint is the non-participation (5A.1) constraint that excludes individuals of type N. This constraint requires that

$$Nl(\underline{\theta}) - \frac{l(\theta)^2}{2} - l(\underline{\theta}) + pD(l(\underline{\theta})) \leq 0. \qquad (5A.3)$$

Since this constraint is binding, the utility level of an individual of type $\underline{\theta}$ is limited to

$$U^V(l(\underline{\theta}),\underline{\theta}) = (\underline{\theta} - N)l(\underline{\theta}) - pl(\underline{\theta}), \qquad (5A.4)$$

where the asset value $l(\underline{\theta})$ still has yet to be determined.

The final constraint, by which damages must equal expected harm, requires that

$$\int_{\underline{\theta}}^{\bar{\theta}} [D(l(\theta)) - l(\theta)] f(\theta) d\theta = 0, \qquad (5A.5)$$

which – in order to eliminate the damages payment – can be rewritten using the use of the definition of individual utility as

$$\int_{\underline{\theta}}^{\bar{\theta}} \left[U^V(l(\theta),\theta) - \theta l(\theta) + \frac{l(\theta)^2}{2} + l(\theta) \right] f(\theta) d(\theta) = 0. \qquad (5A.6)$$

The Hamiltonian that corresponds to the social planner's problem is given by

$$\Gamma = \left[\theta l(\theta) - \frac{l(\theta)^2}{2} - (1 + p)l(\theta) \right] f(\theta)$$

$$+ \alpha \left[U^V(l(\theta),\theta) - \theta l(\theta) + \frac{l(\theta)^2}{2} + l(\theta) \right] f(\theta)$$

$$+ \mu(\theta) l(\theta), \qquad (5A.7)$$

where $l(\theta)$ is the control variable, $U^V(l(\theta),\theta)$ is the state variable, α is the co-variable associated with the budget constraint, and $\mu(\theta)$ is the co-state variable. The first-order conditions are described by

$$\frac{\partial \Gamma}{\partial l(\theta)} = [\theta - l(\theta) - (1 + p)] f(\theta) + \alpha[-\theta + l(\theta) + 1] f(\theta) + \mu(\theta) = 0 \quad (5A.8)$$

and

$$\frac{\partial \Gamma}{\partial U^V(l(\theta), \theta)} = \alpha f(\theta) = -\frac{d\mu(\theta)}{d\theta}, \quad (5A.9)$$

with the transversality condition resulting in

$$lim_{\theta \to \bar{\theta}} \mu(\theta) = 0. \quad (5A.10)$$

Equations (5A.9) and (5A.10) allow us to solve for the co-state variable $\mu(\theta)$:

$$\mu(\theta) = \alpha[1 - F(\theta)]. \quad (5A.11)$$

This and (5A.8) imply that the co-variable α is given by

$$\alpha = \frac{\theta - l(\theta) - 1 - p}{2\theta - \bar{\theta} - l(\theta) - 1}, \quad (5A.12)$$

where it has been used that $F(\theta) = (\theta - \underline{\theta})/(\bar{\theta} - \underline{\theta})$ and $f(\theta) = 1/(\bar{\theta} - \underline{\theta})$ for a uniform distribution of types.

Since α is a constant, we can use (5A.12) to solve for

$$\frac{dl(\theta)}{d\theta} = -\frac{\partial \alpha / \partial \theta}{\partial \alpha / \partial l(\theta)} = \frac{\bar{\theta} - l(\theta) - 1 - 2p}{\bar{\theta} - \theta - p}. \quad (5A.13)$$

Equation (5A.13) is a first-order differential equation for the asset value $l(\theta)$. We obtain

$$l(\theta) = -(\bar{\theta} - \theta - p)A + \bar{\theta} - 1 - 2p, \quad (5A.14)$$

where A is a constant resulting from integration. Evaluating (5A.14) for $\theta = \underline{\theta}$, we can determine A to be

$$A = \frac{\theta - 1 - 2p - l(\theta)}{\bar{\theta} - \underline{\theta} - p}, \quad (5A.15)$$

which is a function of the asset value assigned to the type $\underline{\theta}$. With (5A.14), (5A.15), and (5A.2), the utility of potential victims is given by

$$U^V(l(\theta),\theta) = \int_{\underline{\theta}}^{\theta} l(\tilde{\theta})\, d\tilde{\theta} + U^V(l(\underline{\theta}),\underline{\theta}), \qquad (5A.16)$$

where $U^V(l(\underline{\theta}),\underline{\theta})$ is determined by (5A.4).

Consequently, the only remaining unknown is the asset value $l(\underline{\theta})$, which can be obtained by using the constraint (5A.6). With $l(\underline{\theta})$, we can calculate $U^V(l(\theta),\theta)$ and $l(\theta)$, which gives us the damages for each value of θ:

$$D(l(\theta)) = \frac{1}{p}\left[U^V(l(\theta),\theta) - \theta l(\theta) + \frac{l(\theta)^2}{2} + (1+p)l(\theta) \right] \qquad (5A.17)$$

NOTES

1. In Baumann and Friehe (2009), we allow for heterogenous injurers as well. In such a case, with the court being unable to observe an injurer's type ex-post, it can be shown that strict liability has an advantage compared to the liability rule of negligence.
2. Given the systematic deviation from first-best levels for the value of consumed assets, we are aware that it might be worthwhile from an efficiency point of view to distort injurer incentives as well, in line with the theory of second-best (see Lipsey and Lancester 1956).
3. This results from the envelope theorem; an increase in the utility $u(0,N)$ of a type-N individual not participating is tantamount to a relaxation of the non-participation constraint, which must result in an increase in the value of the optimized function SW.

REFERENCES

Arlen Jennifer, Tort damages, in: *Encyclopedia of Law and Economics II* (Bouckaert, B. & G. de Geest (Eds), Cheltenham, UK: Edward Elgar 2000).

Baumann Florian & Tim Friehe, On the superiority of damage averaging in the case of strict liability, 29 *International Review of Law and Economics*, 138–142 (2009).

Berglöf Erik, Mike Burkart, Guido Friebel and Elena Paltseva, Club-in-the-club: Reform under unanimity, 40 *Journal of Comparative Economics*, 492–507 (2012).

Che Yeon-Koo, Equilibrium Formation of Class Action Suits, 62 *Journal of Public Economics*, 339–361 (1996).

Dari-Mattiacci Giuseppe & Gerrit de Geest, Judgement Proofness Under Four Different Precaution Technologies, 161 *Journal of Institutional and the Oretical Economics*, 38–56 (2005).

Finsinger Jörg, The Choice of Risky Technologies and Liability, 11 *International Review of Law and Economics*, 11–22 (1991).

Kaplow Louis & Steven Shavell, Accuracy in the Assessment of Damages, 39 *Journal of Law and Economics*, 191–209 (1996).

Lipsey R.G. & Kelvin Lancaster, The general theory of the second best, 24, *Review of Economic Studies*, 11–32 (1956).

Marceau & Nicolas Steeve Mongrain, Damage Averaging and the Formation of Class Action Suits, 23 *International Review of Law and Economics*, 63–74 (2003).

Miceli Thomas J.& Kathleen Segerson, Do Exposure Suits Produce a "Race to File"? An Economic Analysis of a Tort for Risk. 36 *Rand Journal of Economics*, 613–627 (2005).

Shavell Steven, *Foundations of Economic Analysis of Law*. Cambridge, MA: Harvard University Press (2004).

Visscher Louis, *Tort damages*, in: Tort law and economics (Faure, M. ed., 2nd ed. Cheltenham, UK: Edward Elgar 2009).

Wang Ruqu & Andrew Weiss, Probation, layoffs, and wage-tenure profiles: A sorting explanation, 5 *Labour Economics*, 359–383 (1998).

6. Incentives for care, litigation, and tort reform under self-serving bias
Claudia M. Landeo, Maxim Nikitin, and Sergei Izmalkov

1 INTRODUCTION

In civil litigation, although most cases settle before trial, many do not settle early, and some do not settle at all. Delayed settlement or impasse causes high costs for the parties and for society.[1] Babcock et al. (1995a, 1997), Babcock and Loewenstein (1997) and Loewenstein et al. (1993) propose an explanation for disputes that rests on a judgment error called "self-serving bias." Self-serving bias refers to the litigant's biased beliefs that the court decision will favor his case due to the interpretation of the facts of the dispute in his own favor.[2] In information environments characterized by ambiguity, even when the parties are exposed to the exact same information, they might arrive at expectations of an adjudicated settlement that are biased in a self-serving manner. As a result, higher likelihood of disputes might be observed.[3] Note that the litigation outcomes might influence potential injurers' level of care, i.e., their expenditures on accident prevention (Png, 1987; Landeo et al., 2006, 2007a, 2007b). Hence, the defendant's level of care, social welfare and the effects of tort reform might also be affected by self-serving bias.[4]

Despite the active experimental literature on self-serving bias and pretrial bargaining, and the robustness of these findings, there has been very little theoretical work on this topic. This chapter presents a strategic model of incentives for care and litigation under asymmetric information and self-serving bias, and studies the effects of caps on non-economic damages. We contribute to the theoretical law and economics literature by providing the first assessment of the effects of self-serving bias on incentives for care and social welfare, and the first evaluation of the effects of damage caps on incentives for care in environments that allow for biased litigants. We also contribute to the behavioral economics literature by generalizing the perfect Bayesian equilibrium concept to strategic environments with biased players. Our work underscores the importance of incorporating asymmetric information and cognitive biases in the theoretical analysis of tort reform. It also suggests that our theoretical framework provides a useful tool for assessing the effects of public policy.[5]

In their seminal experimental work on self-serving bias, Babcock et al. (1995a, 1996) and Loewenstein et al. (1993) study the effects of this cognitive bias on the likelihood of disputes. Their experimental environment consists of a pretrial bargaining game between a plaintiff and a defendant.[6] Their findings suggest that subjects exhibit self-serving bias, and that this cognitive bias increases the likelihood of disputes.[7] Importantly, these studies also indicate that self-serving bias is robust to debiasing interventions (Babcock et al., 1995a, 1997).[8] Field data suggest that self-serving bias does not vanish with experience. In fact, seasoned labor negotiators, lawyers, and judges exhibit self-serving bias and other cognitive errors. Babcock et al. (1996) study Pennsylvania school teachers' salary negotiations. In this type of negotiation, it is common for the school district and the union representatives to use agreements in comparable communities as a reference. Their findings indicate that both parties choose their comparable school districts in a self-serving manner. Eisenberg (1994) analyzes data from a survey conducted with experienced bankruptcy lawyers and bankruptcy judges regarding their perceptions of the bankruptcy system and their performance. Comparisons of judges' and lawyers' responses also suggest self-serving bias.[9]

The theoretical law and economics literature on settlement and litigation has been focused on two other sources of disputes, divergent (but unbiased) beliefs about the trial outcome due to uncertainty regarding the judicial adjudication, and asymmetric information about the strength of the plaintiff's case. Priest and Klein (1984) study a framework that allows for *unbiased* errors in the litigants' estimates of the trial outcome. Their findings suggest that disputes occur when, *randomly*, the plaintiff's estimate of the award at trial exceeds the defendant's by enough to offset the incentive for settlement generated by risk aversion and trial costs (see also Landes, 1971; Posner, 1973; Gould, 1973; Shavell, 1982).[10] Reinganum and Wilde (1986) construct a signaling model between an informed plaintiff and an uninformed defendant, and show that, even in cases in which both parties share common beliefs about the likelihood of a judgment in favor of the plaintiff, asymmetric information about the damages suffered by the plaintiff suffices to generate disputes (see also Png, 1983, 1987; Bebchuk, 1984; Nalebuff, 1987; Schweizer, 1989; Spier, 1992).[11]

We build on Reinganum and Wilde's (1986) work on settlement and litigation, and extend their framework in several interesting and important ways. Our main contributions are as follows. First, our setting encompasses two sources of disputes, asymmetric information (but common priors) about the economic losses, and self-serving beliefs (divergent and biased beliefs) about the size of the non-economic damages awarded at trial.[12] Second, our framework incorporates a previous stage to the litigation game. In this stage, the potential injurer chooses his level of care (expenditures on accident prevention).[13] To the best of our knowledge, ours is the first theoretical assessment of the effects of self-serving bias on incentives for care and social welfare. Third, we study the effects of caps on non-economic damages under biased litigants by extending our basic framework.[14] Importantly, our work provides the first theoretical investigation of the effects of damage caps on defendants' level of care in environments with biased litigants. Fourth, we provide a technical contribution to the behavioral economics literature by generalizing the perfect Bayesian equilibrium concept to environments with biased players.[15]

Our benchmark model involves a two-stage game between two Bayesian risk-neutral parties, a potential plaintiff and a potential defendant.[16] In the first stage, a potential injurer decides his level of care, which determines the probability of accidents. This decision depends on the cost of preventing accidents and on the expected litigation loss in case of an accident.[17] We assume that every injured potential plaintiff has an economic incentive to file a lawsuit. Then, if an accident occurs, the second stage, called the litigation stage, starts.

The litigation stage consists of a take-it-or-leave-it game, where a plaintiff and a defendant negotiate prior to costly trial. Using the court to resolve the dispute is costly, and may be subject to error. We assume that the plaintiff (the first mover) has private information about the amount of her economic losses.[18] Given the uncertainty and unpredictability regarding the determination of non-economic damages, and following empirical regularities regarding the elicitation of cognitive biases (Babcock et al. 1997),[19] we assume that the players exhibit self-serving beliefs about the size of the non-economic damages awarded at trial.[20] Following empirical regularities (Ross and Sicoly, 1982; Loewenstein, et al., 1993), we also assume that the litigants are unaware of their own bias and the bias of their opponent (i.e., the biased litigant believes that her opponent shares her beliefs). As a result, each litigant plays a game against *an apparent opponent*, i.e., against an opponent that appears as *actual* to the biased litigant. We denote this strategic setting as the *strategic environment with apparent opponents*, and apply a generalization of the perfect Bayesian equilibrium concept to this environment. We focus our analysis on the universally-divine fully-separating perfect Bayesian equilibrium in which the potential injurer spends resources on accident prevention, each plaintiff's type make a different settlement offer, and the defendant randomizes between accepting and rejecting the offer. Accidents and disputes do occur in equilibrium.

The main findings from our benchmark model are as follows. First, our results suggest that the defendant's bias decreases his expenditures on accident prevention, and hence, increases the likelihood of accidents. Second, both litigants' biases increase the likelihood of disputes. Third, our results indicate that, although self-serving bias helps litigants commit on tough negotiation positions, it is economically self-defeating for the informed plaintiff.[21] Fourth, our findings suggest that that the plaintiff's bias is always welfare reducing. The defendant's bias is welfare reducing if under-deterrence is present (i.e., when the defendant's level of care is lower than the socially optimal level).

We then illustrate the benefits of incorporating self-serving bias into the theoretical analysis of tort reform by extending our basic framework to study the effects of caps on non-economic damages. Experimental evidence on caps (Pogarsky and Babcock, 2001) suggests that this tort reform might influence litigation outcomes not only by directly reducing the expected award at trial but also by indirectly affecting litigants' beliefs about the award at trial.[22] These findings also indicate that the effects of caps on litigants' beliefs depend on the relationship between the size of the cap and the value of the underlying claim. Following these empirical regularities, we extend our benchmark framework by incorporating caps of non-economic damages, and modeling the bias on litigants' beliefs about the size of the award at trial as a function of the cap.

We find that caps on non-economic damages decrease the defendant's level of care (and hence, increase the likelihood of accidents) if the defendant perceives the cap as relatively low (with respect to his biased estimation of the non-economic award at trial). Importantly, we find that the positive effect of damage caps on lowering the likelihood of disputes, commonly attributed to this tort reform,[23] might not necessarily be observed in environments with biased litigants: Caps might induce higher likelihood of disputes if the defendant perceives the cap as relatively low (with respect to his biased estimation of the non-economic award at trial), and the plaintiff perceives the cap as relatively high (with respect to her biased estimation of the non-economic award at trial). As a result, caps on non-economic damages might be welfare reducing. Hence, this tort reform should be adopted with caution.

Our work is part of a small theoretical law and economics literature on disputes and self-serving bias. Farmer and Pecorino (2002) extend Bebchuk's (1984) screening model of settlement and litigation by allowing for self-serving bias.[24] They find conditions under which self-serving bias increases the likelihood of disputes. Deffains and Langlais (2009) present a different extension of Bebchuk's (1984) framework that allows for self-serving bias and risk aversion.[25] Their findings suggest that self-serving bias has an ambiguous effect on the probability of trial and equilibrium settlement amount. To the best of our knowledge, ours is the first formal analysis of incentives for care, litigation outcomes, and caps on non-economic damages in strategic environments characterized by asymmetric information and self-serving bias.

Although this research is motivated on pretrial bargaining and legal disputes, we believe that our findings, insights, and technical contributions might apply to other contexts as well. Bargaining and impasse are prevalent in environments such as labor contract negotiations (Farber, 1978; Kennan and Wilson, 1989, 1993; Babcock and Olson, 1992; Babcock et al., 1996), and partnership dissolution processes (Brooks et al., 2010).[26] The complexity and ambiguity of these environments might elicit self-serving bias.

The rest of the chapter is organized as follows. Section 2 presents the benchmark framework, describes the strategic environment with apparent opponents, outlines the generalization of the perfect Bayesian equilibrium concept, and summarizes the equilibrium solution. Section 3 analyzes the effects of litigants' self-serving beliefs on equilibrium strategies and litigants' payoffs, and discusses the effects of self-serving bias on social welfare. Section 4 extends the theoretical analysis by allowing for caps on non-economic damages, and discusses the direct and indirect effects of caps on potential injurers' incentives for care and likelihood of disputes. Section 5 concludes the chapter and discusses avenues for future research.

2   BENCHMARK MODEL

We model the interaction between two Bayesian, risk-neutral players, a potential injurer and a potential plaintiff, as a sequential game of asymmetric information (but common priors) about the plaintiff's economic losses, and self-serving beliefs (divergent and biased beliefs) about the size of the non-economic damages awarded at trial.

The game proceeds as follows. The potential injurer first decides his optimal level of care (the probability of accidents λ).[27] To achieve a probability of accidents λ, the potential injurer has to spend on care (accident prevention). The cost of care is denoted by $K(\lambda)$. We assume that all potential injurers have the same cost of care, which is common knowledge. We also assume that $K(\lambda)$ is a smooth and continuously differentiable function defined on the interval $(0,1)$, with $K'(\lambda) < 0$, $K'' > 0$, $K(1) = 0$ and $\lim_{\lambda \to +0} K(\lambda) = +\infty$. The optimal level of care, i.e., the optimal λ, is the one that minimizes the defendant's total expected loss $L_D = K(\lambda) + \lambda l_D$, where l_D is the expected litigation loss. We take the expected litigation loss as parametric in order to describe L_D, but ultimately l_D will be derived as the continuation value of the litigation stage, and hence it will reflect the outcomes at the litigation stage.[28] We assume that accident occurrence is common knowledge.

If an accident occurs, Nature decides the plaintiff's economic losses x (plaintiff's type) from a continuum of types, distributed on $(\underline{x},+\infty)$.[29] We define $f(x)$ as the strictly positive probability density function of the distribution of plaintiffs by type. We assume that $f(x)$ is known by the plaintiff and the defendant, and that the realization of x is revealed only to the plaintiff. We assume that the plaintiff also suffers stochastic non-economic losses y (independent of x), with probability density function $g(y)$, support $(\underline{y},+\infty)$, and expected value μ, which are unknown to the players. We assume that only the realization of y is revealed to the plaintiff. However, the plaintiff does not have a credible way to convey this information to the defendant (or to the court). The potential plaintiff then decides whether to file a lawsuit. We assume that the plaintiff's expected payoff from suing is positive. Therefore, every injured plaintiff has an incentive to file a lawsuit.

Next, the litigation stage starts. It is modeled as a take-it-or-leave-it game between a defendant and a plaintiff. The plaintiff has the first move and makes a settlement proposal S to the defendant, where $S \in (-\infty,+\infty)$. After observing the proposal, the defendant, who only knows the distribution of economic losses x, decides whether to accept or reject the proposal. The defendant's decision is based on his updated beliefs about the plaintiff's type. If the defendant accepts the proposal (i.e., settles out-of-court), the game ends and the defendant pays to the plaintiff the amount proposed. If the defendant rejects the proposal, costly trial occurs. The plaintiff and the defendant incur exogenous legal costs (c_P and c_D, respectively). The total legal costs are denoted by $C = c_P + c_D$. Both the individual and total legal costs are common knowledge. The court then decides whether to award compensatory damages to the plaintiff and the amount of the award.[30] Our framework allows for court errors. There is an exogenous probability $(1 - \pi)$ that the court will make a mistake and rule incorrectly against the plaintiff. It rules correctly with the complementary probability π, which is common knowledge.

If the court rules in favor of the plaintiff, it grants a compensatory award to the plaintiff. We assume that the compensatory award includes compensation for economic and non-economic losses.[31] We assume that the realization of the economic losses x are perfectly assessed by the court, and hence the economic damages are equal to x. However, the court does not know the distribution or the realization of the non-economic losses y.

We denote the compensatory award by tx,[32] where $t > 1$ (i.e., the court always awards non-economic damages, in addition to the economic damages). Note that t can be interpreted as the *ratio of the compensatory award to the economic losses*. We denote the non-economic damages by $A = (t - 1)x$, i.e., the non-economic damages A are equal to the compensatory award at trial tx minus the economic damages x. The intuition behind the assumption that the non-economic damages are proportional to the economic damages is that courts estimate non-economic losses (and grant non-economic damages) by using the only variable they know: the realization of economic losses x.

Following empirical regularities (Babcock et al., 1997), we assume that an information environment characterized by ambiguity regarding the court's decision about the non-economic damages (and hence, about the ratio of the compensatory award to the economic losses, t) will elicit litigants' self-serving beliefs about t. Specifically, we assume that the plaintiff believes that the ratio of the compensatory award to the economic losses is equal to $t + h_P$ (an additive bias), and the defendant believes that this ratio is equal to $t - h_D$, where $h_P > 0$ and $h_D > 0$.[33] Hence, the biased type x plaintiff believes that the compensatory award at trial and the non-economic damages will be $(t + h_P)x$ and $(t + h_P - 1)x$, respectively. The biased defendant believes that a type x plaintiff will get a compensatory award at trial equal to $(t - h_D)x$, and non-economic damages equal to $(t - h_D - 1)x$. Importantly, following experimental evidence from social psychology (Ross and Sicoly, 1982) and behavioral economics (Loewenstein, et al., 1993), we also assume that the litigants are neither aware of their own bias nor aware of the bias of the other party. In other words, each litigant presumes that her individual belief about the ratio of the compensatory award to the economic losses is correct and shared by her opponent. Specifically, the plaintiff presumes that $t + h_P$ is the shared belief, and the defendant presumes that $t - h_D$ is the shared belief. As a result, each biased litigant plays a game against *an apparent opponent*. We denote this strategic environment as the "strategic environment with apparent opponents."

2.1   Generalization of the Perfect Bayesian Equilibrium Concept

We generalize the perfect Bayesian equilibrium (PBE) concept to the strategic environments with apparent opponents. In this equilibrium, each litigant believes that her opponent plays an equilibrium strategy that reflects the litigant's biased beliefs about the compensatory award at trial. Then, the litigant's equilibrium strategy corresponds to her best response to the equilibrium strategy of her apparent opponent.

The Definition presents the characterization of the PBE concept in strategic environments with apparent opponents. Let S and b denote the strategies and posterior beliefs, respectively. The subscripts P and D indicate that the player is the plaintiff or the defendant, respectively; and, the superscript a indicates an apparent player.

DEFINITION: *The set* $(S_P, S_D, S_P^a, S_D^a, b_P, b_D, b_P^a, b_D^a)$ *is a PBE of the game with apparent opponents if*
(1A) S_P is the best response of the plaintiff, given S_D^a and b_P;
(1B) S_D is the best response of the defendant, given S_P^a and b_D;
(1C) S_P^a is the best response of the apparent plaintiff, given S_D and b_P^a;
(1D) S_D^a is the best response of the apparent defendant, given S_P and b_D^a;

(2A) b_P is consistent with S_P and S_D^a;
(2B) b_D is consistent with S_D and S_P^a;
(2C) b_P^a is consistent with S_P^a and S_D; and,
(2D) b_D^a is consistent with S_D^a and S_P.

Consistency implies that the beliefs are updated using the Bayes' rule, whenever possible.

This equilibrium concept specifies the litigants' strategies and beliefs, the apparent opponents' strategies and beliefs, and the belief updating rule for both litigants and their apparent opponents. Hence, this equilibrium concept encompasses two perfect PBE, one for the pair plaintiff-apparent defendant, and the other for the pair defendant-apparent plaintiff. We denote this equilibrium as the "PBE of the game with apparent opponents."

2.2   Equilibrium Solution

This section discusses the solution of the game. While intuition is included in the text, the proofs are relegated to the Appendix.

We focus our analysis on the universally-divine (Banks and Sobel, 1987), fully-separating (every type of plaintiff makes a different settlement offer) PBE of the strategic environment with apparent opponents. This equilibrium is empirically relevant. Although the potential injurer always finds it optimal to spend on accident prevention, we still expect accidents to happen with a positive probability in equilibrium. Disputes do occur in equilibrium. They are originated by asymmetric information *and* self-serving bias.

Proposition 1 specifies the equilibrium strategies, and the equilibrium and off-equilibrium beliefs that support these strategies. Define $\underline{S}_P = \pi(t + h_P)\underline{x} + c_D$ and $\underline{S}_D = \pi(t - h_D)\underline{x} + c_D$ as the lowest values of the settlement demand, from the point of view of the biased plaintiff and biased defendant, respectively.

PROPOSITION 1:   *The following strategy profile, together with the players' beliefs, describe the unique universally-divine fully-separating PBE of the game with apparent opponents.*[34]
(A1) The apparent defendant chooses the level of care (probability of accidents) $\lambda^{a*} = \arg\min\{K(\lambda) + \lambda\int_x^{+\infty}[\pi(t + h_P)x + c_D]f(x)dx\}$.
(B1) The apparent defendant chooses the probability of rejection of a settlement demand S $p^a(S) = 1 - e^{-(S - \underline{S}_P)/C}$ *for* $S \geq \underline{S}_P$, *and* $p^a(S) = 0$ *for* $S < \underline{S}_P$.
(C1) The plaintiff of type x chooses the settlement demand $S = \pi(t + h_P)x + c_D$.
(D1) The equilibrium beliefs of the apparent defendant upon observing the settlement demand S are $b^a(S) = (S - c_D)/[\pi(t + h_P)]$ *for* $S \geq \underline{S}_P$, *and the off-equilibrium beliefs are* $b^a(S) = \underline{x}$ *for* $S < \underline{S}_P$.

(A2) The defendant chooses the level of care (probability of accidents) $\lambda^* = \arg\min\{K(\lambda) + \lambda\int_x^{+\infty}[\pi(t - h_D)x + c_D]f(x)dx\}$.
(B2) The defendant chooses the probability of rejection of a settlement demand S $p(S) = 1 - e^{-(S - \underline{S}_D)/C}$ *for* $S \geq \underline{S}_D$, *and* $p(S) = 0$ *for* $S < \underline{S}_D$.
(C2) The apparent plaintiff of type x chooses the settlement demand $S = \pi(t - h_D)x + c_D$.
(D2) The equilibrium beliefs of the defendant upon observing the settlement demand S are $b(S) = (S - c_D)/[\pi(t - h_D)]$ *for* $S \geq \underline{S}_D$, *and off-equilibrium beliefs are* $b(S) = \underline{x}$ *for* $S < \underline{S}_D$.

It is straightforward to show that the litigation stage strategies for the plaintiff and defendant are incentive-compatible and aligned with the players' equilibrium and off-equilibrium beliefs.[35] First, analyze the plaintiff's settlement offer. In equilibrium, the plaintiff of type x makes a settlement demand $S = \pi(t + h_P)x + c_D$, which corresponds to the expected loss at trial for the defendant from the biased plaintiff's point of view. Second, consider the reply from the defendant. In equilibrium, the defendant randomizes between accepting and rejecting the offer as a way to induce the plaintiff to reveal her true type. Given that higher settlement demands are accepted less frequently (and the court perfectly observes the plaintiff's type at trial), the plaintiff's expected payoff from disguising herself as a higher type is lower than her expected payoff from truthfully revealing her type. Note that the plaintiff's settlement demand serves as a signal for the defendant. Given the litigants' biased beliefs, however, this signal is noisy. Third, assess the defendant's choice of care. The defendant's optimal level of care λ (probability of accidents) minimizes her total expected loss $L(\lambda) = K(\lambda) + \lambda l_D$, where $l_D = \int_{\underline{x}}^{+\infty} [\pi(t - h_D)x + c_D] f(x) dx$ are litigation losses expected by the biased defendant. Her incentives for care are, of course, affected by her expected litigation losses. When a potential injurer expects smaller losses due to an accident, she spends less on accident prevention. This, in turn, increases the likelihood of accidents.

Two additional features of this equilibrium deserve to be mentioned. First, every plaintiff's equilibrium settlement proposal observed by the defendant belongs to the set of equilibrium strategies for the apparent plaintiff (the plaintiff who shares the defendant's beliefs). In other words, the biased defendant is never *surprised* when observing the optimal strategy from the biased plaintiff. In fact, the biased defendant attributes offer $S = \pi(t + h_p)x + c_D$ to a plaintiff of type $x_D = \frac{S - c_D}{\pi(t - h_D)} > x$, and rejects it with a higher probability. The second interesting feature refers to the off-equilibrium beliefs. Following Reinganum and Wilde (1986), we adopt the following intuitive off-equilibrium beliefs: if $S < \underline{S}_D$, then $b(S) = \underline{x}$, and if $S < \underline{S}_p$, then $b^a(S) = \underline{x}$, for the defendant and apparent defendant, respectively. That is, if an off-equilibrium demand is made, the defendant (or apparent defendant) believes that it comes from the lowest plaintiff's type $\underline{x}$.[36]

Consider now the game outcomes. We define the probability of trial as the expected probability of rejection (aggregating across plaintiffs' types). It is easy to show that the probability of trial and the litigants' expected payoffs conditional on accident occurrence are as follows. The probability of trial is

$$\int_{\underline{x}}^{+\infty} p(\pi(t + h_p)x + c_D) f(x) dx.$$

The expected payoff for the plaintiff of type x, V_p, is

$$V_P = (1 - p(x)) [\pi(t + h_p)x + c_D] + p(x)(\pi t x - c_P).$$

The expected payoff for the defendant who meets a type x plaintiff is

$$-(1 - p(x)) [\pi(t + h_p)x + c_D] - p(x)(\pi t x + c_D).$$

Then, the defendant's expected payoff (aggregating across plaintiffs' types) is

$$V_D = \int_{\underline{x}}^{+\infty} \{-(1 - p(x)) [\pi(t + h_p)x + c_D] - p(x)(\pi t x + c_D)\} f(x) dx.$$

3   EFFECTS OF SELF-SERVING BIAS

This section describes the effects of the litigants' biases on the equilibrium strategies, litigants' expected payoffs, and social welfare.

3.1   Effects on Equilibrium Strategies

Proposition 2 summarizes the effects of the litigants' biases on the settlement demand, probability of rejection, the probability of trial, and incentives for care. Note that the *unconditional* values refer to the whole game (the litigation stage and the defendant's level of care stages).

PROPOSITION 2:   *The effects of self-serving bias on the equilibrium strategies are as follows.*
(1) For any given plaintiff's type x, the settlement demand is increasing in the plaintiff's bias. The expected settlement demand is also increasing in the plaintiff's bias.
(2) For any plaintiff's type x, the probability of rejection is increasing in both litigants' biases. The probability of trial is also increasing in both litigants' biases.
(3) An increase in the defendant's bias reduces the defendant's expenditures on care and increases the probability of accidents.

The intuition is as follows. Consider first the effects of self-serving bias on the settlement demand. An increase in the plaintiff's bias affects his beliefs of the defendant's loss at trial: The biased plaintiff anticipates a higher defendant's expected loss at trial. As a consequence, the plaintiff increases his settlement demand. Second, consider the effects of self-serving bias on the probability of rejection. The plaintiff's bias affects the probability of rejection through its effect on the settlement demand: A higher plaintiff's bias increases his settlement demand, and hence, increases the probability of rejection. The defendant's bias affects the probability of rejection through its effect on the defendant's beliefs about the plaintiff's economic losses x_D: A higher defendant's bias decreases x_D, and hence, reduces his expected loss at trial. As a result, it increases the probability of rejection. Third, consider the effect of self-serving bias on the potential injurer's level of care and probability of accidents. A larger defendant's bias reduces her expected litigation loss. Hence, she is less concerned about the occurrence of accidents and economizes on care.[37]

Interestingly, our findings regarding the effects of the plaintiff's bias on the settlement offer and the effects of the defendant's bias on the likelihood of rejection suggest that self-serving bias serves the litigants to commit to tough negotiation positions. Note that impasse increases legal expenditures (and hence, reduces the size of the pie). Then, self-serving bias might be *self-defeating* in terms of the litigants' economic payoffs. (See next section for details.)

Our results regarding pretrial bargaining are aligned with the experimental findings on self-serving bias in pretrial bargaining environments (see Babcock et al., 1995a, 1997; Loewenstein, et al., 1993; and Landeo, 2009). In these experiments, subjects are randomly assigned the role of plaintiff or defendant and given detailed materials outlining a personal injury lawsuit. Before pretrial bargaining, each subject predicts the trial outcome after being assured their prediction would not be shared with their adversary. Although the plaintiff and the defendant subjects receive identical case materials, plaintiffs' estimates exceed defendants' estimates by a significant margin. Hence, these studies demonstrate that subjects consistently arrive at self-serving predictions of trial outcomes, and that these self-serving predictions induce higher likelihood of disputes. Although these environments involve ambiguity, both litigants are symmetrically exposed to this ambiguity. Our results regarding the likelihood of disputes are, of course, exacerbated by the presence of asymmetric information. Importantly, the effects of self-serving bias on the defendant's incentive for care (and hence, on the likelihood of accidents) have not been previously explored (theoretically or empirically). Hence these findings provide a novel contribution to the law and economics literature.

The Corollary outlines the effects of self-serving bias on the unconditional probability of trial and the expected legal costs.

COROLLARY: *The effects of self-serving bias on the unconditional probability of trial and expected legal costs are as follows.*
(1) The unconditional probability of trial is increasing in both litigants' biases.
(2) The conditional and unconditional expected legal costs are increasing in both litigants' biases.

These results are intuitive. The unconditional probability of trial is increasing in both litigants' biases due to the effect of the defendant's bias on the probability of accidents and the effects of both litigants' biases on the probability of trial. Regarding the effects on legal costs, note that legal costs, c_P and c_D, are incurred only in case of trial. Note also that the probability of rejection is increasing in both litigants' biases, and higher probability of rejection implies higher legal costs. Finally note that these results also hold for the whole game (unconditional expected legal costs). In fact, the defendant's bias reduces his expenditures on care and makes accidents more likely. As a result, the unconditional expected legal costs also increase.

3.2 Effects on Litigants' Payoffs

Proposition 3 describes the effects of the litigants' biases on their expected payoffs. Unconditional values refer to the whole game.

PROPOSITION 3: *The effects of self-serving bias on the litigants'*
expected payoffs are as follows.
(1) An increase in the defendant's bias increases his expected payoff and
reduces the plaintiff's expected payoff.
(2) An increase in the plaintiff's bias reduces her expected payoff
and her unconditional expected payoff. It increases the defendant's
expected payoff and his unconditional expected payoff if and only if
$h_P \int_{\underline{x}}^{+\infty} \zeta x^2 f(x) dx > \frac{C}{\pi} \int_{\underline{x}}^{+\infty} \zeta x f(x) dx$, *where* $\zeta \equiv e^{-[\pi(t+h_P)x - \pi(t-h_D)\underline{x}]/C}$.

Analyze the effects of the defendant's bias on his expected payoff. The plaintiff of type x demands $\pi(t + h_P)x + c_D$, which is greater than the defendant's expected loss at trial $\pi tx + c_D$. Then, the defendant would be better off by rejecting the demand. The probability of rejection goes up when the defendant's bias is higher. Hence, the defendant's bias will increase his expected payoff. Note that the impact of the defendant's bias on the defendant's unconditional expected payoff is ambiguous: A higher defendant's bias generates lower litigation losses for the defendant but it also reduces her expenses on care (and hence, it increases the likelihood of an accident). Consider now the effects of the defendant's bias on the plaintiff's expected payoff. The plaintiff will be better off if the settlement demand is accepted because her expected gain at trial $\pi tx - c_P$ is smaller than the settlement demand $\pi(t + h_P)x + c_D$. Therefore, an increase on the probability of rejection (due to a higher defendant's bias) will reduce the plaintiff's expected payoff.

Next, assess the effects of the plaintiff's bias on her expected payoff. The plaintiff's bias affects her payoff through its effect on the settlement offer and the probability of trial. An increase in the plaintiff's bias increases the settlement demand. As a result, it increases the plaintiff's expected payoff for a given probability of rejection. However, this higher demand is rejected with a higher probability. We show in the Appendix that the second effect always dominates the first one. Hence, an increase in the plaintiff's bias unambiguously hurts her. Consider now the effects of the plaintiff's bias on the defendant's expected payoff. Similar two effects are observed in case of the defendant's expected payoff. The defendant might be worse off because the settlement demand is higher for a given probability of rejection. However, the higher demand increases the probability of rejection, which benefits the defendant. We show in the Appendix that the second effect dominates the first one under a specific condition. As a result, the plaintiff's bias might benefit the defendant. These results hold in the litigation game and in the whole game (defendant's unconditional expected payoff) because the plaintiff's bias has no impact on the level of care.

Interestingly, in the litigation game under asymmetric information studied by Reinganum and Wilde (1986), the informed plaintiff enjoys a first-mover advantage. In fact, the plaintiff extracts the whole surplus generated by the out-of-court agreement. The defendant gets just what he expects to get at trial. The presence of self-serving bias, however, dilutes this advantage. The payoff losses suffered by the plaintiff due to his own bias suggest that this bias is actually "self-defeating" (in economic terms) in a take-it-or-leave-it strategic environment in which the plaintiff is the first mover. On the other hand, the positive effects of the defendant's bias on her expected payoff, on the other hand, indicate that her bias is "self-serving" (in economic terms) in this strategic environment.[38]

3.3   Effects on Social Welfare

Define the social cost of accidents (welfare loss) as the sum of expenses on accident prevention, the unconditional (economic and non-economic) harm to the plaintiff, and the unconditional legal costs in case of trial, and denote it by $L_W(\lambda)$.

$$L_W(\lambda) = K(\lambda^*) + \lambda^* l_W, \qquad (6.1)$$

where $l_w = E \int_x [x + y + (c_P + c_D)p(x)] f(x) dx.$

Proposition 4 summarizes the effects of the plaintiff's and defendant's biases on welfare loss.

PROPOSITION 4: *An increase in the plaintiff's bias reduces social welfare. An increase in the defendant's bias reduces social welfare if $l_D < l_W$.*

Consider the effects of the plaintiff's bias. The bias of the plaintiff has no impact on accident prevention or on the probability of accident, but it increases the probability of trial. As a result, the bias of the plaintiff is welfare reducing. Analyze now the effects of the defendant's bias. Remember that lD represents the litigation loss as perceived by the biased defendant, then it influences the defendant's level of care. If prior to the increase in the defendant's self-serving bias, $lD < lW$, an increase in the defendant's bias unambiguously decreases social welfare. Two factors are at play here. First, if prior to the increase in the defendant's bias, potential injurers exercise too little care (from a social point of view), then the increase in the defendant's bias reduces the level of care even further, affecting negatively social welfare. Second, the higher defendant's bias increases the probability of trial, which increases lW. As a result, the bias of the defendant is welfare reducing if $lD < lW$.[39]

To the best of our knowledge, ours is the first theoretical study of the effects of self-serving bias on social welfare. Our findings regarding the potential negative impact of litigants' biases on social welfare suggest that effective debiasing mechanisms might be welfare improving (Jolls and Sunstein, 2006).[40]

4   A MODEL OF CAPS ON NON-ECONOMIC DAMAGES UNDER SELF-SERVING BIAS

Caps on non-economic damages are widely used by U.S. states (Avraham and Bustos, 2011). This tort reform has been motivated by the common perception that excessive damage awards promote unnecessary litigation (Danzon, 1986) and the escalation of liability insurance premiums (Sloane, 1993). There are many different cap schemes. Some states use a flat dollar cap, a multiplier of compensatory damages, or a combination of both. Some caps pertain to all civil cases, while others are tailored to specific categories of cases, such as medical malpractice or product liability (Babcock and Pogarsky, 1999).[41] As an illustration, consider the medical malpractice tort reform enacted by Texas in 2003. The Texas Alliance for Patient Access (TAPA) provides the following description of this reform.[42]

> *"Chief among the 2003 reforms was the passage of a non-economic damage cap, widely regarded as the lynch pin of the reform package . . . Texas law now establishes a $750,000 stacked cap for non-economic damages in a health care lawsuit. The capped figure changes depending upon the variety of defendants in a suit. Physicians are capped at $250,000 exposure for non-economic damages; hospitals have a $250,000 cap and an additional $250,000 non-economic damage cap applies if a second, unrelated hospital or health care institution is named in the suit. The cap is applied on a per claimant basis with no exceptions and no adjustment for inflation. Past and future medical bills, lost wages, custodial care and prejudgment interest remain uncapped."*

Experimental evidence on the effects of damage caps on pretrial bargaining (Pogarsky and Babcock, 2001; Babcock and Pogarsky, 1999) suggests that this tort reform might influence litigation outcomes not only by directly reducing the expected award at trial but also by indirectly affecting litigants' beliefs about the award at trial. These findings also indicate that the effects of caps on beliefs depend on the relationship between the size of the cap relative to the underlying claim.[43]

We apply our strategic environment with apparent opponents to the study of caps on non-economic damages. Our framework employs a straightforward cap, i.e., a cap that limits the plaintiff's non-economic damages to a specific dollar amount. We denote the maximum value of non-economic damages by $\bar{A}$. We first study the direct effects of caps (that operate through the reduction of the expected award at trial) using an environment that abstracts from self-serving bias. We then incorporate self-serving bias into the framework to analyze the total effects of caps, direct and indirect effects (that operate through the litigants' beliefs). Following empirical regularities, we model the bias on litigants' beliefs about the size of the award at trial as a function of the cap.

4.1 Direct Effects of Caps: An Environment without Self-Serving Bias

Suppose a cap $\bar{A}$ is imposed on the non-economic damages part of the compensatory award $A = (t - 1)x$. Proposition 5 describes the equilibrium of the game under caps on non-economic damages. Define $\tilde{x} = \frac{\bar{A}}{(t - 1)}$ as the plaintiff's type for which the non-economic damages part of the compensatory award is equal to $\bar{A}$. The court award is tx for $x < \tilde{x}$ and $\bar{A} + x$ for $x \geq \tilde{x}$. Define $\underline{S} = \pi t \underline{x} + c_D$ as the lowest value of the settlement demand.

PROPOSITION 5: *The following set A-D characterizes the unique universally-divine fully-separating PBE of the game with caps on non-economic damages.*
(A) The defendant chooses the level of care (probability of accident)
$\lambda^* = \arg\min \{K(\lambda) + \lambda [\int_{\underline{x}}^{\tilde{x}} [\pi t x + c_D] f(x) dx + \int_{\tilde{x}}^{+\infty} [(\pi (\bar{A} + x) + c_D] f(x) dx]\}$.
(B) The defendant chooses the probability of rejection of a settlement demand S, $p(S) = 1 - e^{-(S - \underline{S})/C}$ for $S \geq \underline{S}$, and $p(S) = 0$ for $S < \underline{S}$.
(C) The plaintiff of type $x \in (\underline{x}, \tilde{x})$ chooses the settlement demand $S = \pi t x + c_D$, and the plaintiff of type $x \in (\tilde{x}, +\infty)$ chooses the settlement demand $S = \pi (\bar{A} + x) + c_D$.
(D) The equilibrium beliefs of the defendant upon observing the settlement demand S are $b(S) = (S - c_D)/[\pi t]$ for $S \in (\underline{S}, \pi (\bar{A} + \tilde{x}) + c_D)$ and $b(S) = (S - c_D)/\pi - \bar{A}$ for $S \geq \pi (\bar{A} + \tilde{x}) + c_D)$, and the off-equilibrium beliefs are $b(S) = \underline{x}$ for $S < \underline{S}$.

Two features of the equilibrium are worth mentioning. First, this is a separating equilibrium. Each plaintiff's type makes a different settlement demand. Second, each plaintiff's type demands the amount that the defendant expects to lose in case of trial. Then, the plaintiff gets the surplus generated by an out-of-court settlement.

Proposition 6 summarizes the direct effects of caps on non-economic damages. Define low-type plaintiffs as those plaintiffs for which their type $x \leq \tilde{x}$, and high-type plaintiffs as those plaintiffs for which their type $x > \tilde{x}$, where $\tilde{x}$ represents the plaintiff's type for which the non-economic damages are equal to $\bar{A}$.

PROPOSITION 6: *The direct effects of caps on non-economic damages are as follows.*
(1) Caps reduce the settlement demands made by high-type plaintiffs, do not affect the settlement demands made by low-type plaintiffs, and hence, reduce the expected settlement demand.
(2) Caps reduce the probability of rejection of settlement offers made by high-type plaintiffs, do not affect the probability of rejection of settlement offers made by low-type plaintiffs, and hence, reduce the probability of trial.
(3) Caps reduce the defendant's expected litigation loss, and hence, increase the likelihood of accidents.

These findings suggest that caps on non-economic damages reduce the likelihood of disputes by lowering the average settlement demand. Although the reduction in the likelihood of disputes has a positive direct effect on welfare (i.e., it reduces the expected legal costs), it might negatively affect welfare by inducing lower incentives for care (and hence, higher likelihood of accidents).[44]

4.2 Total Effects of Caps on Non-Economic Damages: An Environment with Self-Serving Bias

Pogarsky and Babcock's (2001) experimental findings indicate that caps affect the perception of the expected award at trial (i.e., the biased variable) in the same direction for both litigants. Note that the plaintiff's self-serving bias implies that he believes that the award is higher than it actually is. The defendant's self-serving bias, on the other hand, implies that she believes that the award is lower than it actually is. Hence, caps should affect the self-serving bias of litigants in opposite directions. Specifically, a non-binding cap (i.e., a high cap relative to the true damage) should increase the perception of the award for both parties. As a result, the bias for the plaintiff will increase and the bias for the defendant will decrease. A binding cap (i.e., a low cap relative to the true damage), on the other hand, should reduce the perception of the award for both litigants. As a result, the bias of the plaintiff will decrease and the bias of the defendant will increase.

Following these empirical regularities, we model the bias on litigants' beliefs about the size of the award at trial as a function of the cap. We denote a post-cap value by the superscript *cap*. Consider first the case of the plaintiff. We will specify the impact of a cap on non-economic damages on the plaintiff's perception of the ratio of the compensatory award to the economic damages for his type, and then specify the impact of a cap on the whole distribution of plaintiff's types. These steps will allow us to specify the beliefs and strategies of the apparent defendant, who is supposed to behave optimally against the distribution of plaintiff's types.

Upon the imposition of a cap, the plaintiff believes that he and the apparent defendant play the game outlined in the previous subsection. Assume that prior to the cap, the plaintiff's perception of the ratio of the compensatory award to the economic losses is biased $(t + h_p)$. Following empirical regularities, we also assume that upon the announcement of the cap, the bias increases if and only if the perceived non-economic damages, $(t + h_p - 1)x$ are smaller than the cap, $\overline{A}$. Finally, we assume that the plaintiff post-cap bias, $h_p^{cap}(x)$ never becomes negative. Then,

$$h_p^{cap}(x) = \max\{h_p + \alpha_p[\overline{A} - (t + h_p - 1)x], 0\}, \qquad (6.2)$$

where $\alpha_p > 0$ is the cap revision coefficient for the plaintiff.

Consider now the case of the defendant. The defendant does not know the plaintiff's type, but he forms beliefs about the post-cap ratio of the compensatory award to the economic losses for the whole distribution of plaintiff's types. Let x_{med} be the median of the distribution of economic damages.[45] Then, the median of the defendant's perceived biased distribution of the non-economic damages A_{med} is

$$A_{med} = x_{med}(t - h_D - 1). \qquad (6.3)$$

We assume that the defendant expects smaller non-economic awards, i.e., the self-serving bias of the defendant increases, if the cap is smaller than the median of the biased distribution of expected non-economic awards $(\overline{A} < A_{med})$. The self-serving bias falls (the defendant expects a higher award) if the cap is larger than the median of the perceived distribution $(\overline{A} > A_{med})$. In addition, we assume that the bias of the defendant never becomes negative. Then,

$$h_D^{cap} = \max\{h_D + \alpha_D[(t - h_D - 1)x_{med} - \overline{A}], 0\}, \qquad (6.4)$$

where $\alpha_D > 0$ is a revision coefficient for the defendant.

Equilibrium under caps and self-serving bias

Proposition 7 describes the unique universally-divine fully-separating equilibrium in the strategic environment with apparent opponents and caps on non-economic damages. This equilibrium characterizes beliefs and strategies for two pairs of players, plaintiff-apparent defendant and defendant-apparent plaintiff. Define $\tilde{x}_P^{cap} = \frac{\bar{A}}{(t + h_P^{cap} - 1)}$ as the plaintiff's type for which the non-economic damages part of the compensatory award is equal to $\bar{A}$ from the post-cap point of view of the biased plaintiff; and, define $\tilde{x}_D^{cap} = \frac{\bar{A}}{(t - h_D^{cap} - 1)}$ as the plaintiff's type for which the non-economic damages part of the compensatory award is equal to $\bar{A}$ from the post-cap point of view of the biased defendant.

PROPOSITION 7:   *The following strategy profile, together with the players' beliefs, characterizes the unique universally-divine fully-separating PBE of the game with apparent opponents and caps on non-economic damages.*

(A1) The apparent defendant chooses the level of care (probability of accidents) $\lambda_a^* = \arg\min\{K(\lambda) + \lambda[\int_{\underline{x}}^{\tilde{x}_P^{cap}} [\pi(t + h_P^{cap})x + c_D]f(x)\,dx + \int_{\tilde{x}_P^{cap}}^{+\infty} [(\pi(\bar{A} + x) + c_D]f(x)\,dx]\}.$

(B1) Define $\underline{S}_P^{cap} + \pi(t + h_P^{cap})\underline{x} + c_D$. The probability of rejection of a settlement demand S by the apparent defendant is $p_a(S) = 1 - e^{-(S - \underline{S}_P^{cap})/C}$ for $S \geq \underline{S}_P^{cap}$; and $p_a(S) = 0$ for $S < \underline{S}_P^{cap}$.

(C1) The settlement demand of the plaintiff of type $x \in (\underline{x}, \tilde{x}_P^{cap})$ is $S = \pi(t + h_P^{cap})x + c_D$; the settlement demand of the plaintiff of type $x \in (\tilde{x}_P^{cap}, +\infty)$ is $S = \pi(\bar{A} + x) + c_D$.

(D1) The beliefs of the apparent defendant upon observing the settlement demand S are $b_a(S) = (S - c_D)/[\pi(t + h_P^{cap})]$ for $S \in (\underline{S}_P, \pi(\bar{A} + \tilde{x}_P^{cap}) + c_D), b_a(S) = (S - c_D)/\pi - \bar{A}$ for $S \geq \pi(\bar{A} + \tilde{x}_P^{cap}) + c_D$ and $b_a(S) = \underline{x}$ for $S < \underline{S}_P^{cap}$.

(A2) The defendant chooses the level of care (probability of accidents) $\lambda^* = \arg\min\{K(\lambda) + \lambda[\int_{\underline{x}}^{\tilde{x}_D^{cap}} [\pi(t - h_D^{cap})x + c_D]f(x)\,dx + \int_{\tilde{x}_D^{cap}}^{+\infty}[(\pi(\bar{A} + x) + c_D]f(x)\,dx]\}.$

(B2) Define $\underline{S}_D^{cap} + \pi(t - h_D^{cap})\underline{x} + c_D$. The probability of rejection of a settlement demand S by defendant $p(S) = 1 - e^{-(S - \underline{S}_D^{cap})/C}$ for $S \geq \underline{S}_D^{cap}$; and $p(S) = 0$ for $S < \underline{S}_D^{cap}$.

(C2) The settlement demand of the apparent plaintiff of type $x \in (\underline{x}, \tilde{x}_D^{cap})$ is $S_a = \pi(t - h_D^{cap})x + c_D$; the settlement demand of the apparent plaintiff of type $x \in (\tilde{x}_D^{cap}, +\infty)$ is $S_a = \pi(\bar{A} + x) + c_D$.

(D2) The beliefs of the defendant upon observing the settlement demand S are $b(S) = (S - c_D)/[\pi(t - h_D^{cap})]$ for $S \in (\underline{S}_D^{cap}, \pi(\bar{A} + \tilde{x}_P^{cap}) + c_D), b(S) = (S - c_D)/\pi - \bar{A}$ for $S \geq \pi(\bar{A} + \tilde{x}_D^{cap}) + c_D$ and $b(S) = \underline{x}$ for $S < \underline{S}_D^{cap}$.

Total effects of caps

Define a relatively low cap from the point of view of the biased defendant as $\overline{A} < (t - h_D - 1)x_{med}$, i.e., a cap that is lower than the median of the distribution of non-economic awards perceived by the defendant. Define a relatively high cap from the point of view of the biased plaintiff as $\overline{A} > x(t + h_P - 1)$, i.e., a cap that is higher than the plaintiff's expected non-economic award at trial. Proposition 8 summarizes the (total) effects of caps on the potential injurer's level of care and the likelihood of disputes.

PROPOSITION 8: *If the defendant perceives the cap as relatively low, the cap on non-economic damages reduces the level of care and increases the likelihood of accidents. If, in addition, the plaintiff perceives the cap as relatively high, a cap on non-economic damages increases the settlement demand, increases the probability of rejection, and increases the unconditional probability of trial.*[46]

Consider the effects of caps on the level of care. If the litigants are biased, and the cap is perceived as relatively low by the defendant, then the defendant's bias will increase as a result of the cap. This reduces the defendant's expected litigation loss, and hence, its incentives for care. Analyze now the effects of caps on the probability of trial. Remember that in case of unbiased litigants, caps reduce the settlement demands and hence, reduce the probability of rejection and the probability of trial. In an environment with biased litigants, this result might not hold. Specifically, caps will increase the bias of the plaintiff if he perceives the cap as relatively high. As a result, his settlement demand will increase. Caps will also increase the bias of the defendant if the defendant perceives caps as relatively low. Hence, two factors will induce a higher probability of rejection: the higher settlement demand (due to the higher plaintiff's bias), and the higher defendant's bias. As a result, the unconditional probability of trial will also increase.

Our findings are consistent with experimental results on the effects of caps on pre-trial bargaining outcomes. Pogarsky and Babcock (2001) find that caps that are high relative to the expected award at trial increase the likelihood of disputes. They argue that these findings might be the result of a cognitive mechanism called motivating anchoring, in which the high-level cap (relative to the damage level) becomes the focal point on the pre-trial bargaining negotiations. Hence, caps might act as a biasing through law mechanism.

Our results regarding the *indirect effects* of caps (that operate through the litigants' beliefs) on the potential injurer's level of care are novel.

Empirical studies have been focused on the total effects of caps on incentives for care. For instance, Zabinski and Black (2011) study the effects of the medical malpractice tort reform enacted in Texas in 2003. One of the main components of this reform involves caps on non-economic damages.[47] They find evidence suggesting an increase in adverse health events (proxy for overall hospital quality or level of care) associated with this tort reform. Currie and MacLeod (2008) theoretically and empirically study the effects of tort reform on the types of procedures performed, and the health outcomes of mothers and infants, in childbirth cases in the U.S.[48] They find that caps on non-economic damages increase complications of labor and delivery.[49] Although these empirical studies *do not directly* assess litigants' cognitive biases, a possible explanation for the direction of the total effects of caps on incentives for care might be the presence of self-serving bias.

Our results regarding the welfare-reducing effects of damage caps under plausible scenarios suggest that this tort reform should be adopted with caution. Our work underscores the importance of studying incentives for care, litigation, and the effects of tort reform in settings that allow for asymmetry of information and litigant's self-serving beliefs.

5   SUMMARY AND CONCLUSIONS

Behavioral economics studies on self-serving bias in legal and labor environments provide robust evidence of the impact of this cognitive bias on impasse. However, this additional source of disputes has not been previously addressed in the theoretical law and economics literature on liability and litigation. Our work contributes to this literature by presenting a strategic model of incentives for care and litigation and by studying damage caps, in environments that allow for asymmetric information (and common priors) regarding the plaintiff's economic losses, and self-serving bias (divergent and biased beliefs) regarding the non-economic damages awarded at trial. Our theoretical framework involves empirically-relevant assumptions regarding the elicitation of self-serving bias, and the relationship between self-serving bias and caps on non-economic damages. Importantly, we contribute to the theoretical law and economics literature by providing the first assessment of the effects of self-serving bias on incentives for care and social welfare, and the first evaluation of the effects of damage caps on incentives for care in environments that allow for biased litigants. We also contribute to the behavioral economics literature by generalizing the perfect Bayesian equilibrium concept to strategic environments with biased players.

This work provides policy-relevant findings. First, our results suggest that social welfare might be negatively affected by self-serving bias under certain conditions. The negative impact of this cognitive bias on social welfare is explained by the reduction of the level of care and the increase of the likelihood of disputes. Interestingly, our results indicate that, although self-serving bias helps litigants commit to tough negotiation positions, it is economically self-serving only for the defendant. Second, our findings indicate that damage caps might reduce the defendant's level of care. Importantly, our results suggest that the positive effects of caps on reducing the likelihood of disputes, commonly associated with this tort reform, do not necessarily hold in environments with biased litigants. In fact, we show that the presence of self-serving bias might reverse the positive effect of caps on impasse. Hence, policy-makers should adopt this tort reform with caution. Our findings are aligned with empirical and experimental evidence on pretrial bargaining and caps on non-economic damages.

Our work is motivated on pretrial bargaining and legal disputes. However, the strategic environments discussed in this chapter, and our technical contributions, might be applicable to other settings. For instance, our findings regarding the effects of self-serving bias on disputes, and our technical contributions, might apply to collective bargaining negotiations, and to the assessment of the effects of collective bargaining laws on strikes (Currie and McConnell, 1991). Similarly, this research might benefit studies regarding partnership dissolution processes, and the efficiency effects of partnership dissolution mechanisms (Brooks et al., 2010). Extensions to our work might also involve the assessment of legal institutions that affect settlement and litigation, using environments that allow for self-serving litigants. For example, theoretical and experimental studies on lawyers' compensation schemes and agency problems (Miller, 1987; Dana and Spier, 1993), fee-shifting (Spier, 1994a), and the design of damage awards (Spier, 1994b) might be fruitful topics for research. Finally, future theoretical work might address asymmetries in the litigant's perception of her own bias and the bias of the other party, and the effects of these asymmetries on the likelihood of disputes.[50] These and other extensions remain fruitful areas for future research.

APPENDIX

This appendix presents the lemma, and the proofs to the lemma, propositions, and corollary.

LEMMA: *For any positive value of lD, the function $L(\lambda)$ has a unique interior minimum, λ^{*} (0, 1). λ^{*} is decreasing in lD.*

PROOF:

$$L'_D(\lambda) = K'(\lambda) + l_D$$

By assumptions about the function $K(\lambda)$, the derivative of the total loss is monotonically increasing in λ, it is negative for sufficiently small values of λ, and it is positive for sufficiently large values of λ. Hence there exists a unique critical point, λ^*, such that $L'_D(\lambda^*) = 0$, and λ^* is the minimum point of $L_D(\lambda)$.

Totally differentiating the first-order condition $K'(\lambda^*) + l_D = 0$,

$$K''(\lambda^*)d\lambda^* + dl_D = 0.$$

Hence,

$$\frac{\partial\lambda^*}{\partial l_D} = -\frac{1}{K''(\lambda^*)} < 0.$$

An increase in l_D reduces the optimal probability of accident, λ^*, which implies an increase in the level of care, $K(\lambda^*)$. These results also hold for the apparent defendant. Q.E.D.

PROOF OF PROPOSITION 1:   The following steps show that the strategies described above form a perfect-Bayesian equilibrium and satisfy the universal divinity refinement. The equilibrium is unique in terms of equilibrium outcome. Without loss of generality we solve the game for the pair plaintiff–apparent defendant. For the pair defendant–apparent plaintiff we can solve the game in exactly the same way. We find the equilibrium by backward induction, i.e., we first show that the equilibrium of the litigation game is unique, characterize it, and then compute the unique equilibrium level of care of the apparent defendant.

We allow for mixed strategy equilibria of the litigation game. If any type x is mixing, arguments that follow apply to any pure strategy offer S in the support of the mixed strategy of type x.

Part (1)
Here we show that the litigation game equilibrium has to be monotone. Let $AS(X)$ be the set of offers made in equilibrium and accepted with positive probability (which can be smaller than one). Suppose types x_1 and x_2, $x_1 < x_2$, make offers S_1 and S_2, both $S_1, S_2 \in AS(X)$. We will show that $S_1 < S_2$ and $p_1 \equiv p^a(S_1) < p_2 \equiv p^a(S_2)$. Indeed, an incentive compatibility condition for x_2 means

$$(\pi(t + h_P)x_2 - c_P)p_1 + S_1(1 - p_1) \le (\pi(t + h_P)x_2 - c_P)p_2 + S_2(1 - p_2).$$

$$(6A.1)$$

Thus,

$$S_1(1 - p_1) - S_2(1 - p_2) \le (\pi(t + h_p)x_2 - c_p)(p_2 - p_1).$$

Similarly, using the incentive compatibility condition for type x_1,

$$S_1(1 - p_1) - S_2(1 - p_2) \ge (\pi(t + h_p)x_1 - c_p)(p_2 - p_1).$$

The last two inequalities imply that

$$(\pi(t + h_p)x_2 - c_p)(p_2 - p_1) \ge (\pi(t + h_p)x_1 - c_p)(p_2 - p_1).$$

Hence the last inequality requires that $p_2 \ge p_1$ (given that $x_1 < x_2$). Therefore, it must be the case that $S_2 > S_1$ (otherwise x_2 will prefer to demand S_1 rather than S_2). So, $p_2 > p_1$ (otherwise x_1 will demand S_2 rather than S_1).

Part (2)
Next, we show that all types of plaintiff make settlement demands that are accepted with positive probabilities in equilibrium.

Suppose that there exists x such that $S(x) \notin AS(X)$, that is, x makes an offer that is never accepted in equilibrium. This means that $AS(X) \le \pi(t + h_p)x - c_p$ (each element of the set is smaller), as otherwise x would prefer to make an offer that is accepted with positive probability.

Let S^* be the maximum of the set $AS(X)$ and x^* solve $S^* = \pi(t + h_p)x^* - c_p$.[51] Clearly, the equilibrium payoff of player x^* is $\pi(t + h_p)x^* - c_p$, while for any $x < x^*$ the equilibrium payoff of x is at least $(\pi(t + h_p)x - c_p)p^* + S^*(1 - p^*)$, where $p^* = p^a(S^*)$.

Next, consider any offer $S_1 > S^*$. As S^* is the maximal of $AS(X)$, offer S_1 is rejected. We want to show that, using the universal divinity refinement, we can eliminate any $x < x^*$ from the support of the apparent defendant's beliefs given S_1. To do so, we actually use the *Never a Weak Best Response (NWBR) for signaling games* condition (Fudenberg and Tirole, 1991). According to this condition, if: (i) type x is just indifferent between his equilibrium payoff and offering S_1 expecting it being rejected with probability q_1; and (ii) there exist a type x' that strictly prefers offering S_1 with rejection probability q_1 to her equilibrium payoff, then the plaintiff should not believe that offer S_1 comes from x. Any type x that is eliminated under the NWBR condition will be eliminated under the universal divinity criterion.[52]

Consider any $x < x^*$, let q_1 and q_2 solve, respectively,

$$u^*(x) = (\pi(t + h_p)x - c_p)q_1 + (1 - q_1)S_1,$$

where $u^*(x)$ is the equilibrium payoff to type x, and

$$(\pi(t + h_p)x - c_p)p^* + (1 - p^*)S^* = (\pi(t + h_p)x - c_p)q_2 + (1 - q_2)S_1. \tag{6A.2}$$

Thus, q_1 is the probability of rejection of offer S_1 at which type x is indifferent between making S_1 and following her equilibrium action. Similarly, q_2 is the probability at which x is indifferent between S^* and S_1. As $S_1 > S^*$, $p^* < q_2$. Also, as $u^*(x) \geq (\pi(t + h_p)x - c_p)p^* + (1 - p^*)S^*$ [the equilibrium payoff of x is at least as high as when offering S^*], we have $q_1 \leq q_2$. Consider now type x^*. As $p^* < q_2$, the right hand side of equation (A2) becomes larger if x is substituted for x^*. Thus, type x^* strictly prefers S_1 with probability of rejection q_2 to her equilibrium payoff from offer S^*. Since $q_1 \leq q_2$, S_1 with probability of rejection q_1 is also strictly preferred to S^* by x^*. Therefore, conditions (i) and (ii) of NWBR hold for types x and $x' = x^*$. Any type $x < x^*$ is eliminated from the support of beliefs $b^a(S_1)$ for all $S_1 > S^*$, and so $Eb^a(S_1) \geq x^*$.

Consider $S_1 = S^* + \varepsilon$ for a sufficiently small $\varepsilon > 0$, the expected loss to the apparent defendant from rejecting settlement S_1 is $\pi(t + h_p)b^a(S_1) + c_D \geq \pi(t + h_p)x^* + c_D = S^* + c_p + c_D > S^* + \varepsilon$. Thus, it is optimal for the apparent defendant to accept this settlement with probability 1. This means that all the types of the plaintiff $x \leq x^*$ strictly prefer making S_1 to their equilibrium offers – a contradiction.

Part (3)
We have established that all the types of the plaintiff make offers that are accepted with positive probability in equilibrium. It remains to be shown that no pooling of any kind is possible in equilibrium. If there are two types of the plaintiff $x_1 < x_2$ that make the same offer S, then any type $x \in (x_1, x_2)$ makes the same offer. Indeed, if $S(x) > S$, then monotonicity is violated for the pair (x, x_2). Similarly, if $S(x) < S$, then monotonicity is violated for the pair (x_1, x). Let x_1^S and x_2^S be the smallest and the largest types that make S.[53] Then, $\text{Supp } b^a(S) = [x_1^S, x_2^S]$. Since the apparent defendant accepts S with positive probability,

$$S = \pi(t + h_p)Eb^a(S) + c_D < \pi(t + h_p)x_2^S + c_D. \tag{6A.3}$$

In equilibrium, the apparent defendant's beliefs given any offer $S' > S$ satisfy $x \geq x_2^S$. Indeed, this is due to monotonicity (Part (1)), if S' is made and so accepted with positive probability in equilibrium, or to

NWBR (Part (2)), if S' is never made in equilibrium. In either case, the expected payoff to the apparent defendant from rejecting S' is at least $\pi(t + h_p)x_2^S + c_D$. On the other hand, if S' is close enough to S, then inequality (A3) holds for S' as well. Therefore, offer S' has to be accepted with probability 1, which means that all types $x < x_2^S$ want to deviate to S' – a contradiction.

Part (4)

We have shown that all types of the plaintiff make separating settlement demands, and all these demands are accepted with positive probabilities. Furthermore, by monotonicity, the acceptance probability is strictly decreasing with the offer, and so for almost all x and their $S(x)$ the apparent defendant is indifferent between accepting and rejecting the settlement demand. Hence, for $x > \underline{x}_P$,

$$S(x) = \pi(t + h_p)x + c_D.$$

In equilibrium, the plaintiff of type x obtains payoff $u*(x) = p^a(S(x))(\pi(t + h_p)x - c_P) + (1 - p^a(S(x)))S(x)$. Obviously, the equilibrium payoff function is continuous in x. Therefore, as $S(x)$ is continuous and $S(x) > \pi(t + h_p)x - c_P$, the probability of rejection $p^a(S)$ is also continuous at $S \in [\underline{S}_P, +\infty)$, where $\underline{S}_P = \pi(t + h_p)x + c_D$. Consider the incentive compatibility constraint (A1) of type x_2 pretending to be x_1. As $[S_1(1 - p_1) - S_2(1 - p_2)] = S_2(p_2 - p_1) + (S_1 - S_2)(1 - p_1)$ and $S_2 - \pi(t + h_p)x_2 + c_P = c_D + c_P = C$, after combining the terms we obtain

$$(p_2 - p_1)C \le (S_2 - S_1)(1 - p_1).$$

Analogously, by considering the incentive constraint of type x_1 pretending to be type x_2, we obtain

$$(S_2 - S_1)(1 - p_1) \le (p_2 - p_1)C.$$

By combining these two inequalities and by taking limit of x_2 to x_1 we obtain that $p^a(S)$ is differentiable at all $x > \underline{x}_P$ and its derivative satisfies the following first-order differential equation

$$p^{a'}(S)C = 1 - p^a(S).$$

The solution to this equation is:

$$p^a(S) = 1 - \mu e^{-S/C},$$

where μ is a parameter to be determined using the initial condition.

Note that for the apparent defendant it is strictly optimal to accept any offer $S < \underline{S}_p$ no matter what his beliefs $b^a(S)$ are. Therefore, in equilibrium, $p(\underline{S}_p) = 0$. Otherwise, if $p(\underline{S}_p) > 0$, the lowest plaintiff type, $\underline{x}_p$, has an incentive to deviate and demand $\pi(t + h_p)\underline{x}_p + c_D - \varepsilon$, for any sufficiently small $\varepsilon > 0$, which will be accepted with certainty. Substituting the initial condition $p(\underline{S}_p) = 0$ into the equilibrium expression for $p^a(S)$ yields

$$\mu = -e^{\underline{S}_p/T}.$$

Therefore,

$$p^a(S) = 1 - e^{-(S-\underline{S}_p)/T}.$$

For off-equilibrium offers $S < \underline{S}_p$, we cannot further refine beliefs $b^a(S)$ using the universal divinity refinement, as all the plaintiff types are strictly worse making S under any beliefs than in equilibrium.

This completes the characterization of the separating universally divine PBE for the litigation game. It is unique in terms of equilibrium outcome.

Part (5)

Now, given the equilibrium of the litigation game, we compute optimal λ^a.

The expected loss of the apparent defendant in case of an accident is

$$\int_{\underline{x}_p}^{+\infty} (\pi(t + h_p)x + c_D)f(x)dx$$

By the Lemma, the loss-minimization problem of the apparent defendant has a unique solution, which is

$$\arg\min\left\{ K(\lambda) + \lambda \int_{\underline{x}_p}^{+\infty} (\pi(t + h_p)x + c_D)f(x)dx \right\}.$$

Q.E.D.

PROOF OF PROPOSITION 2:

Part (1)

$$\frac{\partial S(x)}{\partial h_p} = \pi x > 0.$$

Aggregating across types:

$$\frac{\partial ES}{\partial h_P} = \frac{\partial \int_{\underline{x}}^{+\infty} [\pi(t + h_P)x + c_D]f(x)\,dx}{\partial h_P} = \pi Ex > 0.$$

Q.E.D.

Part (2)

$$\frac{\partial p(S)}{\partial h_P} = \frac{\partial p}{\partial S}\frac{\partial S}{\partial h_P} = -e^{-(S-\underline{S}_D)/C}\left(-\frac{1}{C}\right)\pi x > 0;$$

$$\frac{\partial p(S)}{\partial h_D} = \frac{\partial p}{\partial \underline{S}_D}\frac{\partial \underline{S}_D}{\partial h_D} = -e^{-(S-\underline{S}_D)/C}\left(\frac{1}{C}\right)(-\pi\underline{x}) > 0.$$

$$\frac{\partial Ep(S(x))}{\partial h_P} = \frac{\partial\left[\int_{\underline{x}}^{+\infty} (1 - e^{-[(\pi(t+h_P)x+c_D)-(\pi(t-h_D)\underline{x}+c_D)]/C})f(x)\,dx\right]}{\partial h_P} =$$

$$= \int_{\underline{x}}^{+\infty} \frac{\partial}{\partial h_P}[1 - e^{-[(\pi(t+h_P)x+c_D)-(\pi(t-h_D)\underline{x}+c_D)]/C}]f(x)\,dx$$

$$= \int_{\underline{x}}^{+\infty}\left[-e^{-[(\pi(t+h_P)x+c_D)-(\pi(t-h_D)\underline{x}+c_D)]/C}\left(-\frac{\pi x}{C}\right)\right]f(x)\,dx > 0.$$

$$\frac{\partial Ep(S(x))}{\partial h_D} = \frac{\partial\left[\int_{\underline{x}}^{+\infty} (1 - e^{-[(\pi(t+h_P)x+c_D)-(\pi(t-h_D)\underline{x}+c_D)]/C})f(x)\,dx\right]}{\partial h_D} =$$

$$= \int_{\underline{x}}^{+\infty} \frac{\partial}{\partial h_D}[1 - e^{-[(\pi(t+h_P)x+c_D)-(\pi(t-h_D)\underline{x}+c_D)]/C}]f(x)\,dx$$

$$= \int_{\underline{x}}^{+\infty}\left[-e^{-[(\pi(t+h_P)x+c_D)-(\pi(t-h_D)\underline{x}+c_D)]/C}\left(-\frac{\pi\underline{x}}{C}\right)\right]f(x)\,dx > 0.$$

Q.E.D.

Part (3)
The biased defendant expects that his conditional (on accident) litigation loss will be

$$\int_{\underline{x}}^{+\infty} (\pi(t - h_D)x + c_D)f(x)dx,$$

which is inversely related to h_D. Hence, by the Lemma, an increase in the self-serving bias of the defendant will reduce the expenditures on care and increase the probability of accident. Q.E.D.

PROOF OF COROLLARY:

Part (1)
The unconditional probability of trial is the product of the probability of accident, which is increasing in the bias of the defendant (Proposition 2, part 3) and the conditional probability of trial, which is increasing in biases of both defendants (Proposition 2, part 2). Hence, the unconditional probability of trial is increasing in the biases of both defendants. Q.E.D.

Part (2)
Conditional on accident occurrence, the expected litigation costs equal

$$C\int_{\underline{x}}^{+\infty} p(S(x))f(x)dx.$$

By Proposition 2, $p(S(x))$ depends positively on h_P and h_D for all x. Hence the integral expression is rising in both litigants' biases.

In the whole game, the (unconditional) expected litigation costs equal

$$\lambda C\int_{\underline{x}}^{+\infty} p(S(x))f(x)dx.$$

An increase in the bias of the defendant reduces the level of care and increases the probability of accident (Proposition 2, part 3), λ. Hence the expected litigation costs increase. The bias of the plaintiff has no impact on the level of care. Therefore, the product of λ and the conditional litigation costs increase. Q.E.D.

PROOF OF PROPOSITION 3:

Part (1)
The expected payoff for the plaintiff of type x is

$$V_P = (1 - p(x))[\pi(t + h_P)x + c_D] + p(x)(\pi tx - c_P).$$

The expected payoff for the defendant when he meets the plaintiff of type x is

$$-(1 - p(x))[\pi(t + h_p)x + c_D] - p(x)(\pi tx + c_D).$$

Aggregating across plaintiff types, we get the expected payoff of the plaintiff:

$$V_D = -\int_{\underline{x}}^{+\infty} \{(1 - p(x))[\pi(t + h_p)x + c_D] - p(x)(\pi tx + c_D)\}f(x)dx$$

The only variable that depends on h_D is $p(x)$.

$$\frac{\partial p(x)}{\partial h_D} = -e^{-[S-(\pi(t-h_D)\underline{x}+c_D)]/C}\left[-\frac{\pi \underline{x}}{C}\right] > 0.$$

Therefore,

$$\frac{\partial V_P}{\partial h_D} = -(h_p x + C)\frac{\partial p(x)}{\partial h_D} < 0,$$

and

$$\frac{\partial V_D}{\partial h_D} = \int_{x=\underline{x}}^{+\infty} h_p x \frac{\partial p(x)}{\partial h_D} f(x)dx > 0.$$

Q.E.D.

Part (2)
First, consider the impact of the plaintiff's bias on the plaintiff's conditional expected payoff. Denote $\zeta \equiv 1 - p(S(x)) = e^{-[\pi(t+h_p)x - \pi(t-h_p)\underline{x}]/C}$.

$$\frac{\partial \zeta}{\partial h_p} = \zeta\left(-\frac{\pi x}{C}\right).$$

Hence, the conditional expected payoff of the plaintiff of type x is

$$V_P = (1 - \zeta)(\pi tx - c_P) + \zeta[\pi(t + h_p)x + c_D]$$

$$\frac{\partial V_P}{\partial h_p} = \frac{\partial \zeta}{\partial h_p}[C + \pi h_p x] + \zeta \pi x = \zeta\left[-\frac{\pi x}{C}(C + \pi h_p x) + \pi x\right]$$

$$= \zeta\left[-\frac{\pi^2 x^2 h_p}{C}\right] < 0.$$

Now consider the impact of the bias on the expected payoff of the defendant who faces the plaintiff of type x. Plaintiff's bias has no impact on the level of care and the probability of accident. Hence it affects the payoff of the defendant through the conditional (on accident) payoff only. The defendant's conditional expected payoff is

$$V_D = -\int_{\underline{x}}^{+\infty} \{(1 - \zeta)(\pi tx + c_D) + \zeta[\pi(t + h_P)x + c_D]\} f(x) dx.$$

Differentiating with respect to h_P yields

$$\frac{\partial V_D}{\partial h_P} = -\int_{\underline{x}}^{+\infty} \left[\pi h_P x \frac{\partial \zeta}{\partial h_P} + \pi x \zeta\right] f(x) dx =$$

$$= -\int_{\underline{x}}^{+\infty} \pi x \zeta \left[1 - \frac{\pi x h_P}{C}\right] f(x) dx.$$

The derivative is greater/smaller than zero (the defendant is benefitted/hurt by an increase in h_P) if

$$h_P \int_{\underline{x}}^{+\infty} \zeta x^2 f(x) dx > \frac{C}{\pi} \int_{\underline{x}}^{+\infty} \zeta x f(x) dx.$$

The bias of the plaintiff has no impact on the decision to take care and the probability of accidents. Therefore unconditional expected payoffs of both litigants move in the same direction as the expected payoffs. Q.E.D.

PROOF OF PROPOSITION 4:
Define social welfare loss as

$$L_W(\lambda) = K(\lambda^*) + \lambda^* l_W,$$

where l_W is

$$l_W = E \int_{\underline{x}} [x + y + (c_P + c_D) p(x)] f(x) dx$$

$$= \int_{\underline{y}}^{+\infty} \left[\int_{\underline{x}} [x + y + (c_P + c_D) p(x)] f(x) dx\right] g(y) d(y) =$$

$$= \int_{\underline{x}} \left[x + \int_{\underline{y}}^{+\infty} y g(y) d(y) + (c_P + c_D) p(x)\right] f(x) dx$$

$$= \int_x [x + E(y) + (c_P + c_D)p(x)]f(x)dx =$$

$$\int_x [x + \mu + (c_P + c_D)p(x)]f(x)dx,$$

and $g(y)$ is the pdf function for y. Here, we used independence between x and y.

Let's prove the first part of the proposition. An increase on the plaintiff's bias affects social welfare through the probability of trial only. This probability increases for each level of damage x. Hence, social welfare loss increases when the plaintiff is more biased. Proceed now to prove the second part of the proposition. Note that λ^* denotes the choice of the defendant. Then, the effect of the defendant's bias on social welfare is

$$\frac{dL_W(\lambda)}{dh_D} = \frac{\partial L_W(\lambda)}{\partial \lambda^*}\frac{\partial \lambda^*}{\partial h_D} + \frac{\partial L_W(\lambda)}{\partial h_D}.$$

Compute the effects on each component. First, consider the direct effect via the probability of the trial.

$$\frac{\partial L_W(\lambda)}{\partial h_D} = \lambda^* \int_x \left[(c_P + c_D)\frac{\partial p(x)}{\partial h_D} \right] f(x)dx.$$

Given the defendant's bias h_D, if she receives an offer of $S = \pi(t - h_D)x + c_D$, she infers $x_D = \frac{S - c_D}{\pi(t - h_D)}$ and rejects it with probability

$$p(x_D) = 1 - e^{-\frac{\pi(t - h_D)(x_D - x)}{c_P + c_D}}.$$

Note that the plaintiff makes an offer $S = \pi(t + h_P)x + c_D$, thus $x_D = \frac{t + h_P}{t - h_D}x$.
Hence, the probability of trial (expressed in terms of the actual x) is

$$p(x) = 1 - e^{-\frac{\pi(t - h_D)}{c_P + c_D}\left(\frac{t + h_P}{t - h_D}x - x\right)}$$

We can express

$$(t - h_D)\left(\frac{t + h_P}{t - h_D}x - x\right) = t\left(\frac{t + h_P}{t}x - \frac{t - h_D}{t}x\right) = t\left(\frac{t + h_P}{t}x - x\right) + h_D x.$$

Therefore the probability of trial is

$$p(x) = 1 - e^{-\frac{\pi(t-h_D)}{c_P+c_D}\left(\frac{t+h_P}{t}x-x\right)}\Psi,$$

where $\Psi(h_D) = e^{-\frac{\pi h_{D_x}}{c^P+c^D}}$.

We have

$$\frac{\partial p(x)}{\partial h_D} = e^{-\frac{\pi(t-h_D)}{c_P+c_D}\left(\frac{t+h_P}{t}x-x\right)}\Psi(h_D)\frac{\pi x}{c_P+c_D}.$$

In turn, the partial derivative expression becomes

$$\frac{\partial L_W(\lambda)}{\partial h_D} = \lambda^*\Psi(h_D)\pi\underline{x}\int_x\left(e^{-\frac{\pi(t-h_D)}{c_P+c_D}\left(\frac{t+h_P}{t}x-\underline{x}\right)}\right)f(x)\,dx = \lambda^*\pi\underline{x}\Psi(h_D)g(h_P).$$

The terms under the integral in $g(h_P)$ resemble the probability of acceptance of a settlement offer. Overall the integral is between 0 and 1 and goes to 0 if h_P goes to ∞. Note that the effect of the defendant's bias h_D operates only through Ψ: the higher the bias, the lower the overall effect. The computation of the indirect effect is simpler. Consider the defendant's loss,

$$L = K(\lambda) + \lambda l_D,$$

where

$$l_D = \int_x [\pi(t - h_D)x + c_D]f(x)\,dx.$$

The FOC implies

$$\frac{\partial K}{\partial \lambda} = -l_D.$$

By implicit function differentiation,

$$\frac{d\lambda^*}{dh_D} = -\frac{\partial l_D}{\partial h_D}\bigg/\frac{\partial^2 K}{\partial \lambda^2} = \pi E(x)\bigg/\frac{\partial^2 K}{\partial \lambda^2} > 0.$$

We can express the indirect effect as

$$\frac{\partial L_W(\lambda)}{\partial \lambda^*}\frac{\partial \lambda^*}{\partial h_D} = (l_W - l_D)\pi E(x)/K''(\lambda^*).$$

Hence, the total effect (direct and indirect effects) of the defendant's bias on social welfare loss is

$$\frac{dL_W(\lambda)}{dh_D} = (l_W - l_D)\pi E(x)/K''(\lambda^*) + \lambda^*\pi\underline{x}\Psi(h_D)g(h_P).$$

If $l_W > l_D$, both terms are positive. Hence, an increase in defendant's bias unambiguously reduces social welfare.[54] Q.E.D.

PROOF OF PROPOSITION 5:

Analyze the game by backward induction. Consider first the litigation game. It starts when the plaintiff files a lawsuit. For $x < \tilde{x}$, it is easy (following the steps of the proof of Proposition 1) to show that this game has a separating equilibrium in which the plaintiff of type x makes a demand $S = \pi t x + c_D$.[55] Upon observing demand S, the defendant forms beliefs $b(S) = (S - c_D)/[\pi t]$ and rejects this proposal with probability $p(S) = 1 - e^{\{-\frac{(S-\underline{S})}{c}\}}$ if $S \geq \underline{S}$ and always accepts the proposal $S < \underline{S}$.

Now consider $x \geq \tilde{x}$. If the suit proceeds to trial, the defendant expects to lose $\pi(\bar{A} + x) + c_D$. It is straightforward to show that the structure of the solution will be very similar to the first case. The plaintiff of type x makes a settlement demand which is equal to the amount the defendant would lose in trial, i.e. $\pi(\bar{A} + x) + c_D$. The defendant correctly deduces the type of the plaintiff, and hence is indifferent between accepting and rejecting the demand. That is, $b(S) = (S - c_D)/\pi - A$ for $S \geq \pi(\bar{A} + \tilde{x}) + c_D$. It is also easy to show that the probability of rejection, $p(S) = 1 - \phi e^{-\frac{S}{c}}$, where ϕ, is a coefficient to be determined using a boundary condition.

Next we show by contradiction that $p(S)$ must be a continuous function at $x = \tilde{x}$. Suppose not and assume that there exist two types, x_1 and $x_1 + \varepsilon$ infinitely close to x_1 such that probability of rejection of $x_1 + \varepsilon$ is greater than the probability of rejection of x_1 by some positive amount $\Lambda > 0$. Then the type $x_1 + \varepsilon$ will benefit from deviating and pretending to be the type x_1. Using the same procedure, one can show the impossibility of the case when the probability of rejection of x_1 is greater than the probability of rejection of $x_1 + \varepsilon$ by a positive amount. Equating $1 - \phi e^{-\frac{S}{c}} = 1 - e^{-\frac{(S-\underline{S})}{c}}$ reveals that. Hence, $p(S) = 1 - e^{-\frac{(S-\underline{S})}{c}}$ is the rejection probability in equilibrium, for all $S \geq \underline{S}$. Thus we verified that conditions (B) – (D) are satisfied in the litigation game.

Proceed now to evaluate the defendant's optimal level of care. The equilibrium settlement offers, the probability of acceptance of each offer and the expected loss at trial allow us to compute the expected litigation loss of the defendant (conditional on accident), $[\int_{\underline{x}}^{\tilde{x}} [\pi t x + c_D] f(x) dx + \int_{\tilde{x}}^{+\infty} [(\pi(A + x) + c_D] f(x) dx]$. Therefore, condition (a) describes the optimal level of care. The solution exists because the function is continuous and the interval [0,1] is compact. Hence, this equilibrium exists. The proof of uniqueness follows the steps described in the proof of Proposition 1. Q.E.D.

PROOF OF PROPOSITION 6:

Part (1)
Consider first the effects on the settlement demand. The result holds trivially because for $x > \tilde{x}, \bar{A} + x < tx$, and therefore, the settlement demand of plaintiffs with $x > \tilde{x}$, $\pi(A + x) + c_D$ becomes smaller than $\pi tx + c_D$, their demand before the cap was imposed. Proposition 5 establishes that for $x \leq \tilde{x}$ the settlement demand is the same with or without cap. Consider now the effects on the expected settlement demand. The result holds trivially if one aggregates across plaintiff's types

$$\int_{\underline{x}}^{+\infty} (\pi tx + c_D) f(x) dx > \int_{\underline{x}}^{\tilde{x}} (\pi tx + c_D) f(x) dx + \int_{\underline{x}}^{+\infty} (\pi(\bar{A} + x) + c_D) f(x) dx.$$

Q.E.D.

Part (2)

$$\pi(A + x) + c_D < \pi tx + c_D \text{ for } x > \tilde{x} = \frac{\bar{A}}{t-1} \text{ implies that}$$

$$\int_{\tilde{x}}^{+\infty} (1 - \exp(-[\pi(A + x) + c_D - \underline{S}]/C)) f(x) dx$$

$$< \int_{\tilde{x}}^{+\infty} (1 - \exp(-[\pi tx + c_D - \underline{S}]/C)) f(x) dx.$$

Therefore,

$$\int_{\underline{x}}^{\tilde{x}} (1 - \exp(-[\pi tx + c_D - \underline{S}]/C)) f(x) dx +$$

$$\int_{\underline{x}}^{+\infty} (1 - \exp(-[\pi(A + x) + c_D - \underline{S}]/C)) f(x) dx$$

$$< \int_{\underline{x}}^{+\infty} (1 - \exp(-[\pi tx + c_D - \underline{S}]/C)) f(x) dx.$$

which means that the probability of trial conditional on accident occurence is lower under caps (the left-hand side) than before caps (the right-hand side). Q.E.D.

Part (3)
Consider first the effects on the expected litigation loss.

$$\int_{\underline{x}}^{+\infty} (\pi t x + c_D) f(x) dx > \int_{\underline{x}}^{\tilde{x}} (\pi t x + c_D) f(x) dx$$

$$+ \int_{\tilde{x}}^{+\infty} (\pi (A + x) + c_D) f(x) dx.$$

The left-hand side is the expected litigation loss before the cap. The right-hand side is the expected litigation loss under the cap. This inequality holds because $A + x < tx$ for $x > \tilde{x}$. Thus, caps reduce the expected litigation loss, and hence, reduce the expenditures on accident prevention and raise the probability of accidents. The last result follows directly from the Lemma and the effects of caps on the expected litigation loss. Q.E.D.

PROOF OF PROPOSITION 7:
The unawareness of the litigants about their own bias and the bias of their opponent generates environments under caps and biased litigants (for the two pairs of litigants, plaintiff-apparent defendant and defendant-apparent plaintiff) that are similar to the environment with caps and unbiased litigants. Then, Proposition 7 essentially reproduces Proposition 5 taking into account the biased litigants' beliefs. Q.E.D.

PROOF OF PROPOSITION 8:
By equation (3), the condition $\bar{A} < (t - h_D - 1) x_{med}$ implies that the self-serving bias of the defendant rises, i.e., $h_D^{cap} > h_D$. Hence, the expected litigation loss of the defendant falls because

$$\int_{\tilde{x}}^{+\infty} [\pi (t - h_D) x + c_D] f(x) dx =$$

$$= \int_{\tilde{x}}^{\tilde{x}_D^{cap}} [\pi (t - h_D) x + c_D] f(x) dx + \int_{\tilde{x}_D^{cap}}^{+\infty} [\pi (t - h_D) x + c_D] f(x) dx >$$

$$> \int_{\tilde{x}}^{\tilde{x}_D^{cap}} [\pi (t - h_D^{cap}) x + c_D] f(x) dx + \int_{\tilde{x}_D^{cap}}^{+\infty} [\pi (\bar{A} + x) + c_D] f(x) dx.$$

The last inequality holds because $h_D^{cap} > h_D$, and because for $x > \tilde{x}_D^{cap} > \tilde{x}_D$, $\bar{A} + x > (t - h_D) x$. Hence, by the Lemma, a lower expected litigation loss implies a lower spending on care and a higher probability of accident.

In case of low type plaintiffs ($x < \tilde{x}_P$), by equation (2), the plaintiff's bias increases, i.e., $h_P^{cap} > h_P$. Therefore, his settlement demand $S = \pi (t + h_P^{cap}) x + c_D$ also increases. Hence, the probability of rejection

$1 - \exp(-[S - \underline{S}_D^{cap}]/C)$ increases for two reasons. First, S is larger under caps. Second, $\underline{S}_D^{cap} < \underline{S}_D$, i.e.,

$$\pi(t - h_D^{cap})\underline{x} + c_D = \underline{S}_D^{cap} < \underline{S}_D = \pi(t - h_D)\underline{x} + c_D.$$

As a result, the expected probability of trial also increases. Q.E.D.

NOTES

1. The direct costs of tort litigation in the U.S. reached $247 billion in 2006 (Towers Perrin Tillinghast, 2007). Tort costs in the U.S. (as a percentage of the gross domestic product) are double the cost in Germany and more than three times the cost in France or the United Kingdom (Towers Perrin Tillinghast, 2005).
2. Babcock, Loewenstein, and colleagues' work builds on seminal research in social psychology regarding self-serving bias (Messick and Sentis, 1979; Ross and Sicoly, 1982; Kunda, 1990, 1987; Danitioso et al., 1990; Darley and Gross, 1983; Dunning et al., 1989; Thompson and Loewenstein, 1992). Self-serving bias is attributed to motivated reasoning, which can be understood as people's propensity to reason (by attending only to some of the available information) in a way that supports their subjectively favored propositions. Kunda (1990) argues that "People rely on cognitive processes and representations to arrive at their desired conclusions, but motivation plays a role in determining which of these will be used on a given occasion" (p. 481). "[S]elf-serving biases are best explained as resulting from cognitive processes guided by motivation because they do not occur in the absence of motivational pressures" (Kunda, 1987; p. 636).
3. Given that self-serving bias reduces the size of the surplus generated by an out-of-court settlement, this cognitive bias might actually be *self-defeating* in economic terms (i.e., it might decrease litigants' payoffs). See Section 3 for details. We will use the terms *likelihood of disputes* and *likelihood of trial*. interchangeably.
4. The common perception that excessive awards at trial promote unnecessary litigation (Danzon, 1986) and the escalation of liability insurance premiums (Sloane, 1993; Economic Report of the President, 2004) has motivated tort reforms such as damage caps (limits on the size of the awards granted at trial).
5. In his seminal work on theoretical law and economics, Shavell (1982) states that "[T]he aim [of a model] is [. . .] to provide a generally useful tool for thought" (p. 56).
6. These studies involve robust experimental designs. Specifically, the authors use laboratory environments, structured bargaining, rich context (i.e., they provide complex information about a legal case to the subjects), and human subjects paid according to their performance.
7. See Landeo's (2009) experimental work on split-awards tort reform (where the state takes a share of the punitive damages awarded to the plaintiff) for additional evidence of self-serving bias in litigation environments.
8. Debiasing interventions refer to techniques intended to reduce the magnitude of the bias. See Babcock et al. (1997) for a description of one of the few effective debiasing mechanisms. Note, however, that this procedure can be applied only after a dispute occurs. See Jolls and Sunstein (2006) for a comprehensive discussion of debiasing interventions based on procedural rules or substantive law.
9. For instance, sixty percent of lawyers report that they always comply with the bankruptcy fee guidelines, but judges report that only eighteen percent of attorneys always comply.
10. See Prescott et al. (2010) for a pretrial bargaining model with complete information and divergent priors, which accommodates self-serving bias under certain conditions. See

also Watanabe (2010) for a recent game-theoretic model of filing and litigation under divergent but *unbiased* priors and complete information. Finally, see Yildiz (2003) for a more general bargaining model without common (but unbiased) priors.

11. See also Landeo et al. (2007b) for a model of liability and litigation under asymmetric information. See Waldfogel (1998) for an empirical test of models of divergent (but unbiased) beliefs and asymmetric information.

12. Compensatory damages involve economic and non-economic damages. Non-economic damages are primarily intended to compensate plaintiffs for injuries and losses that are not easily quantified by a dollar amount (pain and suffering, for instance). These awards have been widely criticized for being unpredictable. See for instance *Prindilus v. New York City Health Hospitals Corporation*, 743 N.Y.S.2d 770 (N.Y. App. Div. 2002).

13. We will use the terms *potential injurer* and *defendant* interchangeably.

14. Caps on non-economic damages have been widely implemented by U.S. states. By 2007, twenty-six U.S. states had enacted some type of caps on non-economic damages (Avraham and Bustos, 2010).

15. Although our work is motivated on civil litigation, our technical contribution applies to other strategic settings with asymmetric information and biased players.

16. We will use the terms *potential plaintiff* and *plaintiff* interchangeably.

17. Given that the defendant's expected litigation loss will be affected by her self-serving bias, the defendant's self-serving bias will also affect his choice of care. Please see the discussion below.

18. As Reinganum and Wilde (1986) argue, although information is exchanged during bargaining, at the end of this process there might still be some residual uncertainty on the part of the defendant about the level of true economic losses.

19. Babcock et al. (1997) argue that environments characterized by ambiguous information might elicit self-serving bias on litigants' beliefs.

20. The process of constructing these biased beliefs is not explicitly modeled in our setting.

21. Although the plaintiff's self-serving bias allows her to commit to a tougher negotiation position (to propose a higher settlement demand), it also negatively affects the likelihood of disputes (probability that the defendant rejects the plaintiff's offer). We show that the second effect dominates. As a result, the plaintiff's expected payoff is also reduced.

22. Landeo's (2009) experimental findings regarding the effects of the split-award tort reform also suggest that this tort reform might affect litigants' beliefs.

23. See Quayle (1992) and Atiyah (1980).

24. The source of information asymmetry in this model is the defendant's probability of being found liable at trial (only known by the defendant). Note that, although the defendant is informed about his probability of being found liable at trial, the authors assume that both players exhibit self-serving bias regarding this parameter. This assumption is not aligned with previous experimental findings on self-serving bias. In fact, Babcock and Loewenstein (1997) suggest that self-serving bias is elicited in environments characterized by ambiguity, which is not the case of the defendant regarding his probability of being found liable at trial. Note also that there is a technical shortcoming in the environment studied by Farmer and Pecorino (2002): The biased litigants choose equilibrium strategies that according to their opponents should be played with zero probability in equilibrium. Our technical extension of the perfect Bayesian equilibrium concept and our empirically-relevant assumptions preclude these problems to occur.

25. In this model, the source of information asymmetry is the plaintiff's probability of succeeding at trial (only known by the plaintiff). Although the plaintiff is informed about his probability of succeeding at trial, both litigants exhibit self-serving bias on this parameter. Contrary to empirical findings, the authors assume that the litigants' self-serving biases are common knowledge. In addition, they assume that plaintiffs have preferences characterized by probabilistic risk-aversion. The defendants are risk-neutral players.

26. Marital dissolution environments (Wilkinson-Ryan and Small, 2008) represent an additional interesting application.
27. The optimal level of care for the potential injurer might not be aligned with the optimal level of care from a social point of view. See Section 3.3 (social welfare analysis).
28. The assumptions about $K(\lambda)$ ensure that, for any positive value of l_D, $L(\lambda)$ has a unique interior minimum $\lambda^* \in (0, 1)$, and that λ^* is decreasing in l_D. See the Lemma and its proof in the Appendix.
29. The introduction of biased beliefs about the size of the award requires the assumption that the distribution of actual types is unbounded from above. If the actual types were distributed over the interval $[x, \bar{x}]$, the plaintiff with the highest type and self-serving beliefs about the size of the award at trial would make an offer that exceeded the equilibrium offer for a plaintiff with type $\bar{x}$, which cannot be an equilibrium strategy from the defendant's perspective.
30. The most common liability rules used by courts in tort cases are the negligence and strict liability rules. Under the negligence rule, the injurer will be held liable only if he exercised precaution below a level usually determined by the court (reasonable care or due care standard). Under strict liability, the court does not have to set any level of due care because the injurer has to bear the costs of the accident regardless of the extent of his precaution. Product liability and medical malpractice cases generally involve the application of strict liability and negligence rules, respectively. We assume that the court applies a strict liability rule. However, our results are robust to environments in which the negligence rule is applied.
31. Economic and non-economic damages are the main components of compensatory damages. For instance, consider the definition of damages in auto accident cases in Texas. Economic damages are defined (very generally) as money damages intended to compensate an injured party for actual economic loss. Non-economic damages, on the other hand, may include physical pain and suffering, mental or emotional pain or anguish, disfigurement, physical impairment, loss of companionship and society, inconvenience, loss of enjoyment of life, injury to reputation, loss of consortium (loss of spousal companionship and services) (Texas Statutes Civil Practice and Remedies Code, Chapter 41: Damages, Sections 41.001(4) and 41.001(12)).
32. We assume that the compensatory award (economic and non-economic damages) is proportional to the economic losses x. However, our results are robust to other specifications of the relationship between compensatory damages and x.
33. For the case of a multiplicative bias (a different strategy to modeling the bias), these ratios would be th_P and th_D respectively, where $h_P > 1$ and $h_D < 1$. Our qualitative results are robust to this alternative modeling strategy. Our qualitative results are also robust to litigants' (additive) biases on π or on c_D. Proofs of robustness of the qualitative results to alternative specifications of the bias are available upon request.
34. Note that the optimal strategies and equilibrium beliefs of the fully-separating equilibrium (described below) hold under any off-equilibrium beliefs. In this sense, there is an equivalence class of fully-separating equilibria with the same equilibrium strategies and equilibrium beliefs but different off-equilibrium beliefs (see Reinganum and Wilde, 1986). Note also that this game has partially-pooling equilibria. However, these partially-pooling equilibria do not survive the Universal-Divinity refinement (Banks and Sobel, 1987). Finally note that there are no pure-pooling equilibria in this game. The Appendix presents the proof of existence and uniqueness (in terms of the equilibrium outcome) of the fully-separating PBE described in Proposition 1. These arguments also hold in the environments described in Propositions 5 and 7.
35. See Appendix for details.
36. Note, however, that our equilibrium strategies are actually supported by any off-equilibrium beliefs. In fact, when the defendant observes a settlement demand $S < S_D$, he will accept the offer with certainty regardless of his beliefs about the plaintiff's type. In this sense, a class of fully-separating equilibria, characterized by the equilibrium strategies (and equilibrium beliefs) described in Proposition 1 and any set of off-

equilibrium beliefs, exists (see Reinganum and Wilde, 1986). Hence, our equilibrium outcomes (and our analysis of the effects of litigants' biases) are robust to any set of off-equilibrium beliefs.

37. Note that uncertainty and ambiguity regarding the court's non-economic damages award is assumed to be a permanent feature of civil litigation. Hence, potential injurers are also exposed to these environments, and hence, to self-serving biases.

38. Remember, however, that the litigants' biases help them commit to tough negotiation positions. Note also that there might be other non-economic benefits from self-serving bias. Research in social psychology suggests that these biases are beneficial to the well-being of individuals. For instance Taylor and Brown (1988) argue that self-serving bias might positively affect mental health, including the ability to engage in productive and creative work, and the ability to be happy or contended. This might explain the resilience of this cognitive bias to debiasing mechanisms. See Bar-Gill (2007) for an interesting theoretical analysis of the persistence of optimistic beliefs, under an evolutionary game-theoretic approach.

39. If $lD > lW$, on the other hand, the effect of an increase in the defendant's bias on social welfare is ambiguous. Two factors affect social welfare in opposite directions. First, before the increase in the defendant's bias, the defendant exercised too much care. Then, a reduction in the level of care is welfare improving. Second, the increase in the probability of trial due to the higher defendant's bias is welfare reducing. However, the second factor might still dominate. In fact, the parameters that positively affect the likelihood that $lD > lW$ (larger π and smaller hD) also increase the quantitative importance of the probability-of-trial effect.

40. Jolls and Sunstein (2006) propose the use of the law as a debiasing mechanism. Specifically, debias through law refers to an intervention oriented to reduce the magnitude of the bias through the use of procedural rules (such as rules governing the adjudicative process) or substantive law (such as consumer safety law and product risk communication regulations). See also Babcock et al. (1997), Thaler and Sunstein (2008), and Simon et al. (2008).

41. Babcock and Pogarsky (1999) argue that "the variety of statutory damage limitations share a common feature–they circumscribe a previously unbounded array of potential trial outcomes" (p. 345).

42. See http://www.tapa.info/html/Texas Legislative Reforms.html for details. We thank Bernie Black for providing detailed information about this tort reform.

43. Babcock and Pogarsky (1999) analyze the effect on settlement rates of a damage cap set lower than the value of the underlying claim, using a bargaining experiment. They find that damage caps constrain the parties' judgments and produce more settlement. Pogarsky and Babcock (2001) extend this work by studying the effects of size of the damage caps relative to the actual damage on litigation outcomes. They find that litigants' beliefs about the size of the award are affected by the cap, in case of a relatively high cap, and that this motivating anchoring generates higher likelihood of dispute and higher settlement amounts. These studies also show that low caps (relative to the true damages) might act as *debiasing through law* mechanisms. Landeo (2009) finds that the split-awards tort reform can also act as a *debiasing through law* mechanism.

44. Note that the reduction in the level of care negatively affects welfare only if the defendants are under-deterred.

45. Note that x_{med} is defined as follows: $\int_{\underline{x}}^{x_{med}} x f(x)\,dx = \int_{x_{med}}^{+\infty} x f(x)\,dx.$

46. These two conditions imply $x < \frac{A}{(t + h_p - 1)} < \frac{A}{(t + h_p - 1)} < x_{med}$. Hence, the last result holds in case of plaintiffs' types lower than the median type.

47. See Silver et al. (2008).

48. Two tort reforms are studied, reform on the joint and several liability rule and caps on non-economic damages.

49. See also Arlen (2000) for a discussion regarding the effects of damage caps on reducing defendant's incentives to take optimal care.

50. This phenomenon is called "illusion of asymmetric inside." It is characterized by the

conviction that one perceives events as they are but that the perception of other people might be biased (Pronin et al. 2004). We thank Janice Nadler for pointing out this literature.

51. If the maximum does not exist, let $S^* = \sup_S AS(X)$, and choose an increasing sequence $S_n \to S^*$, $S_n \in AS(X)$. For each S_n, we have $\pi(t + h_p)Eb^a(S_n) + c_D = S_n$ as the apparent defendant is indifferent between accepting and rejecting offer S_n. Therefore, $Eb^a(S_n)$ converges as well. Since supports of $b^a(S_n)$ are also ordered (as sets) by monotonicity, convergence of averages means that supports themselves converge (as sets) to $\frac{S^* - c_D}{\pi(t + h_p)}$. Then, $\sup\{\bigcup_n \text{Supp } b^a(S_n)\} = \frac{S^* - c_D}{\pi(t + h_p)} < x^* = \frac{S^* + c_p}{\pi(t + h_p)}$, so x^* is not the smallest type without a possibility of an accepted offer in equilibrium.

52. See Fudenberg and Tirole (1991; pp.451–454) for details.

53. If either type is making some other offer in equilibrium, then, by continuity, it is indifferent between making that offer and S. Without loss of generality, we may assume that both types offer S in equilibrium.

54. Note that this condition is sufficient but not necessary. An increase in π and a reduction in h_D reduce the (positive) difference between tx (the first term in the expression for l_W) and $\pi(t - h_D)x$ (the first term in the expression for l_D), and hence make $l_D > l_W$ more likely. However, the same parameters increase the direct (probability-of-trial) effect of the bias on the social welfare loss. Hence, even if $l_W < l_D$, the effect of the defendant's bias might still be welfare reducing.

55. See proof of Proposition 1 for any of the two pairs, plaintiff-apparent defendant or defendant-apparent plaintiff.

REFERENCES

Arlen, J. (2000). "Tort Damages: A Survey," in *Encyclopedia of Law and Economics*, ed. Bouckaert, B. and De Geest, G. Cheltenham: Edward Elgar.

Atiyah, P.S. (1980). *"Accidents, Compensation and the Law"*. London: Weidenfeld and Nicholson.

Avraham, R. and Bustos, A. (2010). "The Unexpected Effects of Caps on Non-Economic Damages." *International Review of Law and Economics* 30, 291–305.

Babcock, L. and Loewenstein, G. (1997). "Explaining Bargaining Impasse: The Role of Self-Serving Biases." *Journal of Economic Perspectives* 11, 109–26.

Babcock, L., Loewenstein, and G., Issacharoff, S. (1997). "Creating Convergence: Debiasing Biased Litigants." *Law and Social Inquiry* 22, 913–26.

Babcock, L., Wang, Xianghong, and Loewenstein, G. (1996). "Choosing the Wrong Pond: Social Comparisons in Negotiations that Reflect a Self-Serving Bias." *Quarterly Journal of Economics* 111, 1–19.

Babcock, L., Loewenstein, G., Issacharoff, S., and Camerer, C. (1995a). "Biased Judgments of Fairness in Bargaining." *American Economic Review* 11, 109–26.

Babcock, L., Farber, H., Fobian, C., and Shafir, E. (1995b). "Forming Beliefs about adjudicated Outcomes: Perceptions of Risk and Reservation Values." *International Reviewof Law and Economics* 15, 289–303.

Babcock, L. and Olson, C. (1992). "The Causes of Impasse in Labor Disputes." *Industrial Relations* 31, 348–60.

Babcock, L. and Pogarsky, G. (1999). "Damage Caps and Settlement: A Behavioral Approach." *Journal of Legal Studies* 28, 341–70.

Banks, J.S. and Sobel, J. (1987). "Equilibrium Selection in Signaling Games." *Econometrica* 55, 647–61.

Bar-Gill, O. (2007). "The Evolution and Persistence of Optimism in Litigation." *Journal of Law, Economics and Organization* 22, 490–507.

Bebchuk, L.A. (1984). "Litigation and Settlement under Imperfect Information." *Rand Journal of Economics* 15, 404–15.

Brooks, R., Landeo, C.M., and Spier, K.E. (2010). "Trigger Happy or Gun Shy: Dissolving Common-Value Partnerships with Texas Shootouts." *RAND Journal of Economics* 41, 649–73.

Currie, J. and MacLeod, B.W. (2008). "First Do No Harm? Tort Reform and Birth Outcomes." *Quarterly Journal of Economics* 123, 795–830.

Currie, J. and McConnell, S. (1991). "Collective Bargaining in the Public Sector: The Effect of Legal Structure on Dispute Costs and Wages." *American Economic Review* 81, 693–718.

Danitioso, R., Kunda, Z., and Fong, G.T. (1990). "Motivated Recruitment of Auto-biographical Memories." *Journal of Personality and Social Psychology* 59, 229–41.

Danzon, P. (1986). "The Frequency and Severity of Medical Malpractice Claims: New Evidence." *Law and Contemporary Problems* 57, 76–7.

Darley, J. and Gross, P. (1983). "A Hypothesis-Confirming Bias in Labelling Effects." *Journal of Personality and Social Psychology* 44, 20–33.

Deffais, B. and Langlais, E. (2009). "Legal Interpretative Process and Litigants' Cognitive Biases." Mimeo, Université Paris X-Nanterre and Nancy University.

Dunning, D., Meyerowitz, J. and Holzberg, A. (1989). "Ambiguity and Self-Evaluation: The Role of Idiosyncratic Trait Definitions in Self-Assessment of Ability." *Journal of Personality and Social Psychology* 57, 1082–90.

Economic Report of the President. (2004) United States Government Printing Office, Washington, 203–21.

Eisenberg, T. (1994). "Differing Perceptions of Attorney Fees in Bankruptcy Cases." *Washington University Law Quarterly* 72, 979–95.

Farber, H. (1978). "Bargaining Theory, Wage Outcomes, and the Occurrence of Strikes: An Econometric Analysis." *American Economic Review* 68, 262–84.

Farmer, A. and Pecorino, P. (2002). "Pretrial Bargaining with Self-Serving Bias and Asymmetric Information." *Journal of Economic Behavior and Organization* 48, 163–76.

Fudenberg, D. and Tirole, J. (1991). "*Game Theory*". Cambridge: MIT Press.

Gould, J.P. (1973). "The Economics of Legal Conflict." *Journal of Legal Studies* 2, 279–300.

Jolls, C. and Sunstein, C. (2006). "Debiasing through Law." *Journal of Legal Studies* 35, 199–241.

Kennan, J., and Wilson, R. (1993). "Bargaining with Private Information," *Journal of Economic Literature* 31, 45–04.

Kennan, J., and Wilson, R. (1989). "Strategic Bargaining Models and Interpretation of Strike Data," *Journal of Applied Econometrics, Supplement 4*, S87-S130.

Kunda, Z. (1990). "The Case of Motivated Reasoning." *Psychological Bulletin* 108, 480–98.

Kunda, Z. (1987). "Motivated Inference: Self-Serving Generation and Evaluation of Causal Theories." *Journal of Personality and Social Psychology* 53, 636–47.

Landeo, C.M. (2009). "Cognitive Coherence and Tort Reform." *Journal of Economic Psychology* 6, 898–912.

Landeo, C.M. and Nikitin, M. (2006). "Split-Award Tort Reform, Firm's Level of Care and Litigation Outcomes." *Journal of Institutional and Theoretical Economics* 162, 571–600.

Landeo, C.M., Nikitin, M., and Babcock, L. (2007a). "Split-Awards and Disputes: An Experimental Study of a Strategic Model of Litigation" *Journal of Economic Behavior and Organization* 63, 553–72.

Landeo, C.M., Nikitin, M., and Baker, S. (2007b). "Deterrence, Lawsuits and Litigation Outcomes under Court Errors." *Journal of Law, Economics, and Organization* 23, 57–97.

Landes, W. (1971). "An Economic Analysis of the Courts." *Journal of Law and Economics* 14, 61–107.

Loewenstein, G., Issacharoff, S., Camerer, C., and Babcock, L. (1993). "Self-Serving Assessments of Fairness and Pretrial Bargaining." *Journal of Legal Studies* 22, 135–59.

Messick, D. and Sentis, K. (1979). "Fairness and Preference." *Journal of Experimental Social Psychology* 15, 418–34.

Miller, G. (1987). "Some Agency Problems in Settlement." *Journal of Legal Studies* 16, 189–215.

Nalebuff, B. (1987). "Credible Pretrial Negotiation." *RAND Journal of Economics* 18, 198–210.

Png, I.P.L. (1987). "Litigation, Liability, and the Incentives for Care." *Journal of Public Economics* 34, 61–85.

Png, I. (1983). "Strategic behaviour in suit, settlement, and trial," *Bell Journal of Economics*, 14: 539–50.

Pogarsky, G. and Babcock, L. (2001). "Damage Caps, Motivated Anchoring, and Bargaining Impasse." *Journal of Legal Studies* 30, 143–59.

Posner, R. (1973). "Economic Analysis of Law," Boston: Little-Brown.

Prescott, J.J., Spier, K.E., and Yoon, A. (2010), "Trial and Settlement: A Study of High-Low Agreements." Mimeo, University of Michigan, Harvard University, and University of Toronto.

Priest, G.L. and Klein, B. (1984). "The Selection of Disputes for Litigation." *Journal of Legal Studies* 1, 1–55.

Prindilus v. New York City Health Hospitals Corporation, 743 N.Y.S.2d 770 (N.Y. App. Div. 2002).

Pronin, E., Gilovich, T., and Ross, L. (2004). "Theoretical Note. Objective in the Eye of the Beholder: Divergent Perceptions of Bias in Self versus the Others." *Psychological Review* 111, 781–99.

Quayle, D. (1992). "Civil Justice Reform." *American University Law Review* 41, 559–61.

Reinganum, J.F. and Wilde, L.L. (1986). "Settlement, Litigation, and the Allocation of Litigation Costs." *RAND Journal of Economics* 17, 557–66.

Ross, M. and Sicoly, F. (1982). "*Egocentric Biases in Availability and Attribution*," in Judgment under Uncertainty: Heuristics and Biases (eds), Kahneman, D., Slovic, P., and Tversky, A., 179–189. New York: Cambridge University Press.

Schweizer, U. (1989). "Litigation and settlement under two-sided incomplete information," *Review of Economic Studies*, 56: 163–78.

Shavell, S. (1982). "Suit, Settlement, and Trial." *Journal of Legal Studies* 11, 55–81.

Silver, C., Hyman, D.A., and Black, B.L. (2008). "The Impact of the 2003 Texas Medical Malpractice Damages Cap on Physician Supply and Insurer Payouts: Separating Facts from Rhetoric." *Texas Advocate*, 25–34.

Simon, D., Krawezyk, D., Bleicher, A., and Holyoak, K. (2008), "Constructed Preferences: Transient Yet Robust." *Journal of Behavioral Decision Making* 21, 1–14.

Sloane, L. (1993). "The Split-Award Statute: A Move Toward Effectuating the True Purpose of Punitive Damages," *Valparaiso University Law Review* 28, 473–512.

Spier, K.E. (1994a). "Pretrial Bargaining and the Design of Fee-Shifting Rules." *RAND Journal of Economics* 25, 197–214.

Spier, K.E. (1994b). "Settlement and the Design of Fee-Shifting Rules." *Journal of Law, Economics, and Organization* 10, 84–95.

Spier, K.E. (1992), "The Dynamics of Pretrial Negotiation," *Review of Economic Studies* 59, 93–108.

Taylor, S. and Brown, J.D. (1988), "Illusion and Well-Being: A Social Psychological Perspective on Mental Health," *Psychological Bulletin* 103, 193–210.

Thaler, R.H. and Sunstein, C.R. (2008). "*Nudge: Improving Decisions about Health, Wealth, and Happiness*". New Heaven: Yale University Press.

Thompson, L. and Loewenstein, G. (1992). "Egocentric Interpretations of Fairness in Interpersonal Conflict." *Organizational Behavior and Human Decision Processes* 51, 176–97.

Towers Perrin Tillinghast (2007). *Update on U.S. Tort Cost Trends*. Valhalla, NY: Towers Perrin.

Towers Perrin Tillinghast (2005). *U.S. Tort Costs and Cross-Border Perspectives: 2005 Update*. Valhalla, NY: Towers Perrin.

Waldfogel, J. (1998). "Reconciling Asymmetric Information and Divergent Expectations Theories of Litigation." *Journal of Legal Studies* 51, 451–76.

Watanabe, Y. (2010), "Learning and Bargaining in Dispute Resolution: Theory and Evidence from Medical Malpractice Litigation." Mimeo, Northwestern University.

Wilkinson-Ryan, T. and Small, D. (2008). "Negotiating Divorce: Gender and the Behavioral Economics of Divorce." *Law and Inequality* 26, 109–32.

Yildiz, M. (2003). "Bargaining without a Common Prior. An Immediate Agreement Theorem." *Econometrica* 71, 793–811.

Zabinski, Z. and Black, B. (2011), "The Effect of Tort Reform on Health Care Quality: Evidence from Texas." Mimeo, Northwestern University.

7. Tort standards and legal expenditures: a unified model

Jef De Mot and Ben Depoorter

1. INTRODUCTION

Law and economics scholars have long debated the efficiency benefits of various liability standards. Specifically, a lively debate exists even to date as to whether a comparative negligence or contributory negligence provides better incentives to adopt efficient care (see, e.g., Artigot i Golobardes and Gómez Pomar 2009; Bar-Gill and Ben-Shahar 2003). Whereas the early literature concluded that contributory negligence was more efficient (e.g., Brown 1973; Diamond 1974; Posner 1977), scholars subsequently questioned the alleged superiority of comparative negligence on various grounds (Haddock and Curran 1985; Shavell 1987;[1] Cooter and Ulen 1986;[2] Bar-Gill and Ben-Shahar 2003).[3,4]

Whereas the efficiency-promoting aspects of various tort standards remain a contentious matter, there is a widespread consensus that a comparative negligence standard imposes higher administrative costs than a simple negligence standard (Landes and Posner 1987; White 1989) or a simple negligence standard with a defense of contributory negligence (Shavell 1987; Bar-Gill and Ben-Shahar 2001). White (1989), for instance, argues that a comparative negligence standard likely generates higher litigation and administrative costs than contributory negligence because courts must assess the degree of negligence by both parties and not just whether the parties were negligent. De Mot (2013) argues that this wisdom obviously applies to settings involving exogenous litigation costs, but that the literature has not considered whether it holds in a more realistic setting where litigation costs are endogenously determined.[5] He shows that in a setting with endogenous litigation costs, comparative negligence can be less costly than contributory negligence. This contribution expands on and simplifies this prior model by De Mot (2013).[6] We develop a single model that sheds new light on the litigation expenditures of tort litigants under the *three* negligence standards (simple negligence, contributory negligence, and comparative negligence) when litigation costs are endogenous. This unified model demonstrates how and when trial expenditures are lower under a given negligence standard compared to the other standards and examines the impact of the relative merits of a claim on the likely expenditures by litigants under various tort standards.

We proceed as follows. The following section sets out a general model that incorporates simple negligence, contributory negligence and comparative negligence. Section 3 compares the litigation expenditures for these three negligence rules.

2. MODEL

Under a simple negligence rule, the injurer is liable if and only if her level of precaution is below the legal standard regardless of the precaution level exercised by the victim. Under a rule of (negligence with a defense of) contributory negligence, the negligent injurer escapes liability by proving that the victim's precaution fell short of the legal standard of care. Comparative negligence divides the cost of harm between the parties in proportion to the contribution of their negligence to the accident.[7]

At trial, litigants select their level of legal expenditures. When a simple negligence rule applies, there is one choice variable on each side: the litigation effort regarding the negligence of the defendant. By contrast, when contributory and comparative negligence rules apply, there are two choice variables on each side: the litigation effort regarding the negligence of the defendant and the litigation effort regarding the negligence of the plaintiff. Both parties are assumed to be risk-neutral. Each contender aims to maximize his expected income. We assume that each party is responsible for her own legal costs regardless of the outcome (the American rule thus applies). The Litigation Success Functions[8] incorporate the insight that in litigation, relative success depends on the actual degree of fault (or the exogenous merits) and on the efforts invested on each side. If the defendant exercised a care level that is far below the due care standard, the actual degree of fault of the defendant will be high.[9] The actual degree of fault is assumed to be a value between 0 and 1. Regarding the defendant's negligence, an actual degree of fault of 0 implies that the defendant will never be held liable, regardless of the other side investments in litigation. An actual degree of fault of 1 implies that the plaintiff will always win, regardless of the defendant's litigation expenditures. For any other true degree of fault, either party always has a positive probability of winning the issue. Regarding the plaintiff's negligence, a true degree of fault of 0 means that the plaintiff will always win that issue, no matter how much the other side spends. An actual degree of fault of 1 implies that the defendant always wins that issue. Both litigants (but not the court) are aware of the actual degree of fault as it relates to the liability question (the defendant's and plaintiff's negligence). The plaintiff and the defendant select their strategies simultaneously and we examine the Nash equilibrium of this game. The parties have equal stakes and have common knowledge of all the underlying functions and parameters (the actual level of fault, the amount at stake etc.). For the sake of simplicity, the amount at stake is set equal to 1. If both parties are deemed negligent under the comparative negligence standard, we assume that the relative shares of the parties are determined exogenously.[10]

Using a standard contest function, the probability that the court will hold the defendant negligent equals:

$$P_d = \frac{X_1 F_1}{X_1 F_1 + Y_1(1 - F_1)} = \frac{1}{1 + \left(\dfrac{Y_1}{X_1}\right)\left(\dfrac{1 - F_1}{F_1}\right)}$$

where X_1 equals the expenditures of the plaintiff for the liability of the defendant, Y_1 equals the expenditures of the defendant for the liability of the defendant and F_1 is the actual degree of fault of the defendant ($0 \leq F_1 \leq 1$).[11,12]

Similarly, with respect to contributory and comparative negligence, the probability that the court will hold the plaintiff negligent equals:

$$P_p = \frac{Y_2 F_2}{Y_2 F_2 + X_2(1 - F_2)}$$

where X_2 equals the expenditures of the plaintiff for the liability of the plaintiff, Y_2 equals the expenditures of the defendant for the liability of the plaintiff and F_2 is the true degree of fault of the plaintiff ($0 \leq F_2 \leq 1$).[13,14]

We can now write the following functions for the plaintiff's expected value, encompassing each of the three negligence rules:

$$EVp_1 = P_d(1 - P_p) + P_d P_p \sigma - X_1 - X_2$$

Clearly, the case of simple negligence is captured ($\sigma = 1$), as well as the case of contributory negligence ($\sigma = 0$) and the case of comparative negligence ($0 < \sigma < 1$). Note that we assume that σ is exogenously determined.[15]

Similarly, the defendant's expected loss under the three negligence rules equals:

$$EL_{def} = P_d(1 - P_p) + P_d P_p \sigma + Y_1 + Y_2$$

If we now fill in the formulas (contest functions) for P_p and P_d in the plaintiff's expected value and the defendant's expected loss, we obtain the following Nash equilibria (see the Appendix):

$$X_1^* = Y_1^* = F_1(1 - F_1)(1 - F_2 + \sigma F_2)$$

$$X_2^* = Y_2^* = F_2(1 - F_2)(F_1 - \sigma F_1)$$

3. COMPARISON OF THE THREE NEGLIGENCE STANDARDS

3.1. Expenditures Towards Establishing Negligence on Behalf of the Defendant

Under simple negligence ($\sigma = 1$), the parties' expenditures on establishing/refuting negligence on behalf of the defendant equals $X_1^* = Y_1^* = F_1(1 - F_1)$. Under contributory negligence ($\sigma = 0$), the parties' expenditures equal $X_1^* = Y_1^* = F_1(1 - F_1)(1 - F_2)$. Under comparative negligence, the parties' expenditures are $X_1^* = Y_1^* = F_1(1 - F_1)(1 - F_2 + \sigma F_2)$.

The likely litigation investments in determining the negligence issue are highest under simple negligence, lowest under contributory negligence, and somewhere in between for comparative negligence: $F_1(1 - F_1) > F_1(1 - F_1)(1 - F_2 + \sigma F_2) > F_1(1 - F_1)(1 - F_2)$. Legal expenditures are highest under simple negligence because, unlike under contributory and comparative negligence, the plaintiff does not run the risk of being held liable himself. By contrast, when contributory and comparative negligence standards apply, the risk of being held liable reduces the expected benefit of the expenditures devoted to establishing negligence on behalf of the defendant. Intuitively, the value of spending additional resources on determining negligence by the plaintiff is lower under contributory and comparative because some (or *all* in the case of contributory negligence) of the damage is shifted to the plaintiff if the latter is held liable as well.

Next, the expected value of expenditures on determining the defendant's negligence is lower under contributory negligence than comparative negligence. That is because, (only) under contributory negligence, expenditures into establishing negligence on behalf of the plaintiff have absolutely no value when the plaintiff is also found negligent.[16]

3.2. Expenditures to Determine Negligence on Behalf of the Plaintiff

Under simple negligence, expenditures towards establishing negligence on behalf of the plaintiff equal 0 – since a simple negligence standard does not inquire into the care level of the plaintiff. Under contributory negligence, the parties' expenditures equal $X_2^* = Y_2^* = F_1 F_2 (1 - F_2)$. Under comparative negligence, the parties' expenditures are $X_2^* = Y_2^* = F_2 (1 - F_2)(F_1 - \sigma F_1)$.

Because the expected value of expenditures to establish or rebut a plaintiff's negligence is lower under comparative negligence than contributory negligence, the expenditures are likely smaller under comparative negligence: $F_2 (1 - F_2)(F_1 - \sigma F_1) < F_2 (1 - F_2) F_1$. That is because, if the plaintiff is held liable under contributory negligence, he or she bears the entire loss; whereas under comparative negligence a plaintiff who is held negligent only bears part of the losses.[17]

3.3.   Total Expenditures and the Merits of the Claim

Under a standard of simple negligence litigants' total expenditures equal $2F_1 (1 - F_1)$. Expenditures are $2F_1 (1 - F_1)(1 + F_2 - F_1)$ under contributory negligence and $2F_1 (1 - F_1)(1 - F_2 + \sigma F_2) + 2F_2 (1 - F_2)(F_1 - \sigma F_1)$ under comparative negligence.

In a model with fixed expenditures, legal expenditures will always be higher under contributory negligence than under simple negligence since there are more issues for the court to decide under the former rule. However, in a model where litigation expenditures are endogenous, the costs may be lower under a contributory negligence standard. This is the case when $2F_1 (1 - F_1) > 2F_1 (1 - F_1)(1 + F_2 - F_1)$, thus when $F_2 > F_1$ (i.e. the inherent fault of the plaintiff is larger than the inherent fault of the defendant).

Similarly, trial expenditures can either be higher or lower under comparative negligence than under simple negligence. The expenditures are higher under simple negligence if $2F_1 (1 - F_1) > 2F_1 (1 - F_1)(1 - F_2 + \sigma F_2) + 2F_2 (1 - F_2)(F_1 - \sigma F_1)$, thus when $F_2 > F_1$.

Finally, are total trial expenditures always lower under contributory negligence than under comparative negligence? The total expenditures are smaller under a comparative negligence standard than under contributory negligence when $2F_1 (1 - F_1)(1 - F_2) + 2F_1 F_2 (1 - F_2) > 2F_1 (1 - F_1)(1 - F_2 + \sigma F_2) + 2F_2 (1 - F_2)(F_1 - \sigma F_1)$, thus when $F_2 < F_1$. In other words, the stronger (weaker) the plaintiff's claim,[18] the more likely it is that the expenditures will be smaller (higher) under comparative negligence than under contributory negligence. The intuition is the following. First, when the actual degree of fault of the defendant increases, the importance of the outcome of the issue of the plaintiff's negligence increases under both rules, but more so under contributory negligence than under comparative negligence (because of the all-or-nothing character of contributory negligence). Second, when the actual level of fault of the plaintiff decreases, the importance of the outcome of the issue of the defendant's negligence increases under both rules, but more so under contributory negligence than under comparative negligence (due to the sharing element of comparative negligence).

APPENDIX

The plaintiff's expected value equals $EV_{pl} = P_d(1 - P_p) + P_p P_d \sigma - X_1 - X_2$, thus

$$EV_{pl} = \frac{X_1 F_1}{X_1 F_1 + Y_1(1 - F_1)} \left(1 - \frac{Y_2 F_2}{Y_2 F_2 + X_2(1 - F_2)} \right)$$

$$+ \frac{X_1 F_1}{X_1 F_1 + Y_1(1 - F_1)} \frac{Y_2 F_2}{Y_2 F_2 + X_2(1 - F_2)} \sigma - X_1 - X_2$$

The expected loss of litigation for the defendant equals $EL_{def} = P_d(1 - \alpha P_p) + P_p P_d \sigma + Y_1 + Y_2$, thus

$$EL_{def} = \frac{X_1 F_1}{X_1 F_1 + Y_1(1 - F_1)} \left(1 - \frac{Y_2 F_2}{Y_2 F_2 + X_2(1 - F_2)} \right)$$

$$+ \frac{X_1 F_1}{X_1 F_1 + Y_1(1 - F_1)} \frac{Y_2 F_2}{Y_2 F_2 + X_2(1 - F_2)} \sigma + Y_1 + Y_2$$

With respect to the plaintiff's expected value, the first-order conditions regarding the defendant's negligence and the plaintiff's negligence are:

$$\frac{\partial P_d}{\partial X_1}(1 - P_p) + P_p \frac{\partial P_d}{\partial X_1} \sigma = 1, \text{ thus } \frac{\partial P_d}{\partial X_1}(1 - P_p) + P_p \frac{\partial P_d}{\partial X_1} \sigma = 1 \quad (7A.1)$$

$$- P_d \frac{\partial P_p}{\partial X_2} + \frac{\partial P_p}{\partial X_2} P_d \sigma = 1, \text{ thus } - P_d \frac{\partial P_p}{\partial X_2} + \frac{\partial P_p}{\partial X_2} P_d \sigma = 1 \quad (7A.2)$$

With respect to the defendant's expected loss, the respective first-order conditions are:

$$\frac{\partial P_d}{\partial Y_1}(1 - P_p) + P_p \frac{\partial P_d}{\partial Y_1} \sigma = -1, \quad \text{thus} \quad \frac{\partial P_d}{\partial Y_1}(1 - P_p) + P_p \frac{\partial P_d}{\partial Y_1} \sigma = -1 \quad (7A.3)$$

$$- P_d \frac{\partial P_p}{\partial Y_2} + \frac{\partial P_p}{\partial Y_2} P_d \sigma = -1, \text{ thus } - P_d \frac{\partial P_p}{\partial Y_2} + \frac{\partial P_p}{\partial Y_2} P_d \sigma = -1 \quad (7A.4)$$

We can easily see that $X_1^* = Y_1^*$ and $X_2^* = Y_2^*$. If we put $X_1^* = Y_1^*$ and $X_2^* = Y_2^*$ in (1), we get:

$$X_1^* = Y_1^* = F_1(1 - F_1)(1 - F_2 + \sigma F_2)$$

If we put $X_1^* = Y_1^*$ and $X_2^* = Y_2^*$ in (2), we get: $X_2^* = Y_2^* = F_2(1 - F_2)(F_1 - \sigma F_1)$

NOTES

1. It has been argued that the efficiency characteristics of both rules are equivalent when information is perfect and decision-makers are error-free. The reason is that under both rules, if parties of one type take due care, then parties of the other type will reason that they alone will be found negligent if they do not take due care (see Shavell 2004). Note that it is assumed that due care is set at the optimal level.

2. Cooter and Ulen (1986) show that under conditions of evidentiary uncertainty, comparative negligence gives moderate incentives to deviate from the standard of care to both parties. Contributory negligence gives the strongest incentives to one party and the weakest incentives to the other. Comparative negligence is then the most efficient rule because it minimizes the total amount of deviation from due care when parties are symmetrically situated.

3. Some scholars have demonstrated that comparative negligence provides better incentives to take efficient care levels than negligence or contributory negligence if injurers as well as victims are heterogeneous (see Emons and Sobel (1991) and Feess and Hege (1998)) or if parties make precaution decisions sequentially (see Rea (1987) and Grady (1990)).

4. Bar-Gill and Ben-Shahar (2003) challenge the assumption that parties are symmetrically situated: one party could be better situated to take care. Also, they show that small intermediate deviations are not necessarily preferred to large deviations that may result from other liability rules (they use computer simulations to show this). Note that some empirical studies point out that comparative negligence weakens incentives to take precaution (see White 1989), is associated with higher automobile liability insurance premiums (see Flanigan, Johnson, Winkler and Ferguson 1989). According to Dari-Mattiacci and De Geest (2005), the current empirical literature does not allow us to make inferences about incentives of potential tortfeasors. Although there can be more accidents under comparative negligence, injurers who exercise care have, on average, lower care costs. In other words, under comparative negligence, there are more accidents, and less is spent on precaution, but what is spent on precaution is relatively well spent.

5. Recent contributions to the economic literature on litigation stress the importance of treating litigation expenditures as endogenously determined. See Sanchirico (2007).

6. De Mot (2013) compares contributory negligence with comparative negligence, but not with simple negligence. On the other hand, this contribution provides a less complex model of comparative negligence (it assumes that the shares of the parties are determined exogenously).

7. In the United States as well as in Europe, comparative negligence rather than contributory negligence is the general rule in tort law. In the US, negligence with contributory negligence was the dominant tort-liability rule in common law countries for most of the last 200 years. This changed however within the last 40 years. The prevailing liability standard in all but a few of US states is one of comparative negligence. Most civil law jurisdictions in Europe adopted the principle of comparative negligence long before the US made this change.

8. One for the defendant's negligence and one for the plaintiff's negligence (see further).
9. Phrased differently, the exogenous merits of the plaintiff's claim regarding the defendant's negligence will be high.
10. For a model in which the shares are endogenous, see De Mot, 2013.
11. Note that $\frac{\partial P_d}{\partial X_1} > 0$; $\frac{\partial P_d}{\partial Y_1} < 0$; $\frac{\partial^2 P_d}{\partial X_1^2} < 0$; $\frac{\partial^2 P_d}{\partial Y_1^2} > 0$.
12. As described above, the Litigation Success Function incorporates the insight that the outcome of a lawsuit depends on the actual degree of fault and the efforts of the parties. An example may illustrate this. Suppose the defendant took an amount of care that is substantially below the due care standard. The actual degree of fault will be high (e.g. $F_1 = 0.8$). However, this does not *automatically* imply that the defendant will be held negligent with a high probability. For instance, if the defendant greatly outspends the plaintiff ($Y_1 >> X_1$; e.g. the defendant invests heavily in the formulation of legal arguments to support due care is not the appropriate standard; or invests in misrepresenting facts so that due care seems to have been taken, etc.), then the ultimate probability of victory for the plaintiff may be relatively low.
13. Note that $\frac{\partial P_p}{\partial X_2} < 0$; $\frac{\partial P_p}{\partial Y_2} > 0$; $\frac{\partial |P_p}{\partial X_2^2} > 0$; $\frac{\partial |P_p}{\partial Y_2^2} < 0$.
14. Note that both P_p and P_d can take on any value between 0 and 1. I stress that both parties have the same estimate of P_p and the same estimate of P_d (there are no divergent expectations; more formally: $P_p^{pl} = P_p^{def}$ and $P_p^{pl} = P_d^{def}$). Note also that there's no systematic relationship between P_p and P_d (e.g. their sum is not equal to one). The reason is that P_p and P_d are differently defined as is typical in the economic analysis of civil procedure. In the model of this article, P_p and P_d concern the estimates of two different issues (the probability that respectively the plaintiff and the defendant will be held negligent), not the overall estimates that the plaintiff will win at trial. Traditionally, P_p and P_d represent the subjective probabilities of the plaintiff and the defendant that the plaintiff will win at trial. In our model, P_p represents the estimate of both parties that the plaintiff will be held negligent, and P_d represents the estimate of both parties that the defendant will be held negligent.
15. For a model in which σ is endogenous, see De Mot (2013).
16. In a more complicated model in which σ is endogenous, there is a second reason why the expenditures can be higher under comparative negligence: additional investments may convince the court to conclude that the defendant's negligence is relatively large (or small). Under contributory negligence, the degree of negligence doesn't matter for the ultimate division of the loss. Under comparative negligence, however, it matters a great deal, because the relative degree of negligence influences the division of the loss. See De Mot, supra note 1.
17. In a model in which σ is endogenous, the expenditures regarding the plaintiff's negligence can be either larger or smaller under comparative negligence than under contributory negligence. The expenditures can be smaller under comparative negligence because of the reason discussed in the text above. The expenditures can be larger under comparative negligence because additional investments can lead the court to conclude that the plaintiff's fault is relatively small (or large). See De Mot, supra note 1, who shows that even in this more complex model, total expenditures can be smaller under comparative negligence.
18. Taking both the defendant's and the plaintiff's behavior into account.

REFERENCES

Artigot i Golobardes, Mireia and Fernando Gómez Pomar. 2009. 'Contributory and Comparative Negligence in the Law and Economics Literature.' in M. Faure (ed.), Tort Law and Economics, in G. De Geest (ed.), *Encyclopedia of Law and Economics*, Cheltenham: Edward Elgar, 46–79.

Bar-Gill, Oren and Omri Ben-Shahar. 2001. 'Does Uncertainty Call for Comparative

Negligence?' *Harvard Law School John M. Olin Center for Law, Economics and Business Discussion Paper Series.* Paper 346.

Bar-Gill, Oren and Omri Ben-Shahar. 2003. 'The Uneasy Case for Comparative Negligence.' *American Law and Economics Review* 5: 433–69.

Brown, John Prather. 1973. 'Toward an Economic Theory of Liability.' *Journal of Legal Studies* 2: 323–50.

Cooter, Robert D. and Thomas S. Ulen. 1986. 'An Economic Case for Comparative Negligence.' *New York University Law Review* 61: 1067 ff.

Dari-Mattiacci, Giuseppe and Gerrit De Geest. 2005. 'The Filtering Effect of Sharing Rules.' *Journal of Legal Studies* 34: 207–37.

De Mot, Jef, 2013. Comparative versus Contributory Negligence: A Comparison of the Litigation Expenditures, *International Review Of Law And Economics*, 33: 54–61

Diamond, Peter A. 1974. 'Single Activity Accidents.' *Journal of Legal Studies* 3: 107–64.

Emons, Winand and Sobel, Joel. 1991. 'On the Effectiveness of Liability Rules when Agents Are Not Identical,' 58 *Review of Economic Studies*, 58 (2): 375–90.

Fees, Eberhard and Ulrich Hege, 1998. 'Efficient Liability Rules for Multi-Party Accidents With Moral Hazard.' *Journal of Institutional and Theoretical Economics (JITE)*, 154(2), 422–50.

Flanigan, G.B., J.E. Johnson, D.T. Winkler, and W. Ferguson. 1989. 'Experience from Early Tort Reforms: Comparative Negligence Since 1974.' *The Journal of Risk and Insurance* 56: 525–34.

Grady, Mark F. 1990. 'Multiple tortfeasors and the economy of prevention.' *Journal of Legal Studies* 19: 653–78.

Haddock, David D. and Christopher Curran. 1985. 'An Economic Theory of Comparative Negligence.' *Journal of Legal Studies* 14: 49–72.

Konrad, Kai A. 2009. '*Strategy and Dynamics in Contests*.' Oxford: Oxford University Press, 256.

Landes, William M. and Richard A. Posner. 1987. '*The Economic Structure of Tort Law*', Cambridge, MA: Harvard University Press, 330.

Posner, Richard A. 1977. '*Economic Analysis of Law, 2nd edition*,' Boston and Toronto: Little Brown.

Rea, S. 1987. 'The Economics of Comparative Negligence.' *International Review of Law and Economics* 7: 149–62.

Sanchirico, Chris. 2007. *The Economics of Evidence, Procedure, and Litigation, Vol. II*, in Economic Approaches to Law (anthology series from Edward Elgar Publishing Co.)

Shavell, Steven. 1987. '*Economic Analysis of Accident Law*.' Cambridge, MA: Harvard University Press, 312.

Shavell, Steven. 2004. '*Foundations of Economic Analysis of Law*.' Cambridge, MA: Harvard University Press.

White, Michelle J. 1989. 'An Empirical Test of the Comparative and Contributory Negligence Rules in Accident Law.' *Rand Journal of Economics* 20: 308–30.

8.   Litigation success functions
Jef De Mot

1.   INTRODUCTION

Law and economics scholars have traditionally focused more on the reasons for trial than on the trial itself. More recently however, some studies have paid more attention to the legal battle itself. These studies have analyzed the impact of legal rules on the expenditure decisions of the parties at trial and have examined how these effects may change some standard results of the literature. Many of these articles use an explicit function for the probability of a plaintiff victory. These litigation success functions usually take the following form:

$$p(X,Y) = \frac{X^a F}{X^a F + Y^a(1-F)} = \frac{\left(\dfrac{X}{Y}\right)^a F}{\left(\dfrac{X}{Y}\right)^a F + (1-F)}$$

with X and Y the expenditures of the plaintiff and the defendant respectively, F the degree of defendant fault (with $0 \leq F \leq 1$), and a the force exponent that indicates the relative importance of expenditures vis-à-vis the defendant's fault (or briefly, a productivity parameter of the expenditures). This function obviously has the following features:[1] (1) The determinants of success include both the degree of defendant fault and the litigation effort of the parties; (2) The probability of a plaintiff victory depends on the ratio of the effort levels, hence the name 'ratio form' that is used for this functional form; (3) For a very close case ($F = 1/2$), the outcome at trial depends only upon the litigation efforts; (4) Given equal efforts, the outcome depends only on the degree of fault; (5) If the defendant is totally in the wrong ($F = 1$), she always loses as long as the plaintiff makes some effort ($X > 0$); and (6) If the defendant is totally without fault ($F = 0$), she always wins as long as she makes some effort ($Y > 0$).

Some authors have used a simplified version of this function such as $p(X,Y) = \frac{XF}{XF + Y(1-F)}$, implicitly assuming that $a = 1$, or $p(X,Y) = \frac{X}{X+Y}$, implicitly assuming that $F = 1/2$ and $a = 1$. Some other authors use a slightly different function, $p(X,Y) = \frac{e^M X^a}{e^M X^a + Y^a}$, with M reflecting the objective merits of the case (with M varying between $-\infty$ and $+\infty$).[2] When $M > 0$, the merits favor the plaintiff, when $M < 0$ the merits favor the defendant, and when $M = 0$ they favor neither party. However, it's easy to see that both functions are equivalent. We can see this by setting F equal to $\frac{e^M}{e^M + 1}$. When $M = -\infty$, $F = 0$, when $M = 0$, $F = 1/2$, and when $M = +\infty$, $F = 1$.

This chapter unfolds as follows. Section 2 discusses some results of the literature that uses these litigation success functions. Section 3 examines strengths and weaknesses of these functions and section 4 concludes.

2.   SOME RESULTS OF THE LITERATURE

In this section, we first look at the main results of the basic model (2.1). Then we consider an extension: a comparison of adversarial and inquisitorial systems of adjudication (2.2).

2.1   Basic Model: Determinants of the Expenditures and Plaintiff Success Rate

In the basic model, both parties select their level of legal expenditures once and simultaneously. The expenditures are investments made to persuade a fact-finder. The amount at stake equals J. Both parties are assumed to be risk-neutral. Each contender aims to maximize his expected income. Each party is assumed to be responsible for his or her own legal expenses regardless of the outcome (the American rule of cost allocation applies). The actual merit of the claim is known by both litigants but is unknown to the court. We obtain solutions for the litigation efforts under the Nash-Cournot protocol.

The plaintiff wants to maximize his expected value:

$$EV_{pl} = \frac{X^a F}{X^a F + Y^a (1 - F)} J - X$$

The defendant wants to minimize his expected loss:

$$EV_{def} = \frac{X^a F}{X^a F + Y^a (1 - F)} J + Y$$

The first-order conditions are:

$$aF(1 - F) X^{a-1} Y^a J = (X^a F + Y^a (1 - F))^2$$

$$aF(1 - F) X^a Y^{a-1} J = (X^a F + Y^a (1 - F))^2$$

From these conditions, it follows that the parties always spend an equal amount regardless of the level of fault ($X^* = Y^*$ for all F). We can now easily find the equilibrium expenditures of the parties:

$$X^* = Y^* = aF(1 - F)J$$

The expenditures of the parties increase with the productivity parameter a and with the amount at stake J. They are highest for close cases ($F = 1/2$) and lowest for cases with extreme high or low merit ($F = 0$ and $F = 1$). In Figure 8.1 below, the x-axis represents F, the y-axis a and the z-axis the expenditures of one of the parties (J was set equal to 1, F varies between 0 and 1 and a between 0 and 3).

The plaintiff's probability of winning equals $P_{pl}(X^*, Y^*) = F$ and thus equals the exogenous quality of the case.

The expected value of the plaintiff and the expected loss of the defendant equal respectively:

$$EV_{pl} = FJ - aF(1 - F)J$$

$$EL_{def} = FJ + aF(1 - F)J$$

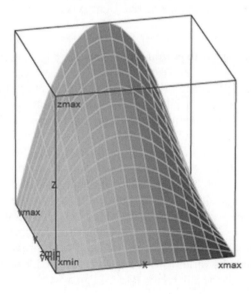

Figure 8.1

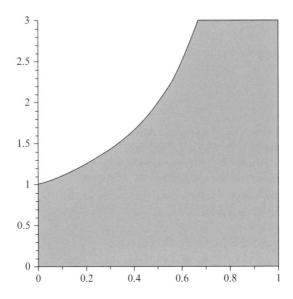

Figure 8.2

The plaintiff's expected value is always positive for relatively low values of *a*, but can be negative for larger values of *a*. The green area in Figure 8.2 below represents combinations of *F* and *a* for which the plaintiff's expected value is positive. The x-axis represents *F* and the y-axis *a*.

2.2   Adversarial versus Inquisitorial Systems

Parisi (2002) compares the litigation expenditures in an adversarial and an inquisitorial system of adjudication.[3] In an inquisitorial proceeding, the presiding judge dominates the trial. He determines the order in which evidence is taken and evaluates the content of the gathered evidence. In an adversarial system, the process develops through the efforts of the parties before a passive decision maker who takes a decision on the sole basis of the evidence presented by the parties. Of course, the distinction between adversarial and inquisitorial proceedings embraces many more dimensions of the legal process than the ones described here. To be able to consider the range of real world alternatives without artificial or incomplete distinctions, Parisi considers the adversarial nature of the process as a continuous variable (through the variable I, see further). The simple model shows that the expenditures of the parties are larger in an adversarial system.

The following notations are used:

X: the effort of the plaintiff.

Y: the effort of the defendant.

Z: the judicial effort exerted by the court in independent investigation and examination of independently obtained evidence.

I: variable that captures the weight attached to the inquisitorial findings in determining the size of the award. Greater values of I indicate that the judge, as opposed to the litigants, has greater control over the process or that the evidence obtained directly by the judge is, ceteris paribus, given greater weight than the evidence provided by the parties.

S: a parameter that denotes the level of scrutiny to which evidence provided by the parties is subjected (e.g. S may symbolize procedural safeguards against the admission of certain types of evidence, like hearsay).

C: the unit cost of litigation effort (C is assumed to be constant).

R_p^e and R_d^e: the total expected return of the plaintiff and the defendant respectively.

R_I: represents the award level that would be given if no adversarial effort is exerted and is a function of the underlying merits of the case and the judicial discovery efforts Z.

R_A: represents the award amount that results from the parties' evidence. It is a function of S.

The plaintiff's objective is to maximize:

$$R_p^e = IR_I(Z) + (1 - I)R_A(S)\frac{X}{X + Y} - CX$$

The defendant wishes to minimize:

$$R_d^e = -IR_I(Z) - (1 - I)R_A(S)\frac{X}{X + Y} - CY$$

The first-order conditions for the optimal levels of effort, X^* and Y^*, are respectively:

$$\frac{\partial R_p^e}{\partial X} = (1 - I)R_A(S)\frac{Y}{(X + Y)} - C = 0$$

$$\frac{\partial R_d^e}{\partial Y} = (1 - I)R_A(S)\frac{X}{(X + Y)} - C = 0$$

It's easy to see that $X^* = Y^*$. We can now find the equilibrium levels of effort:

$$X^* = Y^* = \frac{(1 - I)R_A(S)}{4C}$$

The total expenditures in litigation, at cost C, is:

$$C(X^* + Y^*) = \frac{(1 - I)R_A(S)}{2}$$

The parties will exert litigation effort in proportion to the value of the adversarial component of the case and the weight attached to adversarial evidence in the decision-making process. Note that in a purely adversarial system, the parties will spend half of the value of the case in litigation. This result is in line with some insights from other literature on adversarial and inquisitorial systems. For example, Froeb and Kobayashi (2001) have analogized the fact-finding process in an adversarial system to an 'extremal' estimator based on the difference between the most favorable pieces of evidence produced by each party.[4] As a consequence, with the involvement of the judge diminishing, the litigants' differences will surface more noticeably, and we should expect greater total expenditures. Adams (1998) has pointed out that in civil law jurisdictions, trial is not a single continuous event.[5] The active participation of the judge blurs the distinction between trial and pretrial. In a two-stage process (pretrial and trial), given the uncertainty over the usefulness and relevance of each piece of information in the later trial stage, the litigants tend to look for much more evidence than is actually utilized in the trial stage. In civil law jurisdictions however, the court confines the scope of the supply of information by the parties to those issues that are rather obscure to him. This provides the parties with an opportunity to get some preliminary feedback from the court as to the likely relevance of costly information, thus avoiding expenditures that may prove unnecessary at a later stage.

3.   STRENGTHS AND WEAKNESSES OF THE FORMULA

3.1   Strengths

One interesting feature of the ratio form is that it can be derived in four different ways: stochastic, axiomatic, optimally-derived, and micro-founded.[6] In stochastic derivations, effort is a noisy contributor to some output and the outcome of the contest is determined by a comparison of the outputs of the players. Axiomatic derivations link combinations of axioms to functional forms. In optimal design derivations, a designer with specific objectives about effort or other variables designs the contest, and the functional form is then a result of such a design. Micro-founded derivations derive contest functions by characterizing environments in which they naturally emerge as win probabilities of the contestants (e.g. incomplete information, search-based and Bayesian foundations).

Another strength of the ratio form is that several models using it have produced results that have been empirically confirmed. A first example concerns 'strategic reciprocality'.[7] To describe this phenomenon, it is necessary to introduce some definitions. A party's effort is called *provocative* when a marginal increase in her effort leads to an increase in her opponent's effort. A party's effort is called *deterring* when a marginal increase in her effort leads to a decrease in her opponent's effort. The *favorite* is the party with a greater than 50 percent probability of winning and the *underdog* is the party with a less than 50 percent probability of winning. Strategic reciprocality means that at the (Nash) equilibrium one party's effort is provocative and one party's effort is deterring. The models using the ratio form lead to such a result: the effort of the favored party is deterring and the effort of the underdog is provocative. In other words: the underdog will spend less when the favored party increases his effort and the favored party will spend more when the underdog increases his effort. This can be explained intuitively. When the favored party increases his effort, the case becomes (even) less close. It becomes less worthwhile for the underdog to spend more. When the underdog increases his effort, the case becomes a closer one. It becomes more worthwhile for the favorite to spend more. Sheperd (1999) has made an empirical study of the economics of pretrial discovery.[8,9] His findings are in accordance with strategic reciprocality. The author examined 369 U.S. federal cases in which the attorneys of *both* sides provided information about the number of days they devoted to seeking discovery.[10] Further information was available through court docket sheets and written questionnaires. Sheperd finds that plaintiffs and defendants behave very differently when conducting discovery. When the plaintiff engages in excessive discovery,[11] the defendant retaliates. The plaintiff on the contrary retreats when the defendant engages in excessive discovery.[12,13,14]

A second result that has been empirically validated concerns the influence of an increase in the stakes on the expenditures of the parties. In theoretical models that use the ratio form, an increase in the stakes induces both parties to increase their effort since the marginal value of effort rises. Clearly, $aF(1 - F)J$ increases with J. Empirical studies have indeed found a strong correlation between the stakes and the efforts of litigants. Kakalik et al. (1998) find that 'higher stakes are associated with significantly higher total lawyer work hours, significantly higher lawyer work hours on discovery, and significantly longer time to disposition'. More exactly, 'median total lawyer work hours were more than two and a half times larger for cases with monetary stakes over $500,000 than for cases with monetary stakes of $500,000 or less, while mean total lawyer work hours were almost four times larger'.[15] Willging et al. (1998) find that 'the size of the monetary stakes in the case had the strongest relationship to total litigation costs of any of the characteristics we studied.'[16]

Third, in its simplest version ($P(X,Y) = \frac{X}{X+Y}$), the model predicts that each party spends one fourth of the amount at stake in litigation expenditures. Also in the more complex case of $P(X,Y) = \frac{FX}{FX + (1-F)Y}$, each party spends approximately one fourth of the amount at stake if the case is a close one (F≈1/2). In an experimental study, Eastman and Viswanath (2003) analyze the litigation expenditure decisions of parties in a setting which allows litigants to believe that they can outsmart (or be outsmarted by) the other litigant in making spending decisions.[17] Litigants were told that their probability of victory was equal to the ratio of their effective litigation spending to that of the other side. The instructions explained that effective litigation spending could be equal to actual dollars spent, but could also be higher or lower than actual spending. The litigants were told that the effectiveness of their spending would be determined based on an outside evaluation. The case involves a car accident with stipulated damages of $100,000. Litigants were given the option of spending on several categories (e.g. legal research, hiring a detective etc.). They were not given the opportunity to settle the case. The authors find that the respondents spent an average of $30,000, which is relatively close to and statistically not different from the prediction of rational choice theory ($25,000).

Fourth, the model predicts that the parties will spend the same amount (no matter how low or high the quality of the case). This finds some confirmation in the same experimental study of Eastman and Viswanath (2003).[18] In most cases, the parties spent a similar amount.

3.2   Weaknesses

We have seen that the ratio form can be derived in several ways (see 3.1). However, other functional forms can also be derived in different ways: the logit function and the probit function. These three functions differ in their assumptions on the distributions of the error terms. In the Tullock model the error terms have an inverse exponential distribution, in the logit model they are extreme value distributed and in the probit model they are normally distributed. Empirical tests have not yet been successful in showing which model best captures the characteristics of a particular contest and gives the most accurate predictions.[19]

Some predictions of the ratio form have not been confirmed. For example, the model predicts that the expenditures of litigants increase *linearly* with the amount at stake. However, empirical research by Kakalik et al. (1984) found that the expenditures of the parties do not rise in proportion to the amount awarded, but rather concavely.[20] This cannot be seen as a fundamental flaw of the ratio form. If we would introduce fixed costs on top of variable costs in the basic model, then the expenditures would not rise linearly with the amount at stake anymore.

Some other criticisms do not explicitly concern the type of function that is used for the plaintiff's probability of victory, but rather the solution concept that is employed. Most articles rely on the Nash-Cournot protocol: the parties choose their expenditures in ignorance of the opponent's simultaneous choice. However, social interactions are usually too complex to be captured by any simple model. In some contexts, other solution concepts may be more satisfactory. For example, under the Stackelberg solution concept, one side commits to a level of effort, to which the other side then makes an optimizing response. Using this solution concept, Hirshleifer and Osborne (2001) find some interesting differences with the model that relies on the Nash-Cournot protocol: the litigation efforts of the parties are almost always unequal and the side with the better case tends to fight harder. Outcomes tilt disproportionally in favor of the side with the more meritorious case.[21]

4. CONCLUSION

Specific litigation success functions can be helpful in analyzing the consequences of legal rules. The function most intensively used in the literature, the ratio form, has strong theoretical underpinnings and leads to results which have been empirically validated. However, more theoretical and empirical research is necessary to determine whether other functional forms better capture the expenditure decisions for some types of disputes.

NOTES

1. See Jack Hirshleifer and Evan Osborne, Truth, Effort and the Legal Battle, 108 *Public Choice*, 169–95 (2001).
2. See e.g., Avery W. Katz, Judicial Decisionmaking and Litigation Expenditure, 8 *International Review of Law and Economics*, 127–43 (1988).

3. Francesco Parisi, Rent-Seeking Through Litigation: Adversarial and Inquisitorial Systems Compared, 22 *International Review of Law and Economics*, 193–216 (2002).
4. Luke M. Froeb and Bruce H. Kobayashi, Evidence Production in Adversarial vs. Inquisitorial Regimes, 70 *Economic Letters*, 267–72 (2001).
5. Maurice A. Adams, *Civil Procedure in the USA and Civil Law Countries*, in The New Palgrave Dictionary of Economics and the Law (Peter Newman ed., 1998).
6. See e.g., Hao Jia, Stergios Skaperdas and Samarth Vaidya, Contest Functions: Theoretical Foundations and Issues in Estimation, 31, *International Journal of Industrial Organization*, 195–306 (2013).
7. Katz, supra note 3.
8. George B. Sheperd, An empirical study of the economics of pretrial discovery, 19 *International Review of Law and Economics*, 245–63 (1999). Sheperd uses data from a survey that researchers at Columbia University conducted in 1962 and 1963 to assess the consequences of the discovery provisions in the Federal Rules of Civil Procedure. The author argues that the data are still relevant despite their age (over 40 years). This is because the discovery rules have not changed substantially after the survey. Although approximately one third of the states introduced a requirement of automatic disclosure, discovery not within the scope of automatic disclosure is still subject to the 'old' rules. Moreover, about two thirds of states still follow the system without automatic disclosure.
9. During pretrial discovery, the parties can force each other to disclose documents and other evidence relevant for the case.
10. With exclusion of the days the litigant devoted to responding to the requests of the other party.
11. Excessive according to the defendant.
12. Excessive according to the plaintiff.
13. See Sheperd, supra note 2, at 260. Sheperd also looks at 'normal' (contrary to excessive) discovery behavior: plaintiffs choose an amount of discovery that reflects the case's underlying fundamentals, like the amount at stake or the number of factual issues. They do not raise their level of discovery when the defendant increases his discovery effort. The defendant however does not look at the fundamentals of the case, but rather mimics the plaintiff: when the plaintiff chooses one unit of discovery, he chooses one unit of discovery himself.
14. Note that the result of Sheperd implies that discovery may produce efficiency and justice since the plaintiff bases his discovery amount on the fundamentals of the case. At the same time, the fact that the defendant behaves strategically without looking at the fundamentals of the case directly leads to social waste and injustice. See Sheperd, supra note 2, at 263.
15. James S. Kakalik, Deborah R. Hensler, Daniel McCaffrey, Marian Oshiro, Nicholas M. Pace and Mary E. Vaiana, Discovery Management: Further Analysis of the Civil Justice Reform Act Evaluation Data, 39 B.C.L. REV., pp. 613 and 648 (1998).
16. Thomas E. Willging, Donna Stienstra, John Shapard, and Dean Miletich, An Empirical Study of Discovery and Disclosure Practice Under the 1993 Federal Rule Amendments, 39 B.C.L. REV, 532 (1998).
17. Wayne Eastman and P.V. Viswanath, Repeated Interaction, Deep Pockets and Litigation Spending, working paper (2003), available at http://webpage.pace.edu/pviswanath/research/papers/litigation.pdf.
18. Eastman and Viswanath, supra note 18.
19. Jia, Skaperdas and Vaidya, supra note 7.
20. James S. Kakalik E.A., Variation in Asbestos Litigation Compensation and Expenses (1984).
21. Hirshleifer and Osborne, supra note 1.

9. The optimal amount of distorted testimony when the arbiter can and cannot commit*

Winand Emons and Claude Fluet

1 INTRODUCTION

How much testimony should an arbiter require when he knows that the parties to the conflict spend considerable resources to misrepresent evidence in their favor? When he hears no witnesses, no resources are wasted on fabricating evidence, yet the judge's adjudication will be erroneous, leading to a social loss from inaccurate decisions. If parties testify, the decision will be more accurate, yet resources are wasted on fabricating evidence. Requiring, for example, testimony from two parties rather than one will lead to a duplication of the costs to produce misleading information. The purpose of this chapter is to analyze this trade-off between procedural costs and the benefits of truth-finding.

An arbiter has to decide on an issue which we take to be a real number; for example, the adjudicated value is the damages that one party owes to the other. The defendant wants the damages to be small whereas the plaintiff wants them to be large. The parties thus have conflicting interests. The arbiter can decide the case solely on the basis of his priors. Alternatively, he can ask for further evidence from the two parties to the conflict.

Both parties know the actual realization of the damages. Presenting evidence involves a fixed cost. Moreover, they can boost the evidence in either direction. Distorting the evidence is, however, costly. The further a party moves away from the truth, the higher the cost; for example, expert witnesses charge more the more they distort the truth. The parties have different abilities to falsify.

We study the inquisitorial procedure where the arbiter decides about the amount of testimony.[1] The arbiter first announces whether he wants to hear none, one, or both parties. When he can commit, he announces an adjudication rule which maps the parties' reports into an adjudicated value. For simplicity, we take this adjudication function to be linear. When he cannot commit, he adjudicates in a sequentially rational fashion after he has heard the testimony. The arbiter minimizes the sum from the loss of inaccurate adjudication plus the weighted parties' submission costs.

He thus trades-off the social benefits of truth-finding against the cost of obtaining evidence.

We first look at the case where the arbiter can commit to an adjudication function. When he hears no party, he adjudicates the prior mean. When he decides to hear the parties, the adjudicated value is a weighted average of the true value and the mean. The more weight he gives to the parties' submission costs, the more the adjudicated value is biased towards the mean. The arbiter commits ex ante not to give too much weight to the evidence presented by the parties, thereby inducing them not to boost the evidence excessively.

When the arbiter hears only one party, this party lies more than his extent of lying when both parties submit. When only one party presents evidence, the arbiter gives more weight to the party's submission, thereby inducing him to falsify more. Accordingly, confronting the parties in adversarial hearings induces either of them to distort the evidence less than when only one party is heard. Yet when both parties are heard, both are involved in boosting the evidence.

The optimal number of parties to submit evidence depends on the fixed submission cost and the weight given to the cost of obtaining evidence. When the fixed cost of presenting evidence and the weight given to submission costs are small, the arbiter hears both parties. For intermediate values he goes for one party, and for large values he hears no party at all. Accordingly, even when the cost of obtaining evidence is accounted for, it may still be optimal to hear both parties: the duplication of the fixed submission costs is more than compensated by the lower cost of boosted evidence.

The parties' submissions are monotone in the true value at stake. Therefore, the arbiter can ex post infer the true value. By the choice of the adjudication function he can, however, commit not to adjudicate the true value. This implies a loss from inaccurate adjudication. The arbiter is thus tempted to renege ex post on the adjudication function to minimize the loss from inaccurate adjudication.

In a second step we look, therefore, at the scenario where the adjudicator can no longer ex ante commit to adjudication schemes. If the parties' statements reveal the truth, the arbiter will ex post adjudicate the true value. More weight is therefore now given to the parties' presentations than in the commitment case. This implies that the parties will boost the evidence more. Roughly speaking, in the no commitment scenario the arbiter can give either "full weight" to the parties' evidence or no weight at all by not listening to them in the first place. This in turn implies that it becomes more likely that the arbiter doesn't require any evidence at all from the two parties.

We thus develop a simple framework which allows us to determine when an arbiter should hear two, one, or no party at all. The lower the fixed costs of making a presentation and the less the arbiter weighs the submission costs, the more parties should be heard in the proceedings. The ability to commit to an adjudication scheme turns out to be crucial. The inability to commit makes it more likely that the arbiter hears no party at all and adjudicates solely on the basis of his priors. If it is optimal to receive evidence, the inability to commit also makes it more likely that the two parties will be heard rather than a single one.

It is standard in the literature to view accuracy in adjudication and procedural economy as the objectives at which legal procedures should aim. Adversarial systems of discovery clearly motivate parties to provide evidence. Nevertheless, they are often criticized for yielding excessive "influence" expenditures in the sense of Milgrom (1988): they lead to unnecessary duplication and costly overproduction of misleading information. Tullock (1975, 1980) provides a well-known statement of this opinion. Our contribution is to tackle the cost/accuracy trade-off on the basis of the so-called "costly state falsification" approach; see Lacker and Weinberg (1989), Maggi and Rodríguez-Clare (1995), Crocker and Morgan (1998), and Kartik (2009).[2]

One approach to court decision making views the trial outcome as an exogenous function of the litigants' levels of effort or expenditure. See Cooter and Rubinfeld (1989) for a review of the earlier literature; other examples include Bernardo, Talley, and Welch (2000), Farmer and Pecorino (1999), Katz (1988), and Parisi (2002). In these papers adjudication is a zero-one variable where a party either wins or loses. Parties engage in a rent-seeking game, leading to excessive expenditures. Our approach differs in that the arbiter's adjudication function is not specified exogenously; we derive the optimal adjudication function. In our model, the outcome is based on the evidence provided by the parties, rather than on unobservable effort. Moreover, in our set-up the arbiter understands the parties' incentives to "falsify" the submitted evidence.

Our approach also differs from other expenditure-based models which consider guilty or innocent defendants; see, for example, Rubinfeld and Sappington (1987). A defendant's type is private information. The defendant's level of effort determines the probability that he will be found innocent. This probability function is exogenously given and differs between types. The arbiter minimizes the sum of the losses from type 1 and type 2 errors plus the defendant's expected effort cost with respect to the standard of proof and the penalty for conviction. When effort is not observable, both types of defendant provide effort, yet the innocent defendant more than the guilty one. The major difference to our set-up is that the judge faces just one defendant who can be of two types. Rubinfeld and Sappington do not address the question of how many witnesses should be heard.

We also differ from another well-known strand of literature in which parties cannot falsify the verifiable evidence as such, but are able to misrepresent it by disclosing only what they see fit; see Sobel (1985), Milgrom and Roberts (1986), and Shin (1998). Finally, our chapter is related to the literature comparing adversarial with inquisitorial procedures of truth-finding; see Shin (1998), Dewatripont and Tirole (1999), and Palumbo (2001). In the inquisitorial system a neutral investigator searches for evidence, in the adversarial system the parties to the conflict present the evidence. The last two papers compare the two procedures in terms of the costs to motivate agents to gather and produce verifiable information. By contrast, we look at the question how much testimony from interested parties should be used. Our judge or arbiter is therefore an active agent since he directs how the procedure will evolve.[3]

Closest to the chapter at hand are our papers Emons and Fluet (2009 and 2011). In Emons and Fluet (2009) we also study the inquisitorial procedure. There the arbiter cannot commit to an adjudication scheme; he has to adjudicate in a sequentially rational fashion. Furthermore, there agents have identical falsification costs. In Emons and Fluet (2011) we focus on the adversarial procedure where the parties decide whether or not to testify; moreover, in this paper we compare the efficiency properties of the adversarial and the inquisitorial procedures.

The chapter is organized as follows. In the next section we describe our basic set-up. The following two sections derive the optimal procedures for the case where the judge can commit to an adjudication scheme. In the subsequent section we look at the case where the judge cannot commit. Section 6 concludes.

2   THE MODEL

The issue to be settled is the value of $x \in \mathbb{R}$. The adjudicator – regulatory commission, court, etc – has prior beliefs represented by the density $f(x)$ with full support over the real line and mean μ. Units are normalized so that the variance equals unity.[4] The arbiter's initial beliefs may be taken as being shaped from information publicly available at the beginning of the proceedings.

The arbiter can adjudicate solely on the basis of his priors. Alternatively, he can require further evidence to be submitted from perfectly informed but self-interested actors denoted A and B. Party A would like the adjudicated value of x to be large while party B would like it to be small. For example, the adjudicated value may be the damages that should be paid to the plaintiff A by the defendant B; in a divorce case it may be the amount of support A should get from B; in regulatory hearings about the rental charge for a local loop the incumbent wants the charge to be high whereas the entrant wants it to be low.

Submissions by the parties are costly. A submission is of the form "the value of the quantity at issue is x_i", $i = A, B$. It should be thought of as a story or argument rendering x_i plausible, together with the supporting documents, witnesses, etc. The cost of a presentation is

$$c_i(x_i, x) = \gamma + \frac{1}{2}\gamma_i(x_i - x)^2, \quad i = A, B,$$

where $\gamma \geq 0$ and $\gamma_i > 0$. x is the actual value, which is observed by the party, and x_i is the testimony or the statement submitted.

A distorting presentation is more costly than simply reporting the naked truth as it involves more fabrication. We take a quadratic function to capture the idea that the cost of misrepresenting the evidence increases at an increasing rate the further one moves away from the truth: it becomes more difficult to produce the corresponding documents or experts charge more the more they distort the truth.[5]

The parties' capacity to falsify – their "credibility" – is common knowledge. Falsification costs may differ between the parties, but for simplicity the cost of reporting the true state of the world, γ, is the same. Total submission cost is $C = 0$ if no evidence is required from the parties. It is $C = c_i$ if only party i, $i = A, B$, submits. Otherwise it is $C = c_A + c_B$.

The arbiter is concerned about the loss from inaccuracy in adjudication and the parties' submission costs. Accordingly, there is a potential trade-off between procedural costs and the social benefits of correct adjudication. From the arbiter's perspective, the total social loss is

$$L = l + \theta C,$$

where l is the loss from inaccurate adjudication or "error costs", C is total submission costs, and $\theta \geq 0$ is the rate at which the arbiter is willing to trade-off submission costs against accuracy. If, for example, $\theta = 0$, accuracy is his only concern; for $\theta > 0$, the arbiter is willing to sacrifice some accuracy to save on submission costs.

Let $\hat{x}$ denote the arbiter's decision. The loss from inaccurate adjudication is

$$l(\hat{x}, x) = \frac{1}{2}(\hat{x} - x)^2.$$

If the true value is adjudicated, error costs are zero. The more the decision errs in either direction, the higher the losses from inaccurate adjudication. Losses increase at an increasing rate the further one moves away from the truth.

At the start of the proceedings, the arbiter determines a procedure. This consists of two elements: first, the procedure specifies which party, if any, is required to submit evidence; secondly, it specifies how the arbiter's decision will depend on the evidence submitted. We denote the first part by the decision $d \in \{N, S, J\}$ where N stands for no party being heard, S for only a single party being heard (this would specify which one), and J for joint simultaneous submissions.

The second element of the procedure is an adjudication rule $\hat{x}(\cdot)$ determining $\hat{x}$ as a function of the evidence submitted. For simplicity we focus on linear adjudication functions. When both parties are heard, i.e., $d = J$, the adjudicated $\hat{x}$ is given by

$$\hat{x} = ax_A + bx_B + c.$$

Here the arbiter chooses a, b, and c so as to minimize the expected value of the social loss L. If the arbiter only hears, say, party B, i.e., in procedure S, $\hat{x} = bx_B + c$. For $d = N$, $\hat{x} = \mu$. The linear scheme allows us to easily compare the different scenarios of listening to both, to only one, and to no party.

The arbiter's decision implies a gain of $\hat{x}$ for party A and a loss of $\hat{x}$ for party B. The parties' payoffs as a function of the true state of the world x, of their presentations x_A and x_B, if any, and of the adjudicated $\hat{x}$ are therefore

$$\pi_A(\hat{x}, x_A, x) = \hat{x} - c_A(x_A, x) \quad \text{and}$$
$$\pi_B(\hat{x}, x_B, x) = -\hat{x} - c_B(x_B, x).$$

To summarize, the sequencing is as follows: (i) the arbiter announces a procedure; (ii) parties submit a presentation if asked to do so; (iii) the quantity at issue is adjudicated according to the announced adjudication function. In making their presentation, the parties seek to maximize their payoffs π_A and π_B. In choosing the procedure, the arbiter seeks to minimize the expected loss $E(L) := \overline{L}$. We first solve for the best adjudication functions under each procedure.

3   ADJUDICATION RULES

Both Parties Submit

With both parties submitting evidence, i.e., $d = J$, the expected loss is

$$\overline{L}_J = E\{l(\hat{x}(x_A, x_B), x) + \theta[c_A(x_A, x) + c_B(x_B, x)]\}.$$

The arbiter chooses the adjudication rule $\hat{x}(\cdot, \cdot)$ so as to minimize $\overline{l}_J$ subject to the incentive constraints

$$x_A(x) = \arg\max_{x_A} \hat{x}(x_A, x_B(x)) - c_A(x_A, x) \quad \text{and}$$
$$x_B(x) = \arg\max_{x_B} - \hat{x}(x_A(x), x_B) - c_B(x_B, x).$$

These constraints describe the Nash equilibrium of the parties' submission game. Since the agents' payoff functions are concave in their testimony, the equilibrium reports are given by the first-order conditions

$$x_A = x + \frac{a}{\gamma_A} \quad \text{and} \quad x_B = x - \frac{b}{\gamma_B}. \tag{9.1}$$

Substitution yields

$$\overline{L}_J = E\left\{\frac{1}{2}\left[a\left(x + \frac{a}{\gamma_A}\right) + b\left(x - \frac{b}{\gamma_B}\right) + c - x\right]^2\right\} + \theta\left[2\gamma + \frac{a^2}{2\gamma_A} + \frac{b^2}{2\gamma_B}\right].$$

The first term in the expression is the expected error cost $\overline{l}_J$. Minimizing this term with respect to c yields

$$c = \frac{b^2}{\gamma_B} - \frac{a^2}{\gamma_A} - \mu(a + b - 1).$$

Substituting in $\overline{l}_J$ and recalling the unit variance assumption, we get

$$\overline{L}_J = \frac{1}{2}(a + b - 1)^2 + \theta\left[2\gamma + \frac{a^2}{2\gamma_A} + \frac{b^2}{2\gamma_B}\right].$$

Minimizing with respect to a and b, we finally obtain

$$a = \frac{\gamma_A}{\gamma_A + \gamma_B + \theta} \quad \text{and} \tag{9.2}$$

$$b = \frac{\gamma_B}{\gamma_A + \gamma_B + \theta}. \tag{9.3}$$

The parameters describe the weight given to the parties' reports. The weights depend on the parties' relative credibility and on the arbiter's concern for submission costs. If, say, party A has a lower cost of lying than party B, i.e., $\gamma_A < \gamma_B$, the arbiter gives less importance to A's rather than B's report. Moreover, the weights sum to less than unity and the more the arbiter cares about submission costs, the less weight he gives to both parties' reports. The weights are such that in equilibrium the extent of lying is the same for both parties, i.e., $|x_i - x| = 1/(\gamma_A + \gamma_B + \theta), i = A, B$.

The adjudicated value is

$$\hat{x} = ax_A + bx_B + c = \left(\frac{\theta}{\gamma_A + \gamma_B + \theta}\right)\mu + \left(\frac{\gamma_A + \gamma_B}{\gamma_A + \gamma_B + \theta}\right)x. \tag{9.4}$$

This is the weighted average of the mean μ and the true value x. Thus, $\hat{x}$ is biased towards the prior mean. Perfect accuracy in adjudication only obtains when the arbiter does not care about submission costs, i.e., $\lim_{\theta \to 0}\hat{x} = x$. Conversely, if he cares a lot about submission costs, $\hat{x}$ approaches the prior mean, i.e., $\lim_{\theta \to \infty}\hat{x} = \mu$. The extent of lying is maximal when perfect accuracy obtains and minimal when the mean is adjudicated, i.e., $\lim_{\theta \to 0}|x_i - x| = 1/(\gamma_A + \gamma_B)$ and $\lim_{\theta \to \infty}|x_i - x| = 0, i = A, B$.[6]

Expected error costs and total submission costs are

$$\bar{l}_J = \frac{\theta^2}{2(\gamma_A + \gamma_B + \theta)^2} \text{ and}$$

$$C_J = 2\gamma + \frac{\gamma_A + \gamma_B}{2(\gamma_A + \gamma_B + \theta)^2}.$$

Society's total loss is

$$\bar{l}_J = \bar{l}_J + \theta C_J = \frac{\theta}{2(\gamma_A + \gamma_B + \theta)} + 2\theta\gamma. \tag{9.5}$$

Only One Party Submits

Under procedure $d = S$ only one party is heard. Assume B is more credible, i.e., $\gamma_A < \gamma_B$, and he is therefore the party required to submit. The adjudication function is now $\hat{x} = bx_B + c$. Minimizing $\bar{L}_S$ with respect to b and c subject to the constraint that x_B maximizes B's payoff yields

$$b = \frac{\gamma_B}{\gamma_B + \theta}, \quad c = \frac{b^2}{\gamma_B} - \mu(b - 1),$$

and the adjudicated value is

$$\hat{x} = bx_B + c = \frac{\gamma_B}{\gamma_B + \theta} x + \frac{\theta}{\gamma_B + \theta} \mu. \tag{9.6}$$

Expected error costs and submission costs are

$$\bar{l}_S = \frac{\theta^2}{2(\gamma_B + \theta)^2} \quad \text{and}$$

$$C_S = \gamma + \frac{\gamma_B}{2(\gamma_B + \theta)^2}.$$

The total expected loss is

$$\bar{L}_S = \bar{l}_S + \theta C_S = \frac{\theta}{2(\gamma_B + \theta)} + \theta\gamma. \tag{9.7}$$

The extent of lying by B is now $|x_B - x| = 1/(\gamma_B + \theta)$. This is greater than the amount of lying by B when both parties are heard. The reason is that greater weight is now given to the party's submission, thereby inducing him to falsify more. Thus, confronting the parties induces either of them to distort the evidence less than when only one testimony is heard. Yet when both parties are heard, both are involved in boosting the evidence.

No Party Submits

Under procedure $d = N$, no party testifies and submission costs are therefore zero. The arbiter then minimizes expected error costs solely on the basis of the priors $f(\cdot)$, implying $\hat{x} = \mu$. The expected total loss is $\bar{L}_N = 1/2$, i.e., half the variance of x.

4   OPTIMAL PROCEDURE

Let us now determine the optimal number of parties to submit evidence. The arbiter chooses whether no party N, only party B under procedure S, or both parties J are required to submit evidence so as to minimize the expected loss. We assume $\gamma_A < \gamma_B$ throughout.

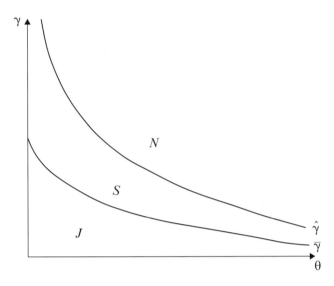

Figure 9.1   Optimal procedures in the commitment case

Proposition 1: *i) If* $\gamma \leq \gamma_A/(2(\gamma_B + \theta)(\gamma_A + \gamma_B + \theta)): = \bar{\gamma}$, *the judge requires joint submission J and adjudicates according to (9.4);*
ii) If $\bar{\gamma} < \gamma \leq \gamma_B/(2\theta(\gamma_B + \theta)):=\hat{\gamma}$, *single submission S by party B is optimal and the judge adjudicates according to (9.6);*
iii) If $\gamma > \hat{\gamma}$, *no submission N minimizes the expected social loss and* $\dot{x} = \mu$.

The result follows because $\bar{L}_J \leq \bar{L}_S$ for $\gamma \leq \bar{\gamma}$ and $\bar{L}_S \leq \bar{L}_N$ for $\gamma \leq \hat{\gamma}$. Moreover, since only the more credible party B is heard under procedure S, $\bar{\gamma} < \hat{\gamma}$ so that there is never a direct switch from J to N.

Figure 9.1 shows in the (γ, θ) plane the regions where the arbiter requires both, only one, or no party to submit evidence. If, for example, $\gamma = 0$ so that non-falsified submissions generate no costs, it is optimal to have both parties submit, irrespective of their credibility and irrespective of θ. The intuition is straightforward. Comparing (9.4) and (9.6), it is readily seen that the arbiter puts less weight on his priors under joint submissions than when only a single, albeit the most credible party, submits. The expected error cost is accordingly smaller under joint submissions. Furthermore, when $\gamma = 0$, total submission costs are also smaller under joint submissions since each party's testimony is accorded an appropriately small weight. Put differently, competition between advocates reduces falsification because each advocate has less influence on the outcome.

When $\gamma > 0$, duplication imposes a dead weight loss. However, when

γ is not too large, it remains optimal to hear both parties. Although we may now have $C_J > C_S$, the fact that $\bar{l}_J < \bar{l}_S$ may more than compensate. Finally, requiring parties to submit evidence is never optimal if γ is sufficiently large and $\theta > 0$. The adjudicated value then rests only on priors, as the submission costs of either J or S exceed the error cost of N.

Note that the threshold $\bar{\gamma}$ is increasing in γ_A, party A's credibility. The more the parties are alike in terms of credibility (recall that $\gamma_A < \gamma_B$), the larger the range over which J is better than S. A larger γ_A lowers the error costs and thus the social loss from joint submission, making J more attractive relative to S, the value of which is independent of γ_A.

5 NO COMMITMENT

So far we have assumed that once a procedure has been chosen the arbiter can commit to the announced adjudication rule. However, it is clear that the true x can be inferred from the evidence submitted under either procedure J or S. An arbiter seeking to minimize error and submission costs would then be tempted to renege on the announced adjudication rule. Ex post, submission costs are sunk and the sequentially optimal action, from the arbiter's point of view, is to adjudicate $\hat{x} = x$.[7]

The inability to commit restricts the set of feasible adjudication rules. A rule must now be part of an equilibrium where, at the last stage of the game the arbiter adjudicates sequentially rationally after updating his beliefs. Under procedure J, the adjudication function must satisfy

$$\hat{x}(x_A, x_B) = \arg\min_{\hat{x}} \left[\frac{1}{2}(\hat{x} - x)^2 | x_A, x_B \right] = E[x | x_A, x_B].$$

If reports are monotone in the true x, the latter can be inferred from any party's action, i.e., along the equilibrium path the posterior distribution is degenerate and we have

$$\hat{x}[x_A(x), x_B(x)] \equiv x \qquad (9.8)$$

Since error costs will be zero, the best adjudication rule under procedure J is the one which minimizes total submission costs subject to (9.8). We now have

$$\hat{x}(x_A, x_B) = ax_A + bx_B + c$$

$$= a\left(x + \frac{a}{\gamma_A}\right) + b\left(x - \frac{b}{\gamma_B}\right) + c \equiv x,$$

where we substituted for x_A and x_B from the equilibrium conditions (9.1) and imposed constraint (9.8). This implies

$$a + b = 1 \quad \text{and} \quad c = \frac{b}{\gamma_B} - \frac{a}{\gamma_A}.$$

These constraints reflect the fact that the adjudication rule (through the parameters a, b, and c) can be picked only to the extent that the arbiter's strategy, at the last stage of the game, is part of a sequential equilibrium. Note that a and b now sum to unity, by contrast with the commitment case.[8]

Choosing a and b to minimize total submission costs, subject to the foregoing constraints, now yields

$$a = \frac{\gamma_A}{\gamma_A + \gamma_B} \quad \text{and} \tag{9.9}$$

$$b = \frac{\gamma_B}{\gamma_A + \gamma_B}. \tag{9.10}$$

Compared to the specification (9.2) and (9.3) for the commitment case, it is readily seen that the arbiter gives more weight to each party's submission, thereby inducing more falsification. A similar argument for procedure S, under which only party B is heard, yields

$$b = 1 \quad \text{and} \quad c = \frac{b}{\gamma_B}.$$

Under procedure J or S the total loss is now (using the superscript n to denote non commitment):

$$\bar{L}_J^n = \theta C_J^n = \theta \left(2\gamma + \frac{1}{2(\gamma_A + \gamma_B)} \right) \quad \text{and} \tag{9.11}$$

$$\bar{L}_S^n = \theta C_S^n = \theta \left(\gamma + \frac{1}{2\gamma_B} \right). \tag{9.12}$$

Under the procedure N the loss is of course the same as before.

The inability to commit on the part of the arbiter influences the choice of procedure. Whenever he receives evidence, the arbiter is now unable to put any weight on his priors, i.e., testimony has a larger effect on his ruling than in the commitment case. Therefore, the parties have a stronger incentive to falsify. The consequence, as shown in the following proposition, is that the arbiter will now be more inclined to choose procedure N rather than J or S and procedure J rather than S.

Proposition 2:   *Under no commitment $\hat{x} = x$ if evidence is submitted; otherwise, $\hat{x} = \mu$. Let $\hat{\theta} = \gamma_B(\gamma_A + \gamma_B)/(2\gamma_A + \gamma_B)$.*
(i) For $\theta \le \hat{\theta}$, the optimal procedure is J if $\gamma \le \overline{\gamma}^n$, S if $\overline{\gamma}^n < \gamma \le \hat{\gamma}^n$, and N otherwise, where

$$\overline{\gamma}^n := \frac{\gamma_A}{2\gamma_B(\gamma_A + \gamma_B)} < \frac{\gamma_B - \theta}{2\theta\gamma_B} =: \hat{\gamma}^n.$$

(ii) For $\theta > \hat{\theta}$, the optimal procedure is J if $\gamma \le \tilde{\gamma}^n$ and N otherwise, where

$$\tilde{\gamma}^n := \frac{\gamma_A + \gamma_B - \theta}{4\theta(\gamma_A + \gamma_B)} < \overline{\gamma}^n.$$

This result follows because $\overline{L}_J^n < \overline{L}_S^n$ for $\gamma \le \overline{\gamma}^n$. For $\theta \le \hat{\theta}$, $\overline{L}_S^n \le 1/2$ for $\gamma \le \hat{\gamma}^n$. For $\theta > \hat{\theta}$, $1/2 < \overline{L}_J^n$ for $\gamma > \tilde{\gamma}^n$.

With commitment hearing both parties is optimal when γ is sufficiently small, independently of θ. Without commitment, this is no longer true. See Figure 9.2. It is now better not to receive any submission at all if $\theta > \gamma_A + \gamma_B$. Thus, no commitment implies a larger parameter region for

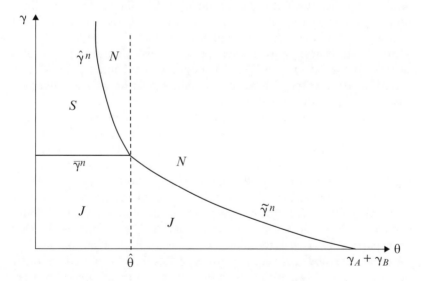

Figure 9.2   Optimal procedures in the no commitment case

which the parties should not be heard. In the commitment case a large θ means that the arbiter gives little weight to the agents' testimony. Without commitment the arbiter cannot commit to give little weight to the reports. He can only give full weight to the reports or no weight at all by choosing N in the first place.

Consider first the case where $\theta \leq \hat{\theta}$. The critical values of γ at which the procedure switches from J to S and from S to N differ from the commitment case. Specifically, for $\theta > 0$,

$$\bar{\gamma} < \bar{\gamma}^n < \hat{\gamma}^n < \hat{\gamma}.$$

Accordingly, $\bar{\gamma} < \bar{\gamma}^n$ implies procedure J is now preferred to S over a larger set of values. Without commitment perfect accuracy is attained under J and S. Under both procedures the amount of lying is independent of θ. Hence, $\bar{\gamma}^n$ is independent of θ. With commitment perfect accuracy also obtains for θ sufficiently small. Therefore, $\lim_{\theta \to 0} \bar{\gamma} = \bar{\gamma}^n$. Yet, $\bar{\gamma}$ decreases with θ. The higher θ, the more $\hat{x}$ under commitment is pushed towards the mean – less weight is given to the parties' submissions. There is no such effect under no commitment because the true x is always adjudicated.

Moreover, the region over which procedure S rather than N is used is smaller. Since under no commitment the amount of lying by B doesn't decrease with θ, the arbiter switches to N for lower values of θ. To put it differently, when θ is not too large, under no commitment it is less likely that only a single party will be heard; it is more likely that both parties will be heard or that no submissions will be required.

For $\theta > \hat{\theta}$, hearing only a single party is never desirable. The arbiter switches directly from J to N. S is dominated by either J or N. $\tilde{\gamma}^n$ is decreasing because the higher θ the more the arbiter weighs the submission costs in choosing the procedure.

To summarize: When the adjudicator cannot commit, he knows ex ante he will be giving too much weight to the parties' submissions, i.e., allow them to influence the adjudication too much. Thus, he knows they will invest "a lot" in falsifying. The only way out of this excessive falsifying may be to refuse to hear the parties at all. At other times, it is better to hear both parties even though only one should be heard under commitment. Under commitment, when the fixed submission cost becomes sufficiently large, it becomes more attractive to hear one rather than both parties. However, the more the decision is then pushed towards the mean, thereby reducing incentives to falsify. Without commitment perfect accuracy always obtains so that switching to a single party is less attractive.

6   CONCLUDING REMARKS

In this chapter we analyze a stylized model of the trade-off between accuracy in adjudication and misrepresentation costs under the inquisitorial procedure. We show that the cost of misrepresentation (net of fixed submission costs) is lower when both parties are heard than when only one party submits evidence: hearing both parties duplicates fixed submission costs but lowers misrepresentation costs. Accordingly, it is preferable to hear both parties when fixed costs are low. We, therefore, qualify Tullock's (1975) statement that the duplication of misrepresentation costs is necessarily inefficient.

We also point out the crucial role of commitment. When the judge cannot commit not to infer (and adjudicate) the truth from the parties' statements, it is more likely that he hears both or no party at all than if he can commit. The inability to commit, which is presumably more likely than commitment, makes it more attractive to hear two rather than one party.

A few qualifications and remarks are in order. Under commitment, the linear adjudication scheme allowed us to readily obtain our results. Nevertheless, relaxing this restriction will not change the qualitative nature of our results. The truly optimal adjudication rule is not linear and it will depend on the prior $f(x)$. Yet, the same qualitative results hold: if they are called to submit evidence, the parties always falsify; the procedure should switch from joint to single and to no submissions as the fixed cost of submitting gets larger.[9]

Under no commitment, once the procedure has been chosen, the arbiter becomes a player in the game. His adjudication strategy must then be part of a sequential (or perfect Bayesian) equilibrium. There are many such equilibria. Choosing the best adjudication "rule" amounts to picking the best equilibrium in terms of minimizing submission costs. In Emons and Fluet (2009) we show that the linear strategy described in the text does indeed characterize the best sequential equilibrium. Hence, in the no commitment case the linearity assumption plays no role.

Similarly, the quadratic cost functions allowed us to obtain closed form solutions. Our conjecture is that most of our results also hold under more general falsification cost functions.

Our results are driven by the fact that the arbiter can only adjudicate one value that one party loses and the other party gains. If we relax this adding-up constraint, the arbiter could obviously do better. The judge could use, for example, the following mechanism: if both parties make the same report, he adjudicates this value. If the parties report different values, the judge punishes both of them heavily for perjury.[10] In reality, however, perjury cases are very rare and there is plenty of evidence indicating that slanted testimony is endemic in courts.[11] Since perjury law seems to be ineffective, we didn't include this possibility in the adjudication function. Moreover, non-judicial proceedings—for example, regulatory hearings—usually have no such provisions.

NOTES

*   We thank Bruno Deffains, Oliver Fabel, Marie-Cécile Fagart, Christian Ghiglino, Gerd Mühlheusser, and Harris Schlesinger for helpful comments. The usual disclaimer applies.
1.   According to Jolowicz (2000, p. 220) under the inquisitorial system "it is for the judge to examine the witnesses, if any, it is for the judge to decide whether to summon the parties for interrogation and it is the judge who acts to obtain the assistance of an expert when required." Under the adversary system (Jolowicz, 2000, p. 28) "it is for the parties to determine not only the issues which the court is to decide, but also the material on which the decision will be based. The evidence presented to the court will be that which the parties choose to present and none other. The judge may not require that a particular witness be summoned to give evidence or that a particular document be produced; he may not even question the witnesses himself except for the purpose of clarifying some doubt as to the meaning of what a witness has said under examination by counsel."
2.   For example, Crocker and Morgan (1998) analyze the falsification of insurance claims. The agent is privately informed about the true value of the loss and is able to misrepresent this quantity at a cost.
3.   Yet another approach can be found in Froeb and Kobayashi (1996, 2001) and Daughety and Reinganum (2000) who model the adversarial provision of evidence as a game in which two parties engage in strategic sequential search.
4.   We assume full support over the real line in order to avoid boundary conditions. The probability of extreme values of x can be made, however, arbitrarily small.
5.   Using quadratic falsification costs is standard in the literature. Maggi and Rodríguez-Clare (1995) interpret γ_i as capturing the publicness of information. If $\gamma_i = 0$, falsification is costless, therefore, information is purely private. As γ_i increases, it becomes more costly to falsify information and for an arbitrarily large γ_i the public-information model obtains.
6.   In Parisi (2002) the judge decides what weight he will give to his own appointed experts (similar to our priors) and what weight he gives to the parties' testimonies. The greater the latter weight, the greater the incentives for the parties to engage in rent-seeking. The weight Parisi gives to the parties, testimony plays a similar role as does the weight given to x in (9.4).
7.   In Emons and Fluet (2009) we analyze yet another form of commitment. There the arbiter can commit not to read the testimonies with a certain probability. If he doesn't read the reports, he adjudicates the mean; if, however, he reads the testimonies, he adjudicates in a sequentially rational fashion.
8.   These parameters reflect how the arbiter interprets out-of-equilibrium moves. Substituting for c and b, the adjudicated value is

$$\hat{x} = a\left[x_A - \frac{a}{\gamma_A}\right] + (1 - a)\left[x_B + \frac{1 - a}{\gamma_B}\right].$$

Along the equilibrium path, the expressions in both square brackets equal x. If one party deviates from his equilibrium strategy, the expressions will differ and one will differ from the true x. Observing the discrepancy between the two expressions, the arbiter will not know which party deviated. Parameter a is the probability he ascribes to the possibility that A did not deviate (i.e., to the deviation arising from B). Hence, a is the weight given to party A's submission, duly corrected for the party's overstatement.

9. Using the revelation principle, the optimal scheme can be obtained by considering a direct truthful mechanism $\hat{x}(t_A, t_B), x_A(t_A), x_B(t_B)$ where t_A and t_B are the messages sent by the parties (messages differ from the costly submissions themselves).

10. See Demski and Sappington (1984) for an analysis of information extraction in a multiagent context.

11. For example, in a continuing scandal in New York City, police engaged in a pattern of perjury so common that they called it "testilying;" in impeachment proceedings former President Clinton admitted making misleading statements about his sexual conduct while steadfastly denying that he committed perjury. For more evidence on slanted testimony see Cooter and Emons (2003).

REFERENCES

A.E. Bernardo, E. Talley, and I. Welch. A Theory of Legal Presumptions, 16 *Journal of Law, Economics, and Organization*, 1–49, (2000).

R. Cooter and W. Emons Truth-Revealing Mechanisms for Courts, 159 *Journal of Institutional and Theoretical Economics*, 259–279, (2003).

R. Cooter and D. Rubinfeld Economic Analysis of Legal Disputes and their Resolution, 27 *Journal of Economic Literature*, 1067–1097, (1989).

K.J. Crocker and J. Morgan Is Honesty the Best Policy? Curtailing Insurance Fraud through Optimal Incentive Contracts, 106 *Journal of Political Economy*, 355–375, (1998).

A. F. Daughety and J. F. Reinganum On the Economics of Trials: Adversarial Process, Evidence, and Equilibrium Bias, 16 *Journal of Law, Economics, and Organization*, 365–394, (2000).

J.S. Demski, and D. Sappington Optimal Incentive Contracts with Multiple Agents, 33 *Journal of Economic Theory*, 152–171, (1984).

M. Dewatripont and J. Tirole Advocates, 107 *Journal of Political Economy*, 1–39, (1999).

W. Emons and C. Fluet Accuracy versus Falsification Costs: The Optimal Amount of Evidence under Different Procedures, 25 *Journal of Law, Economics, and Organization*, 134–156, (2009).

W. Emons and C. Fluet, Adversarial versus Inquisitorial Testimony, Discussion Paper, University of Bern, http://staff.vwi.unibe.ch/emons/downloads/emons_fluet.pdf, (2011).

A. Farmer and P. Pecorino Legal Expenditure as a Rent-Seeking Game, 100 *Public Choice*, 271–288, (1999).

L.M. Froeb and B.H. Kobayashi Naive, Biased, yet Bayesian: Can Juries Interpret Selectively Produced Evidence?, 12 *Journal of Law, Economics, and Organization*, 257–276, (1996).

L.M. Froeb and B.H. Kobayashi Evidence Production in Adversarial vs. Inquisitorial Regimes, 72 *Economics Letters*, 267–272, (2001).

J.A. Jolowicz *On Civil Procedure*. Cambridge: Cambridge University Press, (2000).

N. Kartik Strategic Communication with Lying Costs, 76 *Review of Economic Studies*, 1359–1395, (2009).

A. Katz Judicial Decisionmaking and Litigation Expenditure, 8 *International Review of Law and Economics*, 127–143, (1988).

J. Lacker and J. Weinberg Optimal Contracts under Costly State Falsification, 97 *Journal of Political Economy*, 1345–1363, (1989).

G. Maggi and A. Rodríguez-Clare Costly Distortion of Information in Agency Problems, 26 *Rand Journal of Economics*, 675–689, (1995).

P.R. Milgrom Employment Contracts, Influence Activities, and Efficient Organization Design, 96 *Journal of Political Economy*, 42–60, (1988).

P.R. Milgrom and J. Roberts Relying on the Information of Interested Parties, 17 *Rand Journal of Economics*, 18–32, (1986).

G. Palumbo Trial Procedures and Optimal Limits on Proof-Taking, 21 *International Review of Law and Economics*, 309–327, (2001).

F. Parisi Rent-seeking through Litigation: Adversarial and Inquisitorial Systems Compared, 22 *International Review of Law and Economics*, 193–216, (2002).

D.L. Rubinfeld and D.M. Sappington Efficient Awards and Standards of Proof in Judicial Proceedings, 18 *Rand Journal of Economics*, 308–315 (1987).

H.S. Shin Adversarial and Inquisitorial Procedures in Arbitration, 29 *Rand Journal of Economics*, 378–405, (1998).

J. Sobel Disclosure of Evidence and Resolution of Disputes: Who Should Bear the Burden of Proof?, in A. E. Roth, (ed.) (1985), *Game Theoretic Models of Bargaining*, Cambridge University Press, Cambridge, 341–361.

G. Tullock On the Efficient Organization of Trials, 28 *Kyklos*, 745–762, (1975).

G. Tullock, *Trials on Trials: The Pure Theory of Legal Procedure*, New York, Columbia University Press, (1980).

10. Do exclusionary rules convict the innocent?

Dhammika Dharmapala, Nuno Garoupa, and Richard McAdams

I. INTRODUCTION

In criminal jury trials, though relevant evidence is presumptively admitted, specific policies can compel exclusion. Some of these exclusionary rules are controversial constitutional interpretations, such as *Miranda*'s[1] exclusion of unwarned custodial confessions or *Mapp v. Ohio*'s[2] exclusion of evidence obtained from a search or seizure that violates the Fourth Amendment. Other exclusions have an older pedigree and a statutory basis, such as the rule against hearsay and restrictions on the use of prior crimes' evidence and statements made in discussions over a settlement or plea. To be sure, there is a stark difference in the rationales for these rules: hearsay and prior crimes evidence is said to be unreliable in ways that the jury will not fully appreciate and the evidence is therefore excluded in the name of accuracy. By contrast no one claims that the evidence obtained by unreasonable searches or seizures, nor statements made in negotiations between the parties, is unreliable. Here the purpose of its exclusion is to deter police from violating the Fourth Amendment and to facilitate pre-trial resolution. However, these differences do not matter for this chapter where we address the general topic of excluding factually relevant evidence, that is, the kind of evidence that would rationally influence the jury's verdict if it were admitted. We do not offer a comprehensive analysis of these exclusionary rules, but add to the existing literature by identifying a new domain for economic analysis, which is to analyze how juries respond to the existence of such a rule.

The conventional wisdom in criminal procedure scholarship assumes that the exclusion of evidence leaves juries to decide cases as if the excluded evidence never existed. Not hearing the excluded evidence, the jury knows neither of its existence nor content. Yet this analysis is incomplete. Even if the jury does not hear certain evidence, if the jury knows of the existence of the exclusionary rule it may be aware that there is some probability that relevant evidence was excluded in the present case. If the exclusions were equally likely to favor either side they might neutralize each other and have no net effect. For example, the exclusion of pre-trial settlement negotiations does not favor either party because the jury has no way of knowing which side conceded the most.

But the jury might know that some evidentiary exclusions are asymmetric: the criminal defendant can exclude the prosecutor's evidence obtained through governmental violations of the Fourth or Fifth Amendments (i.e. an illegal search, seizure, or interrogation), but a private defendant cannot violate those Amendments and therefore the prosecution cannot exclude defense evidence on the same grounds. Similarly, one might reasonably believe that the rule that excludes prior crimes evidence from being used to prove that a person acted in conformity to a criminal character[3] is much more likely to bar the prosecutor's evidence against the defendant than the defendant's evidence against prosecutorial witnesses. Thus, we can plausibly wonder if the jury will react to its knowledge of asymmetric exclusion by giving asymmetric weight to the possibility that it has not heard all of the extant evidence of the defendant's guilt. The jury knows that the prosecutor knows of all the extant evidence and might infer from the prosecutor's decision to bring a weak case some probability that the judge has excluded relevant evidence of guilt.

In discussing the rule against admission of the defendant's prior crimes, Lauden & Allen (2011, pp. 134–135) recently raised the possibility of jury inferences of this kind:

> We predict that jurors start with an assumption that defendants have prior records and that the assumption affects their deliberations virtually no matter what judges may tell them. We also predict that the biggest discrepancy between judges' and jurors' views of the evidence will be located in the set of cases in which jurors are not directly informed of defendant's priors, and thus must engage in surmise. We also predict that a fair amount of surmising is going on as a result of the other mechanisms we have mentioned for indirectly indicating the nature of a defendant's priors. Last, we predict that one product of that surmising is likely to be to disadvantage the innocent defendant.

One can broaden their point by making the same claim for other exclusionary rules. In any criminal case, juries might infer that there is a possibility that the court has excluded probative evidence of the defendant's guilt because it was obtained in violation of the defendant's Fourth or Fifth Amendment rights. This inference would increase the jury's willingness to convict given the evidence at trial, which means it would lower the prosecution's effective burden of proof, making the jury more likely to convict the innocent.[4]

Our analysis shows that, once juries' inferences and behavior is explicitly taken into account, the impact of exclusionary rules on the prosecution's effective standard of proof is complex, depending on a number of relevant factors. First, if juries are completely unaware of the existence of exclusionary rules (i.e. "naïve"), then the evidentiary threshold that juries require to convict is unaffected. Innocent suspects (i.e. those who would be acquitted in a world without exclusionary rules) are not adversely affected by the exclusionary rule, though guilty suspects who benefit from the exclusion of evidence are better off. This simple scenario corresponds to the conventional wisdom in most criminal procedure scholarship. A second possibility is that juries are aware of the existence of (asymmetric) exclusionary rules, though not fully Bayesian in accounting for the possibility of the exclusion of evidence in their particular case, nor in taking full account of the strategic responses of the prosecutor to the exclusionary rule. Under this assumption of "limited updating" we show that the effective standard of proof goes down. This entails the possibility that innocent suspects are worse off, and is consistent with the result already recognized in the small economic literature on this issue (Edman 2001; Jacobi 2011).

This simple picture, however, is incomplete. If juries are perfectly Bayesian (i.e. fully rational in accounting for the impact of exclusionary rules and in taking full account of the strategic responses of the prosecutor), we show that the outcomes depend crucially on the probability distribution of suspects and on the preferences of the prosecutor. In particular, the prosecution's effective standard of proof may increase, decrease, or remain unchanged relative to the benchmark threshold in the absence of an exclusionary rule. We characterize circumstances in which each of these outcomes may occur and the various impacts on innocent and guilty suspects.

The central intuition for why the prosecution's effective standard of proof need not always fall when the jury is aware of the existence of an exclusionary rule is the following. The existence of an exclusionary rule, taken in isolation, induces juries to lower their threshold for convicting suspects (in view of the possibility that some factually relevant evidence of guilt has been excluded). An opportunistic prosecutor (i.e. one who seeks to maximize the fraction of suspects convicted) will thus be tempted to exploit the asymmetry of information with respect to the jury. Such a prosecutor would indict an additional increment of suspects who would otherwise go unprosecuted because of the weakness of the evidence against them (i.e., many are actually innocent) and for whom *no evidence has been excluded*, but whom the jury might now convict given its reduced threshold. A rational jury will anticipate this strategic behavior on the part of the prosecutor, and seek to correct for it by raising the prosecution's effective standard of proof. Whether the equilibrium involves a higher or lower standard of proof relative to that which would prevail in the absence of an exclusionary rule turns out to depend on the shape of the probability density function of suspects. For instance, we provide an example in which the prosecution's effective standard of proof is higher under an exclusionary rule. Thus, we conclude that the impact of exclusionary rules on trial outcomes and on the welfare of innocent and guilty suspects is not susceptible to any simple generalizations.

Our chapter provides the first economic model showing that the effect of an exclusionary rule on the effective standard of proof and, in consequence, on innocent and guilty individuals is ambiguous once we allow for Bayesian juries and strategic prosecutors. The policy implications depend very much on the extent to which juries are closer to the naïve model or the Bayesian model. Nonetheless, our model shows that – depending on the sophistication of juries, the motivations of prosecutors, and the probability distribution of suspects – exclusionary rules need not help the guilty (as conventional criminal procedure scholarship generally presumes) nor hurt the innocent (as some recent economic literature has argued).

The chapter is organized as follows. Section II briefly reviews the relevant literature. Section III introduces the basic version of the model. We then consider various assumptions about the jury's knowledge and inferences. Section IV concludes the chapter.

II.   LITERATURE REVIEW

Our chapter intersects with several literatures. Most obviously, there is an economic literature on the exclusionary rule (e.g. Atkins & Rubin 2003; Calabresi 2003; Cicchini 2010; Mialon & Mialon 2008; Mialon & Rubin 2008). This literature considers various aspects of the impact of exclusionary rules, for instance on police behavior and on the deterrence of crime. However, none of the published literature considers the jury's inferences from the existence of exclusionary rules.

There is a significant economic literature on jury behavior. For instance, Schrag and Scotchmer (1994) analyze the impact of restrictions on character evidence pertaining to defendants' past convictions on jury behavior. The emphasis, however, is on the effects of jury prejudice against defendants with past criminal records and the impact on the deterrence of crime, rather than on the questions addressed in this chapter. Froeb and Kobayashi (1996) analyze inferences by naïve and potentially biased juries in the context of civil litigation, focusing on the strategic production of evidence by the parties. However, their paper does not address exclusionary rules in criminal trials. To the best of our knowledge, an unpublished student paper (Edman 2001) was the first to formally model jury responses to exclusionary rules. Since we presented the first version of our model at ALEA (American Law and Economics Association) in 2008, Jacobi (2011) has also proposed a formal model of this topic. Both Edman (2001) and Jacobi (2011), however, draw more determinate conclusions than we think are warranted, as explained below.

Lester, Persico and Visschers (2012) look at the exclusion of evidence in criminal trials. They assume that jurors have a cognitive cost of processing evidence and explain why the judge should have broad powers to exclude less relevant evidence. Exclusion of evidence by the judge is a device to help the jury focus on more important evidence.

There is also a large literature on wrongful conviction (e.g. Garrett 2008; Gould & Leo 2010) that seeks to identify the causes of this type of error, though it has not considered the possibility that exclusionary rules affect the prosecution's effective burden of proof. An economic literature on the optimal standard of proof in criminal trials also exists (e.g. Miceli 1990), but it does not generally consider the impact of exclusionary rules. This chapter is also related to a literature on the behavior of prosecutors and the rules of evidence (e.g. Garoupa & Rizzolli 2011). Finally, there is a small literature on the principal-agent problem in criminal law (e.g. Dharmapala, Garoupa & McAdams 2011), but it has not focused on the jury as we do now.

III. MODEL

Assume that there is a continuum of suspects for a given crime, with the size of the population normalized to 1. The prosecutor P observes each suspect's probability of guilt $p \in [0, 1]$. The probability density function $g(p)$ and the cumulative density function $G(p)$ represent the distribution of suspects over p, with $G(1) = 1$. After observing a suspect's p, the prosecutor P chooses whether or not to indict the suspect. For those suspects that P indicts, P can present evidence $q \in [0, 1]$ in court. The decision of whether to convict or acquit an indicted suspect is made by the jury, denoted J. In making this decision, the jury J has an objective function that trades off Type I and Type II errors (i.e. false acquittals and false convictions). J convicts if, and only if, its inference about p, denoted r, exceeds a threshold of reasonable doubt p^* (i.e. J convicts iff $r \geq p^*$).

P's objective function is modeled in two different ways. The first model is of a benevolent prosecutor who has exactly the same preferences as the jury. The second model is of an opportunistic prosecutor who cares about the proportion of suspects convicted, perhaps because of career concerns. In both models, P's strategy consists of a decision about what subset of suspects to indict (for example, a possible strategy might be to indict all suspects with p in the range [0.95, 1]). Note that, regardless of P's objective function, we restrict P to presenting only truthful evidence of guilt at trial. This entails that $q \leq p$, whether P is benevolent or opportunistic, and regardless of any exclusionary rules that may be applicable (as discussed below).

With no exclusionary rule there are no constraints on the production of evidence in court, so $r = q = p$. In particular, suppose the cost function for the jury is:

$$\int_0^{p^*} pL_1 g(p)\,dp + \int_{p^*}^1 (1 - p)L_2 g(p)\,dp$$

where the first integral is the expected cost of false negatives and the second integral is the expected cost of false positives. False negatives impose a cost L_1 and false positives impose a cost L_2 (typically, we would expect that $L_2 > L_1$, but this is not necessary for the results derived below). The jury chooses p* to minimize the expected cost, yielding:

$$p^* = \frac{L_2}{L_1 + L_2}$$

Hence, the threshold goes up if false positives become relatively more costly.

The equilibrium can be characterized straightforwardly as follows: P indicts suspects for whom $p \geq p^*$, presenting evidence $q = p$; J convicts defendants for whom $r = q = p \geq p^*$; when P is opportunistic, her payoff is $(1 - G(p^*))$. This equilibrium is independent of the prosecutor's preferences. A benevolent prosecutor mimics the behavior of the jury because they share the same preferences and the same information set. An opportunistic prosecutor also mimics the behavior of the jury because there is no gain from indicting suspects with p less than p^* since they will be acquitted at trial.

III.A   Exclusion of Evidence with Naïve or Non-Bayesian Juries

With an exclusionary rule P again observes p; however, with probability n, some element e of the evidence is not admissible in court – i.e. if the evidence is p then the evidence presented in court must be $q = p - e$, where e is sufficiently small in the relevant range to satisfy $q \geq 0$. With probability $1 - n$, the evidence is admissible, so the evidence presented in court is $q = p$. Note that the focus here is on cases where e is relatively small, so that the excluded evidence is not dispositive of the suspect's guilt. When e is sufficiently large, q will be close to zero, and it will presumably be impossible for P to indict the suspect. In such circumstances the question of what inferences the jury might draw is moot as there will be no trial.

A straightforward, albeit extreme, assumption about the jury is that it is *fully* naïve in the sense that it is unaware of the existence of the exclusionary rule. Then, the jury will choose the same threshold p^* as in the absence of the exclusionary rule. Innocent suspects (those with $p < p^* -$ i.e. suspects who would be acquitted in the absence of an exclusionary rule) are not harmed. However, some guilty suspects (with $p < p^*$) are better off – specifically, those for whom evidence is excluded and $e > p - p^*$ are not indicted and convicted (as they would have been in the absence of the exclusionary rule). Even an opportunistic P cannot exploit the asymmetry of information with respect to the jury. The jury is unaware of the exclusionary rule, and so there is no scope for P to indict innocent suspects in the hope that the jury will convict them in the belief that evidence has been excluded.

The above scenario is quite similar to the implicit premise underlying much of conventional criminal procedure scholarship on exclusionary rules. However, it relies on an extreme form of naivety among juries. An alternative assumption is that juries are only partially naïve and engage in what we term "limited updating" – they are aware of the existence of the exclusionary rule and take it into account when determining the threshold for conviction. However, the jury does not fully take account of P's strategic response to the exclusionary rule.

When the jury is aware of the possibility that some evidence is subject to exclusion, the threshold probability that the jury uses to convict defendants will, in general, be affected. Specifically, define p^{**} to be the new threshold for the jury to convict. This means that the jury convicts if and only if $q \geq p^{**}$. The cost function for the jury is now:

$$(1 - n)\left[\int_0^{p^{**}} pL_1 g(p)\,dp + \int_{p^{**}}^1 (1 - p)L_2 g(p)\,dp\right] + n\left[\int_0^{p^{**}+e} pL_1 g(p)\,dp\right.$$

$$\left. + \int_{p^{**}+e}^1 (1 - p)L_2 g(p)\,dp\right]$$

where the first two integrals refer to suspects with fully admissible evidence and the last two integrals refer to suspects for which evidence was excluded. By straightforward computation, the new threshold is $p^{**} = p^* - ne$, assuming $g(p^{**}) \cong g(p^{**} + e)$. In fact, more generally we can show that:

$$p^{**} = p^* - n \frac{g(p^{**} + e)}{(1 - n)g(p^{**}) + ng(p^{**} + e)} e$$

As the likelihood and the size of excludable evidence go up the threshold goes down. The explanation is quite intuitive. Exclusion of evidence increases false negatives (because it deters indictment by prosecutor) and decreases false positives (because fewer suspects are indicted in total). As a consequence the threshold goes down.

As before, the prosecutor observes p before deciding whether to indict the suspect. We now assume that the prosecutor is also able to determine how much of the evidence is admissible before deciding whether to indict the suspect (i.e., that the prosecutor can anticipate what evidence will be excluded). The prosecutor only indicts if the admissible evidence is such that $q \geq p^{**}$ (otherwise, an acquittal will take place). This means that with probability $1 - n$, the prosecutor is able to present evidence $p \geq p^{**}$ and with probability n, $p - e \geq p^{**}$. The implication is that for suspects with $p \, \varepsilon \, [p^{**}, p^{**} + e]$ there is a probability n that they will not be indicted as there is insufficient evidence to guarantee a conviction. Some "innocents" (i.e. suspects for whom the true p is below p^*) are worse-off (in particular, those with $p \, \varepsilon \, [p^{**}, p^*]$ and for whom no evidence is excludable) and some "guilty" suspects (for whom the true p is above p^*) may be better off (in particular, those with $p \geq p^*$ and excludable evidence such that $e > p - p^{**}$). Note that once again the goals of the prosecutor play no role. All indicted suspects have $p \geq p^{**}$ and the prosecutor cannot strategically exploit the asymmetry of information.

III.B   Exclusion of Evidence with a Sophisticated Jury

We now assume that J is sophisticated (or Bayesian). J makes an inference from the admissible evidence knowing that some exclusion of evidence takes place with probability n. Moreover, J takes full account of P's strategic response to the exclusionary rule. Suppose in particular that J is confronted at trial with evidence $q < p^{**}$. There are two possible scenarios in which this could happen:

(i) $p = q + e > p^{**}$ and evidence was excluded
(ii) $p = q < p^{**}$ and evidence was not excluded.

The probabilities of (i) and (ii) depend on the actions taken by the prosecutor, in particular the extent to which the prosecutor strategically exploits the asymmetry of information. Define S as the probability that J places on the event that the prosecutor is opportunistic (an opportunistic prosecutor indicts suspects with probability $p < p^{**}$ using the asymmetry of information to seek to convey the message that the weak case is due to exclusion of evidence). The probabilities of (i) and (ii) are n and $(1-n)S$ respectively. The likelihood that the "true" probability of guilt is p greater than p^{**} is given by Bayes' formula:

$$\frac{n}{n + (1 - n)S}$$

It follows immediately that if the prosecutor is benevolent ($S = 0$) the probability is one since there is no possibility of opportunism. If the evidence observed by the jury is less than p^{**} it is because the remaining evidence was excluded. However, if there is some probability that a prosecutor is opportunistic ($S > 0$), the probability is less than one. The reason why the observed probability q is less than p^{**} could be because the prosecutor is opportunistic and indicts "innocent" people. When the prosecutor is opportunistic for sure ($S = 1$), the probability is n reflecting the possibility of "true" exclusion of evidence. Consequently, J's inferred probability of guilt is:

$$r = \frac{n(q + e) + (1 - n)Sq}{n + (1 - n)S} = q + \frac{n}{n + (1 - n)S}e$$

J's inferred probability of guilt is $(q + e)$ when $S = 0$ (benevolent prosecutor) and $q + ne$ when $S = 1$ (opportunistic prosecutor). They reflect the possibility of "true" exclusion of evidence, which is maximal when the prosecutor is benevolent (so that the probability of guilt fully discounts for the excludable evidence) and minimal when the prosecutor is opportunistic.

The jury is willing to convict individuals with evidence such that $p \; \varepsilon \; [p^{**} - e, p^{**}]$ as long as on average the "true" probability is expected to be above the threshold p^{**}.

J will infer that $r \geq p^{**}$ and convict if

$$q + \frac{n}{n + (1 - n)S}e \geq p^{**}$$

In other words, the lowest level of evidence that the prosecutor can consider to present for an indictment is:

$$q \geq p^{**} - \frac{n}{n + (1 - n)S}e$$

A benevolent prosecutor (one with $S = 0$) can indict suspects with p as low as $p^{**} - e$ since the jury knows that weak evidence against an indicted suspect is due to exclusion and not to strategic behavior. In this sense, J fully delegates to P the discretion to select suspects to indict. An opportunistic prosecutor with $S = 1$ can only go down to $p^{**} - ne$, since the jury does not trust the prosecutor and hence does not delegate the discretion to select cases to the same extent.

Let us define $a = n/[n+(1-n)S]$. The choice of p^{**} by the jury now involves minimizing the following expected cost function:

$$(1 - n)\left[\int_0^{p^{**} - ae} pL_1g(p)\,dp\right.$$

$$+ \int_{p^{**} - ae}^{p^{**}}\left[(1 - p)SL_2 + p(1 - S)L_1\right]g(p)\,dp + \left.\int_{p^{**}}^1 (1 - p)L_2g(p)\,dp\right]$$

$$+ n\left[\int_0^{p^{**} + (1-a)e} pL_1g(p)\,dp + \int_{p^{**} + (1-a)e}^1 (1 - p)L2g(p)\,dp\right]$$

The first three integrals refer to suspects for whom evidence is not subject to exclusion (but for whom the prosecutor might take advantage of the information asymmetry) and the second set of integrals refer to those for which evidence is "truly" excludable.

By straightforward computation, the new threshold is $p^{**} = p^*$ under a uniform distribution of suspects, or a distribution that is sufficiently close to being uniform (i.e. assuming $g(p^{**} - ae) \cong g(p^{**}) \cong g(p^{**}+(1 - a)e)$). The intuition is that there are two effects that exactly cancel out when the distribution is uniform. On the one hand the exclusionary rule, taken in isolation, induces J to reduce its threshold. On the other hand the strategic response to the exclusionary rule by an opportunistic P induces J to increase its threshold. However, as we will see below, this result relies crucially on the probability density function that is assumed.

Notice that even when $p^{**} = p^*$, individuals are affected in different ways. For suspects with admissible evidence the threshold is actually $p^* - ae$, that is, lower than before. For suspects with excludable evidence the threshold is actually $p^* + (1 - a)e$. "Innocents" are generally worse-off since now suspects with $p < p^*$ could be indicted and convicted if evidence is admissible and $p > p* - ae$. As for the "guilty", some of them are better off, namely, those for whom $p > p*$ but since evidence is not admissible have $p < p* + (1-a)e$.

Let us assume that the jury knows the prosecutor is benevolent, i.e. $S = 0.5$ Immediately we know that $a = 1$ and the expression above can be reduced to:

$$\int_0^{p**} pL_1 g(p)\,dp + \int_{p**}^1 (1 - p)L_2 g(p)\,dp$$

If the jury knows the prosecutor is benevolent, the excluded evidence is perfectly anticipated by the jury and therefore the threshold decision is similar to a situation where there is no exclusion, $p** = p*$ for any probability density function $g(p)$.

Suppose now that the jury knows that the prosecutor is opportunistic, $S = 1$. It is the case that $a = n$. The expression above is now:

$$(1 - n)\left[\int_0^{p** - ne} pL_1 g(p)\,dp \right.$$

$$+ \left. \int_{p** - ne}^1 (1 - p)L_2 g(p)\,dp\right]$$

$$+ n\left[\int_0^{p** + (1 - n)e} pL_1 g(p)\,dp + \int_{p** + (1 - n)e}^1 (1 - p)L_2 g(p)\,dp\right]$$

The threshold in this case can be easily derived from computing the first-order condition:

$$p** = p* + n(1 - n)\frac{g(p** - ne) - g(p** + (1 - n)e)}{(1 - n)g(p** - ne) + ng(p** + (1 - n)e)}e$$

As shown before, for some distributions we have $p** = p*$, in particular when $g(p** - ne) \cong g(p** + (1 - p)e)$. However, when the distribution is skewed to the left, in the sense that we are in the negatively sloped part of the probability density function, we should have $g(p** - ne) > g(p**+ (1 - n)e)$ and consequently $p** > p*$. If more individuals are located on the lower tails of the distribution the threshold should go up. Strategic indictment of innocent suspects by P impacts a larger pool of individuals, therefore J has to increase the threshold to address the problem. If the distribution is skewed to the right, in the sense that we are in the positively sloped part of the probability density function, we have $g(p** - ne) <$

$g(p^{**} + (1-n)e)$ and consequently $p^{**} < p^*$. In this case, because the pool affected by the strategic behavior of the prosecutor is smaller, we have a somewhat similar outcome to that when J engages in limited updating with respect to the possibility of exclusion.

These possibilities are illustrated graphically in Figures 10.1–10.3. Figure 10.1 depicts a uniform distribution of suspects, Figure 10.2 a right-skewed distribution of suspects, and Figure 10.3 a left-skewed distribution of suspects. The outcomes in the various cases considered above are summarized in Table 10.1.

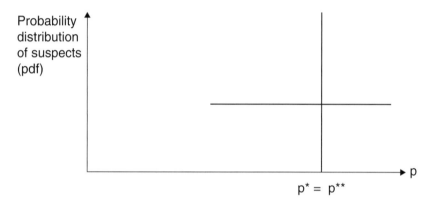

Figure 10.1   Uniform distribution of suspects

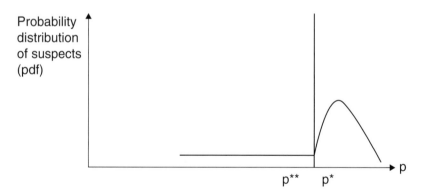

Figure 10.2   Right-skewed distribution of suspects

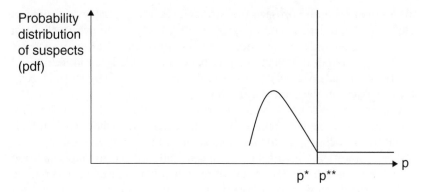

Figure 10.3   Left-skewed distribution of suspects

Table 10.1   Outcomes

		Prosecutor	
		Benevolent	Opportunistic
Jury	Naïve	J's threshold for conviction is unaffected; some guilty suspects may benefit, but innocent suspects do not suffer	J's threshold for conviction is unaffected; some guilty suspects may benefit, but innocent suspects do not suffer
	Limited Updating	J's threshold for conviction falls; some innocent suspects may suffer	J's threshold for conviction falls; some innocent suspects may suffer
	Sophisticated	No effect of exclusionary rules	J's threshold for conviction may increase or decrease, depending on the distribution of suspects

IV.   CONCLUSION

Our simple model shows that the impact of exclusionary rules on the prosecution's effective standard of proof is far from being simple and depends on a complex set of factors. If juries engage in limited updating, the impact of the exclusionary rule is unambiguous and detrimental to innocents since the critical threshold for evidence decreases. However, with Bayesian juries (that fully and rationally anticipate the existence of an

206   *Research handbook on economic models of law*

exclusionary rule and prosecutors' strategic responses), the overall effect is ambiguous and depends on the probability density function as well as on the motivation of the prosecution. With a uniform distribution of suspects the threshold does not change but impacts differentially on innocent and guilty individuals. With a distribution skewed to the left (right) and a strategic prosecutor, the critical threshold goes up (down).

Our model does not directly address the behavior of the defendant. However, an immediate prediction is that defendants who have not benefited from exclusionary rules should signal it to the jury (for example, by testifying about not having a previous criminal record or no incriminating evidence being found in an illegal search and seizure). If there is a credible way for the defendant to inform the jury that no evidence was excluded, the prosecutor has fewer opportunities to be strategic and the effective standard of proof would adjust appropriately.

We have assumed that the excluded evidence is detrimental to the defendant. In some cases it could be relevant to admit the possibility of the excluded evidence being instead detrimental to the case of the prosecution (for example, rape shield laws may exclude some defense evidence that the jury would consider relevant). This would inevitably complicate the model (e.g. Garoupa & Rizzolli 2011). We have also ignored the possibility that evidence can be manipulated or, at the limit, fabricated by the enforcement agency. Exclusion of evidence could have an effect in limiting the incentives for such behavior hence improving the jury perception about the quality of evidence presented in court. Such complications reinforce our main insight: the impact of exclusionary rules on criminal procedure is highly complex and relies on the interaction of a number of factors. From an economic perspective, it cannot be said that the exclusion of evidence unambiguously hurts the innocent and helps the guilty.

NOTES

1. *Miranda v. Arizona*, 384 U.S. 436 (1966).
2. *Mapp v. Ohio*, 367 U.S. 643 (1961).
3. Federal Rule of Evidence 404(b).
4. If one defines "exclusionary rule" as any rule that excludes legally relevant evidence, then certain evidentiary privileges (doctor-patient relationship, attorney-client relationship, etc.) might place some evidence beyond the reach of defendants as well as prosecutors. We ignore these examples, among other reasons, because their symmetry plausibly means that their effects on prosecutors and defendants are offsetting in the aggregate, so the jury would make no net adjustment to the standard of proof. One might further broaden "exclusionary rules" to describe the exclusion of evidence that is legally irrelevant but that would nonetheless affect the jury's verdict. In American courts, criminal juries have the power to "nullify" law by acquitting the defendant despite believing that he is formally guilty. Juries might like to know technically irrelevant facts to decide

whether to nullify. For example, suppose a jury would like to acquit marijuana pos-sessors whose purposes are medicinal, despite their formal legal guilt, but to convict all other marijuana possessors. Because evidence of medicinal use or purposes is technically irrelevant, standard rules exclude it. For this jury, the rule is exclusionary; not knowing which cases are medicinal, they will want to raise the overall burden of proof. We ignore this special case in the text.

5. Alternatively, the prosecutor can credibly inform the jury that some evidence was excluded. Consider the following example. Suppose defendants can only be indicted for sexual crimes if they failed a polygraph test according to the prosecutorial agency guidelines. Polygraph tests are not admitted as evidence. However, the jury knows that if a certain individual has been indicted for a sexual crime, it must be the case that such individual has failed the polygraph test.

REFERENCES

Atkins, Raymond A. and Paul H. Rubin. Effects of Criminal Procedure on Crime Rates: Mapping Out the Consequences of the Exclusionary Rule, 46 J.L. & Econ. 157 (2003).

Calabresi, Guido. The Exclusionary Rule, 26 Harv. J.L. & Pub. Pol'y 111 (2003).

Cicchini, Michael D. An Economics Perspective on the Exclusionary Rule and Deterrence, 75 Mo. L. Rev. 459 (2010).

Dharmapala, Dhammika, Nuno Garoupa and Richard McAdams. Punitive Police? Agency Costs, Law Enforcement, and Criminal Procedure, mimeograph on file with authors.

Edman Carl. Rational Jurors and Extrinsic Exclusionary Rules (2001) (unpublished paper submitted in partial fulfillment of the requirements of the John M. Olin Fellowship in Law and Economics, Georgetown University Law Center).

Froeb, Luke M. and Bruce H. Kobayashi. Naïve, Biased, yet Bayesian: Can Juries Interpret Selectively Produced Evidence?, 12 J.L. & Econ. & Org. 257–76 (1996).

Garoupa, Nuno and Matteo Rizzolli. The Brady Rule May Hurt the Innocent, 13 Am. L. & Econ. Rev. 168–200 (2011).

Garrett, Brandon L. Judging Innocence, 108 Colum. L. Rev. 55 (2008).

Gould, Jon B. and Richard A. Leo. One Hundred Years Later: Wrongful Convictions After a Century of Research, 100 J. Crim. L. & Criminology 825 (2010).

Jacobi, Tonja. The Law and Economics of the Exclusionary Rule, 87 Notre Dame L. Rev. (2011).

Laudan, Larry and Ronald J. Allen. The Devastating Impact of Prior Crimes Evidence and Other Myths of the Criminal Justice Process, 101 J. Crim. L. & Criminology 493 (2011).

Lester, Benjamin, Nicola Persico and Ludo Visschers. Information Acquisition and the Exclusion of Evidence in Trials, 28 J.L. Econ. & Org. 163–82 (2012).

Mialon, Hugo M. and Sue H. Mialon. The Effects of the Fourth Amendment: An Economic Analysis, 24 J.L. Econ. & Org. 22–44 (2008).

Mialon, Hugo M. and Paul Rubin. The Economics of the Bill of Rights, 10 Am. L. & Econ. Rev. 1–60 (2008).

Miceli, Thomas J. Optimal Prosecution of Defendants when Guilt is Uncertain, 6 J.L. Econ. & Org. 189–201 (1990).

Schrag, Joel and Suzanne Scotchmer. Crime and Prejudice: The Use of Character Evidence in Criminal Trials, 10 J.L. Econ. & Org. 319–42 (1994).

11. Search, seizure and false (?) arrest: an analysis of fourth amendment remedies when police can plant evidence
Dhammika Dharmapala and Thomas J. Miceli

1. INTRODUCTION

The prosecution of criminal defendants is a process fraught with uncertainty, and requires a delicate balance between the search for the truth and the protection of citizens' right to be free from unreasonable invasions of their privacy. An important legal safeguard in this context is the Fourth Amendment to the U.S. Constitution, which provides that: 'The right of the people to be secure in their persons, houses, papers, and effects, against unreasonable searches and seizures, shall not be violated, and no warrants shall issue, but upon probable cause. . .' (U.S. Const., Amendment IV). The Supreme Court has interpreted this amendment to require that police, when feasible, obtain a warrant prior to search, which a judge will only issue on a finding of probable cause (the 'warrant requirement'), and further, that any illegally obtained evidence will be excluded from trial (the 'Fourth Amendment exclusionary rule').[1]

Scholars have vigorously debated the desirability of these remedies for violations of the Fourth Amendment. A major focus of the debate has been on the relative merits of the warrant requirement and exclusionary rule on the one hand, and a reasonableness standard enforced by tort liability for the government or its agents on the other. Amar (1997, Chapter 1), for example, argues that the plain language of the Fourth Amendment does not *require* warrants, probable cause, or exclusion of evidence, but only that searches and seizures be *reasonable*. Further, the courts, in recognizing the impracticality of the warrant requirement in many contexts, have historically granted many exceptions to it (for example, the use of metal detectors in airports). Finally, Amar claims on historical grounds that the Framers themselves envisioned tort liability (in the form of a civil action for trespass) rather than exclusion as the principal remedy for unlawful seizures of evidence.

Posner (1981) has also argued for the replacement of the exclusionary rule by tort liability, based on economic rather than textual or historical considerations. As noted above, the primary objective of rules against unreasonable search is to balance citizens' right to privacy against the goal of truth-seeking in criminal proceedings. Given this trade-off, economic efficiency requires that searches should be allowed up to the point where the expected probative value of the evidence being sought equals the harm to the victim of the search.[2] Under such a standard, claims of an unlawful search would involve an *ex post* judicial determination of whether this condition was met at the time the search was conducted, in the same way that negligence is determined after the occurrence of an accident, with liability being assessed if it was not.

According to this logic, the threat of tort liability forces the police to internalize the social costs and benefits of conducting a search. Some errors in their calculations will no doubt occur (just as some injurers are found negligent), but as long as they are acting in good faith (a point we expand on below), liability provides the correct incentives.[3] Exclusion of evidence does not offer any further protection of privacy rights but only serves the interests of guilty defendants, which, it is claimed, are not meant to be protected by the Fourth Amendment (Posner, 1981; Amar, 1997). Moreover, it is argued that the exclusionary rule coupled with the warrant requirement is likely to deter too many searches.[4]

These arguments for the superiority of tort liability over the exclusionary rule, however, implicitly assume that police act in an essentially public-spirited manner. That is, police seek to uncover the truth in their role as evidence gatherers. At worst, they place too small a weight on the costs imposed on innocent suspects who are searched, and this overzealousness may result in Fourth Amendment violations. However, tort liability will induce them to internalize these social costs. Unfortunately, as suggested by a number of recent police scandals in major US cities, the motivations of police may not always be quite so benign.[5] In particular, when police seek to maximize the number of convictions they obtain, there may be some officers who have an incentive and opportunity to plant evidence on innocent suspects in an effort to frame them. Even if this practice is rare, it can seriously compromise the ability of courts to distinguish the innocent from the guilty.

This chapter analyzes Fourth Amendment remedies – comparing tort liability and the exclusionary rule – in circumstances where a subset of police officers are willing to plant evidence. We argue that a system based on tort liability is unlikely to deter such police misbehavior (as opposed to good faith errors). This is true because, while the purported search that uncovered the 'evidence' was presumably unreasonable before the fact (because the suspect is, after all, truly innocent), as a practical matter courts will generally not be able to distinguish planted from legitimate evidence after the fact. On the other hand, the exclusionary rule (and in particular, the warrant requirement) requires police to present some evidence of guilt to a presumably impartial judge *prior* to conducting the search.[6] While this does not eliminate the possibility that evidence will be planted, it greatly reduces the threat of false convictions because the police will only be able to search a small subset of suspects whose probability of guilt surpasses the threshold required for the issue of a warrant. In this way, the exclusionary rule (with a warrant requirement) enhances the ability of courts to convict the guilty and acquit the innocent while protecting the privacy rights of citizens.

The major contribution of this chapter is thus to identify and analyze a set of circumstances in which the exclusionary rule (and in particular, the warrant requirement) leads to superior outcomes compared to a system that relies solely on tort liability as a remedy for Fourth Amendment violations. This result is important, firstly, because it challenges the consensus among law-and-economics scholars, and increasingly among scholars of constitutional criminal procedure, in favor of tort liability (Posner, 1981; Amar, 1997). Secondly, it provides a possible explanation of a long-standing puzzle in the economic approach to the law of evidence. Despite the apparently greater efficiency of tort liability (as claimed in the literature discussed above), the warrant requirement and exclusionary rule are well-established features of criminal procedure. Established for Federal criminal proceedings in 1914,[7] the exclusionary rule remedy had been adopted by about half of US states by 1961, when it was made mandatory by *Mapp*.[8] The widespread use of this approach and its longevity clearly stand in need of explanation from an economic standpoint.

The rest of the chapter is organized as follows. Section 2 briefly reviews the related literature. Then, Section 3 presents the basic model, which consists of an asymmetric information game between police and the court. Police care only about maximizing the probability of a conviction less the cost of search, but they come in two types: 'good' (those unwilling to plant evidence), and 'bad' (those willing to plant evidence). After an arrest, the court seeks to deliver the correct verdict but is uncertain about the reliability of the evidence presented by the arresting officer. This creates a trade-off between Type I and Type II errors which, given the court's objective of minimizing error costs, defines the efficient 'threshold of reasonable doubt.' We initially characterize the equilibria of this model in the absence of remedies for Fourth Amendment violations. Then, in Section 4 we incorporate tort liability and show that this remedy provides no additional deterrence against planting evidence compared to the basic model. In contrast, Section 5 shows that an exclusionary rule with a warrant requirement does increase deterrence, thereby lowering the probability that an innocent defendant will be convicted and raising social welfare.

Section 6 considers a number of extensions, while Section 7 discusses the implications and concludes.

2.   RELATED LITERATURE

There is a very large literature within legal scholarship that addresses Fourth Amendment jurisprudence (as discussed, for example, in Stuntz (1991) and Amar (1997)). However, there is relatively little formal economic analysis of issues in criminal procedure. The most closely related work to this chapter is Mialon and Mialon (2008a), which also formally models the impact of the Fourth Amendment. However, it emphasizes a different set of issues, focusing on the strategic interaction of citizens and the police (rather than on the strategic interaction of police and courts, as in this chapter). Also relevant are economic models analyzing the consequences of the Fifth Amendment privilege against self-incrimination (Seidmann and Stein, 2000; Seidmann, 2005; Mialon, 2005). Other examples of the economic analysis of various issues in criminal law and procedure also implicate issues discussed in this chapter. For instance, Miceli (1990) analyzes the optimal standard of proof in criminal trials, while Mialon and Mialon (2008b) study the optimal evidentiary standard for the issuance of search warrants. The impact of plea bargaining on trial outcomes and social welfare has also attracted attention (Grossman and Katz, 1983; Reinganum, 1988).

While this chapter focuses more on the warrant requirement, it is related to a growing economic literature on the impact of exclusionary rules (including, but not restricted to, the Fourth Amendment exclusionary rule). Schrag and Scotchmer (1994) analyze the effects of rules excluding character evidence from criminal trials. Jacobi (2011) argues that the exclusion of evidence leads juries to modify the evidentiary standard they use when determining guilt, potentially leading to the conviction of innocent defendants. Dharmapala, Garoupa and McAdams (2011) analyze the strategic responses of both juries and prosecutors to rules requiring the exclusion of evidence. Lester, Persico and Visschers (2012) develop a model that explains exclusionary rules in terms of the cognitive costs faced by juries in processing information. There is also a substantial economic literature on civil procedure that in some cases addresses related issues. Daughety and Reinganum (1995) examine the effects of rules excluding the admission of evidence about pretrial settlement negotiations in civil trials. The production of evidence by parties in trials has also been modeled (e.g., Daughety and Reinganum, 2000; Sanchirico, 2000).

Finally, this chapter is related to the literature on corruption and wrongful conduct by the police and other law enforcement agencies (e.g., Bowles and Garoupa, 1997), including models in which police may extract bribes from innocent parties in exchange for not making false arrests (e.g., Polinsky and Shavell, 2001). In the model of this chapter, in contrast, police are motivated not by monetary gain *per se*, but by a desire for convictions. Benoit and Dubra (2004) and Muehlheusser and Roider (2008) develop models that analyze why police officers who engage in wrongful conduct may be protected by those who do not (for instance, through a refusal by the latter to testify against the former). This can explain, for example, why the 'bad' types introduced in the model below may be able to survive. More generally, Hylton and Khanna (2007) develop an account of constitutional criminal procedure protections that emphasizes their role in constraining rent-seeking by law enforcement officials.

3.   THE BASIC MODEL

This section describes the basic model of strategic interaction between two actors – a police officer (hereafter denoted P) and a criminal court (denoted C) – in the absence of either an exclusionary rule (ER) or a system of tort liability (TL) for Fourth Amendment violations. The equilibria of the game, denoted Γ^0, are then derived and discussed.

3.1   Description of the Game

The game Γ^0 is a dynamic game with asymmetric information; it can be divided into four stages – investigation, search, arrest and trial. The information asymmetry arises because P can be one of two types, Good (G) or Bad (B). P is privately informed about his type (which is unobservable to C, and also to the other actors who are introduced in later sections). The two types of P differ not (as in standard asymmetric information games) in their payoffs (described below), but rather in the set of actions available to them. The 'bad' type of P (P_B) can 'plant' evidence on suspects in order to 'frame' them, whereas the 'good' type of P (P_G) is assumed not to have this option available. While C cannot observe a particular P's type, it is common knowledge that a fraction $\beta \in (0, 1)$ of the population from which P is drawn are of the 'bad' type.

In the first stage of the game, P chooses whether or not to expend effort investigating a crime. (In reality, the choice of whether to investigate may not be made by an individual police officer; the choice in this game can, however, be regarded as the choice of a level of effort to exert, with a low level being normalized to zero.) Regardless of his type, P incurs an effort cost $k > 0$ from investigating (and 0 cost from not doing so). If P investigates, 'probable cause' (interpreted here as evidence of guilt that exceeds some given threshold) is found against a particular suspect with some probability $\varphi \in (0, 1)$. Note that the terminology of 'probable cause' is used here to reflect current Fourth Amendment jurisprudence; however, nothing in the formal analysis below would change if the evidence of guilt that exceeds some given threshold were interpreted instead as some form of 'reasonableness' standard.

The next stage of the game involves P deciding whether to search a suspect. If P has investigated at the previous stage and found probable cause against a particular suspect, then, if P searches that suspect, there is a probability g that dispositive evidence is found establishing that suspect's guilt. Note that g is a *conditional* probability, conditioned on probable cause having previously been found against that particular suspect. A search involves an effort cost $s > 0$.

An important feature of this stage of the game is that P_B (but *not* P_G) can choose to plant evidence on a suspect. For P_B, planting evidence entails a positive effort cost denoted by ρ, where $\rho \in (0, s]$. That is, the planting of evidence requires some effort on the part of the bad type of police officer, but (weakly) less than would be entailed by a genuine search.[9]

In the next stage, P decides whether to arrest a suspect. This can be a suspect against whom first probable cause, and then dispositive evidence of guilt, was found; however, P is also able to arrest any other potential suspect. If a suspect is arrested, then there is a trial; otherwise, the game ends. If there is a trial, C decides whether to convict or acquit the suspect. For now, let λ be the probability that the court convicts a suspect against whom evidence exists. (See below for a description of C's role.)

Among the feasible strategies for each type of P, some are strictly dominated. For example, the strategy for P_G of investigating but never searching or arresting gives a payoff of $-k$, which is strictly dominated by a strategy of not entering, which gives a payoff of 0. Similarly, the strategy for P_B of investigating, and then always planting and arresting can be raised by k by simply planting and arresting without investigating. In addition to eliminating strictly dominated strategies, the following (innocuous) restriction on P's strategies is imposed: any strategy that involves arresting a suspect when no evidence (whether real or planted) exists is ruled out. Allowing strategies of this type would not change any of the equilibria derived below, as C can infer from a trial where there is no (real or purported) evidence against the suspect that the suspect is innocent, and would thus always acquit.

Imposing this restriction, and eliminating strictly dominated strategies, essentially leaves P_G with a choice between not entering the game, and following proper procedure, where the latter involves investigating, searching if and only if probable cause is found, and arresting if and only if evidence of guilt is found. If we normalize the (gross) payoff from conviction to be one, we write P_G's expected return from the strategy of following proper procedure as[10]

$$u_G = \varphi(g\lambda - s) - k \qquad (11.1)$$

The maximum value for this expression is achieved when the court convicts with certainty (i.e., $\lambda = 1$), in which case (1) becomes $\varphi(g - s) - k$. In order for P_B ever to enter the game and follow proper procedure, we therefore need to assume that this expression is strictly positive:

A1: $\varphi(g - s) - k > 0$.
Note also that $\varphi(g - s) - k < 1$, as φ and g are both probabilities.

Now consider the strategy choices facing P_B. Recall that he has the same two options as P_G, but can also choose to plant evidence. As noted above, if he does this, he will always prefer to do it without first investigating and/or searching. His expected payoff from this strategy is

$$u_B = \lambda - \rho \qquad (11.2)$$

which is also maximized when $\lambda = 1$. To make the model interesting, we assume that P_B prefers planting evidence to following proper procedure, i.e. that (11.2) exceeds (11.1), for all λ. This will always be true if the following condition holds, which we assume:

A2: $\rho < \varphi s + k$.
Given A2, bad police officers will always choose to plant evidence when they enter the game.

Consider now the behavior of the court, C, whose strategy set consists simply of the decision to convict or acquit the suspect, in the event that there is a trial. Recall that C does not observe P's type; thus, if there is a trial, C must form some belief about P's type (and hence about the suspect's guilt). This belief is denoted by μ, where $\mu = \Pr[\theta = G]$. Recall that the prior belief is based on the knowledge that the fraction of good types in the population of police officers is $1 - \beta$; the updated belief is formed using Bayes' Rule whenever possible. C's payoff reflects a desire to reach the correct verdict (i.e. to convict guilty suspects and acquit innocent ones), combined with a tradeoff between Type I and Type II errors. If there is a trial, C's payoff is:

$$u_C = \begin{cases} 0 & \text{if (innocent, acquit) or (guilty, convict)} \\ -q & \text{if (innocent, convict)} \\ -(1-q) & \text{if (guilty, acquit)} \end{cases} \qquad (11.3)$$

This follows the formulation in Feddersen and Pesendorfer (1998), and has been widely used in the literature (e.g. Dharmapala and McAdams, 2003; Seidmann, 2005).

The parameter q captures the disutility from wrongly convicting an innocent suspect; the higher is q, the greater the disutility. Thus, q reflects the threshold of 'reasonable doubt' that is required for conviction; it is assumed that $q \, \varepsilon \, (1/2, 1)$. Given a belief μ that the suspect is guilty, the expected payoff to C from convicting is $-(1 - \mu)q$, whereas the expected payoff from acquitting is $-\mu(1-q)$. Hence, this payoff function implies that C will convict whenever $\mu > q$ (as a tiebreaking assumption, assume that C acquits when indifferent). If a trial does not take place, then (because it is implicitly assumed that a crime has taken place, so that the lack of a trial implies that the perpetrator has not been found) C is assumed to receive an arbitrary, strictly negative payoff, equal to $-v$ (where $v > 0$).

Note that it is possible to consider the above payoff function as characterizing not only C's utility, but also as representing one aspect of social welfare (as in Grossman and Katz (1983) and Reinganum (1988), where social welfare is equated with the payoff of the jury). That is, the court's tradeoff between Type I and Type II errors can be viewed as representing society's preferences over these two kinds of miscarriages of justice. Of course, a full welfare analysis would have to consider other kinds of costs and benefits (such as the level of crime, resources expended on trials, the utility of the police) that are beyond the scope of this chapter. Thus, we generally refer to the court's payoff, rather than to social welfare; however, the broader interpretation should be borne in mind.

3.2   Equilibria

In the game described above, there always exists what we term a 'passive' pooling equilibrium, where neither type of P investigates. This is supported by out-of-equilibrium beliefs that would lead C to acquit, in the event that a trial was to occur. Formally:

Proposition 1: Γ^0 has a 'passive' perfect Bayesian pooling equilibrium, where the equilibrium strategies are 'not enter' for both types of P, and 'acquit' for C ($\lambda=0$). C's beliefs are $\mu^* \in [0, q]$, and equilibrium payoffs are:

$$u_G{}^* = u_B{}^* = 0 \text{ and } u_C{}^* = -v$$

Proof: To show that this is an equilibrium given the equilibrium strategy profile for P, note first that because there is no trial in equilibrium, C's beliefs are unconstrained by Bayes' Rule. Thus, $\mu^* \in [0, q]$ is admissible. Given these beliefs, C's payoff is maximized by acquitting if a trial occurs (recall that C convicts whenever $\mu > q$). Given C's beliefs and equilibrium strategy, suppose that P_G deviates by investigating, thereby incurring a cost of either k or, if the investigation leads to a search, $(k+s)$. As C acquits, and $k > 0$ and $s > 0$, P_G's deviation payoff will be strictly negative, whereas $u_G = 0$ in equilibrium. Given C's beliefs and equilibrium strategy, suppose that P_B deviates by planting evidence, thereby incurring a cost of ρ. As C acquits, and $\rho > 0$, P_B's deviation payoff will be strictly negative, whereas $u_B = 0$ (a similar argument holds if P_B deviates by investigating rather than planting). Thus, this is an equilibrium.

Since this equilibrium is uninteresting, we now consider the case where both types of P enter the game. We focus on pure strategy equilibria in which both good and bad police enter. Given A2, bad types, if they enter, will always prefer to plant evidence than to follow proper procedure, and so they would never play a mixed strategy that involves randomizing between those two options. Nor would an equilibrium exist in which they randomize between entering and not entering (implying that $\lambda - \rho = 0$) for in that case, good types would not enter (again, by A2).

Under the assumptions made above, P_B will always plant evidence, while P_G will investigate and only pursue an arrest if evidence of guilt is found. Thus, there will be two kinds of cases brought to trial – those in which P is the good type and the suspect is guilty, and those in which P is the bad type, and the suspect is (probably) innocent. (We allow the possibility that P_B will end up framing a guilty person by chance.) The court thus has to infer the probability that a given suspect is guilty. Note that the court cannot simply use the prior belief that a fraction $(1 - \beta)$ of police officers are of the good type, as there is some probability that P_G does not find probable cause and/or evidence of guilt, and so never arrests a suspect. The *ex ante* probability that P_G ends up making an arrest is φg, so the fraction of police officers who are of the good type and make an arrest is $(1 - \beta)\varphi g$. In contrast, P_B always arrests someone, so the fraction of bad types who make arrests is simply β, and a fraction φg of those defendants is guilty (by chance). Thus, when C is faced with a P who has arrested a suspect and is testifying at trial, the inferred probability that the suspect is guilty will be:

$$\frac{(1 - \beta)\phi g + \beta\phi g}{(1 - \beta)\phi g + \beta} = \frac{\phi g}{(1 - \beta)\phi g + \beta} \tag{11.4}$$

where the numerator is the 'number' of guilty suspects (some of whom are accidentally apprehended by the bad type), and the denominator is the 'number' arrested. If this inferred probability exceeds q, then C will convict; otherwise, C will acquit. Note that (11.4) is decreasing in β, implying that as the fraction of bad types rises, the court will be less likely to convict. In the limit, if $\beta = 0$ (all police are good), then (11.4) reduces to one, and only truly guilty suspects are arrested. Thus, the court will convict since $1 > q$. Conversely, if $\beta = 1$, (11.4) reduces to φg, which is the probability that a randomly chosen person is guilty. We assume that the court would never convict in this case; that is,

A3: $\varphi g < q$.
If C's optimal strategy is to convict, then a different kind of pooling equilibrium – one where both types of P enter the game – can be sustained. This 'active' pooling equilibrium requires the following condition to be satisfied:

$$\frac{\phi g}{(1 - \beta)\phi g + \beta} > q \tag{11.5}$$

Proposition 2: Suppose that assumptions A1–A3 and condition (11.5) hold. Then, Γ^0 has an 'active' perfect Bayesian pooling equilibrium, where the equilibrium strategies are 'enter' for both types of P, and 'convict' for C ($\lambda = 1$). In this equilibrium, C's beliefs are

$$\mu^* = \frac{\phi g}{(1 - \beta)\phi g + \beta} \tag{11.6}$$

and the equilibrium (expected) payoffs are:

$$u_G^* = \varphi(g - s) - k$$

$$u_B^* = 1 - \rho$$

$$u_C^* = \frac{-\beta(1 - \phi g)q}{(1 - \beta)\phi g + \beta}$$

Proof: Given the equilibrium strategy profiles for P_G and P_B, the belief μ^* is clearly correct (see the argument in the text). Given μ^*, from (11.3), C's expected payoff from convicting is given by:

$$u_C^* = \Pr[\text{defendant is guilty}]\cdot 0 + \Pr[\text{defendant is innocent}]\cdot(-q)$$

$$= -(1 - \mu^*)q$$

which, using (11.6), gives the equilibrium expected payoff above. Convicting is optimal for C because the payoff from acquitting is

$$u_C = \Pr[\text{defendant is guilty}] \cdot (-(1-q)) + \Pr[\text{defendant is innocent}] \cdot 0$$

$$= -\mu^*(1-q)$$

and condition (11.5) (i.e. $\mu^* > q$) implies that this is lower than u_C^*. In equilibrium, P_G incurs the investigation cost k, and has probability φg of obtaining a conviction, while the search cost s is incurred with probability φ; this gives the equilibrium u_G^*. P_B obtains a conviction with probability 1, while incurring only the planting cost ρ; this gives the equilibrium u_B^*. Given C's beliefs μ^* and the equilibrium strategies of P, it is optimal for each type of P to play the equilibrium strategy. In particular, a deviation by P_G to a strategy of non-entry would lead to a payoff $u_G = 0$, whereas the payoff from entering is $\varphi(g-s) - k > 0$ (by A1). Similarly, a deviation by P_B to a strategy of non-entry would lead to a payoff of $u_B = 0$, whereas the payoff from playing u_B^* is $1 - \rho > 0$. A deviation by P_B to P_G's strategy would also not be profitable, as $1 - \rho > \varphi(g-s) - k$ (by A2). Thus, this is an equilibrium.

In this equilibrium, C is willing to convict all defendants, even while knowing that a certain fraction of them (most of those arrested by P_B) are factually innocent.

Finally, we show that there exist no separating equilibria (i.e. the court is never able to distinguish between the two types of police, given the information available):

Proposition 3:   Given the assumptions above, there exists no separating equilibrium of Γ^0.

Proof: Consider a candidate-equilibrium where P_G enters and P_B does not. Given these strategies for P, C will infer that $\mu = 1$, and hence will convict. But, this is not an equilibrium, as P_B has an incentive to enter, thereby receiving a payoff of $1 - \rho > 0$, which is greater than the 0 payoff in the candidate-equilibrium. Consider next a candidate-equilibrium where P_B enters and P_G does not. Given these strategies for P, C will infer that $\mu = \varphi g$, and hence will acquit (by A3). But, this is not an equilibrium as P_B has an incentive to deviate to a strategy of non-entry, thereby receiving a payoff of 0, whereas the payoff in the candidate-equilibrium is $-\rho < 0$. Hence, there can be no separating equilibrium.

The intuition for the lack of a separating equilibrium is simply that, whenever a good type of P is willing to enter, entry is even more beneficial from the point of view of a bad type (recalling that the latter does not incur the investigation costs k, nor the difference between ρ and s). Thus, it is impossible for the good type of P to distinguish herself from the bad type.

4.   INTRODUCING TORT LIABILITY

In this section, we consider the imposition of tort liability on police officers for searches without probable cause. As discussed earlier, tort liability is the favored remedy for unlawful searches of many commentators on the Fourth Amendment, including Posner (1981) and Amar (1997). The introduction of tort liability involves adding another player, a civil court, denoted T. A suspect who has been searched can (costlessly) seek damages by filing suit. Note, however, that under the assumptions made above, P_G never searches without probable cause (as the *ex ante* probability of success is zero).[11] Thus, if a suspect has been searched but not arrested, it can be inferred by T that P was of the good type, and no damages will be awarded. Hence, we assume that only those suspects who are arrested (regardless of whether they are convicted) bring suit. T then decides whether to hold P liable or not: the strategy set is {Liable, Not liable}. If T determines that P is liable, then damages of $D > 1$ are assessed against P (we ignore any wealth constraints, and assume that D is paid personally by P). T's payoff if there is a trial is analogous to C's payoff:

$$
u_T = \begin{cases} 0 & \text{if (liable, violation) or (not liable, no violation)} \\ -t & \text{if (liable, no violation)} \\ -(1-t) & \text{if (not liable, violation)} \end{cases} \tag{11.7}
$$

Here, $t \in [1/2, 1)$ captures the tradeoff between Type I and Type II errors in the sanctioning of police. Because civil trials only require a preponderance of evidence rather than a reasonable doubt standard, we would expect that $t < q$ (however, this is not essential to the results below).

As we assume that all criminal defendants file suit, the only circumstances in which no suits are filed are when there are no arrests and hence no violations (either there are no searches, or the only searches are carried out by the good type of P). Thus, when there is no suit, T's payoff can be assumed to be 0 (again, this is not crucial to the results). If a suit is filed, T forms a belief by inferring the probability that a Fourth Amendment violation occurred (i.e. that P searched unreasonably). Because P_G never has an incentive to commit such a violation, this probability is equal to the probability that P is of the bad type, which is simply the complement of

C's belief μ (and so will be denoted using the same notation). Of course, in equilibrium, the beliefs of C and T have to be mutually consistent. Note that T will find P liable whenever the belief that P is of the bad type exceeds the threshold t: i.e. $(1 - \mu) > t$. The game with the added tort liability stage will be denoted Γ^T.

In analyzing Γ^T, the first point to note is that a passive pooling equilibrium continues to exist. In this equilibrium, C believes it is sufficiently likely that P is of the bad type that it is willing to acquit all defendants, and in anticipation of this outcome, neither type of P enters. Because the prospect of acquittal deters entry by P, there are no searches. Hence, there is no possibility of unreasonable searches, and no civil suits are filed against the police. Consequently, the beliefs and actions of T (off the equilibrium path) do not affect the equilibrium specified in Proposition 1.

Now suppose that Condition (5) is satisfied so that C believes that it is sufficiently likely that P is of the good type to convict all defendants. This induces both types of P to enter, and leads to the equilibrium specified in Proposition 2 above. When we add a civil court T to the model, suits will be filed by all defendants. Faced with deciding the outcome of a suit against a police officer, T will infer the probability that the officer is of the bad type. Given the strategies of each type of P in the Proposition 2 equilibrium, T's inference will be that P is bad with probability $1 - \mu$. C would only have convicted the defendant if $\mu > q$, however, which implies that $\mu > 0.5$ (recalling that $q > 0.5$ by assumption). This of course implies that $1 - \mu < 0.5$, and (as $t \geq 0.5$ by assumption) that $1 - \mu < t$. That is, in any equilibrium where C is willing to convict (and hence the P's are willing to enter), T's optimal strategy will be to find the police officer not liable. Hence, the equilibrium outcomes are essentially unchanged from those of Proposition 2:

Proposition 4: Suppose that assumptions A1–A3 and Condition (11.5) hold. Then, Γ^T has an 'active' perfect Bayesian pooling equilibrium, where the equilibrium strategies are for both P_G and P_B to 'enter,' for C to 'acquit,' and for T to find P 'not liable.' In this equilibrium, both C and T hold beliefs

$$\mu^* = \frac{\varphi g}{(1 - \beta)\varphi g + \beta}$$

and the equilibrium payoffs are:

$$u_G^* = \varphi g - k - \varphi s$$

$$u_B^* = 1 - \rho$$

$$u_C^* = \frac{-\beta(1 - \varphi g)q}{(1 - \beta)\varphi g + \beta}$$

$$u_T^* = \frac{-\beta(1 - \varphi g)(1 - t)}{(1 - \beta)\varphi g + \beta}$$

Proof: The proof is analogous to that for Proposition 2 for P and C. To show that is optimal for T to find P not liable, consider a deviation by T to the alternative strategy of finding P liable. The expected utility of this is – $t\mu^*$, as compared to $-(1 - \mu^*)(1 - t)$ for finding P not liable. But the latter exceeds the former given $1 - \mu^* < t$, so the expected utility from playing 'Not liable' is higher. Note also that T's equilibrium beliefs are correct given these strategies.

Finally, as the creation of a tort liability regime does not in itself lead to any new information about police characteristics becoming available, there is no separating equilibrium:

Proposition 5:   Given the assumptions above, there exists no separating equilibrium of Γ^T.

Proof: Straightforward.

To summarize, the equilibrium outcomes of the game with tort liability are essentially identical to those in the basic game analyzed earlier. The introduction of tort liability makes no difference in our model because the only circumstances in which a police officer would be found liable are those in which C would not be willing to convict in any event. Under such conditions, police of both types are deterred from entering in the first place because C will not convict, and the existence of a tort liability system does not provide any additional deterrence of wrongful conduct by bad types of P.

5.   INTRODUCING THE EXCLUSIONARY RULE

This section returns to the basic game of Section 3, denoted Γ^0, and introduces an alternative procedural regime that involves two new elements. The first is that, between the first and second stages of the game, P has the option of applying (costlessly) to a judge for a search warrant. This involves introducing a judge or magistrate as a new player, but for the sake of simplicity, she is assumed to be a nonstrategic player. The judge can observe whether or not probable cause was found in stage 1 against the suspect whom P seeks to search, and is assumed to issue a warrant if and only if probable cause was found. The second element is that, in the fourth stage of the game (the criminal trial), the court excludes any evidence that was (actually or allegedly) found in the absence of a search warrant. While this is admittedly a simplification, it is assumed that exclusion amounts to the acquittal of the defendant. These modifications to Γ^0 are intended to represent in stylized form the major features of the line of Fourth Amendment jurisprudence established by *Mapp*, and this regime will be referred to as the exclusionary rule (ER) and denoted Γ^{ER} (although, as discussed in Section 6 below, the warrant requirement is more crucial to the results than the exclusion of evidence *per se*). Under this regime, there is assumed to be no possibility of tort actions against P by suspects.

These changes to the game entail that P now faces a new choice of whether to apply for a search warrant or not. However, it turns out that, for both types of P, failing to apply when probable cause is found is always strictly dominated. Since failing to obtain a search warrant implies that the suspect is never convicted, any strategy for P that involves investigating and *not* applying for a search warrant is strictly dominated by a strategy that involves not investigating at all (as this saves the investigation cost k). Applying for a warrant when there has been no investigation, or when an investigation has failed to find probable cause, is pointless, given that magistrates can observe this, and never issue warrants in such circumstances. Thus, it can be assumed that a police officer always applies for a search warrant if, and only if, probable cause is found. It is important to stress that, because of the assumption that the magistrate who issues warrants can observe or verify whether or not probable cause was found, P cannot falsify the evidence used to obtain a search warrant. Moreover, there is no possibility of collusion between P and the magistrate. The effects of relaxing these assumptions are discussed in Section 6 below.

The court C also faces a new decision regarding whether to exclude evidence. It will be assumed, however, that it always does so if a search warrant is not produced at trial (and, moreover, a warrant cannot be successfully falsified by P). This assumption is made without loss of generality in this framework – it turns out that the only circumstances in which evidence would be excluded are those in which the court would disregard the evidence in any case because it is unreliable (i.e., has too high a probability of having been planted by a bad P). This is a consequence of the assumption that no good P ever commits a Fourth Amendment violation; as discussed earlier (as well as in Section 6 below), relaxing this assumption would only strengthen the chapter's results. Finally, the assumption of a nonstrategic magistrate is also without substantial loss of generality, as the most natural assumption concerning her objective function – that it is identical to that of C – would lead to essentially the same behavior as postulated above.

The new game Γ^{ER}, like those analyzed previously, has a passive pooling equilibrium where neither type of P enters. Recall that in the equilibrium of Proposition 1, C's beliefs lead to a strategy of always acquitting, and the prospect of acquittal is sufficient to deter P from entering. In these circumstances, remedies for Fourth Amendment violations are irrelevant, and so this class of equilibria continues to exist under both a tort liability regime and an exclusionary rule regime.

We thus turn to the case where both types of P enter. The most important change caused by the ER regime is that P_B can no longer follow a strategy of not investigating, and then planting. Were this approach followed, no search warrant could be produced at trial, and so the (purported) evidence would be excluded and the defendant acquitted. To obtain a conviction, P_B must investigate (and therefore expend effort at cost k). If probable cause is not found, a warrant cannot be obtained, and there is no benefit to planting evidence on a suspect. On the other hand, if probable cause is found, then a search warrant is obtained (recalling that the magistrate cannot distinguish between P_B and P_G *per se*). Once the warrant is issued, however, P_B has an incentive to plant evidence on the suspect against whom the warrant was obtained. This incentive arises most clearly when $\rho < s$ (i.e. the effort costs of planting are strictly lower than those of carrying out a genuine search). However, if C is anticipated to convict, the incentive exists even when $\rho = s$, because planting enables P_B to obtain convictions against *every* suspect against whom probable cause is found, rather than simply those who are actually guilty.

Consider the inference problem faced by C when a trial occurs. The probability that P_G will end up making an arrest is (as before) $(1 - \beta)\varphi g$. The probability that P_B will make an arrest, however, is lower than in Γ^0, as an arrest in Γ^{ER} requires that probable cause has been found. Thus, the probability that P_B will make an arrest is $\beta\varphi$. Consequently, the probability that a defendant is truly guilty is given by the expression:

$$\frac{(1 - \beta)\varphi g + \beta\varphi g}{(1 - \beta)\varphi g + \beta\varphi} = \frac{\varphi g}{(1 - \beta)\varphi g + \beta\varphi} \tag{11.8}$$

If this probability exceeds q then C will convict:

$$\frac{\varphi g}{(1 - \beta)\varphi g + \beta\varphi} > q \tag{11.9}$$

Note that this is a stronger condition compared to (11.5) (i.e., is satisfied for larger values of q) because P_B's are able to bring fewer suspects to trial (i.e., only those against whom probable cause is found). Thus, there is a smaller proportion of truly innocent defendants. The beliefs in (11.8) sustain an equilibrium in which both types of P enter: this is the active pooling equilibrium of the game under the ER regime.

Proposition 6:   Suppose that assumptions A1–A3 and Condition (11.9) hold. Then, Γ^{ER} has an 'active' perfect Bayesian pooling equilibrium, where the equilibrium strategies are for P_G and P_B to 'enter,' and for C to 'convict.' C's beliefs are

$$\mu^* = \frac{\varphi g}{(1 - \beta)\varphi g + \beta\varphi} \tag{11.10}$$

and the equilibrium payoffs are:

$$u_G^* = \varphi(g - s) - k$$

$$u_B^* = \varphi(1 - \rho) - k$$

$$u_C^* = \frac{-\beta\varphi(1 - g)q}{(1 - \beta)\varphi g + \beta\varphi}$$

Proof: Given the equilibrium strategy profile for P, the belief μ^* is clearly correct (as argued in the text). Given μ^*, C's expected payoff is given by:

$$u_C^* = \Pr[\text{defendant is guilty}]\cdot 0 + \Pr[\text{defendant is innocent}]\cdot(-q)$$

$$= -(1 - \mu^*)q,$$

which, using (11.10), gives the above expression. Conversely, C's payoff from acquitting is

$$u_C = \Pr[\text{defendant is guilty}]\cdot(-(1 - q)) + \Pr[\text{defendant is innocent}]\cdot 0$$

$$= -\mu^*(1-q)$$

Condition (11.9) (i.e. $\mu^* > q$) implies that this is lower than u_C^*. In equilibrium, P_G incurs the investigation cost k, and has probability φg of obtaining a conviction, while the search cost s is incurred with probability φ; this gives the equilibrium u_G^*. P_B also incurs the investigation cost k, and obtains a conviction with probability φ (i.e. whenever probable cause is found), while incurring the planting cost ρ (also with probability φ); this gives the equilibrium u_B^*. Given C's beliefs μ^* and an optimal strategy of convicting, it is optimal for each type of P to play the equilibrium strategy. Consider a deviation by P_G to a strategy of non-entry. This would lead to a payoff $u_G = 0$, whereas the payoff from entering is $\varphi(g - s) - k > 0$ (by A1). Likewise consider a deviation by P_B to a strategy of non-entry. This would lead to a payoff of $u_B = 0$, whereas the payoff from playing u_B* is $\varphi(1 - \rho) - k > 0$ (by A1, because $\varphi(1 - \rho) - k > \varphi(g - s) - k$). A deviation by P_B to P_G's strategy would also be unprofitable, as $\varphi(1 - \rho) - k > \varphi(g - s) - k$ (as $\rho \leq s$ and $g < 1$ by assumption). Thus, this is an equilibrium.

The intuition here is very similar to that for Proposition 2. What is noteworthy, however, is that the ER regime substantially reduces the scope for P_B to plant evidence, and forces bad police to incur investigation costs that could be avoided in the basic game, and under TL. However, ER does not lead to any separating equilibria:

Proposition 7:   Given the assumptions above, there exists no separating equilibrium of Γ^{ER}.

Proof: Analogous to proof of Proposition 3.

The intuition here (as before) is that whenever entry is profitable for P_G, it will also be profitable for P_B, given that the latter incurs a (weakly) lower cost of planting, ρ, relative to the former's cost of search s, and also because P_B has a higher *ex ante* probability of obtaining a conviction than does P_G. As P_G's have no credible means of distinguishing themselves from P_B's, a separating equilibrium is impossible. (However, see Section 6 for a discussion of the situation where costs of investigation differ for the two types.)

Having characterized the equilibrium outcomes in three games – Γ^0, Γ^T, and Γ^{ER} – it remains to compare the properties of these equilibria. The existence of the same passive pooling equilibrium in each of these games makes it difficult to compare the outcomes of instituting different Fourth Amendment remedies.[12] However, one approach is to focus on the active pooling equilibria in each regime. It is only in these equilibria that any police investigations, arrests and trials occur at all, and so these equilibria may be argued to be more relevant (since in practice investigations, arrests and trials are all observed, and would presumably continue to be observed under any realistic institutional structure). The results in Section 4 showed that the TL regime leads to identical outcomes to the basic game Γ^0 (where there is no Fourth Amendment remedy). Thus, the (active pooling equilibrium) outcomes of Γ^0 and Γ^{TL} can be considered together, and contrasted with the (active pooling equilibrium) outcome of Γ^{ER}.

Let u_C^0, u_C^T and u_C^{ER} denote the equilibrium expected payoff of C in the active pooling equilibria of Γ^0, Γ^T, and Γ^{ER}, respectively.

Proposition 8:   Restricting attention to equilibria where arrests are made (i.e. to active pooling equilibria), $u_C^{ER} > u_C^0 = u_C^T$ (i.e. the court's payoff is strictly higher in Γ^{ER} than in Γ^0 or Γ^T).

Proof: From Propositions 2 and 4:

$$u_C^0 = u_C^T = \frac{-\beta(1 - \varphi g)q}{(1 - \beta)\varphi g + \beta}$$

From Proposition 6:

$$u_C^{ER} = \frac{-\beta\varphi(1 - g)q}{(1 - \beta)\varphi g + \beta\varphi}$$

Consider $u_C^{ER} - u_C^0$:

$$u_C^{ER} - u_C^0 = \frac{-\beta\varphi(1 - g)q}{(1 - \beta)\varphi g + \beta\varphi} - \frac{-\beta(1 - \varphi g)q}{(1 - \beta)\varphi g + \beta}$$

$$= \frac{\beta\varphi g(1 - \varphi)q}{[(1 - \beta)\varphi g + \beta\varphi][(1 - \beta)\varphi g + \beta]}$$

$$> 0$$

(by the definitions of the parameters given earlier).

   This implies that the ER regime leads to a higher level of welfare for C. As discussed earlier, C's payoff can be interpreted as a proxy for social welfare (at least for the welfare derived by society from accuracy in criminal trials), and so it could be argued that the ER regime leads to a higher level of social welfare, in this particular respect. This constitutes the chapter's main result, and shows that there exist circumstances in which the ER regime may be superior (from the standpoint of accuracy in criminal adjudication) to a TL regime.

6.   EXTENSIONS

6.1   Heterogeneous Costs of Investigation

The preceding analysis has assumed that both types of P face the same effort cost k of undertaking an investigation. This appears reasonable as a basic assumption, because there does not seem to be any compelling reason why one type is likely to find investigation more or less costly than the other. However, it may be argued that in some circumstances the good type may not only be a better police officer in terms of being unwilling to plant evidence, but may also be superior in terms of investigative skills (for instance, the bad type's willingness to plant may arise from an inability to solve crimes through legitimate methods). While such an argument is not necessarily compelling in general, it is nonetheless of some interest to examine the case where the bad type faces a higher effort cost of investigation than does the good type.

Let k_G and k_B be the investigation costs of P_G and P_B, respectively, and suppose that $k_G < k_B$. Furthermore, suppose that the above assumptions hold for $k = k_G$ (so that it is optimal for P_G to enter when it is anticipated that C will convict). For k_B, the following assumption is made:

A4: $k_B > 1$.
This assumption implies that it is never optimal for P_B to enter and investigate (even if C is anticipated to convict). Note that A4 is slightly stronger than required, but it is simpler to formulate the assumption in this way.

The assumptions above entail that k_G and k_B are *sufficiently* different (for sufficiently small differences in these costs, the results derived in previous sections would be unchanged). Even when they hold, however, the equilibria of Γ^0 and Γ^T derived in Sections 3 and 4 are unaffected by the heterogeneity in investigation costs. Recall that in these equilibria, P_B's equilibrium behavior involves either not entering, or entering and not investigating. Thus, the investigation cost is not incurred in equilibrium. Under the assumption of heterogeneous costs made here, deviation to any strategy that involves investigation becomes even less profitable for P_B than under the assumptions made in Sections 3 and 4; however, equilibrium behavior is unaffected. Thus, the results concerning Γ^0 and Γ^T are robust to assuming that P_B's investigations costs are higher.

This robustness does not apply, however, to Γ^{ER}. Recall that the active pooling equilibrium of Γ^{ER} involves P_B investigating (and hence incurring the effort cost of doing so). Thus, when k_G and k_B are sufficiently different, P_B will no longer be willing to pool with P_G, and instead will prefer not to enter (as, under the ER regime, entry requires that the investigation costs be expended in order to obtain a warrant and secure a conviction). In these circumstances, the active pooling equilibrium of Γ^{ER} no longer exists; instead, there exists a perfectly separating equilibrium in which P_G enters while P_B does not:

Proposition 9:   Suppose that A1 and A2 apply to k_G, and that A4 applies to k_B; then, there exists a perfectly separating equilibrium of Γ^{ER}, where the equilibrium strategies are for P_G to enter, P_B not to enter, and C to convict. C's beliefs are $\mu^* = 1$, and the equilibrium payoffs are:

$$u_G{}^* = \varphi(g - s) - k_G$$

$$u_B{}^* = 0$$

$$u_C{}^* = 0$$

Proof: Given P's strategy, C's beliefs are clearly correct (i.e. only P_G enters, so any defendant who is arrested and tried is guilty). Given these beliefs, it is optimal for C to convict: the equilibrium expected payoff is 0, while the expected payoff from acquitting is $-(1 - q) < 0$. Given C's beliefs and strategy, P's equilibrium strategy is optimal. If P_G were to deviate to a strategy that involves not entering, it would yield a payoff of 0, whereas the equilibrium payoff is $\varphi(g - s) - k_G > 0$ (by A1). Suppose P_B were to deviate by switching to a strategy that involves entering and planting. This would yield a payoff of $\varphi(1 - s) - k_B < 0$ (by A4), whereas the equilibrium payoff is 0. It is also not profitable for P_B to deviate by adopting P_G's strategy as it would lead to a payoff of $\varphi(g - s) - k_B < 0$ (by A4). Thus, this is an equilibrium.

In this equilibrium, C's payoff (and hence society's payoff from accuracy in criminal adjudication) is at the maximum possible level. Thus, the earlier conclusions concerning the superiority of the ER regime (in Section 5) are substantially reinforced when different types of P face heterogeneous costs. Moreover, in these circumstances, the informational assumptions required concerning the warrant process can be relaxed (relative to the assumptions of Section 5). Recall that the magistrate issuing search warrants was assumed in Section 5 to be able to observe whether or not probable cause was found. When k_G and k_B are sufficiently different, all that is required for the separating equilibrium is that the magistrate be able to observe whether or not an investigation actually occurred (the finding of probable cause, as well as the cost incurred in the investigation can both be P's private information). Thus, heterogeneity in investigation costs substantially strengthens the case for the superiority of the ER regime; however, this superiority can be established (as in Section 5) even with an identical k, and (as noted above) there is no compelling reason why the heterogeneity assumptions made here would always be true.[13]

6.2 Criminal Liability for Planting Evidence

In the analysis so far, there has been no mention of the possibility that P_B may face criminal liability for planting evidence and framing suspects. These activities are of course illegal, and so this section considers the consequences of extending the model in this direction. Incorporating criminal liability into the model is straightforward, and involves essentially the same setup as the game with tort liability (Γ^T in Section 4 above). The main difference is that the second court is now also a criminal court, and it is possible for the state to prosecute police officers for planting evidence on suspects. This court can be assumed to have the same payoff function as the civil court in Section 4 (given by Eq. (5)), except that it will generally require a *higher* standard of proof to convict the police officer than the civil court would require to award damages against the police officer for a Fourth Amendment violation. This means, however, that the results of Section 4 apply *a fortiori* to this case: if there is a sufficient likelihood of planting to convict P, then there would never be a sufficient likelihood of guilt to convict the suspect who is arrested by the same P. That is, the prospect of acquittal of the suspect will always be sufficient to deter P_B from entering and planting, so the existence of criminal liability for planting will not have any additional deterrent effect on this behavior. Consequently, none of the results derived above in Sections 3–5 would be affected by the existence of criminal liability for P for planting evidence.[14]

6.3 Separating the Warrant Requirement from the Exclusionary Rule

In characterizing the alternative institutional structures associated with Fourth Amendment remedies, a TL regime has been contrasted with an ER regime. However, the latter has *combined* the warrant requirement and the exclusionary rule. This reflects current Fourth Amendment jurisprudence, but it is not conceptually necessary that the two be linked. Note that in Γ^{ER}, evidence is never excluded in equilibrium. Moreover, evidence would be excluded (off the equilibrium path) only in cases where C infers a sufficiently high likelihood that P is of the bad type (and hence that the evidence is unreliable because it has been planted). Thus, the exclusionary rule *per se* has no independent effect: C would discount the purported evidence even in the absence of a requirement to exclude it. This means that all the results relating to Γ^{ER} would be unaffected if the exclusionary rule itself did not exist, as long as a warrant requirement was in place.

In reality, of course, there are many reasons why reliable evidence may be excluded under an ER regime (such as mistakes by good types of P). Even if evidence is unreliable, moreover, juries may not always be able to infer this (due for example to cognitive biases or limited attention), and so it may be optimal to exclude the evidence. Abstracting from such considerations, however, the model of the ER regime in this chapter yields a significant insight: the particular benefit of the ER regime identified here (that it can deter the planting of evidence by police because of the requirement that there is some auditing of the investigation prior to search, through the warrant process) is due primarily to the warrant requirement and not the exclusionary rule *per se*. Thus, it is possible to envisage a system in which the warrant requirement stands by itself. The warrant requirement does not of course include any remedy for warrantless searches, but courts could appropriately discount the value of evidence obtained without a warrant to take into account the possibility of its having been planted. In effect, acquittal becomes the remedy when this probability is sufficiently high. Alternatively, the warrant requirement could be combined with tort liability for police officers who carry out unreasonable searches, a regime that would also offer protection to individuals who may be harassed by the police by being targeted for search, but without being framed. All the results obtained in Sections 5 and 6.1 above for Γ^{ER} would also hold in these regimes.

7. DISCUSSION AND CONCLUSION

The discussion of Fourth Amendment remedies among law and economics scholars (and, increasingly, among constitutional criminal procedure scholars) has tended towards a consensus that a system of tort liability is superior on a number of grounds (such as efficiency and conformity with the intentions of the framers) to the current regime that combines a warrant requirement and an exclusionary rule (albeit with many exceptions). The aim of this chapter has been to develop an asymmetric information model of the process of criminal investigation, search, arrest and trial that demonstrates that there are circumstances in which the latter regime is preferable according to the (widely accepted) criterion of accuracy in adjudication. In particular, when some subset of police officers is willing to plant evidence on suspects (rather than to pursue truth-seeking investigations), the use of the warrant requirement and exclusionary rule provides a mechanism for auditing police investigations at a stage prior to search. By reducing the opportunities to plant evidence, it reduces the incidence of false convictions due to planting (although this is not, of course, the kind of abuse it is designed to remedy).

The remainder of this section briefly discusses some caveats to the model and its conclusions. First, the model assumes that the 'good' type of police cannot produce evidence (either about the facts of the case, or about their character) at trial to distinguish themselves from the 'bad' type. While this may seem unrealistic, nonetheless, the model's basic conclusions hold as long as the types are indistinguishable *to some degree* from the perspective of the court; that is, the 'good' type would always have to be able to distinguish itself *perfectly* to change the nature of the results.

The model also assumes that the judge who decides whether to issue warrants can accurately observe the results of the police investigation (or, in the heterogeneous-cost variant, at least whether an investigation occurred). If this were not the case, or if the judge were to collude with the police and always issue warrants, then the outcomes under the two remedies would be identical. However, as long as the judge has some ability to verify investigations, and some degree of independence, the basic conclusions of the model hold.

It has been assumed in the model that officers of the 'good' type never carry out unreasonable searches. In reality, they may make good faith errors and thereby commit Fourth Amendment violations (without being involved in planting evidence). This could be incorporated into the model, but its effect is to reduce the payoff to the 'good' type from investigating. Thus, it would reduce the fraction of 'good' types who would enter in an active pooling equilibrium, and change the cutoff probability above which the court is willing to convict; however, the results would not be fundamentally altered. Even if the exclusionary rule were to deter good faith errors 'excessively' (relative to tort liability), the accuracy-in-adjudication effect identified by the model would still operate.

In the comparison across the two Fourth Amendment remedies, the standard of reasonableness has been held fixed. If the tort liability regime involves a more socially efficient standard of reasonableness, then that would qualify some of the conclusions of the model. However, this would be an argument not for abandoning the warrant requirement and exclusionary rule, but rather for modifying the standard of evidence required for warrants to be issued.

It should be emphasized that this chapter has not sought to undertake a general social welfare analysis of the alternative remedies. This would require the incorporation of factors such as the effects on crime levels, the utility of police officers, and the administrative costs of the court system. Rather, the focus has been on one specific (and relatively uncontroversial) aspect of social welfare – the accuracy of courts' conviction and acquittal decisions.

Finally, it may be thought that the model takes too pessimistic a view of police motivation. Note, however, that the model assumes that the basic agency problem between the public and the police (of motivating police to expend effort to seek convictions, rather than to shirk) has been solved. The remaining problem arises from asymmetric information between police and the public regarding the details of police practices and the evidence against suspects (and it seems a reasonable assumption that such an information asymmetry exists). Thus, this model is in some respects *less* pessimistic about police motivation than some existing models of police corruption (e.g. Bowles and Garoupa, 1997; Polinsky and Shavell, 2001) that assume that police are motivated by monetary gain in seeking bribes from suspects. Moreover, the model's basic conclusions hold even if the fraction of police willing to plant evidence is very small. Note also, in conclusion, that the approach adopted here can be placed in the context of the 'public choice' tradition in economics that models public officials as self-interested actors (e.g. Hylton and Khanna, 2007).

NOTES

1. See, for example, *Weeks v. United States*, 232 U.S. 383 (1914); *Mapp v. Ohio*, 367 U.S. 643 (1961) extended these provisions to the states.
2. Formally, if B is the harm to the victim in terms of impaired privacy, p is the probability that evidence will be discovered that is decisive for conviction, and L is the social loss of not convicting the defendant, then a search is justified on economic grounds (and hence is reasonable) if $B < pL$ (see Posner (2011, p. 954), and *U.S. v. Carroll Towing*, 159 F.2d 169 (2d Cir. 1947), which established the Hand formula for negligence). For a more general economic analysis of the law of evidence, see Posner (1999).
3. Of course, there are many practical problems with a system of tort liability. There may, for instance, be agency problems if individual officers are immune from liability. However, this could be corrected by subjecting officers to dismissal, loss of pay, or criminal sanctions for violations. Another problem is the difficulty in measuring the damages from an illegal search (Stuntz, 1991).
4. To see why, note that if probable cause is interpreted to mean 'more likely than not,' then a search warrant will only be issued if $p > .5$, whereas the reasonableness standard would allow searches if $p > B/L$. Probable cause will therefore result in overdeterrence whenever $B/L < p < .5$, which will be true when the intrusion (B) is small but the value of the evidence (L) is large, a fairly common circumstance.
5. These include the 'Sheetrock' scandal in Dallas (e.g. P. Duggan, "Sheetrock' Scandal Hits Dallas Police: Cases Dropped, Officers Probed after Cocaine 'Evidence' Turns out to be Fake' *Washington Post*, Jan. 18, 2002) and the 'Ramparts' scandal in Los Angeles (e.g. M. Lait and S. Glover, '2 Ex-Officers Accused of Evidence Planting' *Los Angeles Times*, Oct. 21, 2000).
6. Of course, this assumes that judges are more trustworthy than police officers, a point emphasized by Stuntz (1991). Also, it is not crucial to this argument whether warrants are issued on the basis of probable cause, or based on the reasonableness standard discussed earlier; efficiency considerations would, however, favor the latter.
7. *Weeks v. United States*, 232 U.S. 383 (1914).
8. *Mapp v. Ohio*, 367 U.S. 643 (1961). See Atkins and Rubin (2003, Appendix A, p. 174) for a list of these states. A number of other countries, including Canada, Australia, Germany and Italy, use a discretionary exclusionary rule (p. 161).

9.   One way to think of 'good' types is that their cost of planting evidence is infinite.
10. A cost to P of arresting a suspect who is subsequently acquitted could be incorporated into the analysis without affecting the basic results.
11. Of course, this rules out an important class of cases where police may harass innocent individuals without seeking to frame them. In such instances, as Posner (1981, p. 54) points out, the warrant requirement and exclusionary rule are irrelevant, while tort liability may deter the misconduct. The focus here is not on this class of cases, but this issue is discussed further in Section 6.
12. Comparing Condition (5) and Condition (8), it is clear that the latter is satisfied for a larger subset of the parameter space than is the former. Thus, it could be argued that an active pooling equilibrium can be supported more easily under ER than under TL. However, whether this is a benefit from the standpoint of C (and of society) depends crucially on the value of the arbitrary parameter v, and so cannot be determined with any confidence.
13. Note however that, even if the cost differences went the other way (i.e. $k_G > k_B$), there could never be a 'bad' separating equilibrium where P_B enters and plants while P_G does not enter; C would be certain to acquit in such circumstances, and, moreover (given criminal liability for planting), P_B's planting would be detected with certainty.
14. Of course, in reality, it may be that there are circumstances in which P may be prosecuted successfully for planting evidence (e.g. if there is an unanticipated discovery of evidence of planting after the initial trial). However, the main point here is that, in this simplified framework, it is possible to ignore the effects of criminal liability.

REFERENCES

Amar, A.R., *The Constitution and Criminal Procedure: First Principles* Yale University Press: New Haven and London (1997).

Atkins, R. & P. Rubin, Effects of Criminal Procedure on Crime Rates: Mapping Out the Consequences of the Exclusionary Rule, 46 *Journal of Law and Economics*, 157–79 (2003).

Benoit, J.P. & J. Dubra, Why do Good Cops Defend Bad Cops? 45 *International Economic Review*, 787–809 (2004).

Bowles, R. & N. Garoupa, Casual Police Corruption and the Economics of Crime, 17 *International Review of Law and Economics* 75–87 (1997).

Daughety, A. & J. Reinganum, Keeping Society in the Dark: On the Admissibility of Pretrial Negotiations as Evidence in Court, 26 *Rand Journal of Economics*, 203–21 (1995).

Daughety, A. & J. Reinganum, On the Economics of Trials: Adversarial Process, Evidence, and Equilibrium Bias, 16 *Journal of Law, Economics, & Organization*, 365–94 (2000).

Dharmapala, D., N. Garoupa & R.H. McAdams, Do Exclusionary Rules Convict the Innocent? John M. Olin Law & Economics Working Paper No. 569 (2d Series), University of Chicago Law School (2011).

Dharmapala, D. & R.H. McAdams, The Condorcet Jury Theorem and the Expressive Function of Law: A Theory of Informative Law, 5 *American Law and Economics Review*, 1–31 (2003).

Feddersen, T.J. & W. Pesendorfer, Convicting the Innocent: The Inferiority of Unanimous Jury Verdicts, 92 *American Political Science Review*, 23–35 (1998).

Grossman, G. & M. Katz, Plea Bargaining and Social Welfare 73 *American Economic Review*, 749–57 (1983).

Hylton, K.N. & V. Khanna, A Public Choice Theory of Criminal Procedure, 15 *Supreme Court Economic Review*, 61–118 (2007).

Jacobi, T., The Law and Economics of the Exclusionary Rule, 87 *Notre Dame Law Review*, 585–675 (2011).

Lester, B., N. Persico & L. Visschers, Information Acquisition and the Exclusion of Evidence in Trials, 28 *Journal of Law, Economics, & Organization*, 163–82 (2012).

Mialon, H.M., An Economic Theory of the Fifth Amendment, 36 *Rand Journal of Economics*, 833–48 (2005).

Mialon, H.M. & S.H. Mialon, The Effects of the Fourth Amendment: An Economic Analysis, 24 *Journal of Law, Economics, & Organization*, 22–44 (2008a).

Mialon, H.M. & S.H. Mialon, The Economics of Search Warrants, Working paper 0810, Department of Economics, Emory University (2008b).

Miceli, T.J., Optimal Prosecution of Defendants whose Guilt is Uncertain, 6 *Journal of Law, Economics, & Organization*, 189–201 (1990).

Muehlheusser, G. & A. Roider, Black Sheep and Walls of Silence, 65 *Journal of Economic Behavior and Organization*, 387–408 (2008).

Polinsky, A.M. & S. Shavell, Corruption and Optimal Law Enforcement, 81 *Journal of Public Economics*, 1–24 (2001).

Posner, R.A., Rethinking the Fourth Amendment 1981 *Supreme Court Review*, 49–80 (1981).

Posner, R.A., An Economic Approach to the Law of Evidence. 51 *Stanford Law Review*, 1477–546 (1999).

Posner, R.A., Economic Analysis of Law (8th ed., Aspen 2011).

Reinganum, J., Plea Bargaining and Prosecutorial Discretion, 78 *American Economic Review*, 713–28 (1988).

Sanchirico, C.W., Games, Information and Evidence Production: With Application to English Legal History, 2 *American Law and Economics Review*, 342–80 (2000).

Schrag, J.L. & S.M. Scotchmer, Crime and Prejudice: The Use of Character Evidence in Criminal Trials, 10 *Journal of Law, Economics, & Organization*, 319–42 (1994).

Seidmann, D., The Effects of a Right to Silence, 72 *Review of Economic Studies*, 593–614 (2005).

Seidmann, D. & A. Stein, The Right to Silence Helps the Innocent: A Game–Theoretic Analysis of the Fifth Amendment Privilege, 114 *Harvard Law Review*, 430–510 (2000).

Stuntz, W., Warrants and Fourth Amendment Remedies, 77 *Virginia Law Review*, 881–943 (1991).

12. Crime, expectations, and the deterrence hypothesis
Matthew J. Baker and Niklas J. Westelius

INTRODUCTION

The *deterrence hypothesis*, first formalized by Becker (1968), states that criminals are rational agents that weigh the costs and benefits of their actions in deciding whether or not to engage in criminal activity. Since its initial statement, empirical models of the deterrence hypothesis have occupied a prominent place in economics. The standard approach to assessing the deterrence hypothesis is through investigation of the contemporaneous relationship between crime rates and variables that capture as well as possible the costs and benefits of committing crime. Results are of interest not only as tests of the deterrence hypothesis, but also in the role results play in informing policy. Further, the empirical investigation of the deterrence hypothesis has occupied a central position in the study of a variety of controversial issues, such as whether or not capital punishment is a deterrent to crime (Cameron 1994, Katz, Levitt, and Shustorovich 2003, Donohue and Wolfers 2005), the relationship between crime and gun control (Lott and Mustard 1997, Donohue 2004) and the impact of legalized abortion on crime rates (Donohue and Levitt 2001, Joyce 2004).

We argue that the typical econometric model of the deterrence hypothesis is flawed. Our contention is based on the observation that empirical models of aggregate crime rates fail to take into account what should be one of the most important aspects of the crime commission decision if criminals are indeed rational – that decisions to commit crimes have long term consequences. If one expands the model to include this possibility, expectations of *future* enforcement rates and economic conditions should matter in determining crime rates today, as should past crime commission decisions. Along these lines, we develop a simple two-period model that illustrates the basic ideas, and then expand this model into an infinitely-lived, representative-agent model of the crime commission decision. The model is set up so that the representative agent has reasons to take into account past crime rates and future economic conditions in making crime commission decisions. The dependence is induced by ideas that are part of the macroeconomic rational expectations models of behavior. Put simply, past crime rates enter the representative agent's utility function through habit persistence in crime, while future conditions matter because of the dependence of the agent's current time constraint on past criminal activity.

Estimates of our model suggest that both future expectations and past behavior exert an important impact on current crime rates. Our best estimates of contemporaneous elasticities of crime with respect to proxies of enforcement and punishment are small (on the order of −0.05) but are generally in agreement with previous research. Once expectations of future conditions and past behavior are included in the model, the resulting multiplier effects generate long run elasticities that are much larger than short run elasticities, but elasticities generally depend upon both the nature of the change (i.e., whether transitory or permanent), and also how criminals perceive the change. These results are tentative; the empirical model is plagued somewhat by weak identification.

Our findings have important policy implications, not only because of the implication that long run elasticities of crime rates with respect to measures of enforcement are larger than short run elasticities. If expectations of future conditions are important in driving current crime rates, the policy maker's credibility and ability to commit to a course of action assume central importance in assessing the merits of policy changes.

1   LITERATURE REVIEW

The literature on the deterrence hypothesis is voluminous and has several branches. Results vary with the time frame examined, the aggregation level of the data, and the econometric model employed. One common econometric approach – the approach followed in this chapter – centers on a yearly state level panel of state crime rates, proxies for enforcement, punishment, demographics, and economic conditions running from 1970 to the present. Usually, incarceration rates are used to proxy punishment severity, while proxies of the likelihood of apprehension such as the relative size of the police force are used to measure enforcement.

In contrast to the pessimistic view of the importance of the magnitude of punishment in crime drawn by Cameron (1988), most work has found that apprehension and punishment matter, a result in line with initial work on the deterrence hypothesis by Ehrlich (1973) and others. Spelman (2000) summarizes several recent estimates of the elasticity of crime with respect to incarceration rates, and reports that the typical estimated elasticity is on the order of −0.05 to −0.20, but estimates as large as −0.38 have been obtained.[1]

Estimates of the impact of enforcement are more variable, and some of this variation may perhaps be attributed to reliance on different proxies for the intensity of enforcement. Some researchers rely on direct proxies for apprehension and conviction probabilities (for example, Ehrlich (1973) and Lott and Mustard (1997)). These measures are computed by calculating the number of arrests per offense. Research employing probability-style measures of enforcement typically finds quite large elasticities of crime with respect to apprehension, but are subject to the critique that, when such measures of enforcement are used, the same quantity (number of offenses) appears in the denominator on the right hand side of the model and in the numerator of the left hand side variable, strongly biasing results in favor of finding a negative relationship (Spelman, 2000).[2] The most common alternative approach employs a less direct measure of the likelihood of apprehension which does not depend directly on crime rates, such as the relative size of the police force. Typical estimates of elasticities of crime with respect to the relative size of the police vary, but are probably around −0.40 (see Levitt 1997, 2004). At any rate, the bulk of empirical research on the deterrence hypothesis indicates that deterrence matters; apprehension rates and proxies for punishment severity appear to be inversely related to aggregate crime rates. Studies based on individual-level data largely corroborate these findings; for example, Grogger (1998) and Machin and Meghir (2004).

The typical empirical study of the deterrence hypothesis also includes measures intended to capture the impact of economic conditions and demographics on crime. Logically, economic conditions and demographics matter because they are important determinants of the opportunity costs of committing a crime. Kelly (2000), using county-level cross sectional data, found that measures of inequality are important in explaining violent crime. Using a state-level panel, Raphael and Winter-Ebmer (2001) argue that unemployment rates are important determinants of crime rates and that the drop in unemployment in the 1990s explains a large portion of the nationwide crime drop through the 1990s. Gould, Weinberg, and Mustard (2002) study the impact of wages and unemployment rates on crime rates and find that both matter in determining crime rates; they further find that wages have a larger impact on crime rates than unemployment rates. By contrast, Levitt (2004) argues that the magnitude of the effect of unemployment on crime is small and it is unlikely changes in unemployment rates played a large role in the drop in crime through the 1990s.[3]

While most empirical work on crime rates includes demographic control variables, few studies elaborate on the impact of these demographics. An exception is Levitt (1998a), who provides both theoretical and empirical support for the position that the age distribution matters in driving crime rates.[4] Thus, results vary as to the importance of demographics, economics, enforcement and apprehension in determining crime rates, inclusion of these things in an empirical model is well motivated by theory. The fact remains, however, that crime rates appear to be relatively inelastic with respect to demographic variables, economic conditions, enforcement, and punishment.

An interesting feature of the empirical research on the determinants of crime is that it has moved away from estimation of models with a specific, explicit theory of criminal behavior in mind.[5] In the next section, we show how thinking about the long run impact of criminal decisions leads to a different sort of model in which past behavior and expectations of future conditions matter in driving current crime rates. While one must be careful in interpreting our results because of potential identification problems, our model produces estimated elasticities comparable with those of previous research, but the inclusion of future expectations and past behavior changes interpretation of these elasticities. The result is that short-run and long-run elasticities of crime rates with respect to exogenous variables may differ profoundly.

A further point of interest of our results is the possibility that some empirical anomalies may disappear when expectations are built into the econometric model. A common aspect of research on crime is that in crime regressions, estimated coefficients sometimes take on signs opposite those predicted by theory. For example, it is not uncommon to find that the size of the police force and the crime rate are positively correlated in the data.[6] While these anomalies are often attributed to endogeneity problems, our results suggest that the problems may emerge because of a failure to correctly build expectations into the model.

2   THEORY

We begin by describing a simple two-period model of aggregate crime rates that capture the basic ideas expressed in the literature about the way market returns, expectations, and crime rates interact. In the ensuing subsection, we provide a synopsis as to how this model can be taken to aggregate crime rate data. We then conclude with an expansive derivation of an econometric specification of the model deriving from the optimizing behavior of a representative agent, in the spirit of a representative-agent macroeconometric model.

2.1   A Simple Two-period Model

Consider a unit mass of agents – potential criminals – who make a crime commission decision in each of two periods. There are two types of costs to committing crime to the potential criminal. The first type of cost is a direct cost in the form of a fine or jail sentence, which we denote x_t, $t = 1, 2$. x can be thought of as expected lost time due to crime commission – either working to pay off a fine, or time spent incarcerated. The second type of cost is an opportunity cost. If an agent chooses to commit a crime, the agent forgoes an opportunity to engage in productive activity, i.e., working in the honest labor market, which generates an expected return of y_t, $t = 1, 2$. We assume that x_t is fixed across the two time periods in the sense that agents' previous decisions do not change x_t. We do, however, assume that y_2 – the returns to honest work in the second period – depend in part on whether or not the agent engaged in crime in the first period. To be specific, let y_2 denote the returns to honest employment in the second period given the agent has not engaged in crime in the past, and let κy_2 denote what a previous criminal can earn in the market, so $\kappa < 1$ reflects decrease in productivity due to engaging in crime. This could reflect several things – employer reluctance to hire a convicted crimimal, or a forgone chance to engage in learning-by-doing in the productive sector in the first period. Excepting the dependence of earnings on previous criminal activity, we suppose punishments and returns to work are constant across agents, with the gains to crime commission distributed according to the cumulative distribution function $F(b)$, $b \in [-\infty, \infty]$, with density function $f(b) = F'(b)$.

It is helpful for the time being to picture the second period as time t (i.e., the current period), and the first period as time $t - 1$ (i.e., the previous period). We can now demonstrate how current crime rates depend upon past crime rates. In the second period, supposing that some agents have committed crime in the first period, we have two sets of conditions to examine; the decisions of previous criminals and previous non-criminals. Those agents who have previously committed a crime will opt for crime commission if:

$$b - x_2 \geq \kappa y_2$$

While those who did not previously commit crime will commit crime in the current period if:

$$b - x_2 \geq y_2$$

Suppose that in the previous period, there was some b_1^* for which if $b \geq b_1^*$, agents in the previous period decided to commit crimes. This means that the aggregate crime rate in period one is $c_1 = 1 - F(b_1^*)$. The aggregate crime rate in period two is then:

$$c_2 = [1 - F(b_1^*)][1 - F(\kappa y_2 + x_2)] + F(b_1^*)[1 - F(y_2 + x_2)]$$

The current aggregate crime rate c_2 can also be written to reflect the explicit dependence of the second-period crime rate on the first-period crime rate:

$$c_2 = c_1[1 - F(\kappa y_2 + x_2)] + (1 - c_1)[1 - F(y_2 + x_2)]$$

Perhaps more informatively, the current crime rate can also be written as:

$$c_2 = 1 - F(y_2 + x_2) + c_1[F(y_2 + x_2) - F(\kappa y_2 + x_2)] \qquad (12.1)$$

From expression (12.1), one can see clearly the role of the assumption that committing a crime in the first period entailed some sort of implication for future labor market returns; without this assumption, c_2 would lose its dependence on c_1, as the last term on the right in (12.1) would vanish if $\kappa = 1$. The comparative statics are as follows:

$$\frac{\partial c_2}{\partial c_1} = F(y_2 + x_2) - F(\kappa y_2 + x_2) \geq 0$$

$$\frac{\partial c_2}{\partial y_2} = -(1 - c_1)f(y_2 + x_2) - c_1 \kappa f(\kappa y_2 + x_2) \leq 0$$

$$\frac{\partial c_2}{\partial x_2} = -(1 - c_1)f(y_2 + x_2) - c_1 f(\kappa y_2 + x_2) \leq 0$$

$$\frac{\partial c_2}{\partial \kappa} - c_1 y_2 f(\kappa y_2 + x_2) \leq 0 \qquad (12.2)$$

The comparative statics in (12.2) are all familiar, except perhaps the first, which says that the current crime rate should be increasing in past crime rates. This is because past criminals have a lower opportunity cost of committing crimes in the present. The second and third comparative statics reflect the logic of the basic economic model of criminal deterrence – if current opportunity costs and penalties are higher from committing crime, there is less crime in the current period. The last comparative static says that the current crime rate is decreasing in the coefficient κ; a higher value of κ means a higher opportunity cost from committing crime for previous criminals (a smaller fraction of current returns are lost due to previous criminal acts), so the current crime rate falls as κ increases. Of course, all of the above results are conditional on a past crime rate, in that we took the value of b_1^* as given.

Accordingly, we now turn to illustrating how the current crime rate depends upon future conditions. It is helpful to now picture period one as the present, and period two as the future. We also assume perfect foresight on the part of agents, so that the conditions that will prevail in period two are known by all agents.[7] To find a value for b_1^*, we need to consider that criminals weigh both current and future benefits from committing crime in making commission decisions. Let EV_c be the expected utility earned in the second period – now the future – by a current criminal, and EV denote the expected utility earned by a current honest worker. Supposing that agents do not discount the future, the current crime commission decision now turns on the condition:

$$b - x_1 + EV_c \geq y_1 + EV$$

So an agent indifferent between committing and not committing a crime today has a value of b_1, b_1^* say, that satisfies:

$$b_1^* = x_1 + y_1 + EV - EV_c$$

Evidently, agents for whom $b_1 > b_1^*$, commit crime. An agent commits crime in the present if the current benefits, plus the expected future benefits to being a criminal are greater than the current and expected future benefits to productive work. Expected future returns for those agents committing a crime in the present are:

$$EV_c = P(b \geq \kappa y_2 + x_2) E[b - x_2 | b \geq \kappa y_2 + x_2] + P(b < \kappa y_2 + x_2) y_2$$

While expected future returns for those agents who do not commit a crime:

$$EV = P(b \geq y_2 + x_2) E[b - x_2 | b \geq y_2 + x_2] + P(b < y_2 + x_2) y_2$$

These two expressions simplify to:

$$EV_c = \int_{\kappa y_2 + x_2}^{\infty} bf(b)\, db - x_2 + (\kappa y_2 + x_2) F(\kappa y_2 + x_2)$$

and

$$EV = \int_{y_2 + x_2}^{\infty} bf(b)\, db - x_2 + (y_2 + x_2) F(y_2 + x_2)$$

Forming the expression $EV - EV_c$ and differentiating describes how relative returns respond to changes in model parameters:

$$\frac{\partial(EV - EV_c)}{\partial y_2} = F(y_2 + x_2) - \kappa F(\kappa y_2 + x_2) > 0$$

and

$$\frac{\partial(EV - EV_c)}{\partial x_2} = F(y_2 + x_2) - F(\kappa y_2 + x_2) > 0$$

Now, returning to the current, period-one crime rate, we have:

$$c_1 = 1 - F(x_1 + y_1 + EV - EV_c)$$

The comparative statics with respect to current economic conditions and enforcement are familiar. For example,

$$\frac{\partial c_1}{\partial x_1} = -f(x_1 + y_1 + EV - EV_c) < 0$$

With a similar result for $\frac{\partial c_1}{\partial y_1}$. These are the contemporaneous effects of economic conditions and enforcement on crime rates, which reflect the usual deterrence effects. But we also have:

$$\frac{\partial c_1}{\partial x_2} = -f(x_1 + y_1 + EV - EV_c)\frac{\partial(EV - EV_c)}{\partial x_2} < 0$$

with a similar result for $\frac{\partial c_1}{\partial y_2}$. Hence, current crime rates depend upon future economic conditions y_2 and future enforcement x_2.

Before continuing on to discuss what such a model might mean for analysis of aggregate crime rates, we can expand a bit on the above results. First, while we have placed perhaps restrictive assumptions on model parameters that guarantee signs of partial derivatives, and hence the nature of the dependence between current crime rates, past crime rates, and current and future conditions, in a more general model these things might be ambiguous. We might have assumed that past criminals are punished more heavily; this would amount to introducing a term like $\kappa_x x_2$, $\kappa_x > 1$. This would result in the crime commission decision in the second period for previous criminals to turn on the condition:

$$b \geq \kappa y_2 + \kappa_x x_2$$

In this augmented model, it might well be the case that previous criminals were less likely to commit crime if κ_x is sufficiently large. There are other effects that also might run in the other direction; for example, if there was learning by doing in criminal activity and not just in market-based activities. Our basic point is not that the dependence runs in a particular direction, but that there is dependence. This dependence will emerge so long as there are some material differences between criminals and non-criminals that emerge across time periods. The magnitude and direction of the dependence between decisions to commit crime is an empirical matter, which we now turn to discussing in a brief synopsis of how the important features of the model map into the data. A subsequent section delves into details of the derivation.

2.2 Synopsis

To expand the basic logic of the previous section in a way that allows analysis of aggregate crime rates, it is necessary to build expectations into the model and allow for model quantities to interact in a more general way. We first present the basic results in an informal way, and present a more formal derivation in the next section. Let the crime rate at time t (in a given jurisdiction) be given by c_t, let x_t denote a column vector of crime control policy variables (e.g., the relative size of the police force or the incarceration rate), and let y_t denote a column vector of variables measuring economic and demographic conditions that proxy incentives to commit crime (e.g., unemployment rates, poverty rates, or the age distribution of the population). A model of the aggregate crime rate in which both past crime rates as well as current and future expected values of x_t and y_t are allowed to affect today's crime rate may be written as follows:

$$c_t = \gamma c_{t-1} + Ax_t + By_t + E_t \left[\sum_{i=1}^{\infty} \rho^i (Ax_{t+i} + By_{t+i}) \right] \qquad (12.3)$$

The row vectors A and B in (12.3) capture the impact of exogenous variables on the crime rate, and ρ reflects the degree to which potential criminals discount future conditions in reaching a decision to commit crime in the present. E_t denotes the expectations operator with respect to the information set at time t. The parameter γ captures the degree of persistence in the crime rate – that is, the degree to which past crime rates influence current crime rates.

The usual empirical model of crime only takes into account contemporaneous effects of x_t and y_t on the current crime rate, which amounts to assuming that $\gamma = \rho = 0$ in equation (12.3), meaning that criminals are assumed to place no weight on future conditions in deciding whether or not to commit a crime in the current period, and that past criminal outcomes have no role in predicting current criminal behavior.[8] Equation (12.3) allows for a much richer and more realistic setting where the current crime rate is allowed to be affected by past crime rates and expected future conditions. At the same time, the model in equation (12.3) nests the usual model of crime rates.

As we hopefully established in the previous section, there are several compelling microeconomic foundations for model (12.3). To elaborate a bit on this, in studies based on individual-level data, crime commission decisions have been observed to have large and persistent effects on labor market outcomes for offenders (see, for example, Lott 1992, Waldfogel 1994, and Nagin and Waldfogel 1996).[9] If the implications of committing a crime are long-lasting, one expects that both past behavior and expectations of the future matter in deciding to engage in a criminal act, because the fact that a current potential criminal has committed a crime in the past alters lifetime returns from legitimate work (particularly if apprehended and punished).

Forward-looking behavior may also be motivated by the fact that punishment for a crime is not instantaneous. A crime committed today may not be immediately discovered, and the criminal may not be apprehended and punished until some unspecified time in the future. Moreover, the structure of the legal system might cause criminals to be forward looking. If a criminal is caught and punished for a crime, this directly increases the costs of committing crime in the future, as in virtually every legal system repeat offenders are punished more vigorously than first time offenders. A final justification for inclusion of forward-looking terms is that the decision to commit a crime today might lead to more crimes in the future, so the criminal has to make some guess as to the relative productivity of the criminal lifestyle both in the present and in the future. Such an assessment involves a joint evaluation of future labor market conditions, the future likelihood of apprehension, and the future severity of punishment. And even if one is uncomfortable with the idea that future expectations matter in driving crime rates, the model (12.3) nests the hypothesis that expectations do not matter, as will become clear when we describe our estimating equations.

If one accepts this motivation for inclusion of expectations for the model in equation (12.3), how is equation (12.3) to be estimated? Iterating (12.3) forward and applying the expectations operator results in the following expression:

$$c_t = \alpha_0 c_{t-1} + \Pi_1 x_t + \Pi_2 y_t + \alpha_1 E_t[c_{t+1}]$$

(12.4)

where $\alpha_0 = \frac{\gamma}{1 + \rho\gamma}$, $\alpha_1 = \frac{\rho}{1 + \rho\gamma}$, $\Pi_1 = \frac{1}{1 + \rho\gamma}A$, and $\Pi_2 = \frac{1}{1 + \rho\gamma}B$. Equation (12.4) allows us to replace the problem of characterizing future expected values of all right-hand side variables with the problem of characterizing current expectations of the one-period-ahead crime rate. There are antecedents to follow in estimating equation (12.4). Forward-looking terms routinely appear in estimation of the expectations-augmented Phillips curve (Fuhrer 1997) and also in the empirical literature on rational addiction (Becker et. al. 1994), to give two examples.

We briefly note that Equation (12.4) has implications for interpretation of estimated coefficients. Assessing the impact of changes in x_t or y_t on crime rates requires first finding a rational expectations solution to (12.4); one cannot simply read off the values of estimated coefficients in (12.4) as elasticities. In Section 4, we will discuss how this can be done and how one might then interpret the estimated coefficients.

2.3 A Derivation

We now show how the model (12.4) can be derived from a model in which a rational representative agent takes into account the future and the past in making decisions about how much criminal behavior to engage in. Our representative agent derives utility from consumption *and* crime; thus, the operative assumption is that goods acquired through the commission of crime are fundamentally different than those acquired through other means. We specify the representative agent's utility function as follows:

$$U(Z_t, C_t) = \alpha Z_t + \chi \frac{(C_t - \gamma C_{t-1})^{1-\eta}}{1 - \eta} \qquad (12.5)$$

The representative agent consumes Z_t units of an aggregate consumption good, and consumes C_t units of crime. Implicit in the utility specification (12.5) is the assumption that consumption of crime is habit-forming. That is, a higher past level of criminal activity increases the agent's marginal utility of crime in the current period. This assumption implies that higher levels of past crime encourage an agent to commit higher levels of crime today. Finally, the marginal utility of consumption is constant while the marginal utility of crime is diminishing.[10]

We continue our convention of referring to enforcement variables using X's and variables influencing returns to criminal activity or the opportunity costs from engaging in criminal activity using Y's. The representative agent is endowed with one unit of labor each period which may be allocated to either the production of consumption goods (i.e., "honest" labor) or to criminal activity. Let the probability of apprehension and conviction at time t be denoted by X_{1t} ($0 \le X_1 \le 1$), and the loss of labor endowment if caught and punished be denoted by X_{2t}. Then, the *effective* labor endowment constraint facing the agent can then be written as a function of the enforcement variables X as follows:

$$N_t^Z + N_t^C = 1 - X_{1t}X_{2t} \qquad (12.6)$$

where N_t^Z and N_t^C represent the labor supply to the production of consumption goods and crime, respectively.[11]

We assume for simplicity that the crime production technology exhibits constant returns to scale and is directly proportional to time spent engaging in crime:

$$C_t = N_t^C \qquad (12.7)$$

In addition to directly influencing utility, we assume that criminal activity also generates a return in terms of the consumption good. We assume, however, that total economy-wide returns from crime in terms of the consumption good are zero, so that crime is purely redistributive in that any goods acquired through crime are stolen from someone else. Hence, the budget constraint facing the representative individual can be written as:

$$Z_t = Y_{1t}N_t^C - Y_{1t}\overline{C_t} + Y_{2t}N_t^Z \qquad (12.8)$$

where Y_{1t} and Y_{2t} are the real marginal returns to crime and honest labor, respectively. Crime per capita is represented by $\overline{C_t}$, and thus the average expected loss of income due to crime is $Y_{1t}\overline{C_t}$.

The key to the agent's forward-looking behavior is the relationship between past criminal activity and an individual's effective labor endowment in the present.[12] As discussed previously, past criminal activity is likely to affect an individual's current labor market outcomes negatively. This induces the representative agent to worry in the current period about how crime commission will influence future labor endowment. It is reasonable to assume that the impact on current effective labor lessens the further back in time that the criminal activity occurred. Consequently, we model the potential loss in today's labor endowment – that is, the current punishment from crime, X_{2t}, as a discounted sum of current and past criminal activity:

$$X_{2t} = \Psi \sum_{i=0}^{\infty} \sigma^i C_{t-i} \qquad (12.9)$$

where $0 \leq X_{2t} \leq 1$, σ is a discount rate measuring the rate at which the influence of past criminal acts on present effective labor supply dissipates, and Ψ is a scaling parameter.[13] The choices of policy makers, which we do not model but consider exogenous, in part determine Ψ and σ.

We follow the usual method for analyzing such a model, which is to find equations describing the agent's utility-maximizing decisions, posit a steady state, and then linearize around this steady state to generate a model that is easily estimated using common linear methods.[14] The maximization problem facing the infinitely-lived representative agent can now be described as:

$$\max_{Z,C} \sum_{i=0}^{\infty} \beta^i U(Z_{t+i}, C_{t+i}) \qquad (12.10)$$

subject to

$$s.t \ Z_t = Y_{2t}(1 - X_{1t}X_{2t} - C_t) + Y_{1t}(C_t - \overline{C_t}) \qquad (12.11)$$

where β is the discount factor. Using Lagrangian multipliers φ we can rewrite the optimization problem as:

$$\max_{Z,C} \sum_{i=0}^{\infty} \beta^i E_t \{ U(C_{t+i}, Z_{t+i}) + \varphi_{t+i}[Y_{2t}(1-X_{1t}X_{2t}) + (Y_{1t} - Y_{2t})C_t - Y_{1t}\overline{C_t} - Z_{t+i}]\}$$

Substituting the functional form for the utility function (12.5) into the maximization problem and differentiating gives the first order conditions:

$$\alpha - \varphi_t = 0$$

and

$$0 = \chi(C_t - \gamma C_{t-1})^{-\eta} + \varphi_t\left[(Y_{1t} - Y_{2t}) - \left(Y_{2t}X_{1t}\frac{\partial X_{2t}}{\partial C_t} \right) \right]$$

$$+ \beta E_t \varphi_{t+1}\left[- \left(Y_{2t}X_{1t}\frac{\partial X_{2t+1}}{\partial C_t} \right) \right]$$

$$+ \beta^2 E_t \varphi_{t+2}\left[- \left(Y_{2t}X_{1t}\frac{\partial X_{2t+2}}{\partial C_t} \right) \right]$$

$$+ \cdots$$

From expression (12.9) we have that:

$$\frac{\partial X_{2t+i}}{\partial C_t} = \Psi\sigma^i$$

Substituting this last result into the first-order conditions and eliminating multipliers gives:

$$\chi(C_t - \gamma C_{t-1})^{-\eta} + \alpha(Y_{1t} - Y_{2t}) = \alpha E_t \Psi \sum_{i=0}^{\infty} (\beta \sigma)^i Y_{2t+i} X_{1t+i} \quad (12.12)$$

Log linearizing equation (12.12), we have:

$$c_t - \gamma c_{t-1} - \frac{(1 - \gamma)(1 - \beta\sigma)}{\eta[A\Phi\Psi - (1 - \beta\sigma)(Y_1 - Y_2)]}(Y_1 y_{1t} - Y_2 y_{2t}) \quad (12.13)$$

$$= -\frac{(1 - \gamma) Y_2 X_1 \Psi}{\eta[Y_2 X_1 \Psi - (1 - \beta\sigma)(Y_1 - Y_2)]} E_t \sum_{i=0}^{\infty} (\beta\sigma)^i (y_{2t+i} + x_{1t+i})$$

where variables denoted by lower case letters represent the percentage deviation around their steady state levels (denoted by upper case letters). To simplify notation, we introduce the following variables:

$$\Gamma_{y1} = \frac{(1 - \gamma)(1 - \beta\sigma) Y_1}{\eta[Y_2 X_1 \Psi - (1 - \beta\sigma)(Y_1 - Y_2)]}$$

$$\Gamma_{y2} = \frac{(1 - \gamma)(1 - \beta\sigma) Y_2}{\eta[Y_2 X_1 \Psi - (1 - \beta\sigma)(Y_1 - Y_2)]}$$

$$\lambda = \frac{(1 - \gamma) Y_2 X_1 \Psi}{\eta[Y_2 X_1 \Psi - (1 - \beta\sigma)(Y_1 - Y_2)]}$$

This allows us to write equation (12.13) as:

$$c_t - \gamma c_{t-1} - \Gamma_{y1} y_{1t} + \Gamma_{y2} y_{2t} = -\lambda E_t \sum_{i=0}^{\infty} (\beta\sigma)^i (x_{1t+i} + y_{2t+i}) \quad (12.14)$$

Iterating expression (12.14) one period forward gives:

$$\beta\sigma E_t[c_{t+1} - \gamma c_t - \Gamma_{y1} y_{1t+1} + \Gamma_{y2} y_{2t+1}] = -\lambda E_t \sum_{i=0}^{\infty} (\beta\sigma)^i (x_{1t+1+i} + y_{2t+1+i})$$

Subtracting (2.3) from (12.14) and rearranging terms gives:

$$c_t = \gamma c_{t-1} + \Gamma_{y1} y_{1t} - \Gamma_{y2} y_{2t} - \lambda(x_{1t} + y_{2t})$$

$$+ \beta \sigma E_t[c_{t+1} - \gamma c_t - \Gamma_{y1} y_{1t+1} + \Gamma_{y2} y_{2t+1}] \qquad (12.15)$$

Assume that y_{1t} and y_{2t} are white noise random variables, meaning that deviations around long-term means is random.[15] Then, equation (12.15) can be rewritten as:

$$(1 + \beta \sigma \gamma)c_t = \gamma c_{t-1} + \Gamma_{y1} y_{1t} - (\Gamma_{y2} + \lambda)y_{2t} - \lambda x_{1t} + \beta \sigma E_t c_{t+1}$$

which gives us:

$$c_t = \left(\frac{\gamma}{1 + \beta \sigma \gamma}\right) c_{t-1} - \left(\frac{\lambda}{1 + \beta \sigma \gamma}\right) x_{1t} \qquad (12.16)$$

$$+ \left(\frac{\Gamma_{y1}}{1 + \beta \sigma \gamma}\right) y_{1t} - \left(\frac{\Gamma_{y2} + \lambda}{1 + \beta \sigma \gamma}\right) y_{2t} + \left(\frac{\beta \sigma}{1 + \beta \sigma \gamma}\right) E_t c_{t+1}$$

If we let $\alpha_0 = \frac{\gamma}{1 + \beta \sigma \gamma}$, $\Pi_1 = \frac{\lambda}{1 + \beta \sigma \gamma}$, $y_t = [y_{1t}, y_{2t}]'$, $\Pi_2 = \frac{1}{1 + \beta \sigma \gamma} [\Gamma_{y1}, -(\Gamma_{y2} + \lambda)]$, and $\alpha_1 = \frac{\beta \sigma}{1 + \beta \sigma \gamma}$, equation (12.16) is of the same form as equation (12.4). Equation (12.16) states that the current crime rate depends upon contemporaneous measures of the rate of returns to criminal and honest activity. Specifically, the current crime rate is positively related to returns to crime, y_{1t}, negatively related to the current returns to honest activity, y_{2t}, and negatively related to the current level of enforcement, x_{1t}. Additionally, the current rate of crime is positively related to the past crime rate. Finally, the current crime rate is positively related to the expected future rate of crime, which serves as a stand-in for expectations of future conditions in general.

Before discussing estimation of the model, we emphasize the critical assumptions of the theoretical model. The critical assumptions are: 1) habit persistence in crime commission, manifest in the way in which past and current crime rates enter the representative agent's utility function (12.5); and 2) the dependence of current punishment on past crime rates. Habit persistence introduces dependence between current crime rates and past crime rates, and the dependence of current punishments on the past introduces dependence between current crime rates and future conditions.

3   MODEL ESTIMATION

3.1   Econometric Specification

Returning now to the reduced-form equation (12.4) or (12.16), our econometric specification can be written as:

$$c_{it} = \hat{\alpha}_0 c_{it-1} + \hat{\Pi}_1 x_{it} + \hat{\Pi}_2 y_{it} + \hat{\alpha}_1 E_t c_{it+1} + e_{i,t} \qquad (12.17)$$

where $e_{i,t}$ is an error term. The obvious difficulty in estimating (12.17) is that there is no available measure of the expectation of future crime rates formed at time t. We therefore construct $E_t c_{it+1}$ by regressing c_{it+1}, the realized one-year-ahead crime rate, on information available at time t – which in this setting includes past values of exogenous variables and crime rates. This amounts to treating the realized value of c_{t+1} as an endogenous variable in specification (12.17) and estimating the model using instrumental variables techniques. The data set provides instruments in the form of past values of exogenous and endogenous variables, and for the time being, we shall rely on this "natural" instrument set in model estimation. Assuming that individuals form expectations rationally, the expectations error, i.e., $\varepsilon_{t+1} = c_{it+1} - E_t[c_{it+1}]$, is uncorrelated with information available at time t, and can be folded into the error term $e_{i,t}$.

3.2   Data

The data set is an expanded version of that used by Spelman (2001) and Ayres and Donohue (2003). Spelman (2001) points out that this is essentially the same data which has been used by Becsi (1999), Levitt (1996), and Marvell and Moody (1994), among many others, and therefore the use of similar data has a rather long tradition in the literature. We update and expand this data set to be as current as possible.[16]

The data consist of a yearly panel of states (including the District of Columbia) covering the years 1970 though 2006. For each state and year our primary dependent variables are state violent and property crime rates, defined as the number of index offenses per 100,000 people, deriving from the *Uniform Crime Reports*.[17] We also include a standard collection of exogenous explanatory variables used to characterize economic conditions, demographics, and proxies of the level enforcement and severity of punishment in each jurisdiction. Measures of economic conditions we include are the state unemployment rate and the poverty rate. Demographic variables include the percentage population in the state that is black; the fraction of the population aged 15 to 17, 18 to 24, and 25 to 35; and the fraction of population living in a metropolitan area. For measures of enforcement, we use police per capita (measured as police per 10,000 population) and the imprisonment rate (prisoners per 100,000 population). Sources and additional details of the data set are described in appendix A. This set of variables comprise a base model of aggregate crime rates, upon which we will expand in subsequent sections.

Summary statistics of crime rates and the set of explanatory variables appear in Table 12.4. From the table, one can see that there is considerable variation in both violent and property crime rates, and that a large part of the variation occurs between rather than within states over time. For demographic variables, while a non-negligible fraction of variation occurs within states over time, there is greater variation between states, rather than within states across time. The opposite is true of basic economic variables – for example, the unemployment rate exhibits more variation within states over time than it does across states. This comes as no surprise, as macroeconomic measures are likely to be highly correlated across states over time and are known to have changed rather substantially in aggregate over the past few decades. While it appears that most of the variability in police per capita is between states, it is interesting to note that this is not so true of incarceration rates, which exhibit very similar degrees of within-state and between-state variation.

3.3   Estimation

We shall first discuss estimation and present results using a standard set of variables, and reserve discussion of more expansive models once some of the issues with model estimation have been developed. Essentially, estimated models are regressions of property and violent crime rates on the set of exogenous variables described in Table 12.1. For comparative purposes, we begin by estimating simple OLS models without any future or past crime rates as explanatory variables, and then estimate models including future and past crime rates without controlling for endogeneity. We then present estimated models obtained using different estimation techniques to address various econometric problems.

In all estimated models, we employ the lagged values of police per capita and the incarceration rate. This is done for two reasons, one practical, and the other because of the circumstances under which these data were collected. Practically speaking, using lagged values in estimation rather than current values eases potential problems with endogeneity, as we can be certain that they are predetermined relative to crime rates. Using lagged values of incarceration rates and police per capita makes further sense as what should matter during the course of the year is the size of the police

Table 12.1   Base model summary statistics

Variable	Mean	Max	Min		Std. Dev.	Obs.
Property crime	4163.74	9512.1	942.20		1303.72	1937
rate				Within =	787.23	$\bar{T} = 38$
				between =	1049.01	n = 51
Violent crime	450.6	2921.8	27.7		314.71	1938
rate				within =	130.58	$\bar{T} = 38$
				between =	289.11	n = 51
Unemployment	5.89	18	1.9		2.04	1887
rate				within =	1.71	$\bar{T} = 38$
				between =	1.11	n = 51
Poverty rate	13.04	35.4	3.7		4.18	1887
				within =	1.94	$\bar{T} = 38$
				between =	3.74	n = 51
Percent pop.	4.83	6.91	2.5		0.84	1836
15 to 17 years				within=	0.79	$\bar{T} = 36$
old				between=	0.29	n = 51
Percent pop.	11.4	16.11	7.56		1.7	1836
18 to 24 years				within =	1.59	$\bar{T} = 36$
old				between =	0.63	n = 51
Percent pop.	15.2	23.58	10.13		2.16	1836
25 to 34 years				within =	1.87	$\bar{T} = 36$
old				between =	1.1	n = 51
Percent pop.	10.68	71.05	0.17		12.06	1835
black				within =	1.11	$\bar{T} = 36$
				between =	12.19	n = 51
Percent pop.	64.01	100	0		22.97	1824
metro				within =	6.86	$\bar{T} = 36$
				between =	22.13	n = 51
Prisoners per	226.89	1821.77	20.34		187.42	1930
capita				within =	149.37	$\bar{T} = 38$
				between =	118.28	n = 51
Police per	2.62	8.85	0.59		0.9	1836
capita				within =	0.36	$\bar{T} = 36$
				between =	0.83	n = 51

force or the incarceration rate – these are stock variables that are being used to explain the flow of crime rates. As these variables are typically measured very close to the end of the year, it would seem that the size at the very beginning of the year would be a better gauge of the level of enforcement and punishment during the year.[18]

Tables 12.2 and 12.3 – pertaining to property and violent crime rates, respectively – display results from initial attempts at estimating (12.17).

Table 12.2 Property crime models

	I	II	III	IV	V
Property crime rate $(t + 1)$		0.507*** (45.445)	0.598*** (12.247)	0.584*** (13.395)	0.658*** (8.179)
Property crime rate $(t - 1)$		0.490*** (44.219)	0.417*** (10.524)	0.426*** (11.852)	0.368*** (5.659)
Police per capita $(t - 1)$	0.355*** (3.259)	−0.016 (−1.614)	−0.015 (−1.461)	−0.009 (−0.969)	−0.015 (−1.451)
Prisoners per capita $(t - 1)$	−0.074*** (−3.036)	−0.005 (−1.372)	−0.005 (−1.310)	−0.005 (−1.382)	−0.003 (−0.832)
Unemployment rate	0.144*** (6.064)	0.008** (2.215)	0.011** (2.473)	0.011*** (2.731)	0.012** (2.478)
Poverty rate	−0.252*** (−6.040)	0.007 (0.937)	0.011 (1.288)	0.008 (0.963)	0.015 (1.510)
Percent pop. 15 to 17 years old	0.087 (0.812)	0.001 (0.045)	−0.017 (−0.987)	−0.018 (−1.158)	−0.021 (−1.160)
Percent pop. 18 to 24 years old	0.519*** (6.775)	0.018 (1.180)	0.015 (0.874)	0.020 (1.451)	0.011 (0.624)
Percent pop. 25 to 34 years old	0.064 (0.688)	0.016 (1.008)	0.004 (0.274)	0.003 (0.237)	0.001 (0.078)
Percent pop. black	−0.200*** (−6.555)	−0.002 (−0.488)	0.003 (0.477)	0.002 (0.442)	0.006 (0.811)
Percent pop. in metro area	0.019** (2.039)	0.002 (0.684)	0.004* (1.695)	0.004** (2.063)	0.004 (1.632)
N	1758	1756	1542	1542	1542
Hansen J	0.000	0.000	33.082	33.082	31.214
p-value			0.608	0.608	0.696
Kleinbergen-Paap rk LM stat.			70.396	70.396	70.396
p-value			0.001	0.001	0.001
Partial F, cr $(t + 1)$			2.598	2.598	2.598
p-value			0.000	0.000	0.000
Estimation Method	OLS	OLS	IV	GMM	LIML

Notes:
All models are estimated in levels using logs, with yearly time dummy variables and state level fixed effects. Standard errors are heteroscedasticity and autocorrelation consistent. *** denotes significance at 99% ** denotes significance at 95% * denotes significance at 90%.

Table 12.3   Violent crime models

	I	II	III	IV	V
Violent crime rate ($t+1$)		0.501*** (31.048)	0.533*** (11.763)	0.526*** (14.115)	0.553*** (6.637)
Violent crime rate ($t-1$)		0.499*** (34.065)	0.473*** (13.646)	0.477*** (16.647)	0.459*** (7.455)
Police per capita ($t-1$)	0.287*** (2.771)	−0.032* (−1.869)	−0.014 (−0.617)	−0.005 (−0.306)	−0.014 (−0.612)
Prisoners per capita ($t-1$)	−0.014 (−0.454)	−0.013** (−2.205)	−0.012** (−1.975)	−0.009* (−1.681)	−0.012* (−1.845)
Unemployment rate	−0.097*** (−2.939)	−0.004 (−0.501)	0.001 (0.145)	−0.003 (−0.464)	0.001 (0.167)
Poverty rate	−0.055 (−1.069)	−0.006 (−0.475)	−0.009 (−0.597)	0.002 (0.185)	−0.007 (−0.402)
Percent pop. 15 to 17 years old	−0.056 (−0.372)	−0.018 (−0.585)	−0.011 (−0.363)	0.007 (0.245)	−0.013 (−0.388)
Percent pop. 18 to 24 years old	0.548*** (4.586)	0.018 (0.725)	0.003 (0.116)	0.013 (0.557)	−0.001 (−0.044)
Percent pop. 25 to 34 years old	0.082 (0.529)	−0.000 (−0.016)	−0.004 (−0.122)	0.021 (0.834)	−0.004 (−0.113)
Percent pop. black	0.035 (0.710)	0.001 (0.088)	−0.007 (−0.767)	−0.009 (−1.271)	−0.007 (−0.795)
Percent pop. in metro area	0.021 (1.438)	−0.001 (−0.164)	0.003 (0.450)	0.001 (0.171)	0.004 (0.488)
N	1759	1759	1546	1546	1546
Hansen J	0.000	0.000	39.541	39.541	39.376
p-value			0.315	0.315	0.321
Kleinbergen-Paaprk LM stat.			68.310	68.310	68.310
p-value			0.001	0.001	0.001
Partial F, cr ($t+1$)			3.030	3.030	3.030
p-value			0.000	0.000	0.000
Estimation Method	OLS	OLS	IV	GMM	LIML

Notes:
All models are estimated in levels using logs, with yearly time dummy variables and state level fixed effects. Standard errors are heteroscedasticity and autocorrelation consistent. *** denotes significance at 99% ** denotes significance at 95% * denotes significance at 90%.

All models on Tables 12.2 and 12.3 include fixed effects and yearly time dummy variables.[19] The first columns of Tables 12.2 and 12.3 report models of property and violent crime rates omitting future and past crime rates as explanatory variables, estimated by OLS. From these results, one can see that while many of the explanatory variables are significant, some of them (such as police per capita and the poverty rate) have signs that are inconsistent with the deterrence hypothesis. The second columns on Tables 12.2 and 12.3 report results of OLS estimation, but now with future and past crime rates included. This inclusion changes the sign of many coefficients, making the estimates more in line with coefficient signs suggested by the deterrence hypothesis. The estimated coefficients on the future and past crime rates are large in magnitude and statistically significant, although the bulk of other explanatory variables are insignificant. OLS, however, is an inappropriate estimation technique as the model suggests that the expectation of the future crime rate, not actual future crime rates, should be in the model.

The next three columns on both Tables 12.2 and 12.3 are estimated using instrumental variables techniques in which we replace the realized value of the future crime rate with its predicted value. As mentioned previously, this amounts to treating the future crime rate as endogenous and using past values of model variables as instruments. In model III on Tables 12.2 and 12.3, we use four lags of all exogenous variables and the second-order lag of the dependent variable – the property or violent crime rate – as instruments for the future crime rate. The results are similar to previous results. Model selection statistics indicate that model III on both Tables 12.2 and 12.3 is not overidentified (the Hansen-Sargan J test statistic suggests the overidentifying restrictions are valid), or underidentified (the Kleinbergen-Paap statistic indicates that the hypothesis that the model is underidentified can be rejected).[20] However, the partial F-statistics from first stage estimation reported on Tables 12.2 and 12.3 indicate that both the property crime and violent crime models may be only weakly identified. A rule of thumb is that first-stage F-statistics should exceed 10 (see Staiger and Stock 1997 and Baum et. al. 2007), and indeed, one must fail to reject the hypothesis of weak identification using more well-developed tests. This is not surprising given the rather large instrument set, and the apparent possibility that some, if not all, of the instruments are weak. As weak instruments can induce bias in instrumental-variables estimates, this potential problem must be treated with some care.

Crime data across states and over time is likely to be heteroscedastic in ways that are difficult to anticipate in the econometric model, which suggests that an estimation method more robust to arbitrary error structure be used. Moreover, one might argue that even if some of the left-hand side

Table 12.4   Summary statistics for expanded models

Variable	Mean	Max	Min			Std. Dev.	Obs.
Percent state	0.59	2.06	0.22			0.2	1887
inc. spent on				within =		0.08	$\bar{T} = 38$
enforcement				between =		0.18	n = 51
Executions per	0.02	1.21	0			0.08	1930
1000 prisoners				within =		0.08	$\bar{T} = 38$
				between =		0.03	n = 51
Shall-Issue Law	0.27	1	0			0.44	1938
				within =		0.34	$\bar{T} = 38$
				between =		0.29	n = 51
Three Strike	0.14	1	0			0.35	1938
Law				within =		0.32	$\bar{T} = 38$
				between =		0.15	n = 51
Real Per Capita	13449.52	28842.29	6261.49			3068.26	1938
Income				within =		2329.68	$\bar{T} = 38$
				between =		2016.05	n = 51
Infant Mortality	11.82	35.5	3.8			4.96	1836
Rate				within =		4.55	$\bar{T} = 36$
				between =		1.99	n = 51
Close Guberna-	0.05	1	0			0.23	1938
torial Election				within =		0.22	$\bar{T} = 38$
				between =		0.03	n = 51
Close Election	0.03	1	0			0.16	1938
won by				within =		0.16	$\bar{T} = 38$
Republican				between =		0.03	n = 51
Population	0.01	0.08	−0.04			0.01	1887
Growth Rate				within =		0.01	$\bar{T} = 38$
				between =		0.01	n = 51

variables in the model are predetermined, correlation between error terms and the dependent variable may still be present. Under these conditions, an estimation method such as GMM may be preferred, and in column IV on Tables 12.2 and 12.3, we estimate the model using GMM. While more robust to potential problems with error terms, the models displayed in column IV, Tables 12.2 and 12.3, have done nothing to deal with weak instrument issues. In fact, some research suggests that GMM and instrumental variables estimates are particularly prone to bias induced by weak instruments, while other estimation methods, such as limited information maximum likelihood (LIML), are less susceptible to weak-instruments bias.[21] The final estimated models on Tables 12.2 and 12.3 (column V on both Tables 12.2 and 12.3) repeat the estimation of the model in column

IV using LIML. While these models still might raise cause for concern, it is encouraging that the LIML estimates are not radically different to the GMM estimates in column IV of Tables 12.2 and 12.3.

Our initial efforts at estimation at least suggest that future and past crime rates are important determinants of current crime rates, but the concerns with these estimated models are several. First, fixed effects estimates in the presence of leads and/or lags of dependent variables can lead to dynamic panel bias (Baltagi 2008, Chapter 8). While there is some argument about how important this bias is, particularly in panels with a long time dimension, the possibility of dynamic panel bias remains. Since an important aspect of our work is obtaining accurate estimates of these parameters, we should be especially careful in avoiding this possibility. Second, some if not all of our instruments may be weak. A small amount of experimentation with the instrument set verifies that its weakness has as much to do with the large number of instruments as it does with many of them being only weak predictors of future crime rates. We therefore seek to improve the specification by expanding the set of explanatory variables, and also exploring some alternative estimation methods less prone to these potential problems.

3.4 Expanded Model Estimation

Perhaps the most straightforward way to combat both dynamic panel bias and problems posed by weak instruments is through introduction of additional variables into the model. This may aid with potential problems with dynamic panel bias, as additional variables may result in better controlling for persistent shocks at the state level. Additional information may also help in alleviating the weak instruments problem by expanding the potential universe of lagged exogenous variables that may be used as instruments, if not by directly suggesting instruments. We therefore expand the base data set to include some additional variables. Some of these variables are atypical in that they are not customarily part of the discussion of the econometric modeling of aggregate crime rates, and some variables that others have argued are important in understanding crime rates but are more controversial. This expanded set of variables includes: the fraction of state income spent on enforcement, a measure of capital punishment presence (specifically, executions per 1000 prisoners), whether or not states have passed a "shall issue" law for carrying a concealed firearm, and whether or not the state has "strike three" criminal sentencing legislation for repeat offenders. We also include the level of state per capita income, as it is commonly included in models of aggregate crime rates (e.g., Lott and Mustard 1997). Finally, we include in the data set the statewide infant mortality rate, as it may pick up some unobserved component of quality of well-being, or possibly even the prevalence of drug usage.

We introduce three further variables that serve solely as additional instrumental variables. The first variable records whether or not a state had a close gubernatorial election in a given year, where we defined a close election to be one in which the top two candidates were less than 6% apart in the statewide popular vote. Our logic was that the resolution of a close election would be known only very late in a given year, and therefore may represent a shock occurring to future policy and economic conditions that cannot have any direct bearing on current conditions. We also include the possibility that the close election was won by an independent or republican candidate, as one could argue that this results in a different sort of policy shock than an election won by a democratic candidate. Lagged population growth rates may capture beliefs that others have about the future course of the state economy, and therefore may also serve as effective instruments.[22]

While adding data is perhaps the most basic way of improving the fit and performance of a model, a complementary alternative is to employ a different method of estimation. Difference-based estimators may help in circumventing dynamic panel bias (Baltagi, 2008, Ch. 8).[23] The chief problem with working with data in differenced form is that differencing renders both leads and lags of the dependent variable endogenous. Thus, when using difference-based estimators, we must treat both the lead and the lag of the dependent variable as endogenous in models estimated in differences.

As a first step towards making these corrections to our estimated models, Tables 12.5 and 12.6 present expanded models for property and violent crime rates, estimated in levels with fixed effects. These models are estimated in levels using either GMM or LIML with heteroscedasticity and autocorrelation consistent standard errors, including time dummy variables and fixed effects, and using four lags of all exogenous variables, in addition to the second and third order lagged difference of the dependent variable, as instruments. Model II on both tables shows results after paring down the instrument set by dropping insignificant variables from first-stage instrumental variable regressions.[24] The model selection statistics indicate the model is neither overidentified or underidentified, and the use of a smaller instrument set increases first-stage partial F statistics substantially. Model III on both Tables 12.5 and 12.6 shows the results of estimating the model with the pared down instrument set using LIML. As before, the aim in estimating models with LIML is to provide some verification that model estimates are not too sensitive to weak instrument bias. In terms of the estimated coefficients on the models, the coefficients

Table 12.5   Expanded property crime models

	I	II	III
Property crime rate $(t + 1)$	0.571***	0.584***	0.633***
	(15.684)	(9.197)	(8.309)
Property crime rate $(t - 1)$	0.437***	0.423***	0.387***
	(15.080)	(8.420)	(6.459)
Police per capita $(t - 1)$	−0.015*	−0.017*	−0.019*
	(−1.763)	(−1.728)	(−1.953)
Prisoners per capita $(t - 1)$	−0.006*	−0.005	−0.004
	(−1.790)	(−1.266)	(−0.877)
Executions per 1000 prisoners $(t - 1)$	−0.006	−0.007	−0.013
	(−0.515)	(−0.565)	(−0.983)
Shall Issue Law – Vernick Coding	−0.001	−0.002	−0.003
	(−0.576)	(−0.565)	(−1.020)
Three Strikes Legislation	−0.001	−0.001	−0.000
	(−0.266)	(−0.449)	(−0.157)
Unemployment rate	0.011**	0.010**	0.011**
	(2.513)	(2.076)	(2.246)
Poverty rate	0.008	0.010	0.014
	(1.118)	(1.021)	(1.382)
Real Per Capita Income	−0.008	−0.009	−0.005
	(−0.436)	(−0.456)	(−0.221)
Infant Mortality Rate	0.018*	0.016	0.015
	(1.959)	(1.282)	(1.104)
Percent pop. 15 to 17 years old	−0.020	−0.014	−0.015
	(−1.278)	(−0.719)	(−0.786)
Percent pop. 18 to 24 years old	0.022	0.020	0.018
	(1.602)	(1.093)	(0.968)
Percent pop. 25 to 34 years old	0.008	0.003	−0.001
	(0.493)	(0.156)	(−0.042)
Percent pop. black	0.001	−0.002	0.000
	(0.148)	(−0.347)	(0.059)
Percent pop. in metro area	0.004**	0.003	0.003
	(2.191)	(1.013)	(1.238)
N	1496	1509	1509
Hansen J	56.645	9.217	9.036
p-value	0.812	0.101	0.108
Kleinbergen-Paap rk LM stat.	94.258	44.500	44.500
p-value	0.019	0.000	0.000
Partial F, cr$(t + 1)$	2.124	8.185	8.185
p-value	0.000	0.000	0.000
Estimation Method	GMM	GMM	LIML

Notes:
All models are estimated in levels using logs, with yearly time dummy variables and state
level fixed effects. Standard errors are heteroscedasticity and autocorrelation consistent.
*** denotes significance at 99% ** denotes significance at 95% * denotes significance at
90%.

Table 12.6   Expanded violent crime models

	I	II	III
Violent crime rate ($t + 1$)	0.517***	0.513***	0.472***
	(15.622)	(10.058)	(7.116)
Violent crime rate ($t - 1$)	0.488***	0.489***	0.517***
	(19.849)	(13.768)	(11.314)
Police per capita ($t - 1$)	−0.012	−0.018	−0.022
	(−0.701)	(−0.779)	(−0.914)
Prisoners per capita ($t - 1$)	−0.010*	−0.012*	−0.014**
	(−1.710)	(−1.777)	(−1.982)
Executions per 1000 prisoners ($t - 1$)	0.007	0.004	0.006
	(0.371)	(0.189)	(0.244)
Shall Issue Law – Vernick Coding	−0.003	−0.003	−0.003
	(−0.786)	(−0.717)	(−0.631)
Three Strikes Legislation	−0.003	−0.002	−0.002
	(−0.704)	(−0.506)	(−0.473)
Unemployment rate	0.002	0.007	0.004
	(0.268)	(0.830)	(0.441)
Poverty rate	0.005	−0.002	−0.007
	(0.421)	(−0.126)	(−0.404)
Real Per Capita Income	0.055	0.077	0.047
	(1.418)	(1.506)	(0.880)
Infant Mortality Rate	0.015	0.021	0.034
	(0.929)	(1.084)	(1.490)
Percent pop. 15 to 17 years old	0.028	−0.008	−0.004
	(0.912)	(−0.233)	(−0.119)
Percent pop. 18 to 24 years old	0.005	0.009	0.019
	(0.194)	(0.284)	(0.587)
Percent pop. 25 to 34 years old	0.007	−0.044	−0.018
	(0.261)	(−1.060)	(−0.407)
Percent pop. black	−0.009	−0.005	−0.004
	(−1.069)	(−0.453)	(−0.328)
Percent pop. in metro area	0.001	0.003	0.002
	(0.261)	(0.430)	(0.314)
N	1500	1504	1504
Hansen J	68.642	8.074	8.081
p-value	0.421	0.233	0.232
Kleinbergen-Paap rk LM stat.	96.930	37.874	37.874
p-value	0.012	0.000	0.000
Partial F, cr ($t + 1$)	2.697	10.205	10.205
p-value	0.000	0.000	0.000
Estimation Method	GMM	GMM	LIML

Notes:
All models are estimated in levels using logs, with yearly time dummy variables and state level fixed effects. Standard errors are heteroscedasticity and autocorrelation consistent.
*** denotes significance at 99% ** denotes significance at 95% * denotes significance at 90%.

for the future and past crime rates are significant, and some enforcement variables and some other explanatory variables – for example, the unemployment rate – are significant and are nearing levels suggested by prior research.

While these estimates suggest that expectations and past behavior are important in explaining current crime rates, they still do not completely address the potential problem of dynamic panel bias. Tables 12.7 and 12.8 present difference-based model estimates to combat this problem. The progression as one moves left to right across Tables 12.7 and 12.8 is roughly the same as that on Tables 12.5 and 12.6. Initial model estimates are presented, the instrument set is reduced by excluding variables insignificant in the first stage regression and the model is estimated again, and then a final set of estimates is presented using LIML to check that estimates are stable under an estimation method more robust to weak identification.

The first three columns on both tables present models in which lagged differences of exogenous variables, and the second-order lagged difference of the dependent variable, are used as instruments. The last three columns on both tables present models in which lagged levels of exogenous variables are used as instruments instead of lagged differences, as some have argued that using level-based instruments for differenced based estimators is useful because of the additional information brought to bear by levels (Baltagi, 2008, Ch. 8).

Model V on Tables 12.7 and 12.8 appears to exhibit the best all-around performance. These models appear not to suffer from identification problems (either over- or underidentification), and have (relatively) large first-stage partial F statistics. Moreover, the estimation method (GMM) is flexible in terms of the assumption on the permitted structure of error terms, and standard errors are adjusted to be robust to heteroscedasticity and autocorrelation consistent. The estimation of the model in logged differences mitigates concerns about dynamic panel bias. As a final robustness check, model VI on Tables 12.7 and 12.8 estimates the model using LIML, with similar results.

If we take model V of both Tables 12.7 and 12.8 as our best specification, we see that a small collection of the usual variables is significant. The estimated coefficient of police per capita in the property crime rate regression (Table 12.7, column V) is -0.05, and the estimated coefficient on prisoners per capita is -0.033. Among other significant variables, unemployment rates, infant mortality rates, and the percent population living in a metropolitan area are significant in the property crime specification with estimated coefficients of 0.032, 0.039, and 0.006, respectively. The estimated coefficient on the one-period-ahead crime rate is 0.773, and

Table 12.7 Expanded property crime models – estimated in differences

	I	II	III	IV	V	VI
Property crime rate ($t + 1$)	0.492***	0.560***	0.628	0.675***	0.773***	0.807***
	(4.950)	(2.892)	(1.541)	(8.715)	(6.533)	(4.293)
Property crime rate ($t - 1$)	0.076	0.186*	0.249	0.294***	0.213*	0.182
	(1.026)	(1.729)	(1.597)	(4.342)	(1.896)	(1.119)
Police per capita ($t - 1$)	-0.031***	-0.037***	-0.040**	-0.047***	-0.050***	-0.046***
	(-2.663)	(-2.707)	(-2.543)	(-4.061)	(-3.738)	(-3.207)
Prisoners per capita ($t - 1$)	-0.049***	-0.041**	-0.038*	-0.033**	-0.033*	-0.038*
	(-3.500)	(-2.496)	(-1.701)	(-2.337)	(-1.944)	(-1.823)
Shall issue law	0.000	-0.016	-0.018	-0.007	-0.016	-0.021
	(0.043)	(-1.081)	(-0.847)	(-0.631)	(-0.891)	(-1.001)
Three strikes legislation	-0.003	-0.002	0.003	-0.003	0.002	0.004
	(-0.294)	(-0.209)	(0.240)	(-0.306)	(0.144)	(0.272)
Executions per 1000 pris. ($t - 1$)	-0.007	-0.010	-0.016	-0.005	-0.019	-0.020
	(-0.469)	(-0.577)	(-0.778)	(-0.261)	(-0.938)	(-0.916)
Unemployment rate	0.030***	0.030**	0.025*	0.027***	0.032**	0.029**
	(3.179)	(2.495)	(1.798)	(2.636)	(2.483)	(2.005)
Poverty rate	0.011	0.006	0.020	0.013	0.020	0.023
	(1.000)	(0.474)	(1.187)	(1.010)	(1.250)	(1.336)
Real per capita income	-0.171**	-0.132	-0.134	-0.113	-0.106	-0.120
	(-2.388)	(-1.551)	(-1.159)	(-1.509)	(-1.065)	(-1.032)
Infant mortality rate	0.028*	0.042**	0.037	0.034**	0.039*	0.035
	(1.912)	(2.214)	(1.619)	(2.048)	(1.743)	(1.411)
Percent pop. 15 to 17 years old	-0.043	-0.026	0.024	-0.013	0.046	0.027
	(-0.639)	(-0.276)	(0.222)	(-0.186)	(0.457)	(0.240)

Percent pop. 18 to 24 years old	0.032	−0.034	0.005	0.025	0.056	0.039
	(0.502)	(−0.405)	(0.049)	(0.401)	(0.645)	(0.378)
Percent pop. 25 to 34 years old	−0.037	−0.068	−0.085	−0.042	−0.063	−0.099
	(−0.555)	(−0.777)	(−0.707)	(−0.634)	(−0.750)	(−1.047)
Percent pop. black	−0.079*	−0.093*	−0.082	−0.034	−0.050	−0.087
	(−1.800)	(−1.706)	(−1.281)	(−0.833)	(−0.899)	(−1.254)
Percent pop. in metro area	0.005***	0.005**	0.005*	0.006**	0.006**	0.005**
	(2.594)	(2.155)	(1.812)	(2.549)	(2.476)	(2.060)
N	1444	1447	1447	1496	1498	1498
Hansen J	58.705	10.311	9.230	44.119	7.672	7.136
p-value	0.726	0.503	0.601	0.983	0.936	0.954
Kleinbergen-Paap rk LM stat.	63.298	21.430	21.430	74.790	38.743	38.743
p-value	0.606	0.044	0.044	0.240	0.001	0.001
Partial F, cr($t+1$)	1.987	5.009	5.009	2.630	8.203	8.203
p-value	0.000	0.000	0.000	0.000	0.000	0.000
Partial F, cr($t-1$)	2.599	6.956	6.956	3.685	8.763	8.763
p-value	0.000	0.000	0.000	0.000	0.000	0.000
Estimation Method	GMM	GMM	LIML	GMM	GMM	LIML

Notes:
All models are estimated in differences using logs, with yearly time dummy variables and state level fixed effects. Standard errors are heteroscedasticity and autocorrelation consistent.
*** denotes significance at 99% ** denotes significance at 95% * denotes significance at 90%.

Table 12.8 Expanded violent crime models – estimated in differences

	I	II	III	IV	V	VI
Violent crime rate ($t + 1$)	0.369***	0.448***	0.481***	0.564***	0.661***	0.807***
	(4.352)	(3.736)	(3.099)	(7.524)	(5.931)	(4.687)
Violent crime rate ($t - 1$)	0.224***	0.279***	0.249**	0.338***	0.299***	0.262**
	(3.424)	(3.141)	(2.122)	(5.462)	(3.300)	(2.017)
Police per capita ($t - 1$)	-0.061***	-0.086***	-0.081***	-0.083***	-0.088***	-0.098***
	(-2.669)	(-3.295)	(-2.909)	(-3.987)	(-3.554)	(-3.499)
Prisoners per capita ($t - 1$)	-0.065***	-0.055**	-0.070**	-0.059**	-0.070**	-0.069*
	(-2.743)	(-1.997)	(-2.097)	(-2.417)	(-2.025)	(-1.795)
Shall issue law	-0.016	-0.020	-0.017	-0.019	-0.018	-0.014
	(-1.174)	(-1.209)	(-0.881)	(-1.276)	(-0.917)	(-0.615)
Three strikes legislation	-0.009	-0.002	-0.006	-0.006	-0.009	-0.010
	(-0.604)	(-0.137)	(-0.336)	(-0.364)	(-0.522)	(-0.520)
Executions per 1000 pris. ($t - 1$)	0.008	0.013	0.008	0.002	0.009	0.005
	(0.272)	(0.405)	(0.232)	(0.076)	(0.242)	(0.120)
Unemployment rate	0.014	0.017	0.023	0.032*	0.037*	0.052*
	(0.814)	(0.840)	(1.018)	(1.756)	(1.692)	(1.960)
Poverty rate	-0.001	0.012	0.009	0.012	0.019	0.018
	(-0.040)	(0.550)	(0.403)	(0.590)	(0.780)	(0.663)
Real per capita income	0.481***	0.430**	0.374*	0.334**	0.377**	0.315
	(3.224)	(2.197)	(1.729)	(2.126)	(1.971)	(1.359)
Infant mortality rate	0.057**	0.040	0.057*	0.065**	0.085**	0.076*
	(2.300)	(1.343)	(1.688)	(2.382)	(2.323)	(1.768)
Percent pop. 15 to 17 years old	0.005	-0.139	-0.107	-0.005	-0.063	-0.173
	(0.040)	(-0.910)	(-0.633)	(-0.040)	(-0.389)	(-0.917)

Percent pop. 18 to 24 years old	−0.053	−0.128	−0.149	−0.087	−0.147	−0.204
	(−0.546)	(−1.150)	(−1.097)	(−0.976)	(−1.308)	(−1.427)
Percent pop. 25 to 34 years old	−0.157	−0.332**	−0.260	−0.171	−0.132	−0.353*
	(−1.185)	(−1.986)	(−1.255)	(−1.240)	(−0.756)	(−1.803)
Percent pop. black	0.007	0.142	0.102	0.045	0.003	0.150
	(0.116)	(1.643)	(1.000)	(0.728)	(0.041)	(1.378)
Percent pop. in metro area	−0.008	−0.008	−0.006	−0.010*	−0.006	−0.007
	(−1.279)	(−1.288)	(−0.895)	(−1.819)	(−0.848)	(−0.950)
N	1449	1452	1452	1500	1504	1504
Hansen J	75.677	8.454	8.221	59.261	9.730	8.438
p-value	0.194	0.981	0.984	0.709	0.782	0.865
Kleinbergen-Paap rk LM stat.	72.307	43.432	43.432	77.470	46.807	46.807
p-value	0.307	0.002	0.002	0.179	0.000	0.000
Partial F, cr ($t + 1$)	1.861	3.752	3.752	2.379	4.878	4.878
p-value	0.000	0.000	0.000	0.000	0.000	0.000
Partial F, cr ($t − 1$)	2.669	5.292	5.292	3.136	6.773	6.773
p-value	0.000	0.000	0.000	0.000	0.000	0.000
Estimation Method	GMM	GMM	LIML	GMM	GMM	LIML

Notes:
All models are estimated in differences using logs, with yearly time dummy variables and state level fixed effects. Standard errors are heteroscedasticity and autocorrelation consistent.
*** denotes significance at 99% ** denotes significance at 95% * denotes significance at 90%.

the coefficient on the past crime rate is 0.213. The estimation results for violent crime yield similar results. The coefficient of the police per capita in the violent crime regression (Table 12.8, column V) is -0.088, while the estimated coefficient of imprisonment rate is -0.070. The unemployment rate has a significant coefficient of 0.037 and the infant mortality rate a coefficient of 0.085. The estimated coefficient of the level of income is 0.377 in the violent crime regression; this is an anomalous result that has occurred in other research. The coefficient on the one-period ahead violent crime rate is 0.661, while the coefficient on the lagged crime rate is 0.299. We now turn to discussing the interpretation of these estimates.

4   INTERPRETATION OF ESTIMATION RESULTS

Estimation results suggest that expectations of future conditions play an important role in determining crime rates. In light of this observation, interpretation of the estimated coefficients on model exogenous variables is no longer straightforward. Consider an increase in the level of enforcement. This change has an immediate impact on the crime rate, but has an indirect impact on current crime rates by altering expectations of future crime rates. This is true even if this change is completely transitory in that it only applies in the current period, because future crime rates depend upon past values of the crime rate. This example highlights two critical aspects of assessing the importance of policy or other changes. First, one must consider that expectations are changed by current changes in exogenous variables. Second, one must know the exact nature of a change (i.e., whether it is believed to be permanent or transitory), and how this change is perceived by potential criminals to correctly assess its impact.

To make these ideas concrete, consider the expectational difference equation (12.4) that we set out to estimate:

$$c_t = \alpha_0 c_{t-1} + \Pi_1 x_t + \Pi_2 y_t + \alpha_1 E_t c_{t+1}, \qquad (12.18)$$

Where x_t is a vector of policy variables, y_t is a vector of control variables, and Π_1 and Π_2 are row vectors of (estimated) coefficients. α_1 is the weight placed on future expectations of exogenous variables in driving current crime rates, and α_0 captures the dependence of current crime rates on past crime rates.

Equation (12.18) can be solved in a way that facilitates interpretation.[25] Consider a simple case in which the vector x_t is equal to a given constant plus some transitory component, so that $x_t = \bar{x} + \varepsilon_{xt}$, with ε_{xt} a vector of randomly distributed terms with mean zero. Similarly, suppose that other exogenous variables are simply given by their mean values with error terms added: $y_t = \bar{y} + \varepsilon_{yt}$. Then, $E_t x_{t+1} = \bar{x}$, and $E_t y_{t+1} = \bar{y}$.[26]

We wish to describe the current crime rate c_t as a function of information available at time t – that is, as a function of past crime rates, exogenous variables, and policy variables. This solution will have the form:

$$c_t = a_0 c_{t-1} + P_1 \bar{x} + P_2 \bar{y} + Q_1 \varepsilon_{xt} + Q_2 \varepsilon_{yt}, \qquad (12.19)$$

where the values for P, Q, and a_0 are to be determined from model estimates. The values of P will describe the impact of *permanent* changes in exogenous variables on the current crime rate, while the values of Q will capture the impact of *transitory* changes in exogenous variables on the current crime rate. Once we have determined the value of a_0, we will be able to assess the impact of permanent changes in exogenous variables on the steady-state, long run crime rate. From equation (12.19), the long run, steady-state crime rate can be written as:

$$\bar{c} = \frac{P_1 \bar{x} + P_2 \bar{y}}{1 - a_0} \qquad (12.20)$$

From (12.20), one can see that the long-run impact on $\bar{c}$ of a unit change in the mean of a given policy measure or exogenous variable is $\frac{P_i}{1-a_0}$; $i = 1, 2$. To find the coefficients of (12.19), iterate equation (12.19) forward one period and apply the expectations operator E_t. This gives the following expression:

$$E_t c_{t+1} = a_0 c_t + P_1 \bar{x} + P_2 \bar{y} \qquad (12.21)$$

Inserting (12.21) into (12.18) gives:

$$c_t = \alpha_0 + \alpha_1 [a_0 c_t + P_1 \bar{x} + P_2 \bar{y}] + \Pi_1 x_t + \Pi_2 y_t \qquad (12.22)$$

Using the specifications $x_t = \bar{x} + \varepsilon_{xt}$, and $y_t = \bar{y} + \varepsilon_{yt}$ in (12.22) and rearranging gives:

$$c_t = \frac{\alpha_0}{1 - \alpha_1 a_0} c_{t-1} + \frac{(\alpha_1 P_1 + \Pi_1) \bar{x}}{1 - \alpha_1 a_0} + \frac{(\alpha_1 P_2 + \Pi_2) \bar{y}}{1 - \alpha_1 a_0} + \frac{\Pi_1 \varepsilon_{xt}}{1 - \alpha_1 a_0} + \frac{\Pi_2 \varepsilon_{yt}}{1 - \alpha_1 a_0}$$

$$(12.23)$$

Matching coefficients between (12.23) to (12.19) results in a series of equations that map estimates of (12.18) into the coefficients of (12.19).

Evidently, the autoregressive component of (12.19) is described by the equation:

$$a_0 = \frac{\alpha_0}{1 - \alpha_1 a_0} \qquad (12.24)$$

Equation (12.24) is a quadratic equation in the estimated lead and lag terms, which can be solved accordingly:

$$\alpha_1 a_0^2 - a_0 + \alpha_0 = 0, \ \ or \ \ a_0 = \frac{1}{2}\frac{1 \pm \sqrt{1 - 4\alpha_0\alpha_1}}{\alpha_1} \qquad (12.25)$$

An implication of (12.25) is that there will exist more than one solution to (12.18). This is not an uncommon occurrence in rational expectations models, and we follow the custom of selecting the stable root. This is generally the negative component of the quadratic in (12.25).[27]

Given a solution for a_0, we have the following equations describing the coefficients of other terms in equation (12.19):

$$P_{ij} = \frac{\alpha_1 P_{ij} + \Pi_{ij}}{1 - \alpha_1 a_0}, \ \ i = 1, 2; \quad Q_{ij} = \frac{\Pi_{ij}}{1 - \alpha_1 a_0}, \ \ i = 1, 2 \quad (12.26)$$

The solutions to these equations are estimated coefficients augmented to take into account that changes also influence expectations of future crime rates. The coefficients of P_{ij} describe the impact of a *permanent* change in policy or in an exogenous variable on the current crime rate. The coefficients of Q_{ij}, alternatively, tell us the impact of a *transitory* change in a policy or exogenous variable on the current crime rate, taking into account the impact of a change on expectations.

If we wish to find the ultimate long run impact of these policy changes, we must first solve the respective equation in (12.26) to get P_{ij}, and then compute $\frac{P_{ij}}{1 - a_0}$ as described in equation (12.20). Performing these calculations and simplifying yields:

$$LRM_{ij} = \frac{P_{ij}}{1 - a_0} = \frac{\Pi_{ij}}{1 - \alpha_0 - \alpha_1} \qquad (12.27)$$

We now have three different ways of thinking about our coefficient estimates. Given coefficient estimates, we can describe the impact of a permanent shock on the current crime rate, a permanent shock on the long-run crime rate, or of a transitory shock on the current crime rate.[28]

As described in the previous section, our belief is that our most reliable estimated models are those in column V of Tables 12.7 and 12.8. The coefficients on the future and past crime rates for the property crime rate are .77 and .21, respectively; solving (12.25) gives $a_0 = .26$. For the violent crime rate, the estimated coefficients of future and past crime rates are .66 and .30, respectively, resulting in $a_0 = .39$. Solving for P_{ij} in equation (12.26) gives:

$$P_{ij} = \frac{\Pi_{ij}}{1 - \alpha_1(1 + a_0)}$$

Thus, estimated coefficients must be inflated by a factor of $(1 - \alpha_1(1 + a_0))^{-1}$ to assess the impact of an anticipated permanent change in an exogenous or policy variable on the current crime rate. For the property crime rate, $(1 - \alpha_1(1 + a_0))^{-1} = 14.6$, while for the violent crime rate, $(1 - \alpha_1(1 + a_0))^{-1} = 7.0$. From equation (12.26), transitory changes influence current crime rates according to the adjusted coefficients:

$$Q_{ij} = \frac{\Pi_{ij}}{1 - \alpha_1 a_0}$$

To assess the impact of transitory changes on current crime rates, estimated coefficients must be inflated by a factor of $(1 - \alpha_1 a_0)^{-1}$. For the property crime rate, $(1 - \alpha_1 a_0)^{-1} = 1.19$, while for the violent crime rate, $(1 - \alpha_1 a_0)^{-1} = 1.24$. These results indicate that permanent changes in exogenous variables have impacts on current crime rates that are orders of magnitude larger than transitory changes.

Using our expression for long run multipliers in equation (12.27), apparently estimated coefficients in the property crime model must be inflated by a factor of 50, and in the violent crime model by a factor of 25. In Table 12.9, the various multipliers are applied to estimated coefficients to give a sense as to how elasticities change with the nature of the change in the exogenous variable and the time frame.

4.1 Discussion

The results displayed on Table 12.9 must be considered with care for several reasons. There are some anomalous results in model estimation (for example, the positive sign attached to real per capita income in violent crime specifications). Estimates from models designed to avoid potential problems such as dynamic panel bias may suffer from weak

Table 12.9   Short and long run elasticities

	Coefficient	Current crime rates Elasticity w.r.t.:		Long-run crime rates Elasticity w.r.t.:
		Transitory change	Permanent change	Permanent change
Property Crime:				
Police Per Capita	−0.050	−0.060	−0.730	−2.5
Imprisonment Rate	−0.033	−0.039	−0.482	−1.65
Unemployment Rate	0.032	0.038	0.467	1.6
Infant Mortality Rate	0.039	0.046	0.569	1.95
Percent pop. Metro Area	0.006	0.007	0.088	0.30
Violent Crime:				
Police Per Capita	−0.088	−0.110	−0.616	−2.2
Imprisonment Rate	−0.070	−0.087	−0.490	−1.75
Unemployment Rate	0.037	0.046	0.259	0.93
Infant Mortality Rate	0.085	0.105	0.595	2.13
Real Per Capita Income	0.377	0.467	2.639	9.43

Notes: Elasticities are computed using GMM estimates from Tables 7 and 8, column V using the methods described in the text.

identification. Since the estimated coefficients on future and past crime rates work their way into the denominators of multipliers, very small changes in model estimates may provoke rather large changes in long run elasticities. Some estimated models produce estimates of lead and lag terms that sum to greater than one, implying that the long run multiplier in response to permanent changes in exogenous variables cannot be computed.

On the other hand, the fact remains that in virtually any model we estimated, lead and lag terms appear to be significant and large, suggesting that past conditions and expectations of the future are of some importance in understanding current crime rates. Qualitatively, this result implies that the exact nature of a change in a given exogenous variable – something heretofore ignored in the econometric literature on crime rates – is critical in understanding its current and eventual impact. The estimates on Table 12.9 of the impact of changes on the current crime rate of a permanent change, for example, only apply if agents believe the change to be permanent, and the policy maker can credibly commit to a permanent change. Therefore, one must view the results on Table 12.9 through a lens which includes an assessment of criminal perceptions and policy maker credibility.

5 CONCLUSIONS

In this chapter we have estimated a model of aggregate crime rates that explicitly takes into account that if crimes are committed by rational agents, crime commission decisions should in part depend upon expectations of future economic conditions, enforcement, and punishment. While none of our estimated models are immune from criticism, virtually all of our estimation results imply that future expectations are important in explaining current crime rates, and that expectations are important in understanding the dynamics of aggregate crime rates. Even if one questions the quantitative results we have presented, their qualitative meaning is important.

Our finding that expectations matter presents both challenges and opportunities for policy makers. On the one hand, it becomes harder to predict the exact effect of planned policy measures on the crime rate because this will depend upon whether the change is perceived to be temporary or long-lasting. On the other hand, if policy makers can commit to a pre-specified and credible course of action, then it may be possible to effectively manage expectations and thus make crime-reducing policies more efficient. For instance, suppose governments are somehow committed to increasing enforcement for a prolonged period of time as soon as economic conditions deteriorate. If such a policy is credible, the impact of a contemporaneous increase in the unemployment rate on today's crime rate would be lessened because of the expectations of increased crime fighting effort in subsequent periods. Such a commitment, if practically feasible, would actually reduce the need for a contemporaneous increase in enforcement and make crime fighting less costly. Of course, to gain the needed credibility may take time and require significant resources in the short run.

The implication that past behavior and expectations of the future are important in driving crime rates has rich and interesting implications for policy. We hope that our approach and results will invite fuller consideration of the role of expectations and credibility in the classic Becker (1968) model.

A   DATA APPENDIX

The data we used in this study basically derives from a version of the data set used in Spelman (2001), made available by John J. Donohue on his website (http://islandia.law.yale.edu/donohue/pubsdata.htm). We checked all the data against historical sources and updated the data set so that it is as recent as possible. The data sources for individual items are as follows:

1. All crime data comes from the uniform crime reports, available from the bureau of justice statistics (http://bjsdata.ojp.usdoj.gov/dataonline/Search/Crime/State /statebystatelist.cfm). This data is also available online in historical editions of the Statistical the United States available at (http://www.census.gov/compendia /statab/).
2. Early poverty rates comes from the Statistical Abstract. We added in data for the District of Columbia to that already in the Spelman's (2000) data. Data from 1970–1974 and 1976 were missing for the District of Columbia, so we interpolated these values. More recent information on poverty rates comes from the Small Area Survey of Income and Poverty Estimates produced by the United States Census (http://www.census.gov/hhes/www/saipe/). From this source we took poverty information for 1993 and from 1996–2005.
3. Age distribution data also derives from the Statistical Abstract, but due to format changes in the reporting of this information, more recent data (from 2001-on) was calculated by hand from Census bureau estimates (http://www.census.gov/popest/estimates.php).
4. There is in fact detailed information on incarceration rates going back for some time. The chief problem with this data is that there is a comparability problem. In practice, this problem appears to have a negligible impact on the data. In years prior to 1971 prison population data also includes persons jailed for some states. We took our data from the Statistical Abstract. We also relied upon some data from Bureau of Justice Statistics sources (http://www.ojp.usdoj.gov/bjs/prisons.htm). As mentioned in the text, the prison population is typically measured on the last day of the year. The District of Columbia drops out of the sample in 2001 because jurisdiction of its prisoners was transferred to the federal government at this time. Some early values are missing; we interpolated values in Delaware and North Carolina in 1968, and Rhode Island and Arkansas over the time period 1968–70.
5. Police data and expenditures data were taken from the Statistical Abstract. These data were checked against data appearing in the

early versions of the Justice Expenditure and Employment Abstracts (JEEA). Since the Statistical Abstract had no data from 1980–81 on expenditure, we took this data from the JEEA. For similar reasons, police employment data from 1980–82 also derives from the JEEA. Missing values which had to be interpolated were 1973, 1984, 1989, 1990, and 1996 for police employment data, and 1973, 1984, 1989, 1990, and 2003 for the expenditure data.

6. Coding of three strikes legislation was developed following Marvel and Moody (2001), while coding of "shall issue" gun permit laws was developed following Donohue (2004). Donohue describes several controversies in the coding of gun control laws, and his data includes several alternative means of codifying this information. We relied upon the coding which Ayres and Donohue (2003) refer to as the "Vernick" coding. We experimented with some of the other ways in which this information was coded but this had no perceptible impact on results.

7. All data on state income come from the Bureau of Economic Analysis's Local Area Personal Income Reports (http://www.bea.gov/bea/regional/reis/). This source also gives population data for each state. The growth rate of state income was calculated as the log difference in income. All income data was deflated using the CPI available from the St. Louis Federal Reserve (base 1982–4, available at http://research.stlouisfed.org /fred2/).

8. Data on the infant mortality rate derives from the Statistical Abstract.

9. Data on state gubernatorial elections came from the *Congressional Quarterly*.

B INSTRUMENT SETS

This section describes the instrument sets used for the various instrumental variables regressions in this chapter.

1. Table 12.2, Model III: Second order lag of the property crime rate, and first, second, third, and fourth order lags of all exogenous variables.

2. Table 12.2, Model IV: Second order lag of the property crime rate, and first, second, third, and fourth order lags of all exogenous variables.

3. Table 12.2, Model V: Second order lag of the property crime rate, and first, second, third, and fourth order lags of all exogenous variables.

4. Table 12.3, Model III: Second order lag of the violent crime rate, and first, second, third, and fourth order lags of all exogenous variables.

5. Table 12.3, Model IV: Second order lag of the violent crime rate, and first, second, third, and fourth order lags of all exogenous variables.

6. Table 12.3, Model V: Second order lag of the violent crime rate, and first, second, third, and fourth order lags of all exogenous variables.

7. Table 12.5, Model I: Second order lag of the property crime rate, whether or not there was a close gubernatorial election, whether or not there was a close gubernatorial election won by a republican or independent, and first, second, third and fourth order lags of the fraction of income spent on enforcement, the population growth rate, and all exogenous variables.

8. Table 12.5, Model II: The lagged fraction of income spent on enforcement, the lagged unemployment rate, the lagged poverty rate, the second order lag of the imprisonment rate, the third order lag of the percentage of population 25 to 34, and the fourth order lag of the percentage population black.

9. Table 12.5, Model III: Same as Table 12.4, Model II.

10. Table 12.6, Model I: Second order lag of the violent crime rate, whether or not there was a close gubernatorial election, whether or not there was a close gubernatorial election won by a republican or independent, and first, second, third and fourth order lags of the fraction of income spent on enforcement, the population growth rate, and all exogenous variables.

11. Table 12.6, Model II: The lagged infant mortality rate, the lagged poverty rate, and the lagged percentage population living in a metropolitan area, the second order lags of the unemployment rate and the percentage population living in a metropolitan area, the third order lag of the unemployment rate, and the fourth order lag of the percentage population living in a metropolitan area.

12. Table 12.6, Model III: Same as Table 12.5, Model II.

13. Table 12.7, Model I: Second order lag of the property crime rate, whether or not there was a close gubernatorial election, whether or not there was a close gubernatorial election won by a republican or independent, and first, second, third and fourth order lags of the fraction of income spent on enforcement, the population growth rate, and all exogenous variables. All instruments are in differences.

14. Table 12.7, Model II: First order lags of the population growth rate, the unemployment rate, the poverty rate, the percentage population aged 25 to 34, and the percentage population living in a metropolitan

area; second order lags of the incarceration rate and the fraction of population 25 to 34; third order lags of the percentage population 25 to 34 and the percentage population living in a metropolitan area, fourth order lags of the percentage population 18 to 24, and fifth order lags of the incarceration rate and the fraction of state income spent on law enforcement. Note that fifth order lags of the last two variables enter into the instrument set as these variables were lagged once to begin with. All instruments are in differences.

15. Table 12.7, Model III: Same as Table 12.7, Model II.

16. Table 12.7, Model IV: Second order lag of the property crime rate, whether or not there was a close gubernatorial election, whether or not there was a close gubernatorial election won by a republican or independent, and first, second, third and fourth order lags of the fraction of income spent on enforcement, the population growth rate, and all exogenous variables. All instruments are in levels.

17. Table 12.7, Model V: Second order lag of the property crime rate, first order lags of the population growth rate, the level of real per capita income, the unemployment rate, the fraction population aged 25 to 34, the percentage population living in a metropolitan area; second order lags of the population growth rate, the unemployment rate, the incarceration rate, and the percentage population living in a metropolitan area; third order lags of the the percentage population 25 to 34, the percentage population living in a metropolitan area, the incarceration rate, and police per capita, fourth order lags of the incarceration rate, the fraction of income spent on enforcement, and the percentage population living in a metropolitan area. All instruments are in levels.

18. Table 12.7, Model VI: Same as Table 12.7, Model V.

19. Table 12.8, Model I: Second order lag of the violent crime rate, whether or not there was a close gubernatorial election, whether or not there was a close gubernatorial election won by a republican or independent, and first, second, third and fourth order lags of the fraction of income spent on enforcement, the population growth rate, and all exogenous variables. All instruments are in differences.

20. Table 12.8, Model II: First order lag of the fraction of state income spent on enforcement, population growth rate, infant mortality rate, unemployment rate, fraction population aged 18 to 24, fraction population living in a metropolitan area, presence of a shall issue law; second order lag of the incarceration rate, the infant mortality rate, fraction population aged 25 to 34, fraction population living in a metropolitan area, the fraction population black, and the presence of a three strikes law; third order lags of the population growth rate,

the unemployment rate, the percentage population living in a metropolitan area, the percentage population black, fourth order lags of the population growth rate, the fraction population aged 18 to 24, and the fifth order lag of the fraction state income spent on enforcement. All instruments are in differences.

21. Table 12.8, Model III: Same as Table 12.8, Model II.
22. Table 12.8, Model IV: Second order lag of the violent crime rate, whether or not there was a close gubernatorial election, whether or not there was a close gubernatorial election won by a republican or independent, and first, second, third and fourth order lags of the fraction of income spent on enforcement, the population growth rate, and all exogenous variables. All instruments are in levels.
23. Table 12.8, Model V: Second order lag of the violent crime rate; first order lags of the population growth rate, the unemployment rate, the percentage population 18 to 24, the percentage population living in a metropolitan area, and the percentage population black; second order lags of the population growth rate, the unemployment rate, the percentage population living in a metropolitan area, the percentage population black; third order lags of police per capita, the percentage population 18 to 24, and the percentage population black, and fourth order lags of the population growth rate, the unemployment rate, and the percentage population living in a metropolitan area. All instruments are in levels.
24. Table 12.8, Model VI: Same as Table 12.8, Model V.

NOTES

1. The state-level estimates summarized by Spelman, in addition to his own estimates, include Marvell and Moody (1994), Becsi (1999), and Levitt (1996). Marvell and Moody (1994) find the elasticity of violent crime with respect to the imprisonment rate is −0.06, while the elasticity of the property crime rate is −0.17. Becsi's (1999) estimates for all types of crime range between −0.05 and −0.09, while Levitt's (1996) estimates are typically larger: his estimates of the violent crime elasticity and property crime elasticity, are, respectively, −0.38 and −0.26.
2. Spelman (2000, p.101–103) notes that this critique appeared in Blumstein, Cohen, and Nagin (1978), which assessed the early literature on deterrence. The critique also figures prominently in Cloninger's (1975) assessment of initial econometric studies of the deterrence hypothesis. Relatedly, Levitt (1998a) asks if it is measurement error, deterrence, or incapacitation that drives the negative correlation between arrest rates and crime rates, and Kessler and Levitt (1999) also contrast deterrence and incapacitation.
3. Raphael and Winter-Ebmer (2001) and Gould, Weinberg, and Mustard (2002) also point out that a large portion of previous literature has found that the impact of unemployment on crime rates is ambiguous.
4. However, Levitt (1999) suggests that demographic changes are of limited usefulness in understanding movements in aggregate crime rates.

5. Indeed, a characteristic of Ehrlich's (1973) early work on the subject was his careful specification of a theoretical model that coincided with his econometric model.

6. One prominent example in which this occurs is Levitt (1996), which also discusses various attempts to deal with this problem using instrumental variables with state level data, with limited success (see Levitt, 1996, p. 339.)

7. As described in a subsequent section, a large part of what follows in bringing the model to the data involves incorporating rational expectations about future enforcement and economic conditions into the model.

8. There are exceptions, one of which is Marvell and Moody (2001), who include past crime rates in their econometric specifications.

9. It should be mentioned that results are not always what one might expect. For example, Waldfogel and Nagin (1996) find that the impact of conviction on earnings depends upon the age of the offender, and that younger offenders may in fact earn higher wages than their peers. They argue that this may be because offenders are likely to search for different types of jobs than others. For our purposes, there is no need to take a precise position as to *how* future prospects are effected, but only that future prospects are influenced by current decisions, and that agents should consider this when reaching current decisions about whether or not to engage in criminal activity.

10. It would be reasonable for the population average of crime consumption, $\overline{C}_t$, to enter negatively into the utility function. But since $\overline{C}_t$ is not a choice variable, such an inclusion would not change results so long as $\overline{C}_t$ is included as an additively separable component of utility.

11. We assume that $X_{1t}X_{2t} < 1$. This means that *all* of the representative agent's time cannot be taken through punishment and/or incarceration. When aggregated up to an economy-wide level, this rules out the absurd possibility that everyone in the population is completely imprisoned.

12. Of course, if the individual is incarcerated, the current effective labor endowment is directly reduced by past criminal activity.

13. We have simplified the punishment mechanism in the sense that it does not matter for the current punishment whether past criminal activity has gone unpunished or not. In a more elaborate model such an assumption may be altered.

14. Two recent sources which provide accessable explanations of the method are De Jong and Dave (2007) and McCandless (2008).

15. Alternatively, the returns to crime and honest labor (y_{1t} and y_{2t}) could be modeled as autoregressive processes. While this might be more realistic, it does complicate the exposition a bit without fundamentally changing results.

16. The data set we used as a building block was downloaded from John Donohue's website (http://islandia.law.yale.edu/donohue/pubsdata.htm). Our data set, along with a Stata do-file replicating results, is available by request.

17. Property index crimes include burglary, larceny, and automobile theft. Violent index crimes include murder, rape, robbery and assault.

18. The data appendix elaborates further on timing issues in the data. Levitt (1996) also uses the prison population lagged one period in model estimation.

19. All models are estimated with heteroscedasticity and autocorrelation consistent standard errors. To correct for autocorrelation, we use the Bartlett kernel with a value of 3, which corresponds to a lag order 2 correction. We settled on this value of 3 using the rule of thumb suggested in Baum et. al. (2007) that the kernel length be of the order of $T^{1/3}$.

20. This test statistic is perhaps less familiar in that its development is a bit more recent. For details, see Kleinbergen and Paap (2006) and Baum et. al. (2007).

21. See Stock and Yogo (2005) and Baltagi (2008).

22. We experimented with some additional instruments, for example, dummy variables capturing the electoral cycle in each state. Because Levitt (1996) also found these variables did not prove to be useful as instruments for policy changes, we do not discuss these results.

23. A further benefit of working with differences is that it anticipates potential stationarity problems in the data. Indeed, many of the series of interest (for example, the crime rates themselves) fail standard panel stationarity tests.
24. Appendix B provides a description of the ultimate instrument sets used in various estimated models.
25. The solution method is that described in Blanchard and Fisher (1985, p. 261–5).
26. This is the simplest possible way of framing our discussion of the implications of estimation results for assessing changes in policy or other variables. We elaborate on more complex specifications below.
27. It bears mentioning that equation (12.25) results in some restrictions that estimated coefficients must satisfy if the equation is to be stable or even generate reasonable solutions. For example, it cannot be the case that $\alpha_0 \alpha_1 > \frac{1}{4}$, as then no solution exists.
28. Of course, the impact of a transitory shock on the long run crime rate is by definition zero.

REFERENCES

Ayres, Ian and John J. Donohue. 2003. "Shooting Down the 'More Guns, Less Crime' Hypothesis," *Stanford Law Review* 55(4): 1371–1398.
Baltagi, Badi H. 2008. *Econometric Analysis of Panel Data, 4th. ed.* Chichester, West Sussex, UK: John Wiley and Sons.
Baum, Christopher F., Mark E. Schaffer, and Steven Stillman. 2007. "Enhanced routines for instrumental variables/generalized method of moments estimation and testing," *Stata Journal* 7(4): 465–506.
Becker, Gary S. 1968. "Crime and Punishment: An Economic Approach." *Journal of Political Economy* 76: 169–217.
Becker, Gary S., Michael Grossman, and Kevin M. Murphy. 1994. "An Empirical Analysis of Cigarette Addiction." *The American Economic Review* 84(3): 396–418.
Becsi, Zsolt. 1999. "Economics and Crime in the United States," *Economic Review of the Federal Reserve Bank of Atlanta* 84: 38–56.
Blanchard, Olivier J. and Stanley Fisher. 1989. *Lectures in Macroeconomics.* Boston: The MIT Press.
Blumstein, Alfred, Jacqueline Cohen, and Daniel Nagin. 1978. "Deterrence and Incapacitation: Estimating the Effects of Criminal Sanctions on Crime Rates," Report of the Panel on Research on Deterrent and Incapacitative Effects. Washington: National Academy of Sciences.
Cameron, Samuel. 1988. 'The economics of crime deterrence: a survey of theory and evidence,' Kyklos 41(2): 301–23.
Cameron, Samuel. 1994. "A Review of the Econometric Evidence on the Effects of Capital Punishment" *Journal of Socio-Economics* 23(1-2): 197–214.
Cloninger, Dale O. 1975. "The Deterrent Effect of Law Enforcement: An Evaluation of Recent Findings and Some New Evidence," *American Journal of Economics and Sociology* 34(3): 323–35.
De Jong, David N., with Chetan Dave. 2007. *Structural Macroeconomics.* Princeton, N.J.: Princeton University Press.
Donohue, John. J. 2004. "Guns, Crime, and the Impact of State Right-to-Carry Laws," *Fordham Law Review* 73(2): 637–52.
Donohue, John J. and Steven D. Levitt. 2001. "The Impact of Legalized Abortion on Crime," *Quarterly Journal of Economics* 116(2): 379–420.
Donohue, John J. and Justin Wolfers. 2005. "Uses and Abuses of Empirical Evidence in the Death Penalty Debate," *Stanford Law Review* 58: 791–846.
Ehrlich, Isaac. 1973. "Participation in Illegitimate Activities: A Theoretical and Empirical Investigation." *Journal of Political Economy*, May, 81(3): 521–65.

Fuhrer, Jeffrey C. 1997. "The (Un)Importance of Forward-looking Behavior in Price Specifications." *Journal of Money, Credit, and Banking*, 29(3): 338–50.

Gould, Eric D., Bruce A. Weinberg, and David B. Mustard. 2002. "Crime Rates and Local Labor Opportunities in the United States: 1979–1997," *Review of Economics and Statistics* 84(1): 45–61.

Grogger, Jeff. 1998. "Market Wages and Youth Crime," *Journal of Labor Economics* 16(4): 756–91.

Joyce, Ted. 2004. "Did Legalized Abortion Reduce Crime?" *Journal of Human Resources* 39(1): 1–28.

Katz, Lawrence, Steven D. Levitt, and Ellen Shustorovich. 2003. "Prison Conditions, Capital Punishment, and Deterrence," *American Law and Economics Review* 5(2): 318–43.

Kessler, Daniel P. and Steven D. Levitt. 1999. "Using Sentence Enhancements to Distinguish between Deterrence and Incapacitation," *Journal of Law and Economics* 42(1): 343–63. *American Law and Economics Review* 5(2): 318–43.

Kelly, Morgan. 2000. "Inequality and Crime," *The Review of Economics and Statistics* 82(4): 530–39.

Kleinbergen, F. and R. Paap. 2006. "Generalized Reduced Rank Tests Using the Singular Value Decomposition." *Journal of Econometrics* 127(1): 97–126.

Levitt, Steven D. 1996. "The Effect of Prison Population Size on Crime Rates: Evidence from Prison Overcrowding Litigation." *Quarterly Journal of Economics* 111(2): 319–51.

Levitt, Steven D. 1997. "Using Electoral Cycles in Police Hiring to Estimate the Effect of Police on Crime," *American Economic Review* 87(3): 270–90.

Levitt, Steven D. 1998a. "Juvenile Crime and Punishment," *Journal of Political Economy* 106(6): 1156–85.

Levitt, Steven D. 1998b. "Why do Increased Arrest Rates Appear to Reduce Crime? Deterrence, Incapacitation, or Measurement Error?" *Economic Inquiry* 36(3): 353–72.

Levitt, Steven D. 1999. "The Limited Role of Changing Age Structure in Explaining Aggregate Crime Rates," *Criminology* 37(3): 581–97.

Levitt, Steven D. 2004. "Understanding Why Crime Fell in the 1990s: Four Factors That Explain the Decline and Six That Do Not," *Journal of Economic Perspectives* 18(1): 163–90.

Lott, John R. 1992. "Do We Punish High Income Criminals Too Heavily?" *Economic Inquiry* 30: 583–608.

Lott, John R. and David B. Mustard. 1997. "Crime, Deterrence, and Right-to-Carry Concealed Handguns," *Journal of Legal Studies* 26(1): 1–68.

Machin, Stephen and Costas Meghir. 2004. "Crime and Economic Incentives. *Journal of Human Resources* 39(4): 56–89.

Marvell, Thomas B. and Carlisle E. Moody. 1994. "Prison Population Growth and Crime Reduction," *Journal of Quantitative Criminology* 10: 109–40.

Marvell, Thomas B. and Carlisle E. Moody. 2001. "The Lethal Effects of Three-Strikes Laws," *Journal of Legal Studies* 30(1): 89–106.

McCandless, George. 2008. *The ABCs of RBCs: An Introduction to Dynamic Macroeconomic Models.* Cambridge, Mass. and London: Harvard University Press.

Nagin, Daniel and Joel Waldfogel. 1998. "The Effect of Conviction on Income Through the Life Cycle,"*International Review of Law and Economics* 18(1): 25–40.

Raphael, Steven and Rudolf Winter-Ebmer. 2001. "Identifying the Effect of Unemployment on Crime," 44(1): 259–83.

Spelman, William. 2000. 'What recent studies do (and don't) tell us about imprisonment and crime,' in Michael Tonry (ed.) *Crime and justice: a review of research vol. 27*, University of Chicago Press: Chicago, 419–94

Spelman, William. 2001. "The Limited Importance of Prison Expansion," in *The Crime Drop in America*, Alfred Blumstein and Joel Waldman, (eds), pp. 97–130. Cambridge and New York: Cambridge University Press.

Staiger, D. and J. H. Stock. 1997. "Instrumental Variables Regression with Weak Instruments," *Econometrica* 65(3): 557–86.

Stock, J. H. and M. Yogo. 2005. "Testing for Weak Instruments in Linear IV Regression," in *Identification and Inference for Econometric Models: Essays in Honor of Thomas Rothenberg* D. W. Andrews and J. H. Stock, (eds). Cambridge: Cambridge University Press.

Waldfogel, Joel. 1994. "Does Conviction Have a Persistent Effect on Income and Employment?" *International Review of Law and Economics* 14(1): 103–19.

13. Active courts and menu contracts*
Luca Anderlini, Leonardo Felli, and Andrew Postlewaite

1. INTRODUCTION

In a recent paper (Anderlini, Felli, and Postlewaite 2011) we showed, by means of a simple example, that Courts that actively intervene in parties' contracts may improve on the outcome these parties could achieve without intervention. In particular if the role of the Court is to maximize the parties' welfare under the veil of ignorance, Court intervention can induce parties to reveal their private information and enhance their ex-ante welfare.

The example in Anderlini, Felli, and Postlewaite (2011) is one in which parties are asymmetrically informed when they write their ex-ante contract. The seller knows the value and cost associated with the widget she provides while the buyer is uninformed. If the seller is restricted to offering a simple trading contract (a price at which to trade the widget in question) without the Court's intervention she will offer the same price whatever the value and the cost of the widget. In other words, different types of seller offer the same trading contract and in equilibrium inefficient pooling arises. Court intervention that takes the form of a restriction on the price at which the parties can trade, induces the different types of seller to separate and reveal their private information. In so doing the inefficiency associated with the sellers' pooling is eliminated and ex-ante welfare increases.

In this chapter we consider a different example from the one in Anderlini, Felli, and Postlewaite (2011). We first show that in this richer example if we follow Anderlini, Felli, and Postlewaite (2011) and restrict the contracts the informed party can offer to the uninformed one at the negotiation stage, Court intervention can improve the parties' ex-ante welfare exactly as in Anderlini, Felli, and Postlewaite (2011). However, if we remove this restriction then multiple equilibria obtain. In this case an active Court still has an important role. It ensures that the inefficient pooling equilibria do not exist alongside the superior ones in which separation occurs.

In particular, the key type of contract the informed party would like to offer to the uninformed one is a menu contract. This is a pooling contract across different types of the informed party that immediately becomes binding, and that contains an array of contractual arrangements. Which contractual arrangement applies is then left to an (incentive compatible) declaration by the informed party.

In two separate papers, Maskin and Tirole (1990, 1992) examine the general case of an "Informed Principal" problem. Among other insights, they point out that, under certain conditions a menu contract equilibrium may Pareto improve over other types of arrangements.

In our setup the informed party, the buyer, has private information and, ex-ante, makes a take-it-or-leave-it offer to the seller. Therefore he is an informed Principal. Our model in fact falls within the case of "Common Values" examined in Maskin and Tirole (1992). As in Maskin and Tirole (1992), it is then possible to construct equilibria of the game in which by means of a menu contract the informed parties can both pool when offering a contract to the uninformed party and reveal their private information in an incentive compatible way after the contract is accepted. Courts' intervention can select the equilibria supported by menu contracts that foster separation of the different types of the informed party.

1.1   Outline

The plan of the rest of the chapter is as follows. In Section 2 we present the model under the assumption that menu contracts cannot be used. The equilibrium characterization of this model is presented in Section 3. We first consider the case in which Courts enforce everything the parties write and then introduce active Courts. In Section 4 we modify the model so as to allow parties, at the negotiation stage, to offer menu contracts. We then provide the equilibrium characterization of this new model first when Courts are passive enforcers and then when Courts are active. Section 5 briefly concludes. For ease of exposition all proofs have been gathered in the Appendix.[1]

2.   THE MODEL

2.1   Passive Courts

A buyer B and a seller S face a potentially profitable trade of three widgets, denoted w_1, w_2 and w_3 respectively.

Widgets w_1 and w_2 require a widget- and relationship-specific investment $I > 0$ on B's part. The buyer can only undertake one of the two widget-specific investments. The value and cost of both w_1 and w_2 are zero in the absence of investment, so that only one of them can possibly be traded profitably.

The cost and value of w_3 do not depend on any investment. To begin with assume that w_3 is *not contractible* at the ex-ante stage. Non-contractibility means that w_3 can be traded regardless of any ex-ante decision. In practice, in this case we can think of w_3 as being traded (or not) at the ex-post stage. When menu contracts are introduced the difference between w_3 being contractible or not at the ex-ante stage will become crucial. In the results presented in this section it is not.

The buyer has private information at the time of contracting. He knows his type, which can be either α or β. Each type is equally likely, and the seller does *not* know B's type.

We take the cost and value of the three widgets to be as in Table 13.1 below, where they are represented *net* of the cost of investment $I > 0$.[2] In each cell of the table, the left entry represents surplus, and the right entry represents cost (obviously the sum of the two gives the value to the buyer, net of investment cost).

Table 13.1

	w_1	w_2	w_3	
Type α	$\Delta_M, \quad c_L$	$\Delta_H, \quad c_L$	$-\Delta_H, \quad c_H$	(13.1)
Type β	$\Delta_N, \quad c_L$	$\Delta_L, \quad c_L$	$\Delta_S, \quad c_S$	

We take these parameters to satisfy the following.

Assumption 1: *Parameter Values:* The values of cost and surplus in the matrix in (13.1) satisfy
(i) $0 < \Delta_L < \Delta_M < \Delta_H$
and
(ii) $\Delta_M + \Delta_H < \Delta_S$
and
(iii) $c_S + \Delta_H + \Delta_S + \dfrac{\Delta_M}{2} < c_H < \Delta_S + 2\Delta_M$
and
(iv) $0 < -\Delta_N < \Delta_H - \Delta_M - \Delta_L$
and
(v) $c_L < c_S$

The costs and values of the three widgets are *observable but not contractible*. We first restrict attention to an environment in which any contract between B and S can only specify the widget(s) to be traded, and price(s).

Menu contracts are ruled out by assumption. The Court can only observe (verify) which one of w_1 or w_2 is specified in any contract, and whether the correct widget is traded or not as prescribed, and the appropriate price paid.

Assume that B has all the bargaining power at the ex-ante contracting stage, while S has all the bargaining power ex-post.

To sum up, the timing and relevant decision variables available to the trading parties are as follows.

The buyer learns his type *before* meeting the seller. Then B and S meet at the ex-ante contracting stage. At this point B makes a take-it-or-leave-it offer of a contract to S, which S can accept or reject. A contract consists of a pair $s_i = (w_i, p_i)$, with $i = 1, 2$ specifying a single widget to trade and at which price. After a contract (if any) is signed, B decides whether to invest or not, and in which of the specific widgets.

After investment takes place (if it does), the bargaining power shifts to the seller and we enter the ex-post stage. At this point S makes a take-it-or-leave-it offer to B on whether to trade any widget not previously contracted on and at which price, which B can accept or reject. Without loss of generality, we can restrict S to make a take-it-or-leave-it offer to B on whether to trade w_3 and at which price p_3. After B decides whether to accept or reject S's ex-post offer (if any), production takes place. First S produces the relevant widgets and then he learns his cost.[3] Finally, delivery and payment occur according to contract terms. The Court's role is the one of a passive enforcer of the terms of the parties' ex-ante and ex-post contract.

2.2   Active Courts

The information of B, S and the Court, and their bargaining power remain as described above. The timing, investment requirements and all the elements of the matrix in (13.1) also stay the same.

The Court announces a set of ex-ante contracts U which will be "upheld" and a set of ex-ante contracts V which will be "voided." There are two contracts in all to be considered, one of the type $s_1 = (w_1, p_1)$ and another of the type $s_2 = (w_2, p_2)$. We restrict the Court to be able to announce that certain contracts will be upheld or voided, *only according to the widget involved*. Therefore U and V are two mutually exclusive subsets of $\{s_1, s_2\}$ with $U \cup V = \{s_1, s_2\}$, so that effectively the Court's strategy set consists of a choice of $V \subseteq \{s_1, s_2\}$.

We restrict the Court to make deterministic announcements; each contract is either in V or not with probability one.

If $V = \varnothing$ so that all contracts are enforced, then the model is exactly as described in Subsection 2.1 above. If on the other hand one or two contracts are in V, in the final stage of the game B and S are free to renegotiate the terms (price and delivery) of any widget in the voided contract, regardless of anything that was previously agreed.[4] Notice that, by our assumptions on bargaining power, this means that S is free to make a take-it-or-leave-it offer to B of a price p_i at which any w_i with voided contract terms is to be delivered.[5]

The Court chooses V so as to maximize its payoff which equals the *sum* of the expected payoffs of B and S.[6, 7]

3. EQUILIBRIA WITH NO MENU CONTRACTS

3.1 Passive Court Equilibria

As we anticipated, when all contracts are enforced, inefficient pooling obtains in equilibrium.

Proposition 1: *Equilibrium With A Passive Court: Suppose the Court enforces all contracts, $V = \emptyset$, and Assumption 1 holds. Then the unique equilibrium outcome of the model is that the two types of buyer pool with probability one: they both invest and trade w_2 at a price $p_2 = c_L$, and they both trade w_3 at a price $p_3 = \Delta_S + c_S$.*

The total amount of expected surplus (net of investment) in this case is given by $\frac{\Delta_S}{2} + \frac{\Delta_L}{2}$. By definition, this is also the Court's payoff.

The equilibrium outcome in Proposition 1 is inefficient in the sense that, in equilibrium w_3 is traded by the type α buyer; this trade generates a net surplus of $-\Delta_H$.

The reason separation is impossible to sustain as an equilibrium outcome with passive Courts is easy to see. In any separating equilibrium, it is clear that the type β buyer would trade w_3 ex-post for a price $p_3 = \Delta_S + c_S$. The type β buyer would also trade w_2 for a price $p_2 = c_L$ (this is in fact true in *any* equilibrium in which the Court does not void contracts for w_2). Given that the type β buyer trades both w_2 and w_3, the type α will always gain by deviating and pooling with the the type β buyer.

3.2 Active Court Equilibria

A Court that actively intervenes and voids contracts for w_2 will be able to induce separation between the two types of buyer and increase expected welfare.

Proposition 2:   *Equilibrium With An Active Court: Suppose the Court is an active player that can choose V as above, and that Assumption 1 holds. Then the unique equilibrium outcome of the model is that the Court sets $V = \{s_2\}$ and the two types of buyer separate: the type α buyer invests and trades w_1 at a price $p_1 = c_L$ and does not trade w_3; the type β buyer does not invest and only trades w_3 at a price $p_3 = \Delta_S + c_S$.*

The total amount of expected surplus (net of investment) in this case is given by $\frac{\Delta_S}{2} + \frac{\Delta_M}{2}$. By definition, this is also the Court's payoff.

When the Court voids contracts for either w_1 or w_2, the corresponding widget will not be traded in equilibrium. This would be true for completely obvious reasons if the Court's voiding makes the trade not *feasible*. It is also true when the Court allows in principle the trade of the widget ex-post acting as a minimal enforcement agency (see footnote 5). This is because a classic hold-up problem obtains in our model, driven by the relationship- and widget-specific investment. Given that the seller has all the bargaining power ex-post, unless an ex-ante contract is in place the buyer will be unable to recoup the cost of his investment and hence will not invest.

To see why the Court's intervention induces the two types of buyer to separate at the contract offer stage consider the incentives of the type α buyer to deviate from the separating equilibrium described in Proposition 2. With a passive Court, pooling with the type α buyer involves positive payoffs *both* in the trade of w_2 and in that of w_3 ex-post. Now that the Court renders the trade of w_2 impossible in equilibrium, the payoff to the type α buyer from deviating to pool with the type β buyer comes only from the ex-post trade of w_3. This decrease is enough to sustain the separating equilibrium of Proposition 2.

The Court's intervention has two direct effects. One is separation, so that the type α buyer no longer inefficiently trades w_3, and the other is the lack of trade of w_2. While the first increases expected welfare, the second reduces it. Overall expected welfare increases by $(\Delta_M - \Delta_L)/2$.

4.   MENU CONTRACTS

Allowing menu contracts changes the terms on which we can justify Court intervention, but still provides a robust rationale for active Courts.

The effect of allowing menu contracts depends critically on whether we maintain the assumption that w_3 is not contractible ex-ante. If we do, Propositions 1 and 2 hold essentially unchanged.[8]

If on the other hand we allow ex-ante contracting on w_3, *as well as* menu contracts, the picture changes. When menu contracts and ex-ante contracting on w_3 are both allowed, if the Court enforces all contracts, *multiple* equilibrium outcomes obtain. Pooling as in Proposition 1 is an equilibrium. However, the model also has an equilibrium in which a (non-trivial) menu contract is offered and the same separating outcome as in Proposition 2 obtains. Clearly, even in this case an active Court has a role in eliminating any possibility for the parties to inefficiently pool in equilibrium. The Court will step in when it expects inefficient pooling to occur.

In order to proceed, we need to be precise about two new elements of the model: the set of possible contracts when ex-ante contracting on w_3 is allowed, and the set of possible menu contracts built on the basis of these.

When w_3 can be contracted ex-ante, two types of contracts need to be considered (still abstracting from menu ones). For want of better terminology we label them *simple* and *bundle*. A simple contract, as before, consists of a pair $s_i = (w_i, p_i)$, with $i = 1, 2, 3$, specifying a single widget to trade and at which price.

A bundle contract consists of an offer to trade a specific widget w_i $i = 1, 2$ *and* the regular widget w_3 at prices p_i and p_3 respectively; a bundle contract is denoted by a triplet $b_{1,3} = (w_i, p_i, p_3)$.[9] So, as well as possible offers of s_3, $b_{1,3}$ and $b_{2,3}$, we now need to consider any possible choice of $V \subseteq \{s_1, s_2, s_3, b_{1,3}, b_{2,3}\}$.

We also need to specify what a menu contract is. This is not hard to define. A menu ex-ante contract is a pair (m^α, m^β) with both m^α and m^β elements of $\{s_1, s_2, s_3, b_{1,3}, b_{2,3}\}$ if ex-ante contracting on w_3 is allowed, and just elements of $\{s_1, s_2\}$ if ex-ante contracting on w_3 is not allowed.[10] The interpretation is that m^α is the contract that rules if the Buyer announces that he is of type α after the contract is accepted and becomes binding, while m^β is the relevant arrangement if the Buyer announces that he is of type β.

With little loss of generality, we take $V \subseteq \{s_1, s_2, s_3, b_{1,3}, b_{2,3}\}$ and $V \subseteq \{s_1, s_2\}$, depending on whether ex-ante contracting on w_3 is allowed or not, even when menu contracts are allowed. In essence, we are restricting the Court to uphold or void on the basis of the applicable part of the menu (in other words on the basis of the part of the menu which rules as a result of the Buyer's declaration).

Proposition 3:   *Menu Contracts and Non-Contractible w_3: Assume that menu contracts are allowed and that w_3 is not ex-ante contractible. Suppose that Assumption 1 holds.*

Then Propositions 1 and 2 still hold. In particular the equilibrium payoff of a passive Court is $\frac{\Delta_S}{2} + \frac{\Delta_L}{2}$ while the equilibrium payoff of an active Court is $\frac{\Delta_S}{2} + \frac{\Delta_M}{2}$.

We can now proceed to the case of w_3 contractible at the ex-ante stage.

Proposition 4:   *Menu Contracts and Contractible w_3 – Passive Court: Assume that menu contracts are allowed and that w_3 is ex-ante contractible. Let Assumption 1 hold, and assume that the Court upholds all contracts, $V = \varnothing$. Then:*

(i) There is an equilibrium of the model in which the trading and investment outcome is as in Proposition 1. The menu contract in this equilibrium is degenerate in the sense that both types of buyer offer the same menu contract and $m^\alpha = m^\beta$. Both types of buyer invest in and trade w_2 and both types of buyer trade w_3. The total amount of expected surplus (net of investment) in this case is given by $\frac{\Delta_S}{2} + \frac{\Delta_L}{2}$.

(ii) There is an equilibrium of the model in which the trading and investment outcome is the same as in Proposition 2: the type α buyer invests in and trades w_1, and the type β buyer trades w_3. The menu contract in this equilibrium is non-degenerate in the sense that both types of buyer offer the same contract and $m^\alpha \neq m^\beta$. The type α buyer invests in and trades w_1, while the type β buyer does not invest in either w_1 or w_2, and trades w_3. The total amount of expected surplus (net of investment) in this case is given by $\frac{\Delta_S}{2} + \frac{\Delta_M}{2}$.

(iii) There is no equilibrium of the model in which the total amount of expected surplus (net of investment) exceeds $\frac{\Delta_S}{2} + \frac{\Delta_M}{2}$.

We, finally, turn to the case of an active Court and show that active Courts do have a role when parties can negotiate menu contracts.

Proposition 5:   *Menu Contracts and Contractible w_3 – Active Court: Assume that menu contracts are allowed and that w_3 is ex-ante contractible. Suppose that Assumption 1 holds. Suppose that the Court voids all contracts involving w_2. In other words suppose that $V = \{s_2, b_{2,3}\}$.*

Then the unique equilibrium trading and investment outcome of the ensuing sub-game is the same as in Proposition 2: the type α buyer invests in and trades w_1, and the type β buyer trades w_3.

Any equilibrium that sustains this equilibrium outcome is non-degenerate in the sense that both types of buyer offer the same menu contract and $m^\alpha \neq m^\beta$. The type α buyer invests in and trades w_1, while the type β buyer does not invest in either w_1 or w_2, and trades w_3.

In equilibrium, the total expected surplus (net of investment) is the maximum possible when menu contracts are allowed and the Court enforces all contracts, namely $\frac{\Delta_S}{2} + \frac{\Delta_M}{2}$.

5. CONCLUSIONS

In a world where contracts are incomplete (parties can write only simple trading contracts) active Courts can enhance the parties' ex-ante welfare by restricting the set of contracts they will enforce in equilibrium (Anderlini, Felli, and Postlewaite 2011).

This chapter shows that active Courts have a role even in a world where parties can negotiate at an ex-ante stage more complex (menu) contracts.

The main finding is that the effect of menu contracts depends critically on whether w_3 (the widget whose cost and value do not depend on investment) is contractible ex-ante or not.

If w_3 is not contractible ex-ante then active Courts enhance the parties' ex-ante welfare by inducing them to reveal their private information and hence prevent inefficient pooling exactly as in Anderlini, Felli, and Postlewaite (2011).

If, on the other hand, w_3 is contractible ex-ante, in other words parties can write more complete contracts, then multiple equilibria emerge. When the Court does not intervene both separation and inefficient pooling are possible in equilibrium.

In the latter case the model still provides a robust rationale for Court intervention: when the Court steps in and voids contracts for w_2, the *only* possible equilibrium is the superior one involving separation. Court's intervention shrinks the equilibrium set, destroying, once again, the inefficient pooling equilibrium.

APPENDIX

Lemma A.1: *Consider either the model with passive Courts or any subgame of the model with active Courts following the Court's choice of V. In any equilibrium of the model with passive Courts, or of the subgame, w_3 is traded with positive probability by the type β buyer. Moreover, the equilibrium price of w_3 is $p_3 = \Delta_S + c_S$.*

Proof: We distinguish four, mutually exclusive, exhaustive cases.

Consider first a possible separating equilibrium in which the two B types each offer a distinct contract at the ex-ante stage. In this case, at the ex-post stage it is a best reply for type β buyers to accept offers to trade w_3 at a $p_3 \leq \Delta_S + c_S$. Their unique best reply is instead to reject any offers to trade w_3 at any $p_3 > \Delta_S + c_S$. By standard arguments it then follows that in equilibrium it must be that w_3 is traded between S and type β buyers at a price $p_3 = \Delta_S + c_S$.

The second case is that of a possible pooling equilibrium in which both types of B offer the same ex-ante contract to S with probability 1. In this case the beliefs of S at the ex-post stage are that B is of either type with equal probability. The type β buyer's best reply to offers to trade w_3 at the ex-post stage is as in the previous case. It is a best reply for type α buyers to accept offers to trade w_3 at a $p_3 \leq c_H - \Delta_H$. Their unique best reply is to reject any offers to trade w_3 at any $p_3 > c_H - \Delta_H$. Since Assumption 1 (parts ii and iii) implies that $c_H - \Delta_H > \Delta_S + c_S$, it now follows by standard arguments that only two outcomes are possible in equilibrium: either w_3 is traded between S and both types of B at a price $p_3 = \Delta_S + c_S$, or w_3 is not traded at all because S does not make an offer that is accepted by either type of B. The seller's expected profit from trading w_3 at $p_3 = \Delta_S + c_S$ is given by $\Delta_S + c_S/2 - c_H/2$, which is positive by Assumption 1 (parts i, ii and iii). Therefore, S will choose to offer to trade w_3 at $p_3 = \Delta_S + c_S$. Hence the conclusion follows in this case.

The third case is that of a possible semi-separating equilibrium in which the type β buyer offers a separating contract at the ex-ante stage with probability strictly between zero and one. In this case, the same logic of the first case applies to show that in equilibrium it must be the case that S and the type β buyers who offer the separating contract trade w_3 at $p_3 = \Delta_S + c_S$.

The fourth and last case is that of a possible semi-separating equilibrium in which the type β buyer offers a separating contract at the ex-ante stage with probability zero. Since some type α buyers are separating, there must be some contract that the type β buyer offers in equilibrium which is offered by the type α buyer with a strictly lower probability. Since the ex-ante probabilities of the two types of buyer are the same, there is some contract offered in equilibrium by the type β buyer such that the seller's beliefs after receiving the offer are that he is facing a type α buyer with probability $v \in (0, 1/2)$. After this contract is offered and accepted, in any Perfect Bayesian Equilibrium, the seller's beliefs when he contemplates making an offer to trade w_3 must also be that he faces the type α buyer with probability v. Using the same logic as in the second case, only two possibilities remain. Either w_3 is traded at $p_3 = \Delta_S + c_S$, or S makes an offer that is not accepted. Given the beliefs we have described, the seller's expected profit from trading w_3 at $p_3 = \Delta_S + c_S$, is $\Delta_S + vc_S - vc_H$, which is positive using $v < 1/2$ and Assumption 1 (parts ii and iii). Hence S will choose to trade w_3 at $p_3 = \Delta_S + c_S$, and the conclusion follows in this case.

Lemma A.2: *Suppose that the Court enforces all contracts. Then in any equilibrium of the model w_2 is traded with probability one by the type β buyer at a price $p_2 = c_L$.*

Proof: Since the cost of w_2 is independent of B's type it is obvious that if it is traded, then it is traded at $p_2 = c_L$.

Suppose by way of contradiction that there exists an equilibrium in which with positive probability w_2 is not traded by the type β buyer. From Lemma A.1 we know that in this equilibrium some type β buyers trade w_3 at a price $p_3 = \Delta_S + c_S$. Therefore, type β buyers have a payoff of at most 0. (This follows from the fact that their expected profit from the w_3 trade is zero, and the maximum profit they can possibly make by trading w_1 is negative.) Consider now a deviation by the type β buyer to offering w_2 at $p_2 = c_L + \varepsilon$ with probability one. It is a unique best response for the seller to accept offers to trade w_2 at any $p_2 > c_L$. It then follows that the type β buyer can deviate to such offer and achieve a payoff of $\Delta_L - \varepsilon$. For ε sufficiently small this is clearly a profitable deviation for the type β buyer.

Lemma A.3: *Suppose that the Court enforces all contracts. Then in any equilibrium of the model the type α buyer offers a contract to trade w_1 with probability zero.*

Proof: Notice that by Lemma A.2 in any equilibrium the type β buyer trades w_2 with probability one. Suppose by way of contradiction that there exists an equilibrium in which the type α buyer separates with positive probability and offers a contract to trade w_1. In this case, the type α buyer's payoff must be Δ_M. This follows from the fact that, by separating, the type α buyer must be trading w_1 at a price $p_1 = c_L$ and, since he separates, S will not trade w_3 with him.

Suppose now that the type α buyer deviates to pool with the type β buyers who trade w_2 at $p_2 = c_L$ and then trade w_3 at $p_3 = \Delta_S + c_S$. By Lemmas A.1 and A.2 we know that the type β buyer behaves in this way with positive probability. Following this deviation the type α buyer's payoff is $\Delta_H + c_H - \Delta_H - \Delta_S - c_S$. The latter, by Assumption 1 (parts i and iii) is greater than Δ_M. Hence this is a profitable deviation for the type α buyer.

Lemma A.4: *Suppose that the Court enforces all contracts. Then in any equilibrium of the model w_2 is traded with probability one by the type α buyer at a price $p_2 = c_L$.*

Proof: Since the cost of w_2 is independent of B's type it is obvious that if it is traded, then it is traded at $p_2 = c_L$.

Suppose that the claim were false. Using Lemma A.3 we then know that, in some equilibrium, with positive probability the type α buyer trades neither w_1 nor w_2. By Lemma A.2 a type α buyer who does not trade w_2

actually separates from the type β buyer. Hence in any equilibrium in which with positive probability the type α buyer trades neither w_1 nor w_2 the type α buyer's payoff is at most zero. (The seller will not trade w_3 with him because of separation, and he makes no profit on either w_1 or w_2 since he does not trade them.)

As in the proof of Lemma A.3 the type α buyer has a profitable deviation from this putative equilibrium. He can pool with the type β buyers who trade w_2 at $p_2 = c_L$ and then trade w_3 at $p_3 = \Delta_S + c_S$. After this deviation the type α buyer's payoff is $\Delta_H + c_H - \Delta_H - \Delta_S - c_S$, which is positive by Assumption 1 (parts i and iii).

Lemma A.5: *Suppose that the Court enforces all contracts. Then in any equilibrium of the model w_3 is traded with probability one by both types of B at a price $p_3 = \Delta_S + c_S$.*

Proof: From Lemmas A.2 and A.4 we know that the two types of B pool with probability one at the ex-ante stage. The same reasoning as in the second case considered in the proof of Lemma A.1 now ensures that in equilibrium w_3 is traded with probability one by both types of B at a price $p_3 = \Delta_S + c_S$.

Proof of Proposition 1: The claim is a direct consequence of Lemmas A.2, A.4 and A.5.

Lemma A.6: *Consider the model with an active Court, and any of the subgames following the Court choosing a V that contains w_i, $i = 1, 2$. In any equilibrium of such subgames neither type of B invests in w_i, and hence it is not traded.*

Proof: If $w_i \in V$ then the terms of its trade can be freely re-negotiated at the ex-post stage, when S makes a take-it-or-leave-it offer to B, regardless of anything previously agreed.

Now suppose that in any equilibrium both types of B invest in $w_i \in V$ with positive probability. Then by standard arguments in any equilibrium it must be that S offers to trade w_i at a price p_i that makes one of the two B types indifferent between accepting and rejecting the offer at the ex-post stage. But since $I > 0$ this must mean that one of the B types has an overall payoff equal to $-I$. Since either type of buyer can always guarantee a payoff of zero (by not investing and not trading) we can then conclude that in any equilibrium of any of these subgames it cannot be the case that both types of B invest in $w_i \in V$ with positive probability.

Suppose then in any equilibrium only one type of B invests in $w_i \in V$

with positive probability. Then by standard arguments in any equilibrium it must be that S offers to trade w_i at a price p_i that makes the type of buyer who is trading w_i indifferent between accepting and rejecting the offer at the ex-post stage. But since $I > 0$ this must mean that this type of B has an overall payoff equal to $-I$. Since, as before, this type of buyer can always guarantee a payoff of zero we can now conclude that in any equilibrium of any of these subgames it must be that neither type of B invests in $w_i \in V$ with positive probability.

Lemma A.7: *Consider the model with an active Court. In any equilibrium of the subgame following the Court setting $V = \{w_2\}$ the type α buyer trades w_1 with probability one.*

Proof: From Lemma A.6 we know that in this case neither type of B invests in w_2, and hence it is not traded.

Suppose that the type α buyer invests in w_1 and trades it. His payoff in this case is at least Δ_M. This is because clearly, in any equilibrium, p_1 is c_L, and at worst he is unable to trade w_3.

Suppose that instead the type α buyer does not invest in w_1 and hence does not trade it. Then his payoff is at most $c_H - \Delta_H - \Delta_S - c_S$. This is because, using Lemma A.1, at best he will be able to trade w_3 at a price $p_3 = \Delta_S + c_S$. Using Assumption 1 (parts i and iii) we know that $\Delta_M > c_H - \Delta_H - \Delta_S - c_S$, and hence the argument is complete.

Lemma A.8: *Consider the model with an active Court. In any equilibrium of the subgame following the Court setting $V = \{w_2\}$ the type β does not invest in either w_1 or w_2, separates from the type α buyer, and only trades w_3 at a price $p_3 = \Delta_S + c_S$.*

Proof: From Lemma A.6 we know that in this case neither type of B invests in w_2, and hence it is not traded.

Suppose that the type β buyer invests in w_1. Then his payoff must be negative. This is because, using Lemma A.1, he either trades w_3 at a price $p_3 = \Delta_S + c_S$ or does not trade w_3 (in either case the profit is zero), and using Lemma A.7 he trades w_1 at a price $p_1 = c_L$.

Since either type of buyer can always guarantee a payoff of zero (by not investing, making offers that must be rejected, and rejecting all ex-post offers) we can then conclude that the type β buyer does not invest in w_1.

Therefore, we know that the type β buyer does not invest in either w_1 or w_2. Using Lemma A.7 and the same reasoning as in the first case of Lemma A.1 we can now conclude that the type β buyer trades w_3 at a price $p_3 = \Delta_S + c_S$.

Lemma A.9:   *Consider the model with an active Court. Suppose that the Court sets* $V = \{w_2\}$, *then the two types of buyer separate: the type* α *buyer invests in* w_1 *and only trades* w_1 *at a price of* $p_1 = c_L$; *the type* β *buyer does not invest in either* w_1 *or* w_2 *and only trades* w_3 *at a price* $p_3 = \Delta_S + c_S$.
By choosing $V = \{w_2\}$ *the Court achieves a payoff of* $\frac{\Delta_S}{2} + \frac{\Delta_M}{2}$.

Proof: The claim is a direct consequence of Lemmas A.7 and A.8.

Lemma A.10:   *Consider the model with an active Court. Suppose that the Court sets* $V = \{w_1\}$. *Then the unique equilibrium outcome is that the two types of buyer pool with probability one: they both invest and trade* w_2 *at a price* $p_2 = c_L$, *and they both trade* w_3 *at a price* $p_3 = \Delta_S + c_S$.
By choosing $V = \{w_1\}$ *the Court achieves a payoff of* $\frac{\Delta_S}{2} + \frac{\Delta_L}{2}$.

Proof: The proof essentially proceeds in the same way as the proof of Proposition 1. In fact by setting $V = \{w_1\}$, the Court simply takes away the possibility that the parties may trade w_1 via Lemma A.6. The details are omitted for the sake of brevity.

Lemma A.11:   *Consider the model with an active Court. Suppose that the Court sets* $V = \{w_1, w_2\}$. *Then the two types of buyer pool: they do not invest in either* w_1 *or* w_2 *and they trade* w_3 *at* $p_3 = \Delta_S + c_S$.
By choosing $V = \{w_1, w_2\}$ *the Court achieves a payoff of* $\frac{\Delta_S}{2} - \frac{\Delta_H}{2}$.

Proof: The claim follows immediately from Lemma A.6 using the same reasoning as in the second case of the proof of Lemma A.1.

Proof of Proposition 2:   Using Assumption 1 (part i), the claim is an immediate consequence of Lemmas A.9, A.10 and A.11.

Proof of Proposition 3:   Throughout the proof, we let $M_\alpha = (m_\alpha^\alpha, m_\alpha^\beta)$ and $M_\beta = (m_\beta^\alpha, m_\beta^\beta)$ denote the menu contract offers of the type α and the type β buyer respectively. We first show that Proposition 1 still holds. The two types of buyer must pool and trade both w_2 and w_3, yielding an equilibrium payoff for a passive Court of $\frac{\Delta_S}{2} + \frac{\Delta_L}{2}$.

There are three main cases to consider. The first is a possible equilibrium in which $M_\alpha \neq M_\beta$. In this case the two types of buyer would separate at the contract-offer stage. The same argument as in Proposition 1 can be used to establish that this cannot happen in any equilibrium of the model when the Court enforces all contracts. In other words, we conclude that there is no equilibrium of the model with passive Courts when menu contracts are allowed and w_3 is not contractible ex-ante in which $M_\alpha \neq M_\beta$.

The second case is that of a possible equilibrium in which $M_\alpha = M_\beta$ and $m_\alpha^\alpha = m_\alpha^\beta = m_\beta^\alpha = m_\beta^\beta$. In this case, the same argument as in Proposition 1 can be used to establish that the only possibility is that of an equilibrium in which the two types of buyer pool and trade both w_2 and w_3, yielding a Court equilibrium payoff of $\frac{\Delta_S}{2} + \frac{\Delta_L}{2}$.

The third case is that of $M_\alpha = M_\beta$, and $m_\alpha^\alpha \neq m_\alpha^\beta$ and $m_\beta^\alpha \neq m_\beta^\beta$. Let $m^\alpha = m_\alpha^\alpha = m_\beta^\alpha$ and $m^\beta = m_\alpha^\beta = m_\beta^\beta$.

Clearly, in equilibrium we need the "truth-telling" constraints to be satisfied: m^α and m^β must be such that the type α buyer does not prefer to declare that he is of type β, and, symmetrically, the type β buyer does not prefer to declare that he is of type α. We will show that these constraints are in fact impossible to satisfy. Since $m^\alpha \neq m^\beta$, after declaring α, the buyer will be unable to trade w_3 since the seller's beliefs must be that he is facing a type α buyer with probability one. Moreover, after declaring β the buyer will trade w_3 ex-post at a price $p_3 = \Delta_S + c_S$. This is because the seller's beliefs in this case are that he is facing a type β buyer with probability one. There are four sub-cases to consider.

The first sub-case is that of m^α and m^β both being contracts for w_1, so that m^α and m^β differ only in the proposed prices. Let these be p_1^α and p_1^β respectively. Hence by declaring α, the type α buyer receives a payoff of $\Delta_M + c_L - p_1^\alpha$, while if he declares β he receives a payoff of $\Delta_M + c_L - p_1^\beta + c_H - \Delta_H - \Delta_S - c_S$. Therefore, to satisfy the truth-telling constraint for the type α buyer we need

$$p_1^\beta - p_1^\alpha \geq c_H - \Delta_H - \Delta_S - c_S \qquad (13A.1)$$

By declaring β, the type β buyer obtains a payoff of $\Delta_N + c_L + I - p_1^\beta$. If instead he declares to be of type α he obtains a payoff of $\Delta_N + c_L + I - p_1^\alpha$. Hence to satisfy the truth-telling constraint for the type β buyer we need

$$0 \geq p_1^\beta - p_1^\alpha \qquad (13A.2)$$

However, (13A.1) and (13A.2) cannot both be satisfied because of Assumption 1 (parts i and iii).

The second sub-case we consider is that of m^α and m^β both being contracts for w_2, so that m^α and m^β differ only in the proposed prices. Let these be p_2^α and p_2^β respectively. Reasoning in the same way as for the first case, the truth-telling constraint for the type α buyer implies

$$p_2^\beta - p_2^\alpha \geq c_H - \Delta_H - \Delta_S - c_S \qquad (13A.3)$$

while the truth-telling constraint for the type β buyer implies that

$$0 \geq p_2^\beta - p_2^\alpha \tag{13A.4}$$

However, just as in the first case, (13A.3) and (13A.4) cannot both be satisfied because of Assumption 1 (parts i and iii).

The third sub-case is that of m^α and m^β being contracts for w_1 and w_2 respectively, with prices offered p_1^α and p_2^β. The truth-telling constraint for the type α buyer implies

$$p_2^\beta - p_1^\alpha \geq c_H - \Delta_M - \Delta_S - c_S \tag{13A.5}$$

while the truth-telling constraint for the type β buyer tells us that

$$\Delta_L - \Delta_N \geq p_2^\beta - p_1^\alpha \tag{13A.6}$$

However, (13A.5) and (13A.6) cannot both be satisfied because of Assumption 1 (parts i, iii and iv).

The fourth sub-case is that of m^α and m^β being contracts for w_2 and w_1 respectively, with prices offered p_2^α and p_1^β. The truth-telling constraint for the type α buyer can be written as

$$p_1^\beta - p_2^\alpha \geq c_H + \Delta_M - 2\Delta_H - \Delta_S - c_S \tag{13A.7}$$

while the truth-telling constraint for the type β says that

$$\Delta_N - \Delta_L \geq p_1^\beta - p_2^\alpha \tag{13A.8}$$

However, (13A.7) and (13A.8) cannot both be satisfied because of Assumption 1 (i, iii and iv).

We conclude that there is no equilibrium of the model with passive Courts when menu contracts are allowed and w_3 is not contractible ex-ante in which $M_\alpha = M_\beta$, and $m_\alpha^\alpha \neq m_\alpha^\beta$ and $m_\beta^\alpha \neq m_\beta^\beta$.

Therefore, we have shown that Proposition 1 still holds. In any equilibrium of the model with passive Courts when menu contracts are allowed and w_3 is not contractible ex-ante the two types of buyer must pool and trade both w_2 and w_3, yielding an equilibrium payoff for a passive Court of $\frac{\Delta_S}{2} + \frac{\Delta_L}{2}$.

There remains to show that Proposition 2 still holds. When menu contracts are allowed and w_3 is not contractible ex-ante, in equilibrium, an active Court chooses $V = \{s_2\}$ and its payoff is $\frac{\Delta_S}{2} + \frac{\Delta_M}{2}$.

Because of a standard hold-up problem caused by the relationship-specific investment (see for instance Lemma A.6 of AFP), in any of the subgames following the Court choosing a V that contains w_i, $i = 1, 2$, in equilibrium, neither type of B invests in w_i, and hence it is not traded.

It follows that without loss of generality whenever V equals either $\{s_1\}$ or $\{s_2\}$ we can restrict attention to menu contracts that specify the *same* widget in both components. Incentive-compatibility then ensures that any equilibrium menu contract would have to specify the *same* price for the single widget appearing in both menu entries. In other words, the only candidates for equilibrium are *degenerate* menus in which $m^\alpha = m^\beta$. Given this, the claim can be proved using the same argument used to prove Proposition 2 above. The details are omitted.

Proof of Proposition 4 (i): Take the degenerate menu offered by both types of buyer to be one that specifies $m^\alpha = m^\beta = s_2 = (w_2, c_L)$. In other words, the candidate equilibrium has the degenerate menu specifying that w_2 will be traded at a price $p_2 = c_L$, regardless of the buyer's announcement. Moreover, in the proposed equilibrium both types of buyer trade w_3 ex-post at a price $p_3 = \Delta_S + c_S$.

In the proposed equilibrium the type α buyer obtains a payoff of $c_H - \Delta_S - c_S$, the type β buyer obtains a payoff of Δ_L, and the seller obtains an expected payoff of $\Delta_S - c_H/2 + c_S/2$.

The argument proceeds in two steps. The first step is to show that neither type of buyer can profitably deviate from the proposed equilibrium by making an offer of a contract of the type s_1, s_2, s_3, $b_{1,3}$ or $b_{2,3}$. The second is to show that neither type of buyer can profitably deviate from the proposed equilibrium by offering a menu contract different from the equilibrium one.

The first step involves several cases.

Using the same argument as in the proof of Proposition 1 we already know that no type of buyer can profit from a unilateral deviation to offering any other simple contract of the type s_1 or s_2. Therefore, it only remains to show that no type of buyer can profit from a unilateral deviation to offering a contract of type s_3, $b_{1,3}$ or $b_{2,3}$.

It is easy to see that (see for instance Lemma A.1 of AFP), regardless of his beliefs, the seller will reject any off-path offer of an s_3 contract specifying a price $p_3' < \Delta_S + c_S$. (This is because $c_H - \Delta_H > \Delta_S + c_S$ by Assumption 1 (parts i and iii), and hence the seller will either trade w_3 ex-post at a price $p_3 = \Delta_S + c_S$ or will not trade it at all, depending on his beliefs.)

Now consider a possible deviation by the type α buyer to offering s_3 with a price $p_3' \geq \Delta_S + c_S$. In this case (a standard hold-up problem arises because of the relationship-specific investment, see for instance Lemma A.6 of AFP), he will not trade either w_2 or w_1. Hence his payoff after the deviation would be $c_H - \Delta_H - p_3'$. Therefore for this to be a profitable deviation we need $c_H - \Delta_H - p_3' > c_H - \Delta_S - c_S$. Since $p_3' \geq \Delta_S + c_S$, this is possible only if $\Delta_H < 0$, which is false by Assumption 1 (part i). We can then conclude that the type α buyer cannot profit from any deviation to offering a contract of the s_3 variety.

Next, consider a possible deviation from the type β buyer to offering s_3 with a price $p_3' \geq \Delta_S + c_S$. In this case (again, a standard hold-up problem arises because of the relationship-specific investment, see for instance Lemma A.6 of AFP), he will not trade either w_2 or w_1. Hence his payoff after the deviation would be $\Delta_S + c_S - p_3' \leq 0$. Since his payoff in the candidate equilibrium is positive, we conclude that the type β buyer cannot profit from any deviation to offering a contract of the s_3 variety.

The next case to consider is a possible deviation by the type α buyer to a bundle contract of the type $b_{2,3}$. Let the prices specified by the contract be denoted by p_2' and p_3'. For this to be a profitable deviation for the type α buyer we need $\Delta_H + c_L - p_2' + c_H - \Delta_H - p_3' > c_H - \Delta_S - c_S$, which implies $c_L + \Delta_S + c_S > p_2' + p_3'$. Let the seller's off-path beliefs, after receiving the offer of $b_{2,3}$, be that he is facing a type α buyer with probability $v \in [0,1]$. For the seller to accept $b_{2,3}$ we need $p_2' - c_L + p_3' - v c_H - (1 - v)c_S \geq \max\{0, \Delta_S + c_S - v c_H - (1 - v)c_S\}$. This is because if he rejects the $b_{2,3}$ offer, then either w_3 will be traded at a price $p_3 = \Delta_S + c_S$, or will not be traded at all, depending on the seller's beliefs. But the last inequality implies $p_2' + p_3' \geq c_L + \Delta_S + c_S$. Hence we conclude that the type α buyer cannot profit from any deviation to offering a contract of the $b_{2,3}$ variety.

Consider now a possible deviation by the type β buyer to a bundle contract of the type $b_{2,3}$. Let the prices specified by the contract be denoted by p_2' and p_3'. For this to be a profitable deviation for the type β buyer we need $\Delta_L + c_L - p_2' + \Delta_S + c_S - p_3' > \Delta_L$, which implies $c_L + \Delta_S + c_S > p_2' + p_3'$. Let the seller's off-path beliefs, after receiving the offer of $b_{2,3}$, be that he is facing a type α buyer with probability $v \in [0,1]$. For the seller to accept $b_{2,3}$ we need $p_2' - c_L + p_3' - v c_H - (1 - v)c_S \geq \max\{0, \Delta_S + c_S - v c_H - (1 - v)c_S\}$. This is because if he rejects the $b_{2,3}$ offer, then either w_3 will be traded at a price $p_3 = \Delta_S + c_S$, or will not be traded at all, depending on the seller's beliefs. But the last inequality implies $p_2' + p_3' \geq c_L + \Delta_S + c_S$. Hence we conclude that the type β buyer cannot profit from any deviation to offering a contract of the $b_{2,3}$ variety.

The next case we consider is that of a possible deviation by the type α buyer to offering a bundle contract of the $b_{1,3}$ variety. Let the prices specified by the contract be denoted by p_1' and p_3'. For this to be a profitable deviation for the type α buyer we need $\Delta_M + c_L - p_1' + c_H - \Delta_H - p_3' > c_H - \Delta_S - c_S$, which implies $\Delta_M + c_L + \Delta_S + c_S - \Delta_H > p_2' + p_3'$, which using Assumption 1 (part iv) in turn implies $\Delta_S + c_S - \Delta_L > p_2' + p_3'$. Let the seller's off-path beliefs, after receiving the offer of $b_{1,3}$, be that he is facing a type α buyer with probability $v \in [0, 1]$. For the seller to accept $b_{1,3}$ we need $p'_1 - c_L + p'_3 - v c_H - (1 - v)c_S \geq \max\{0, \Delta_S + c_S - v c_H - (1 - v)c_S\}$. This is because if he rejects the $b_{2,3}$ offer, then either w_3 will be traded at a price $p_3 = \Delta_S + c_S$, or will not be traded at all, depending on the seller's beliefs. But the last inequality implies $p'_1 + p'_3 \geq \Delta_S + c_L + c_S$. Hence we conclude that the type α buyer cannot profit from any deviation to offering a contract of the $b_{1,3}$ variety.

The last case we need to consider to conclude the first step in the proof is that of a possible deviation by the type β buyer to offering a bundle contract of the $b_{1,3}$ variety. Let the prices specified by the contract be denoted by p'_1 and p'_3. For this to be a profitable deviation for the type β buyer we need $\Delta_N - p'_1 + \Delta_S + c_S - p'_3 > \Delta_L$, which implies $\Delta_S + c_S + \Delta_N - \Delta_L > p'_2 + p'_3$. Let the seller's off-path beliefs, after receiving the offer of $b_{1,3}$, be that he is facing a type α buyer with probability $v \in [0,1]$. For the seller to accept $b_{1,3}$ we need $p'_1 - c_L + p'_3 - v c_H - (1 - v)c_S \geq \max\{0, \Delta_S + c_S - v c_H - (1 - v)c_S\}$. This is because if he rejects the $b_{2,3}$ offer, then either w_3 will be traded at a price $p_3 = \Delta_S + c_S$, or will not be traded at all, depending on the seller's beliefs. But the last inequality implies $p'_1 + p'_3 \geq \Delta_S + c_L + c_S$. Hence we conclude that the type β buyer cannot profit from any deviation to offering a contract of the $b_{1,3}$ variety.

We have now ruled out the possibility that either type of buyer could profitably deviate from the proposed equilibrium by making an offer of a contract of the type s_1, s_2, s_3, $b_{1,3}$ or $b_{2,3}$. The second step in the argument rules out the possibility that either type of buyer can profitably deviate from the proposed equilibrium by offering a menu contract different from the equilibrium one. It involves considering several cases again.

Consider first the possibility that either type of buyer deviates to offering a degenerate menu with $m^\alpha = m^\beta$. In this case, the same argument we used in the first step clearly suffices to prove the claim.

Therefore, there remains to consider the case of some type of buyer deviating to offering a non-degenerate menu contract $M = (m^\alpha, m^\beta)$ with $m^\alpha \neq m^\beta$. Clearly in this case, without loss of generality, we can take it to be the case that the menu M satisfies the *truth-telling* constraints: m^α and m^β must be such that the type α buyer does not prefer to declare that he is of type β, and, symmetrically, the type β buyer does not prefer to declare that he is of type α. If this were not the case, the seller would believe that one of the two menu items will be chosen with probability one when the buyer announces his type. Therefore, the same argument as in the case of a degenerate menu would suffice to prove the claim.

It is convenient to classify the possible deviations to non-degenerate menus M that satisfy the truth-telling constraints into three mutually exclusive subsets.

We say that a menu contract is of class α if it has the property that, if accepted, it constitutes a strictly profitable deviation (given truth-telling) from the proposed equilibrium for the type α buyer, but not for the type β buyer. The class of such menu contracts is denoted by M^α. We say that a menu contract is of class β if it has the property that, if accepted, it constitutes a strictly profitable deviation (given truth-telling) from the proposed equilibrium for the type β buyer, but not for the type α buyer. The class of such menu contracts is denoted by M^β. We say that a menu contract is of class ω if it has the property that, if accepted, it constitutes a strictly profitable deviation (given truth-telling) from the proposed equilibrium for both the type α and the type β buyer. The class of such menu contracts is denoted by M^ω. Clearly, to conclude the proof it suffices to show that no type α buyer can profitably deviate by offering a menu $M \in M^\alpha$, no type β buyer can profitably deviate by offering a menu $M \in M^\beta$, and no buyer of either type can profitably deviate by offering a menu $M \in M^\omega$.

Consider a possible deviation by a type α buyer to a menu $M \in M^\alpha$. In this case, we assign off-path equilibrium beliefs to the seller that he is facing a buyer of type α with probability one. These beliefs clearly satisfy the Intuitive Criterion of Cho and Kreps (1987) (see footnote 7). The seller believes that the m^α component of M will apply with probability one after the buyer declares his type. It follows that the same argument used in the first step of this proof to show that the type α buyer cannot profitably deviate to a contract of type s_1, s_2, s_3, $b_{1,3}$ or $b_{2,3}$ now suffices to show that he cannot profit from a deviation to a menu $M \in M^\alpha$.

Next, consider a possible deviation by a type β buyer to a menu $M \in M^\beta$. In this case, we assign off-path equilibrium beliefs to the seller that he is facing a buyer of type β with probability one. These beliefs clearly satisfy the Intuitive Criterion of Cho and Kreps (1987) (see footnote 7). The seller believes that the m^β component of M will apply with probability one after the buyer declares his type. It follows that the same argument used in the first step of this proof to show that the type β buyer cannot profitably deviate to a contract of type s_1, s_2, s_3, $b_{1,3}$ or $b_{2,3}$ now suffices to show that he cannot profit from a deviation to a menu $M \in M^\beta$.

Consider now a possible deviation by a type α buyer to a menu $M \in M^\omega$. In this case, we assign off-path equilibrium beliefs to the seller that he is facing a buyer of type α with probability one. These beliefs clearly satisfy the Intuitive Criterion of Cho and Kreps (1987) (see footnote 7). The seller believes that the m^α component of M will apply with probability one after the buyer declares his type. It follows that the same argument used in the first step of this proof to show that the type α buyer cannot profitably deviate to a contract of type s_1, s_2, s_3, $b_{1,3}$ or $b_{2,3}$ now suffices to show that he cannot profit from a deviation to a menu $M \in M^\alpha$.

Lastly, consider a possible deviation by a type β buyer to a menu $M \in M^\omega$. As we specified above, in this case we assign off-path equilibrium beliefs to the seller that he is facing a buyer of type α with probability one. These beliefs clearly satisfy the Intuitive Criterion of Cho and Kreps (1987) (see footnote 7). The seller believes that the m^α component of M will apply with probability one after the buyer declares his type.

Recall that the argument used in the first step of this proof to show that the type β buyer cannot profitably deviate to a contract of type $s_1, s_2, s_3, b_{1,3}$ or $b_{2,3}$ applies *regardless* of the seller's off-path beliefs following the deviation. Therefore, that argument also suffices to now show that he cannot profit from a deviation to a menu $M \in M^\omega$.

Proof of Proposition 4 (ii): Take the equilibrium non-degenerate menu contract to be $M = (m^\alpha, m^\beta)$ with m^α of the s_1 variety with a price $p_1 = \Delta_M + c_L - c_H + \Delta_S + c_S$ and m^β of the s_3 variety with a price $p_3 = \Delta_S - \Delta_M + c_S$.

In this candidate equilibrium the type α buyer gets a payoff (under truth-telling) of $\Delta_M + c_L - p_1 = \Delta_M + c_L - \Delta_M - c_L + c_H - \Delta_S - c_S = c_H - \Delta_S - c_S$, while the type β buyer obtains a payoff (under truth-telling) of $\Delta_S + c_S - p_3 = \Delta_S + c_S - \Delta_S + \Delta_M - c_S = \Delta_M$ and the seller gets an expected payoff (under truth-telling) of $(p_1 - c_L)/2 + (p_3 - c_S)/2 = \Delta_S - c_H/2 + c_S/2$. Crucially, notice that the type β buyer has a payoff strictly greater than the one he obtains in the equilibrium constructed in the proof of Proposition 4 (i). The type α buyer and the seller have the same payoffs as the ones they obtain in the equilibrium constructed in the proof of Proposition 4 (i).

We begin by verifying that the proposed equilibrium contract satisfies the necessary truth-telling constraints. The truth-telling constraint for the type α buyer can be written as

$$p_3 - p_1 \geq c_H - \Delta_H - c_L - \Delta_M \tag{13A.9}$$

which is satisfied for $p_1 = \Delta_M + c_L - c_H + \Delta_S + c_S$ and $p_3 = \Delta_S - \Delta_M + c_S$ by Assumption 1 (part i).

The truth-telling constraint for the type β buyer can be written as

$$\Delta_S - \Delta_N \geq p_3 - p_1 \tag{13A.10}$$

which is satisfied for $p_1 = \Delta_M + c_L - c_H + \Delta_S + c_S$ and $p_3 = \Delta_S - \Delta_M + c_S$ by Assumption 1 (part iii and iv).

Consider now a possible deviation by the type α buyer to offering a simple contract of the s_2 variety. At best, he would be able to get a payoff of $c_H - \Delta_S - c_S$. This is because the seller will not accept any offer to trade w_2 for a price below c_L, and the type α buyer, at best (depending on the seller's beliefs) will be able to trade w_3 ex-post for a price of $\Delta_S + c_S$. Since $c_H - \Delta_S - c_S$ is also his payoff in the proposed equilibrium, we conclude that the type α buyer cannot profit from a deviation to offering a simple contract of the s_2 variety.

Next, consider a possible deviation by the type β buyer to offering a simple contract of the s_2 variety. At best, he would be able to get a payoff of Δ_L. This is because the seller will not accept any offer to trade w_2 for a price below c_L, and the type β buyer, at best (depending on the seller's beliefs) will be able to trade w_3 ex-post for a price of $\Delta_S + c_S$. Since $\Delta_L < \Delta_M$, we conclude that the type β buyer cannot profit from a deviation to offering a simple contract of the s_2 variety.

All other possible deviations can be ruled out using the computations (including the off-path beliefs that they use) in the proof of Proposition 4 (i). This is because the equilibrium payoffs to both types of buyer in the equilibrium proposed here are at least as large as the payoffs that they receive in the equilibrium constructed there.

Proof of Proposition 4 (iii):   Suppose that there were an equilibrium in which expected net surplus exceeds $\frac{\Delta_S}{2} + \frac{\Delta_M}{2}$. Then using Assumption 1 (parts i and ii) the equilibrium would have to be of one of the following three varieties. The first variety involves type α buyer trading w_2 only and the type β buyer trading w_1 and w_3. The second variety involves the type α buyer trading w_2 only and the type β buyer trading w_3 only. The third variety involves the type α buyer trading w_1 only and the type β buyer trading w_2 and w_3.

As in the proof of Proposition 3, throughout the argument we let $M_\alpha = (m_\alpha^\alpha, m_\alpha^\beta)$ and $M_\beta = (m_\beta^\alpha, m_\beta^\beta)$ denote the menu contract offers of the type α and the type β buyer respectively.

There are three main cases to consider. The first is a possible equilibrium in which $M_\alpha \neq M_\beta$. In this case the two types of buyer would separate at the contract-offer stage. Because of separation at the contract-offer stage we can take it to be the case that both M_α and M_β are degenerate menus, with $M_\alpha = (m_\alpha, m_\alpha)$ and $M_\beta = (m_\beta, m_\beta)$.

There are two possible ways to obtain an equilibrium of the first variety when $M_\alpha \neq M_\beta$. The first is that $m_\alpha = s_2$ and $m_\beta = s_1$, with the type β buyer trading w_3 ex-post. This possibility can clearly be ruled out in the same way as in the proof of Proposition 1. The second way is to have $m_\alpha = s_2$ and $m_\beta = b_{1,3}$. In such putative equilibrium, the type α buyer would obtain a payoff of Δ_H, since clearly the s_2 contract would have to specify $p_2 = c_L$. Notice also that, given separation, the seller can trade w_3 ex-post for a payoff of Δ_S if he rejects the type β buyer offer of $b_{1,3}$. It follows that the contract $b_{1,3}$ contains prices p_1 and p_3 such that $p_1 + p_3 = \Delta_S + c_L + c_S$. Therefore, by deviating to pooling with the type β buyer, the type α buyer would obtain a payoff of $c_H - \Delta_H - \Delta_S + \Delta_M - c_S$. Using Assumption 1 (part iii) this is a profitable deviation. Therefore we can conclude that the putative equilibrium is not viable.

A possible equilibrium of the second variety when $M_\alpha \neq M_\beta$ can be ruled out by noticing that in any case this will involve trading w_2 at a price $p_2 = c_L$ and w_3 at a price $p_3 = \Delta_S + c_S$. Therefore this possibility can clearly be excluded out in the same way as in the proof of Proposition 1.

There are two possible ways to obtain an equilibrium of the third variety when $M_\alpha \neq M_\beta$. The first is that $m_\alpha = s_1$ and $m_\beta = s_2$, with the type β buyer trading w_3 ex-post. This possibility can clearly be ruled out in the same way as in the proof of Proposition 1. The second way is to have $m_\alpha = s_1$ and $m_\beta = b_{2,3}$. In such putative equilibrium, the type α buyer would obtain a payoff of Δ_M, since clearly the s_1 contract would have to specify $p_1 = c_L$. Notice also that, given separation, the seller can trade w_3 ex-post for a payoff of Δ_S if he rejects the type β buyer offer of $b_{2,3}$. It follows that the contract $b_{2,3}$ contain prices p_2 and p_3 such that $p_2 + p_3 = \Delta_S + c_L + c_S$. Therefore, by deviating to pooling with the type β buyer, the type α buyer would obtain a payoff of $c_H - \Delta_S - c_S$. Using Assumption 1 (parts i and iii) this is a profitable deviation. Therefore we can conclude that the putative equilibrium is not viable.

The second case is that of a possible equilibrium in which $M_\alpha = M_\beta$ and $m_\alpha^\alpha = m_\alpha^\beta = m_\beta^\alpha = m_\beta^\beta$. Clearly, no equilibria of the first, second or third variety can be sustained in this case. This is because in all three varieties, the two types of buyer do not trade the same widget w_1 or w_2.

The third case is that of $M_\alpha = M_\beta$, and $m_\alpha^\alpha \neq m_\alpha^\beta$ and $m_\beta^\alpha \neq m_\beta^\beta$. Let $m^\alpha = m_\alpha^\alpha = m_\beta^\alpha$ and $m^\beta = m_\alpha^\beta = m_\beta^\beta$.

As in the proof of Proposition 3, in equilibrium we need the "truth-telling" constraints to be satisfied: m^α and m^β must be such that the type α buyer does not prefer to declare that he is of type β, and, symmetrically, the type β buyer does not prefer to declare that he is of type α. We will show that these constraints are in fact impossible to satisfy in any of the three varieties of equilibria.

Notice that, since $m^\alpha \neq m^\beta$, whenever m^α is a simple contract for either w_1 or w_2, after declaring α, the buyer will be unable to trade w_3 since the seller's beliefs must be that he is facing a type α buyer with probability one. Moreover, whenever m^β is a simple contract for either w_1 or w_2, after declaring β the buyer will trade w_3 ex-post at a price $p_3 = \Delta_S + c_S$. This is because the seller's beliefs in this case are that he is facing a type β buyer with probability one.

There are two ways to support a possible equilibrium of the first variety when $M_\alpha = M_\beta$, and $m_\alpha^\alpha \neq m_\alpha^\beta$ and $m_\beta^\alpha \neq m_\beta^\beta$. The first is with m^α and m^β being simple contracts for w_2 and w_1 respectively, with prices offered p_2^α and p_1^β. The truth-telling constraint for the type α buyer can be written as

$$p_1^\beta - p_2^\alpha \geq c_H + \Delta_M - 2\Delta_H - \Delta_S - c_S \tag{13A.11}$$

while the truth-telling constraint for the type β says that

$$\Delta_N - \Delta_L \geq p_1^\beta - p_2^\alpha \tag{13A.12}$$

However, (13A.11) and (13A.12) cannot both be satisfied because of Assumption 1 (parts i, iii and iv). The second is with m^α being a simple contract of the s_2 variety and m^β being a bundle contract of the $b_{1,3}$ variety with prices p_2^α, p_1^β and p_3^β respectively. The truth-telling constraint for the type α buyer can be written as

$$p_1^\beta + p_3^\beta - p_2^\alpha \geq c_H + \Delta_M - 2\Delta_H \tag{13A.13}$$

while the truth-telling constraint for the type β says that

$$\Delta_S + c_S + \Delta_N - \Delta_L - c_L \geq p_1^\beta + p_3^\beta - p_2^\alpha \tag{13A.14}$$

However, (13A.13) and (13A.14) cannot both be satisfied because of Assumption 1 (parts i and iii).

When $M_\alpha = M_\beta$, and $m_\alpha^\alpha \neq m_\alpha^\beta$ and $m_\beta^\alpha \neq m_\beta^\beta$, to support an equilibrium of the second variety we would have to have m^α and m^β being simple contracts for w_2 and w_3 respectively, with prices offered p_2^α and p_3^β. The truth-telling constraint for the type α buyer implies

$$p_3^\beta - p_2^\alpha \geq c_H - c_L - 2\Delta_H \tag{13A.15}$$

Using Assumption 1 (parts ii, iii and v), (13A.15) implies that $p_3^\beta > p_2^\alpha$. If the seller rejects the menu contract, he will trade w_3 ex-post at a price of $\Delta_S + c_S$ with equal probability with either type of buyer. Hence by rejecting the offer the seller obtains an expected profit of $\Delta_S - c_H/2 + c_S/2$. By standard arguments the menu contract will leave S indifferent between accepting and rejecting. Hence

$$\frac{1}{2}(p_2^\alpha - c_L) + \frac{1}{2}(p_3^\beta - c_S) = \Delta_S - \frac{1}{2}c_L + \frac{1}{2}c_S \tag{13A.16}$$

which together with $p_3^\beta > p_2^\alpha$ implies that $p_3^\beta > \Delta_S + c_S$. However, the latter implies that the type β buyer would get a negative profit from the putative menu contract equilibrium. This is not possible since he can always not invest and not trade and guarantee a payoff of zero.

There are two ways to support a possible equilibrium of the third variety when $M_\alpha = M_\beta$, and $m_\alpha^\alpha \neq m_\alpha^\beta$ and $m_\beta^\alpha \neq m_\beta^\beta$. The first is with m^α and m^β being simple contracts for w_1 and w_2 respectively, with prices offered p_1^α and p_2^β, and the type β buyer trading w_3 ex-post. The truth-telling constraint for the type α buyer implies

$$p_2^\beta - p_1^\alpha \geq c_H - \Delta_M - \Delta_S - c_S \qquad (13A.17)$$

while the truth-telling constraint for the type β buyer tells us that

$$\Delta_L - \Delta_N \geq p_2^\beta - p_1^\alpha \qquad (13A.18)$$

However, (13A.17) and (13A.18) cannot both be satisfied because of Assumption 1 (parts i, iii and iv). The second is with m^α being a simple contract of the s_1 variety and m^β being a bundle contract of the $b_{2,3}$ variety with prices p_1^α, p_2^β and p_3^β respectively. The truth-telling constraint for the type α buyer can be written as

$$p_2^\beta + p_3^\beta - p_1^\alpha \geq c_H - \Delta_M \qquad (13A.19)$$

On the other hand, the truth-telling constraint for the β type buyer implies that

$$c_L + \Delta_L + \Delta_S \geq p_2^\beta + p_3^\beta - p_1^\alpha \qquad (13A.20)$$

However, inequalities (13A.19) and (13A.20) cannot be both satisfied because of Assumption 1 (parts i, iii, iv and v).

Proof of Proposition 5:   We begin by arguing that the equilibrium constructed in the proof of Proposition 4 (ii) is still viable when the Court sets $V = \{s_2, b_{2,3}\}$. This is straightforward since the Court now makes some deviations impossible. The remaining deviations can be shown not to be profitable in the same way as in the proof of Proposition 4 (ii).

Given that $V = \{s_2, b_{2,3}\}$, since a standard hold-up problem arises because of the relationship-specific investment (see for instance Lemma A.6 of AFP), we can be sure that in no equilibrium of the model will it be the case that either (or both) types of buyer will invest in w_2, and hence it will not be traded.

To show that the type α buyer investing in and trading w_1 and the type β buyer trading w_3 is the unique equilibrium outcome the following three varieties of equilibrium outcomes need to be ruled out. The first variety is one in which both types of buyer invest in and trade w_1. The second variety is one in which both types of buyer trade w_3. The third variety is one in which the type α buyer trades w_3, while the type β buyer invests in and trades w_1.

Consider an equilibrium of the first variety. This outcome cannot be sustained without using menu contracts in equilibrium. This can be proved using the same argument as in the proof of Proposition 2. For the same reason, this outcome cannot be sustained using menu contracts in an equilibrium in which the two types of buyer separate at the contract-offer stage by offering $M_\alpha \neq M_\beta$. Suppose that $M_\alpha = M_\beta$ and both menus are degenerate in the sense that $m_\alpha^\alpha = m_\alpha^\beta = m_\beta^\alpha = m_\beta^\beta$. In this case clearly we must have that the menu contracts specify $p_1 = c_L$. Hence, just as in the proof of Proposition 2, the type β buyer has an incentive to deviate. Lastly, suppose that $M_\alpha = M_\beta$, and $m_\alpha^\alpha \neq m_\alpha^\beta$ and $m_\beta^\alpha \neq m_\beta^\beta$. Then, since both menu items must be simple contracts for w_1 the truth telling constraints trivially imply that $p_1^\alpha = p_1^\beta$. Hence, in equilibrium $p_1^\alpha = p_1^\beta = c_L$, and therefore the type β buyer has an incentive to deviate as before.

Any equilibrium of the second variety can be ruled out in a completely analogous way as any equilibrium of the first variety. The details are omitted.

Consider now an equilibrium of the third variety. From the surplus and cost matrix in (13.1) it is evident that the sum of the payoffs of the two types of buyer and of the seller in any such equilibrium is negative. Hence at least one of the players will have a profitable deviation to not trading at all.

NOTES

*   This chapter was revised while the second author was visiting the Department of Economics at Humboldt University, their generous hospitality is gratefully acknowledged. The third author acknowledges financial support from the National Science Foundation.
1.   In the numbering of Propositions, Lemmas, equations and so on, a prefix of "A" indicates that the relevant item can be found in the Appendix.
2.   The *gross* value is therefore computed as the sum of cost, surplus and I, while the *gross* cost is the cost value reported in Table 13.1.
3.   The reason to assume that production costs are *sunk* before S learns what they are is to prevent the possibility of ex-post revelation games a la Moore and Repullo (1988) and Maskin and Tirole (1999).
4.   As well as negotiating the terms of trade for w_3, as before.
5.   Implicitly, this means that we are taking the view that "spot" trade is feasible ex-post even when contract terms are voided by the Court.

6. Clearly, following a particular choice by the Court multiple equilibrium payoffs could ensue in the relevant subgame. When multiple equilibria arise in some relevant subgames, we deem something to be an equilibrium of the entire model when it is an equilibrium considering the Court as an actual player, complete with its equilibrium *beliefs*. For more on the distinction between a classical "planner" and a planner who is also a player see Baliga, Corchon, and Sjöström (1997).

7. Throughout, by equilibrium we mean a Sequential Equilibrium (Kreps and Wilson 1982), or equivalently a Strong Perfect Bayesian Equilibrium (Fudenberg and Tirole 1991), of the game at hand. We do not make use of any further refinements. However, it should be pointed out that whenever we assert that something is an equilibrium outcome, then it is the outcome of at least one Sequential Equilibrium that passes the Intuitive Criterion test of Cho and Kreps (1987).

8. When w_3 is contractible ex-ante, the prices at which each widget is traded, when w_3 is traded as well as w_1 or w_2, become indeterminate. The equilibrium trading and investment outcomes are as before. See Proposition 3.

9. There is no need to consider any other possible bundles since trading both w_1 and w_2 is never profitable. The two specific widgets are mutually exclusive since, by assumption, the buyer can only undertake one widget-specific investment.

10. We restrict attention to pure strategy equilibria when menu contracts are allowed. That is, we do not allow the buyer to randomize across different menu contracts.

REFERENCES

Anderlini, L., L. Felli, and A. Postlewaite (2011): "Should Courts Always Enforce What Contracting Parties Write?," Review of Law and Economics, 7(1), Article 2.

Baliga, S., L.C. Corchon, and T. Sjöström (1997): "The Theory of Implementation When the Planner Is a Player," Journal of Economic Theory, 77, 15–33.

Cho, I.-K., and D.M. Kreps (1987): "Signaling Games and Stable Equilibria," Quarterly Journal of Economics, 102, 179–221.

Fudenberg, D., and J. Tirole (1991): "Perfect Bayesian Equilibrium and Sequential Equilibrium," Journal of Economic Theory, 53, 236–60.

Kreps, D., and R. Wilson (1982): "Sequential Equilibria," Econometrica, 50, 863–94.

Maskin, E., and J. Tirole (1990): "The Principal Agent Relationship with an Informed Principal, I: Private Values," Econometrica, 58, 379–409.

——(1992): "The Principal Agent Relationship with an Informed Principal II: Common Values," Econometrica, 60, 1–42.

——(1999): "Unforeseen Contingencies and Incomplete Contracts," Review of Economic Studies, 66, 83–114.

Moore, J., and R. Repullo (1988): "Subgame Perfect Implementation," Econometrica, 56, 1191–220.

14. The efficiency of affirmative action with purely historical discrimination
Abraham L. Wickelgren

1   INTRODUCTION

Affirmative action is one of society's most controversial issues. The constitutionality of affirmative action in university admissions is about to be decided by the United States Supreme Court in *Fisher v. University of Texas at Austin*.[1] Opponents of affirmative action argue that affirmative action is discriminatory and leads to more qualified white candidates being passed over for less qualified minorities. They argue that while affirmative action based on disadvantaged status may be justifiable, it should not be based on race.[2] Its proponents, in contrast, argue that affirmative action is necessary to counter the effects of current or past discrimination, to provide role models, or to promote diversity. While each of these arguments has its supporters, the most prevalent justification for affirmative action is the history of racism in the United States. This is likely due to the fact that the premise of this justification is undeniable. Almost no one claims that African-Americans did not suffer unjustly in the past from slavery, the Jim Crow laws, and many other *de jure* and *de facto* forms of discrimination. However, while there is still some evidence of current discrimination in the labor market and in educational opportunities (Harry Holzer and David Neumark 2000 provide an excellent discussion of this evidence), many doubt the existence or magnitude of current discrimination (Washington Post 2001). Similarly, there is no widespread agreement about the importance of role models or diversity in the workforce or in higher education.[3]

The predominance of the historical discrimination argument for affirmative action makes it important to determine whether there is a sound economic rationale for the claim that historical discrimination justifies current affirmative action. This chapter shows that affirmative action can be efficient when there has been past discrimination, even if this discrimination has been entirely eliminated. The reason for this is that past discrimination can have a permanent, though declining, influence on the relationship between ability and wealth for members of a previously discriminated group. This makes membership in that group a useful signal of ability even when controlling for class and educational attainment. Despite the relative prevalence of the historical discrimination argument for affirmative action, most theoretical models of affirmative action have focused on the current discrimination argument, with statistical discrimination receiving the most attention (Andrea Moro and Peter Norman 2003; Jaewoo Ryoo 1995; Stephen Coate and Glenn C. Loury 1993; Shelly J. Lundberg 1991; see Hanming Fang and Andrea Moro 2011 for a survey of this literature). Lawrence M. Kahn (1991) analyzes the effect of affirmative action under customer discrimination. While Kim-Sau Chung's (2000) paper on role models does not require current discrimination, it does require the perception of current discrimination (at least with positive probability). One exception is Susan Athey et al. (2000) on affirmative action and diversity. In their paper, diversity affects a firm's production function through the existence of type-based mentoring.

In contrast, in this chapter I assume that it is common knowledge that discrimination has been eliminated and that race has no direct effect on a firm's production function. I make these assumptions not to argue that current discrimination does not exist or that type-based mentoring is unimportant, but to determine whether affirmative action can be optimal solely on the basis of historical discrimination.

I separate affirmative action into two types. Voluntary affirmative action occurs when non-discriminatory firms or schools decide, without any government inducement, to consider an applicant's membership in a group that suffered from past discrimination in addition to her qualifications. I call such applicants minorities. Externally-induced affirmative action occurs when the government provides incentives to firms or schools to give additional preferences to minorities. I show that voluntary affirmative action is optimal for firms if there has been past discrimination, though the magnitude of the preference given to minorities declines over time. I also show that when innate ability and education are complements in producing good job performance (knowledge is more useful to higher ability people because they are better able to apply it), some externally-induced affirmative action will often be efficient if there has been past discrimination. In this case, government should not only allow voluntary affirmative action but should encourage it. While these results are derived in a labor market context, they also apply to a university seeking to admit students with the greatest probability of succeeding, either at the university or at some future task.[4]

The finding that voluntary affirmative action is privately optimal is quite important, because there is substantial criticism of voluntary affirmative action in both education and employment. Public opposition to any minority preferences is widespread (Lawrence Bobo and Ryan

Smith 1994; Washington Post 2001). Government policies and court decisions are also limiting the use of voluntary affirmative action (at least by governmental organizations). In 1995, the University of California Board of Regents decreed that race could not be a factor in university admissions. Proposition 209 in California (passed in 1996) and Initiative 200 in Washington (passed in 1998) prohibit the government from giving preferential treatment based on race (and other factors) in employment, education, or contracting. The issue of the constitutionality of affirmative action in higher education will be decided soon by the United States Supreme Court. Just nine years after ruling, in *Grutter v. Bollinger*[5] that universities could use affirmative action in admissions, the Court is now set to revisit that decision in *Fisher v. University of Texas at Austin*. If the court were to overturn *Grutter*, this would prohibit the use of voluntary affirmative action. That is, it would prevent the government in its capacity as a firm or university from considering race as a factor in employment or admission. Thus, the finding that it is efficient for a non-discriminatory firm to give preferences to minorities is of important policy relevance. It shows that such a ruling would prevent the government from acting efficiently.[6] Of course, to the extent there can also be positive externalities from affirmative action, i.e., some externally-induced affirmative action is optimal, we may even want government to encourage affirmative action in the private sector in addition to being able to use affirmative action in its own hiring and admission decisions.

The reason why minorities should receive preferences even if there is no current discrimination stems from three important (but non-controversial) assumptions.

1. A person's ability is positively correlated with her parents' ability.[7]
2. The wealth of one's parents (which I call class), in addition to one's ability, affects one's success in school.
3. Job performance depends both on one's ability (which is unobservable) and what one has learned (measured by success in school).

The first two assumptions imply that, when there is discrimination, a minority's expected ability is greater than a non-minority's of the same class. (The minority's parents had to overcome discrimination to reach any given class level, which means she is probably more able than those who reached that same level without overcoming this barrier.) That is, the distribution of ability conditional on class is different for minorities and non-minorities. The second and third assumptions imply that non-discriminatory firms will not eliminate this difference in conditional ability distributions in any one period. While, as soon as discrimination ends, firms will pay otherwise identical (in terms of class and schooling success) minorities more because they are more able (in expectation), they will also pay equally able (in expectation) non-minorities more because they are not otherwise identical (their parents were higher class because they did not suffer from discrimination, which improves their schooling outcome).[8] Thus, the difference in the conditional ability distribution will shrink over time when discrimination ends, but it will never be completely eliminated. Because the expected ability of minorities, conditional on class, remains greater than it is for non-minorities, firms will continue to pay otherwise identical minorities more.[9] This is voluntary affirmative action.

This conclusion is consistent with current empirical evidence on affirmative action programs in the private sector. Holzer and Neumark (1999) show that, in companies that practice affirmative action, minority employees do have somewhat weaker educational and labor market qualifications than white employees but that their job performance is no worse. This is exactly what my model predicts: firms hire minorities who are less qualified but more able than non-minority hires (for a given job) so that for any given job expected job performance is equal across races.

So long as there is no social interest in faster convergence between the races, there is no role for government. When ability and education are complements in producing good job performance, however, there is an efficiency externality associated with faster convergence. This complementarity means that productivity is enhanced the greater the correlation between ability and educational achievement. Because discrimination makes more able minorities poorer than less able non-minorities, it reduces the schooling success of more able minorities relative to less able non-minorities (schooling success depends on class as well as ability). This reduces the total productivity of the next generation. Increasing the speed of convergence between the races, then, will increase the productivity in the future by increasing the correlation between ability and education (in most cases).

Non-discriminatory firms, however, will not internalize this benefit since they will usually not employ their current employees' offspring (and would not get the entire surplus from their increased productivity even if they did). Thus, it is optimal to forgo at least some current efficiency to speed the convergence between the races. This requires externally-induced affirmative action.

While most prior papers in this area have considered static models, there are a series of papers by Loury (1977; 1981a; 1981b) that explicitly model the impact of parents' success on their children's success. Those papers and this chapter are similar in that both show that children can suffer from discrimination against (or the poverty of, for other reasons) their parents. There is one critical difference. Loury's papers all assume that a child's ability is independent of the ability of her parent's. This prevents discrimination from affecting the distribution of ability conditional on class, which is the driving force behind the optimality of affirmative action in this chapter.

The plan of the chapter is as follows. Section 2 analyzes a model where ability and educational attainment independently improve job performance (the Independence model). In order to derive analytic solutions, the Independence model assumes all relevant variables are normally distributed (one cannot derive general analytic solutions using even two-point distributions). Section 2.1 describes the environment in this model. Section 2.2 derives the steady state[10] under discrimination and Section 2.3 shows that after discrimination ends, voluntary affirmative action is optimal. Section 3 examines the a model where ability and schooling are complements (the Complementarity model). Because complementarities are difficult to model when variables can be negative (and normality no longer guarantees analytic solutions in the presence of complementarities), this model uses a two-point distribution. Section 3.1 describes the environment for this model. Section 3.2 begins analysis of the model and, for a special case, analytically demonstrates that some externally-induced affirmative action is always welfare-increasing. Section 3.3 describes simulation results suggesting that under a broader range of conditions some externally-induced affirmative action increases social welfare. Section 4 concludes.

2   INDEPENDENCE MODEL

2.1   The Environment

This is an overlapping generations model with two types of actors, firms and workers. Workers live for two periods: the first period is a schooling stage and the second an employment stage. Each worker has one parent and each worker produces one offspring who begins her schooling stage during her parent's employment stage. Every worker is born with three characteristics, each inherited from her parent: class, ability, and race. That is, each worker has the same ability and race as her parent and her class is given by the wages earned by her parent in her parent's employment stage. (Imperfect, but positive, correlation between the ability of a parent and her offspring would not change the results qualitatively, but it would make the exposition substantially more complicated.) A worker's class and race are observable,[11] her ability is not. The unconditional distri-

bution of ability is normal with mean zero. This is the same for both possible races, *B* and *W*. It is also useful to define the conditional distribution
of ability given class. I call the density for this distribution f_R, $R = B,W$.
In the schooling stage, a worker gets an observable outcome, schooling
success. Schooling success is given by the following:

$$S(C, A) = \alpha A + (1 - \alpha)C + \varepsilon_S \qquad (14.1)$$

The formula for schooling success (*S*), identical for both races, is a linear
combination of ability (*A*) and class (*C*) plus some zero mean, normally
distributed, noise, $\varepsilon_{\tilde{S}} N(0, h_S^{-1})$, with density function ϕ (h_S is the precision of ε_S). In the employment stage, firms pay workers the value of their
expected job performance (there is a competitive labor market). This
expectation is conditional on a worker's three observable characteristics.
If there is no discrimination, expected job performance, and thus wages,
are given by:

$$JP(C, S, R) = \beta E(A|C, S, R) + (1 - \beta)S \qquad (14.2)$$

Expected job performance is a linear combination of expected ability
($E(A|C, S, R)$) and schooling success (*S*). Since f_R is the prior density of
ability given class and race and ϕ is the likelihood function, by Bayes' Rule
the posterior density for ability is:

$$\frac{f_R(C, A)\phi(S - (\alpha A + (1 - \alpha)C))}{\displaystyle\int_{-\infty}^{\infty} f_R(C, A)\phi(S - (\alpha A + (1 - \alpha)C))dA} \qquad (14.3)$$

Expected ability conditional on class, schooling success, and race, then, is
given by:

$$E(A|C,S,R) = \int_{-\infty}^{\infty} A \frac{f_R(C, A)\phi(S-(\alpha A+(1 - \alpha)C))}{\displaystyle\int_{-\infty}^{\infty} f_R(C, A)\phi(S-(\alpha A + (1 - \alpha)C))dA} dA \qquad (14.4)$$

Notice that I assume that firms do not have information about a worker's
ancestors, they only know characteristics of the worker herself. That is,
they do not have information about the schooling success or class of a
worker's parent or grandparent, etc. Because I assume, for simplicity,
that a worker's ability is identical to her parent's ability, this assumption
ensures that the worker's own schooling outcome is a valuable signal
of her ability. If a worker's ability were imperfectly correlated with that

of her parent's, then this assumption would be unnecessary. If there is discrimination in hiring, then expected job performance as valued by the discriminating firm, and hence wages, are given by:

$$JP_D(C, S, R) = \beta E(A|C, S, R) + (1 - \beta)S - D \qquad (14.5)$$

I model discrimination as taste discrimination, as in Gary S. Becker (1971). Firms value the job performance of an employee of one race by an amount D less than an employee with the same expected ability and schooling success of the other race.

   If class is normally distributed, then schooling success is a linear combination of three normal random variables, thus, it is normal also. Moreover, when class is normally distributed, the distribution of ability given class will also be normal. This makes the expected ability variable normal as well. This makes expected job performance, which determines class for the next generation, a linear combination of two normal random variables. Thus, it is reasonable to say that class will be normally distributed, i.e., $(C|R) \sim N(\mu_R, h_{C,R}^{-1})$. With this class distribution, I conjecture that the mean of the conditional distribution of ability given class is an affine function of class, whose slope and intercept terms may vary by race. That is, $(A|C, R) \sim N(\gamma_R C + \delta_R, h_{A,R}^{-1})$. In the next section, I confirm that these forms do generate steady state distributions and determine what restrictions (if any) on the values of μ_R, $h_{C,R}$, γ_R, δ_R, and $h_{A,R}$ are necessary for a steady state to exist.

2.2   Steady State with Discrimination

I now derive the steady state distribution of class and ability conditional on class for races B and W, where B suffers discrimination D, and W is not discriminated against (i.e., $D_B = D$ and $D_W = 0$). This steady state gives the initial conditions (the class and ability given class distributions for each race) that exist when discrimination is eliminated. In order to analyze the effect of historical discrimination on the optimal private and social policies in the present (when I assume there is no discrimination), one must derive the implications of past discrimination on the distribution of ability by race and class. The following Lemma shows how discrimination affects the steady state class distribution for each race.

Lemma 1   *The steady state mean for class conditional on race with discrimination is* $\mu_R = \frac{(\alpha + \beta - \alpha\beta)\delta_R - D_R}{(\alpha + \beta - \alpha\beta)(1 - \gamma_R)}$. *$D_W = 0$ implies* $\mu_W = \frac{\delta_W}{(1 - \gamma_W)}$. *The steady state precision for class conditional on race with discrimination is* $h_{C,R} = \frac{h_{A,R} h_S (h_{A,R} + \alpha^2 h_S)(\alpha + \beta - \alpha\beta)(1 - \gamma_R)(2 - (\alpha + \beta - \alpha\beta)(1 - \gamma_R))}{((\alpha + \beta - \alpha\beta)h_S + (1 - \beta)h_{A,R})^2}$.

Proof. See Appendix.
While the details of the proof are in the appendix, the approach the proof takes is as follows:

C1. Derive an explicit formula for expected ability given class, schooling success, and race by performing the integration in (14.4).

C2. Substitute this formula into (14.5) to obtain an explicit formula for expected job performance (wages) as a function of class, schooling success, and race.

C3. Substitute for S using (14.1). Now expected job performance is a linear combination of C and A, both of which are normally distributed, making the expected job performance conditional only on race normally distributed.

C4 Use the fact that $(A|C, R) \sim N(\gamma_R C + \delta_R, h_{A,R}^{-1})$ and $(C|R) \sim N(\mu_R, h_{C,R}^{-1})$ to determine the mean and variance of the distribution of expected job performance conditional only on race.

C5. In a steady state, the mean and variance of expected job performance conditional on race (which is the class distribution for the next generation) must equal the mean and variance of class distribution conditional on race. Using this, I then solve for μ_R and $h_{C,R}$ to determine the steady state mean and precision for class.

Notice that this steady state precision for class is non-positive if $\gamma_R \geq 1$. Thus, $\gamma_R < 1$ is a necessary condition for a steady state to exist.

Given the steady state distribution for class, one can derive the steady state distribution for ability given class for each race. Because a worker's class is the expected job performance of her parent and her ability is identical to that of her parent, the distribution of ability given class for one generation is the distribution of ability given expected job performance for the prior generation. Thus, the steady state distribution of ability given class is equivalent to the steady state distribution of ability given expected job performance. Deriving this distribution is just a Bayesian inference problem: given the joint prior distribution of ability and class and the signal of expected job performance (wages), one must determine the posterior distribution of ability and class given expected job performance. The resulting steady state distribution of ability given class is provided in the following lemma.

Lemma 2 *The mean of ability given class and race is $\gamma C + \delta_R$ where*
$\gamma = \frac{\alpha h_s (2 - (\alpha + \beta - \alpha\beta))}{h_A (1 - \beta)}$ *and* $\delta_R = \frac{D_R \alpha h_s (2 - (\alpha + \beta - \alpha\beta))}{h_{A,R} (1 - \beta)(\alpha + \beta - \alpha\beta)}$. *The variance of ability given class is independent of race,* $h_{A,W} = h_{A,B} = h_A$.

Proof. See Appendix.

As with the prior lemma, while we leave the details of the proof to the appendix, the strategy of the proof is as follows:

A1. Derive the distribution of expected job performance (the signal) conditional on ability and class.

A2. Use standard results from normal distribution theory about the joint posterior distribution of two random variables given a bivariate normal prior and a univariate normal signal distribution. In this case, the joint posterior of class and ability given the signal of expected job performance is sought. Given the joint posterior, the marginal posterior distribution for ability given job performance (and race) is immediate.

A3. In a steady state, the mean and variance of ability given job performance (and race) must equal the mean and variance of the ability given class and race distribution. Using this, I then solve for γ_R, δ_R and $h_{A,R}$ to determine the steady state mean and precision for ability given class and race.

Notice that since the variance of ability given class is independent of race, $\gamma_R = \gamma$. Since the conditional mean of ability given class is $\gamma C + \delta_R$, it follows from Lemma 2 that conditional on class the mean ability of Bs is greater than the mean ability of Ws. Because Bs are discriminated against, they must be more able on average to reach the same class as Ws.

Recall that the steady state mean and precision for class ((22) and (23)), were given in terms of γ and δ_R. Using the steady state values for γ and δ_R in Lemma 2, one can write the steady state mean and precision for class as follows:

$$\mu_R = \frac{-D_R}{(\alpha + \beta - \alpha\beta)} \tag{14.6}$$

$$h_C = \frac{h_S(h_A + \alpha^2 h_S)(h_A(1-\beta) - \alpha h_S(2 - (\alpha + \beta - \alpha\beta)))(\alpha + \beta - \alpha\beta)(2 - (\alpha + \beta - \alpha\beta))}{h_A(\alpha h_S(\alpha + \beta - \alpha\beta) + h_A(1-\beta))(1-\beta)^2} \tag{14.7}$$

The mean class of Ws is zero while the mean class of Bs is negative due to discrimination. This explains why, even though the unconditional ability distribution is identical for both races, the Bs are conditionally more able than Ws.

2.3   Post-Discrimination Affirmative Action

Now consider what happens, after reaching the steady state with discrimination, when discrimination ends. It is easy to see that firms (even when there is no discrimination) will still use race as a factor in assessing expected job performance. Moreover, while this use of race will decline over time, it will not decline to zero immediately. The intuition is as follows. In the first period after discrimination ends, *B*s are conditionally more able than *W*s. Because schooling success is not a perfect predictor of ability, the difference in prior probabilities will affect a firm's posterior assessment of a worker's ability given their class and schooling success. A *B* with the same schooling success and of the same class as a *W* will have higher expected job performance and thus receive higher wages. This is affirmative action: a minority earns higher wages than an observationally equivalent non-minority; wages are not race blind. This affirmative action persists (though its magnitude declines over time) because the difference between the races of the conditional mean of ability given class persists (though its magnitude declines over time). The reason for this is that expected job performance is not determined solely by expected ability. It is also determined by schooling success. A worker with greater schooling success presumably has more useful knowledge that she can use to improve her job performance. Thus, a less able worker with greater schooling success can have the same expected job performance as a more able worker with a lower degree of schooling success. Because *W*s are, due to past discrimination, in a higher class than equally able *B*s, they will tend to do better in school (class and ability both contribute to schooling success). Thus, if a *W* and a *B* have the same expected job performance, on average the *B* will be more able and the *W* will have done better in school. Thus, *B*s will remain conditionally more able than *W*s even after discrimination ends. That said, this difference will decline over time, reaching zero in the limit.

To determine how the privately optimal amount of affirmative action will vary with the length of time since discrimination has ended, one needs the distribution of ability given class for minorities (which is the distribution of ability given job performance in the previous period). Since I am not looking for a steady state distribution, I do not, unlike in the previous section, evaluate this distribution using steady state values for the unconditional mean and precision of the class distribution. Because the values for γ, h_C and h_A were independent of the level of discrimination, however, one can treat these as constants and use $\gamma = \frac{\alpha h_s (2 - (\alpha + \beta - \alpha\beta))}{h_A(1 - \beta)}$. Thus, to find the minority distribution of ability given job performance t periods after the end of discrimination, one only needs to find the value of the intercept term for the conditional ability distribution (δ_B in the discrimination steady state) t periods after discrimination ends (which I will call $\delta_{B,t}$).

Proposition 1 *Suppose discrimination against one race has reached a steady state and then discrimination is ended. t periods after discrimination has ended, B's expected ability conditional on class will exceed W's by* $\delta_{B,t} = \frac{D_B h_S \alpha (1-\alpha)^{t-1}(1-\beta)^{t-2}(2-(\alpha+\beta-\alpha\beta))}{h_A (\alpha+\beta-\alpha\beta)} > 0.$ *Observationally equivalent B's will receive higher wages than W's by* $\frac{D_B h_S \alpha\beta (1-\alpha)^{t-1}(1-\beta)^{t-2}(2-(\alpha+\beta-\alpha\beta))}{(h_A+\alpha^2 h_S)(\alpha+\beta-\alpha\beta)} > 0.$ *That is, non-discriminatory firms will practice voluntary affirmative action in every subsequent period following the removal of that discrimination. The magnitude of that affirmative action, however, decreases as the number of periods since the end of discrimination increases.*

Proof. See Appendix.
The proof in the appendix uses the following steps:

P1. Use equation (*) in proof of Lemma 2 to find the mean of the joint distribution of class and ability given the distributions for class and ability given class t periods after discrimination has ended, that is, given the unconditional mean for class, $\mu_{B,t}$, and the constant term in the mean of ability given class, $\delta_{B,t}$.

P2. Use the fact that the unconditional mean of ability is zero to find $\delta_{B,t}$ in terms of $\mu_{B,t}$ ($\gamma\mu_{R,t} + \delta_{R,t} = 0 \Rightarrow \delta_{R,t} = -\frac{\alpha h_S (2 - (\alpha+\beta-\alpha\beta))\mu_{R,t}}{h_A(1-\beta)}$).

P3. Find the unconditional mean of minority expected job performance t periods after discrimination ends in terms of $\delta_{B,t}$ and $\mu_{B,t}$, the unknown parameters of the class and ability given class distribution in period t. This is done by following steps C1 through C4 for the procedure for finding the steady state class distribution. This is the mean for the class distribution in period $t + 1$.

P4. Using the relationship between $\delta_{B,t}$ and $\mu_{B,t}$, this gives a recursive formula for $\mu_{B,t+1}$. From this recursive formula, it is easy to find $\mu_{B,t}$ in terms of $\mu_{B,0}$, the steady state mean of class for minorities with discrimination derived above. From this it is easy to derive $\delta_{B,t}$ using step 2.

In Proposition 1, D_B represents the magnitude of the historical discrimination suffered by members of race B, not the existence of any current discrimination. Because $D_B > 0$, Proposition 1 shows that firms will continue to practice at least some affirmative action (give greater wages, or better jobs, to Bs than they give to Ws with otherwise identical observable characteristics) indefinitely after discrimination has ended. The magnitude of this affirmative action, however, will decrease as t increases, and quite rapidly if α and β are not too small.

Proposition 1 has important policy implications. Prohibiting affirmative action can decrease efficiency. When there has been past discrimination, similarly situated candidates of different races are not identical candidates. While the model in this chapter is couched in terms of employment-based affirmative action, the same reasoning would apply to university-based affirmative action. Thus, a court decision prohibiting universities from considering race as a factor in admissions (as could happen in *Fisher*) will prevent these universities from following a policy that admits applicants with the best expected performance (however measured) so long as both ability and past schooling success are important factors in this perform-ance.[12] This is true even when taking class into account. While class does provide some relevant information, it is not a sufficient statistic for race when there has been past discrimination. Thus, proposals to replace race-based affirmative action with class-based affirmative action do not allow universities to admit only the best applicants.

Before proceeding to the case for inducing more affirmative action than is privately optimal, I present some additional comparative statics results on how privately optimal affirmative action varies with the importance of ability in generating schooling success and expected job performance.

Proposition 2 *(a) There is some $t_\beta \in (1, \infty)$ such that affirmative action is decreasing in β (the relative importance of ability in expected job performance) if $t > t_\beta$ (discrimination ended more than t_β periods ago) and is increasing in β if $t < t_\beta$. (b) There is some $t_\alpha < \infty$ such that affirmative action is decreasing in α (the relative importance of ability in schooling success) if $t > t_\alpha$ and is increasing in α if $t < t_\alpha$. $t_\alpha < 1$, affirmative action is decreasing in α for any t, if $\beta < \dfrac{1 - \alpha + \alpha^2 - \sqrt{1 - 2\alpha + 2\alpha^2}}{(1 - \alpha)^2}$.*

Proof. See Appendix.

The more important ability is in generating high expected job perform-ance the greater the magnitude of affirmative action in the periods right after the end of discrimination. Affirmative action will be more durable (be of larger magnitude many periods after the end of discrimination), however, when ability is less important in expected job performance. A similar relationship holds for the effect of the importance of ability in gen-erating schooling success on the magnitude of affirmative action. The only difference is that if ability is not very important for expected job perform-ance, then the magnitude of affirmative action is always decreasing in the importance of ability in generating schooling success.

Proposition 2 does not describe comparative statics results for h_S.[13]

The reason is these results are very sensitive to the simplifying assumption of the model that parent and offspring ability are identical. With this perfect correlation, it turns out that the greater is the precision of schooling success the greater is the optimal amount of affirmative action. The reason is that while increasing h_S does make the schooling signal more valuable, it also increases the correlation between class and ability, making the prior more informative also. When an offspring's ability is identical to that of her parent, this second effect dominates. Undoubtedly, however, the weaker the correlation between parent and offspring ability the more likely it is that improving the precision of the schooling signal will decrease the optimal amount of affirmative action.

3   COMPLEMENTARITY MODEL

3.1   The Environment

In the independence model, ability and class independently contribute to schooling success and ability and schooling success independently contribute to expected job performance. Such independence means that the fact that past discrimination makes Bs more likely to be in a lower class than equally able Ws has no effect on aggregate efficiency.

Discrimination reduced aggregate efficiency only because it caused Bs to have a lower class than they otherwise would and class, indirectly, affects job performance. The relative distortion of the B versus W distribution of ability conditional on class, however, had no direct efficiency consequences. As a result, while it was efficiency enhancing for the government not to prohibit affirmative action, there was no reason for the government to induce firms to practice even more affirmative action to increase the speed of the convergence between the B and W class and ability conditional on class distributions. Whenever the government cares about the speed of this convergence, however, this will not be the case. In this section, I introduce complementarities between ability and schooling success in generating good expected job performance to provide an example in which a government that cares only about aggregate efficiency might want to promote additional affirmative action. To do so, however, it is necessary to depart from the normal distribution assumptions of the previous section. The reason is that with complementarities, normal prior distributions do not generate normal posterior distributions and because complementarities are hard to model when variables can take on negative values. Thus, I alter the above model so that there are only two ability levels, class levels, schooling success levels, and job performance levels. In each case, I let l denote the low level and h denote the high level. The probability of schooling success is given by:

$$P_S(C,A) = r_l + (\alpha A + (1-\alpha)C)(r_h - r_l) \tag{14.8}$$

r_l is the probability a low-class, low-ability worker will have schooling success, while r_h is the probability of schooling success for a high-class, high-ability worker, $r_l < r_h$. As before, α measures the importance of ability relative to class in generating schooling success. Like the prior model, the ability and class enter linearly in the probability (as opposed to the level) of schooling success. From Bayes' Rule, the expected ability of a worker with class C and schooling success $S = h$ is:

$$E(A|C,S = h,R) = \frac{p_{C,h,R}P_S(C,h)}{p_{C,h,R}P_S(C,h) + p_{C,l,R}P_S(C,l)} \tag{14.9}$$

Similarly, the expected ability of a worker with class C and schooling success $S = l$ is:

$$E(A|C,S = l,R) = \frac{p_{C,h,R}(1 - P_S(C,h))}{p_{C,h,R}(1 - P_S(C,h)) + p_{C,l,R}(1 - P_S(C,l))} \tag{14.10}$$

In the above expressions, $p_{C,A,R}$ is the prior probability that a worker of race R has ability A and is born into class C.

As before, both schooling and ability affect job performance, though here it is the probability of high expected job performance. (One can think of this as the probability of getting a good job, which means being in the high class.) Now, however, I assume they are strict complements. Thus, the probability of high expected job performance is given by:

$$P_{JP}(C,S,R) = q_{0,R} + qE(A|C,S,R)S \tag{14.11}$$

There is some base probability that a firm will hire a worker for a good job, given by $q_{0,R}$. I allow this to vary by race to allow for discrimination. If a worker has schooling success, however, then her expected ability can increase this probability by q.[14] Obviously, I restrict $q_{0,R} + q < 1$. I say $q_{0,R} > 0$ either because there is some chance a worker will happen to have a really good interview or has some personal connections that will make a firm judge her qualified for a good job regardless of her qualifications or because there are some idiosyncratic characteristics that are not captured by ability or schooling that might lead a worker to do well at some good job. When there is discrimination, however, firms are less likely to either appreciate the interview of a *B* candidate or hire her because of her connections and they do not value a *B*'s idiosyncratic characteristics as much. All workers, however, can improve on this base probability if they are of higher expected ability and have schooling success. The important point, however, is that higher expected ability is more valuable if one has had schooling success (ability is more useful if one has enough knowledge to use it properly).

I also assume that the *average* probability that a worker gets a good job independent of her qualifications is fixed at q_0. If *B*s suffer from discrimination, so that $q_{0,B} = Dq_0$ ($D \leq 1$), then $q_{0,W} = \frac{q_0(1 - D\lambda)}{1 - \lambda}$, where λ is the fraction of *B*s in the population. Thus, discrimination only creates a transfer of good jobs from *B*s to *W*s in any given period. Notice that, unlike in the prior model, here smaller *D* means greater discrimination.

This setup generates a transition function that determines how the joint distribution of class, ability, and race changes from one period to the next. I call this transition function *pt*. The probability that a worker of race *R* of high ability will be born into the high class given the initial probability distribution of $p_{C,A,R}$ is:

$$pt_{h,h,R}(p_{C,A,R}) = p_{h,h,R}(P_S(h,h,R) P_{JP}(h,h,R) + (1 - P_S(h,h,R)) P_{JP}(h,l,R))$$

$$+ \ p_{l,h,R}(P_S(l,h,R) P_{JP}(l,h,R) \ + \ (1 \ - \ P_S(l,h,R)) P_{JP}(l,l,R)) \tag{14.12}$$

A worker can be high ability and high class only if her parent was high ability and she got a good job. If her parent was high ability and high class, she could have had schooling success and then gotten a good job with probability $P_{JP}(h,h,R)$, or she could have not had schooling success and gotten a good job with probability $P_{JP}(h,l,R)$. The probability of getting a good job when one is high ability and low class is explained similarly. The transition function for other ability-class combinations can be derived in an analogous fashion.

3.2   External Effect of Externally-induced Affirmative Action

In this section I look at the effect of externally-induced affirmative action. This is affirmative action that is not based on the effect of race on estimates of job performance. It is giving more weight to the qualifications of minority candidates than one gives to the qualifications of non-minorities. In this model, externally-induced affirmative action is when the *q* (the weight given to $S*E(A|C,S,R)$) in (11) is larger for Bs than it is for Ws.[15] That is, with externally-induced affirmative action, and no current discrimination, the probability that a worker gets a good job is given by:

$$P_{JP}^{AA}(C,S,R) = q_0 + q_R E(A|C,S,R)S \qquad (14.13)$$

To ensure that I do not allow externally-induced affirmative action to increase the number of good jobs available or result in a net increase in the weight given the expected ability and schooling success, any increase in q for Bs must be compensated by a decrease in q for Ws such that the number of good jobs remains constant. That is, $q_W = \frac{q - \lambda q_B}{1 - \lambda}$. Externally induced affirmative action cannot increase the total number of high-class people, it can only change the racial makeup of that class. These assumptions represent the worst case for affirmative action.

I assume that per period welfare is given by the "true" probability that a worker has high expected job performance. This "true" probability is just the probability of high expected job performance when firms are non-discriminatory (only consider race through its impact on expected ability). Thus, this "true" probability that a worker has high expected job performance is given by (11) with $q_{0,R} = q_0$ and $q_R = q$ for both races.

$$P_{JP}^{T}(C,S,R) = q_0 + q E(A|C,S,R)S \qquad (14.14)$$

Notice that because externally-induced affirmative action causes some misallocation of workers to good jobs in the current period, it can only increase future welfare if it increases the average "true" probability of high expected job performance in the future. To see if that is possible, I first determine how the prior distribution of ability and class affects the unconditional "true" probability of high expected job performance. From (14), I write the unconditional "true" probability of high expected job performance as follows:

$$P_{JP}^{T,UC}(R) = q_0 + q(p_H(\alpha r_h + (1 - \alpha)r_l) + (r_h - r_l)(1 - \alpha)$$

$$(\lambda p_{h,h,B} + (1 - \lambda)p_{h,h,W})) \qquad (14.15)$$

Here p_H is the probability that a worker is of high ability. The unconditional "true" probability of high expected job performance only depends on the prior ability and class distribution through the number of high-ability, high-class workers of both races, $\lambda p_{h,h,B} + (1 - \lambda)p_{h,h,W}$. Externally-induced affirmative action will increase future welfare, then, if and only if it increases the probability that high-ability workers get good jobs above what would happen if the weight given to a worker's expected ability and schooling success were equal for both races.

One can determine the effect of increasing q_B with the corresponding decrease in q_W on the probability that high-ability workers obtain good jobs using the transition equation (12) with P_{JP}^{AA} replacing P_{JP}. Imposing the restriction that $q_W = \frac{q - \lambda q_B}{1 - \lambda}$ and differentiating the transition function for each race with respect to q_B, shows how externally-induced affirmative action affects the probability that high ability workers of each race obtain good jobs and thus make their offspring high class. Because of the complementarity between ability and schooling in producing expected job success, and the fact that high class students are more likely to succeed in school, welfare is greater the greater the fraction of high class, high ability people in the economy. Thus, externally-induced affirmative action creates a positive welfare externality in the future if and only if it increases the combined number of high class, high ability people of both races in the future (that is, if and only if it increases $\lambda p_{h,h,B} + (1 - \lambda)p_{h,h,W}$ in the next generation).

Whether or not externally-induced affirmative action has positive, future external effects will, in general, depend on the prior class-ability joint distribution for each race. Unfortunately, unlike the independence model above, one cannot derive a general analytic solution for the steady state class-ability distribution with discrimination. This is because doing so requires finding the roots of a polynomial of degree greater than four. In the next proposition, however, we present the results from the special case in which a low-ability, low-class person has no chance of getting schooling success.

Proposition 3 *In the complementarity model, when the probability of schooling success for a low-class, low-ability person is zero ($r_l = 0$), then there is a positive future welfare benefit to externally-induced affirmative action.*

Proof. See Appendix.

If $r_l = 0$, one can analytically solve for the steady state joint class-ability distribution for each race under discrimination. We can then use this steady state as our prior, and then evaluate the effect of externally-induced affirmative action on the combined number of high class, high ability people of both races in the next generation.

Because schooling and ability are complements in generating good job performance, welfare is larger when more high-ability people are high class and more low-ability people are low class. Thus, future welfare is increased if firms bias their hiring decisions for good jobs towards people with higher expected ability. Because of historical discrimination, the expected ability of minorities conditional on class is greater than it is for non-minorities. Thus, if firms give the qualifications of minorities more weight, conditional on class, they will be biasing their decisions in favor of high-ability people. Notice that any current welfare effects from job misallocation will be second order at the point of no externally-induced affirmative action (the least productive non-minority in the good job is only marginally more productive than the most productive minority in the bad job when there is no externally-induced affirmative action). So, this proposition establishes that some externally-induced affirmative action is optimal in this case.[16] It does not, however, say how much externally-induced affirmative action is optimal. Certainly, generating immediate converge is excessive since, at this level, the future welfare benefit is of second order while the immediate distortion is of first order.

3.3 $r_l > 0$ Simulation

Now, turn to the case of $r_l > 0$. Because there is no analytic solution to the steady state in this case, one must proceed by simulation. The simulation consists of two steps. First, for any given parameter values I numerically solve for the steady state values of $p_{h,h,R}$ and $p_{h,l,R}$. This steady state distribution of ability and class with discrimination will depend on the value of eight different parameters: r_h, r_l, and α (the three parameters that determine the probability of schooling success given ability and class); q_0 and q (the two parameters that determine the probability of getting a good job given one's expected ability and schooling success); p_H (the fraction of high-ability people); λ (the fraction of Bs in the population); and D (the magnitude of the historical discrimination; recall that larger D means less discrimination). Second, after obtaining the steady state values for $p_{h,h,R}$ and $p_{h,l,R}$ for a given value for each of the eight parameters, I plug these values into (44), the welfare-externality expression in the proof of Proposition 3 in the appendix, to determine if it is positive or negative. Thus, the welfare externality will also depend on the same eight parameters.

In the simulation, I randomly sampled 50,000 different parameter values for each of the eight parameters from the following uniform distributions:

$$r_h \sim U(0,1); r_l \sim r_h * U(0,.99); \alpha \sim U(0,1); p_H \sim U(.01,.5); \lambda \sim U(0,.5);$$

$$q_0 \sim U(0,.5); q \sim U(0,1 - q_0); D \sim U(.5,1) \qquad (14.16)$$

For each of these 50,000 different vectors of parameter values, I computed the welfare externality as just described. I restrict p_H and λ to be less than .5 since it is natural to think of high-ability people and minorities as being in the minority. I restrict q_0 to be less than .5 so that qualifications are sufficiently important in determining one's expected job performance. The restriction on q guarantees that the probability of high expected job performance is always less than one. I limit the magnitude of prior discrimination D to capture the case where discrimination is not too extreme. The reason that the upper bound on r_l is strictly less than r_h and the lower bound on p_H is strictly greater than zero is to eliminate cases where finding numerical solutions to the steady state is especially difficult. The following summarizes the most important results from this simulation.[17]

Result   *When parameters are drawn randomly from the uniform distributions given in (16): (A) The welfare externality is almost always positive (over 99.9% of the time). (B) α and $(q_0 + q)$ have the greatest influence on the sign of the welfare externality: (14.1) For the 50,000 draws in the sample, the welfare externality was positive whenever $\alpha < .89$ and the mean value of α for the 32 draws that produced a negative welfare externality was .975 (one can reject the hypothesis that the mean of α is less than .96 (when the welfare externality is negative) with a p-value of less than .001). (14.2) For the 50,000 draws in the sample, the welfare externality was positive whenever $(q_0 + q) < .72$ and the mean value of $(q_0 + q)$ for the 32 draws that produced a negative welfare externality was .926 (one can reject the hypothesis that the mean of $(q_0 + q)$ is less than .90 (when the welfare externality is negative) can be rejected with a p-value of less than .014).*

While the welfare externality is not always positive, as it was for $r_l = 0$, it is almost always positive (for the distributions used in the simulation). The reason it is not always positive is that there are only different weights for each race, there are not different weights for race and class. Since it is much more difficult for the government to provide incentives for two-dimensional variations in qualification weights than for one-dimensional variations, I restrict attention to one-dimensional affirmative action. It is still true that if firms give the qualifications of minorities more weight, *conditional on class*, they will be biasing their decisions in favor of high-ability people, generating a positive future welfare externality. When preferences are only given by race, however, there are some circumstances where class provides a much better signal of ability than race. Because of discrimination, non-minorities are much less likely to be high class. For some parameter values, this effect outweighs the fact that, conditional on class, minorities are more likely to be high ability than non-minorities, making the welfare externality negative. When $r_l = 0$, any low-class people who have schooling success must be high ability. This means that high class (given schooling success) is not a signal of high ability. Thus, there is no reason to give more weight to non-minorities.

The simulation reveals that α must be quite large (ability matters much more than class for generating schooling success) for externally-induced affirmative action to not have a positive future welfare externality. When class has a big impact on schooling success, discrimination has a much bigger effect on the racial difference in the conditional ability distribution. The greater this difference, the more increasing the relative weight given to minority qualifications means biasing hiring decisions towards high-ability people. When $q_0 + q$ is small, the fraction of non-minorities who are high class in the discrimination steady state is small. This decreases the importance of favoring non-minorities so as to favor high-class people. While it is not possible to conclusively show that either of these variables has a monotonic effect on the sign of the welfare externality,[18] the non-random simulation described in footnote 14 suggests that this is the case.

The simulations also suggest that the welfare externality is more likely to be negative when r_h and p_H are large (high-ability, high-class people are very likely to have schooling success and there are many high-ability people). Their means in the 32 cases where the welfare externality is negative are significantly different from their overall means (with a p-value of less than .001). The effect of these parameters was not nearly as large as the effect of α *and* $(q_0 + q)$: the minimum value of r_h for which the welfare externality was positive was .60 and for p_H the minimum was .13. r_l, λ and D did not seem to have a significant, consistent effect on the sign of the welfare externality. For λ and D one cannot reject the hypothesis that their means for negative welfare externalities is identical to their overall means. This is not to say that they have no effect. There are cases where the welfare externality is positive for small λ and negative for larger λ, but the magnitude of this effect appears to be so small that it cannot be detected with only 32 negative values out of 50,000 observations. For both r_l and D, one can show that their effect is not monotonic for all parameter values. In fact, the mean of r_l/r_h when the welfare externality is negative is statistically significantly less than its overall mean (p-value of .03) despite the fact that the prior section shows that the welfare externality must be positive when $r_l = 0$. Even for larger r_l, there are parameter values where the welfare externality is positive only when r_l/r_h is small just as there are parameter values when the welfare externality is positive only when r_l/r_h is large. The same effect occurs for D.

I also ran a linear regression (on the data from the random simulation) of the welfare externality using each of these eight parameters, the square of each parameter, and interactions between any two of the parameters as independent variables. Table 14.1 gives the results of this

Table 14.1

	Estimate	SE	TStat	PValue
l	−0.00244728	0.000126794	−19.3012	0
rh	0.00133065	0.000110159	12.0793	0
rl	−0.00159307	0.0001438	−11.0784	0
a	0.00213197	0.0000858732	24.8269	0
pH	0.0021741	0.000168356	12.9137	0
q0	0.001906	0.000179033	10.6461	0
q	−0.00011633	0.00011637	−0.999656	0.317482
l B	−0.0000745603	0.00017218	−0.433038	0.664989
D	0.00412993	0.000268997	15.3531	0
rh^2	0.00456862	0.000064416	70.9237	0
rl^2	0.00906039	0.0000938144	96.5778	0
a^2	−0.00179204	0.0000426802	−41.9877	0
pH^2	−0.00127379	0.000169548	−7.51286	0
q0^2	−0.00136484	0.000173033	−7.88774	0
q^2	0.000286793	0.000067572	4.24426	0.0000219713
l B^2	0.000681794	0.000171679	3.97134	0.0000715711
D^2	−0.0000304476	0.000165163	−0.184349	0.853741
rh rl	−0.0131091	0.000133703	−98.0463	0
rha	0.000657292	0.0000505854	12.9937	0
pHrh	0.00922099	0.0000953937	96.6625	0
q0rh	0.00824206	0.000103374	79.7303	0
qrh	0.000895022	0.0000663174	13.496	0
rh l B	0.00322675	0.000101507	31.7883	0
Drh	−0.00969312	0.0000972489	−99.6733	0
rl a	−0.000766204	0.0000667735	11.4747	0
pHrl	−0.0106418	0.000125264	−84.9554	0
q0rl	−0.00968011	0.000134957	−71.7276	0
qrl	−0.00114209	0.0000882612	−12.9399	0
rl l B	−0.00387193	0.000132624	−29.1948	0
Drl	0.0114496	0.000128747	88.9308	0
pHa	−0.000231475	0.0000763188	−3.033	0.00242258
q0a	0.000420241	0.0000810323	5.1861	0
qa	0.000050904	0.0000520074	0.978783	0.327692
al B	0.0000495585	0.0000736942	0.672489	0.501276
Da	−0.000612429	0.0000758685	−8.07224	0
pHq	0.00464486	0.000153295	30.3002	0
pHq	0.000339016	0.000099186	3.41798	0.000631376
PHl B	0.00162647	0.000154472	10.5292	0
DpH	−0.00508933	0.000145456	−34.9888	0
qq0	−0.0000879625	0.000125838	−0.699016	0.484546
q0l B	0.0014452	0.000162485	8.89434	0
Dq0	−0.004663	0.000155331	−30.0197	0
ql B	0.0000683349	0.000104814	0.651966	0.514426
Dq	−0.000405624	0.000100316	−4.04346	0.0000527461
Dl B	−0.00175972	0.000153148	−11.4903	0

regression. It is worth noting that the R-squared for this regression is only .64. Given that, by construction, the welfare externality is a function of these eight parameters and only these eight parameters, there must be a great deal that the quadratic specification for the regression does not capture. Because higher order specifications are difficult to interpret, however, I use the quadratic form. Since the specification appears to fare worst when the parameters are such that the welfare externality is negative, or close to it, the fact that the regression results are not always consistent with the results described above must be due to this mis-specification. The regression results can, however, give some indication of how different parameters affect the magnitude of the welfare externality in a way that above analysis that focuses on the sign cannot. For example, they show that when α is small, increasing α increases the magnitude of the welfare externality, while the reverse is true for larger α. The exact cutoff, of course, will depend on the values of the other parameters. At their mean values, it is about .53, externally-induced affirmative action has the greatest positive externality when ability and class have relatively equal effects on the probability of schooling success.

4   CONCLUSION

This chapter demonstrates that when there has been past discrimination, race provides useful information about ability even after discrimination has been eliminated. When someone has to overcome discrimination, they are likely to be more able than someone in the same position who had no such obstacle. Because ability is inherited, their offspring will, in expectation, be more able. At the same time, the fact that one's parents suffered from discrimination means that a minority child with the same ability as a non-minority child will likely be poorer, resulting in lower educational achievement. Therefore, it is optimal for non-discriminatory employers (or universities) to prefer minorities with the same (or somewhat lower) educational achievement as a non-minority but to prefer (on average) a non-minority student of equal expected ability as a minority student due to the greater educational achievement of the non-minority student (because of her higher class). This leads to a reduction in, but not an elimination of, racial differences, making, some (but less) affirmative action optimal in the next period. Thus, laws, regulations, or court decisions that limit voluntary affirmative action may harm efficiency.

Because voluntary affirmative action does not immediately eliminate racial differences, governmental action is necessary if the speed of convergence between the races is of social concern. While there are many possible reasons why achieving faster racial income equality may improve social welfare, I explicitly examined one possibility based solely on efficiency. If education and ability are complements in generating good job performance, then total welfare is higher when ability and class are highly correlated. When discrimination has made minorities, conditional on class, more able than non-minorities, then inducing firms to give minority qualifications more weight than non-minority qualifications will often increase the correlation of ability and class, improving future productivity. Since externally-induced affirmative action will often reduce current productivity due to job allocation distortion, this only establishes that some externally-induced affirmative action is socially optimal. Immediate convergence is not, in general, optimal.

5   APPENDIX

Proof of Lemma 1. Following the steps described in the text, observe that, by performing the integration on the right hand side of equation (14.4), expected ability given class, schooling success and race can be written as follows:

$$E(A|C,S,R) = \frac{\alpha h_S S + (\gamma_R h_{A,R} - \alpha(1-\alpha)h_S)C + \delta_R h_{A,R}}{h_{A,R} + \alpha^2 h_S} \tag{14A.1}$$

Using this in (14.5), expected job performance (wages) is given by (step C2):

$$JP_D(C,S,R) = (1-\beta)S + \beta\frac{\alpha h_S S + (\gamma_R h_{A,R} - (1-\alpha)h_S)C + \delta_R h_{A,R}}{h_{A,R} + \alpha^2 h_S} - D_R \tag{14A.2}$$

Now use (14.1) to write expected job performance as a stochastic function of ability and class as follows (step C3):

$$\tilde{JP}_D(C,A,R) = \beta\frac{\alpha^2 h_S A + \gamma_R h_{A,R}C + \delta_R h_{A,R} + \alpha h_S \varepsilon_S}{h_{A,R} + \alpha^2 h_S} \tag{14A.3}$$

$$+ (1-\alpha)(1-\beta)C + \alpha(1-\beta)A - D_R + (1-\beta)\varepsilon_S$$

Combining steps C4 and C5, the unconditional mean for JP_D is:

$$(1 - \beta(1 - \gamma_R))\mu_R + \alpha(1 - \beta)(\delta_R - (1 - \gamma_R)\mu_R) - D_R \quad (14A.4)$$

Setting this equal to μ_R and solving for the steady state mean for class yields:

$$\mu_R = \frac{(\alpha + \beta - \alpha\beta)\delta_R - D_R}{(\alpha + \beta - \alpha\beta)(1 - \gamma_R)} \quad (14A.5)$$

For Ws this simplifies to:

$$\mu_W = \frac{\delta_R}{(1 - \gamma_R)} \quad (14A.6)$$

Similar manipulation yields the following formula for the steady state precision for class:

$$h_{C,R} = \frac{h_{A,R}h_S(h_{A,R} + \alpha^2 h_S)(\alpha + \beta - \alpha\beta)(1 - \gamma_R)(2 - (\alpha + \beta - \alpha\beta)(1 - \gamma_R))}{((\alpha + \beta - \alpha\beta)h_S + (1 - \beta)h_{A,R})^2}$$

$$(14A.7)$$

Q.E.D.

Proof of Lemma 2.   To derive the distribution of expected job performance conditional on ability and class (step A1), recall that following steps C1–C3 produced a formula for expected job performance as a function of ability and class, equation (19). Since ε_S is normally distributed, (19) is normally distributed. It is straightforward to show that the mean is:

$$\beta\frac{\alpha^2 h_S A + (\gamma_R C + \delta_R)h_{A,R}}{h_{A,R} + \alpha^2 h_S} + (1 - \alpha - \beta + \alpha\beta)C + \alpha(1 - \beta)A - D_R \quad (14A.8)$$

and the variance is:

$$\left(1 - \beta + \frac{\alpha\beta h_s}{h_{A,R} + \alpha^2 h_S}\right)\Big/ h_S \quad (14A.9)$$

Now turn to step A2. Given that the signal (expected job performance) is normal with this mean and variance, it follows from Bayes' Rule and the properties of the normal distribution that the joint distribution of A and C given expected job performance of JP is (at the steady state values for the mean and variance of C) bivariate normal with mean:[19]

$$\{JP(1 - (\alpha + \beta - \alpha\beta)(1 - \gamma_R)) + (\alpha + \beta - \alpha\beta)\delta_R - D_R,$$

$$(14A.10)$$

$$\frac{1}{\alpha h_S(\alpha + \beta - \alpha\beta) + h_{A,R}(1-\beta)}\langle(1-\beta)\delta_R[h_{A,R}(1+(\alpha+\beta-\alpha\beta)\gamma_R)$$

$$- \alpha h_S(1-\alpha)(\alpha+\beta-\alpha\beta)] +$$

$$JP[h_{A,R}(1-\beta)\gamma_R(1-(\alpha+\beta-\alpha\beta)(1-\gamma_R))$$

$$+\alpha h_S(\alpha+\beta-\alpha\beta)(2-(\alpha+\beta-\alpha\beta)(1-\gamma_R)-\gamma_R)]$$

$$-D_R[h_{A,R}(1-\beta)\gamma_R-\alpha h_S(2-(\alpha+\beta-\alpha\beta))]\}\}$$

and variance-covariance matrix:

$$\frac{1}{h_{A,R}h_S(h_{A,R} + \alpha^2 h_S)}*$$

$$(14A.11)$$

$$\begin{pmatrix} (h_{A,R}(1-\beta) + \alpha h_S(\alpha+\beta-\alpha\beta))^2 & -(h_{A,R}(1-\beta)+\alpha h_S(\alpha+\beta-\alpha\beta))(1-\beta)(\alpha(1-\alpha)h_S-\gamma_R h_{A,R}) \\ -(h_{A,R}(1-\beta)+\alpha h_S(\alpha+\beta-\alpha\beta))(1-\beta)(\alpha(1-\alpha)h_S-\gamma_R h_{A,R}) & (\alpha(1-\alpha)(1-\beta)h_S)^2 + (\gamma_R(1-\beta)h_{A,R})^2 \\ & + (1-2\alpha\gamma_R(1-\beta)^2(1-\alpha)) \end{pmatrix}$$

For step A3, notice that since an offspring's ability is her parent's ability, and her class is her parent's expected job performance, in the steady state the conditional mean of ability given job performance must be $\gamma_R JP + \delta_R$. Using this (and the fact that the unconditional mean for ability is zero) and solving for γ_R and δ_R gives the following:

$$\gamma_R = \frac{\alpha h_S(2-(\alpha+\beta-\alpha\beta))}{h_{A,R}(1-\beta)}; \delta_R = \frac{D_R\alpha h_S(2-(\alpha+\beta-\alpha\beta))}{h_{A,R}(1-\beta)(\alpha+\beta-\alpha\beta)} \quad (14A.12)$$

One can also solve for $h_{A,R}$ in terms of the unconditional precision for ability by using the fact that, when X and Y are distributed bivariate normal, $V(X|Y) = (1 - \rho^2)V(X)$ (where ρ is the correlation coefficient). The resulting expression, however, is very complicated and un-illuminating. One does learn, however, that $h_{A,B} = h_{A,W} = h_A$. This also means $\gamma_R = \gamma$.[20] Q.E.D.

Proof of Proposition 1. Steps P1 and P2 produce the following expression for the conditional mean of ability given job performance (which is the conditional mean of ability given class in the next period) t periods after discrimination:

$$\frac{\alpha h_S (2 - (\alpha + \beta - \alpha\beta))(C - (1 - \alpha)(1 - \beta)\mu_{R,t})}{h_A(1 - \beta)} \qquad (14A.13)$$

Here, $\mu_{R,t}$ is the unconditional mean for class of race R in the tth period after discrimination. Since conditional mean of ability given class is of the form $\gamma_R C + \delta_R$, $\delta_{R,t+1} = -\alpha h_S(2 - (\alpha + \beta - \alpha\beta))(1 - \alpha)\mu_{R,t}/h_A$. For step P3, the mean of the unconditional distribution for expected job performance in period t (which is $\mu_{R,t+1}$), is obtained from (20) by setting $\mu_R = \mu_{R,t}$, $\delta_R = \delta_{R,t}$, $D = 0$, and $\gamma_R = \frac{\alpha h_S(2 - (\alpha + \beta - \alpha\beta))}{h_A(1 - \beta)}$. Thus, one can write:

$$\mu_{R,t+1} = \frac{h_A(1 - \beta)(\alpha + \beta - \alpha\beta)\delta_{R,t} + (h_A(1 - \alpha)(1 - \beta)^2 + \alpha h_S(\alpha(1 - \beta)^2(2 - \alpha) + (2 - \beta)\beta))\mu_{R,t}}{h_A(1 - \beta)}$$

$$(14A.14)$$

Step P4 just involves using $\delta_{R,t} = -\frac{\alpha h_S(2 - (\alpha + \beta - \alpha\beta))\mu_{R,t}}{h_A(1 - \beta)}$ in the above equation to obtain:

$$\mu_{R,t+1} = (1 - \alpha)(1 - \beta)\mu_{R,t} \text{ or } \mu_{R,t} = -(1 - \alpha)^{t-1}(1 - \beta)^{t-1}\frac{D_R}{(\alpha + \beta - \alpha\beta)}$$

$$(14A.15)$$

Then, I can write $\delta_{R,t}$ as follows, for $t \geq 1$:

$$\delta_{R,t} = \frac{D_R h_S \alpha(1 - \alpha)^{t-1}(1 - \beta)^{t-2}(2 - (\alpha + \beta - \alpha\beta))}{h_A(\alpha + \beta - \alpha\beta)} \qquad (14A.16)$$

Now, one can see what the effect of past discrimination, D, has on expected job performance and wages in the periods following the elimination of discrimination. Recall that the explicit formula for expected job performance is given by (18). Post-discrimination, however, we set $D_R = 0$ and $\delta_R = \delta_{R,t}$ and use the explicit expression for γ derived above. Thus, wages t periods after the end of discrimination are given by:

$$JP_t(C, S, R) = (1 - \beta)S + \beta\frac{\alpha h_S(S + C/(1 - \beta))}{h_A + \alpha^2 h_S} \qquad (14A.17)$$

$$+ \frac{D_R h_S \alpha\beta(1 - \alpha)^{t-1}(1 - \beta)^{t-2}(2 - (\alpha + \beta - \alpha\beta))}{(h_A + \alpha^2 h_S)(\alpha + \beta - \alpha\beta)}$$

Q.E.D.

Proof of Proposition 2.   (a) Differentiating the last term in (33) with respect to β gives the following:

$$\frac{D\alpha(1-\alpha)^{t-1}(1-\beta)^{t-1}h_s((3-(2-\beta)t-\beta)\beta^2-\alpha^2(1-\beta)^2(1-(1-t)\beta)+2\alpha(1-\beta)(1-\beta(t-1)(1-\beta)))}{(1-\beta)^2(\alpha+\beta-\alpha\beta)^2(h_A-\alpha^2h_S)}$$

$$(14A.18)$$

This has the sign of the following:

$$(3-(2-\beta)t-\beta)\beta^2-\alpha^2(1-\beta)^2(1-(1-t)\beta)+2\alpha(1-\beta)(1-\beta(t-1)(1-\beta))$$

$$(14A.19)$$

Differentiating this with respect to t yields:

$$-\beta(\alpha(1-\beta)^2(2-\alpha)+(2-\beta)\beta)<0 \qquad (14A.20)$$

At $t = 1$, (35) is:

$$\alpha(1-\beta)(2-\alpha(1-\beta))+\beta^2>0 \qquad (14A.21)$$

As $t \to \infty$, (35) approaches $-\dot\infty$.

(b) Differentiating the last term in (33) with respect to α gives the following:

$$\frac{D\beta(1-\alpha)^t(1-\beta)^th_s(h_A(-\alpha^2(1-\beta)^2(2-\alpha)t-(\alpha t-1)(2-\beta)\beta+\alpha(1-\beta)(\alpha+\alpha\beta-2\beta))+\alpha^2h_s(-\alpha^2(1-\beta)^2(2\alpha+(2-\alpha)t)+\alpha^2(1-\beta)(7-5\beta)-(2-\beta)(\beta+\alpha(2-(4-t)\beta))]}{(1-\alpha)^2(1-\beta)^2(\alpha+\beta-\alpha\beta)^2(h_A-\alpha^2h_S)^2}$$

$$(14A.22)$$

This has the sign of the term in square brackets in the numerator above. Differentiating this term with respect to α yields:

$$-\alpha(h_A+\alpha^2h_S)(\alpha(2-\alpha)(1-\beta)^2+\beta(2-\beta))<0 \quad (14A.23)$$

Evaluating the square bracket term at $t = 1$ gives:

$$-(1-\alpha)(4\alpha^3(1-\beta)h_S+(h_A-\alpha^2h_S)(\alpha(1-\beta)(2\beta+\alpha(1-\beta))-\beta(2-\beta)))$$

$$(14A.24)$$

For there to be a steady state, $h_A - \alpha^2h_S > 0$ otherwise $h_C < 0$. So (40) will be negative if $\alpha(1-\beta)(2\beta+\alpha(1-\beta))-\beta(2-\beta)>0$, which holds whenever $\beta < \frac{1-\alpha+\alpha^2-\sqrt{1-2\alpha+2\alpha^2}}{(1-\alpha)^2}$. Taking the limit of the square bracket term as $t \to \infty$ gives $-\infty$. Q.E.D.

Proof of Proposition 3. Imposing the restriction that $q_W = \frac{q - \lambda q_B}{1 - \lambda}$ and differentiating the transition function, (12), with P_{JP}^{AA} replacing P_{JP} for each race with respect to q_B gives the following effect on $p_{h,h,B}$ and $p_{h,h,W}$ respectively:

$$\frac{p_{h,h,B}^2 r_h^2}{p_{h,h,B} r_h + p_{h,l,B}(\alpha r_l + (1 - \alpha)r_h} + \frac{(p_H - p_{h,h,B})^2(\alpha r_h + (1 - \alpha)r_l)^2}{(p_H - p_{h,h,B})(\alpha r_h + (1 - \alpha)r_l) + (1 - p_H - p_{h,l,B})r_l}$$

(14A.25)

and

$$\frac{\lambda(p_H(\alpha r_h + (1 - \alpha)r_l) + p_{h,h,B}(1 - \alpha)(r_h - r_l))}{(1 - \lambda)(p_H(\alpha r_h + (1 - \alpha)r_l) + p_{h,h,W}(1 - \alpha)(r_h - r_l))}$$

(14A.26)

$$\left(\frac{p_{h,h,W}^2 r_h^2}{p_{h,h,W} r_h + p_{h,l,W}(\alpha r_l + (1 - \alpha)r_h} + \frac{(p_H - p_{h,h,W})^2(\alpha r_h + (1 - \alpha)r_l)^2}{(p_H - p_{h,h,W})(\alpha r_h + (1 - \alpha)r_l) + (1 - p_H - p_{h,l,W})r_l}\right)$$

Thus, there will be a future welfare benefit to externally-induced affirmative action if and only if λ times (42) plus $(1 - \lambda)$ times (42) is positive. That is, if and only if the following is positive:

$$\frac{p_{h,h,B}^2 r_h^2}{p_{h,h,B} r_h + p_{h,l,B}(\alpha r_l + (1 - \alpha)r_h} + \frac{(p_H - p_{h,h,B})^2(\alpha r_h + (1-\alpha)r_l)^2}{(p_H - p_{h,h,B})(\alpha r_h + (1-\alpha)r_l) + (1 - p_H - p_{h,l,B})r_l} +$$

$$\frac{(p_H(\alpha r_h + (1 - \alpha)r_l) + p_{h,h,B}(1 - \alpha)(r_h - r_l))}{(p_H(\alpha r_h + (1 - \alpha)r_l) + p_{h,h,W}(1 - \alpha)(r_h - r_l))} *$$

(14A.27)

$$\left(\frac{p_{h,h,W}^2 r_h^2}{p_{h,h,W} r_h + p_{h,l,W}(\alpha r_l + (1 - \alpha)r_h)} + \frac{(p_H - p_{h,h,W})^2(\alpha r_h + (1-\alpha)r_l)^2}{(p_H - p_{h,h,W})(\alpha r_h + (1-\alpha)r_l) + (1 - p_H - p_{h,l,W})r_l}\right)$$

I will refer to this term as the welfare externality (from externally-induced affirmative action). From (43), one can see that whether or not externally-induced affirmative action has positive external effects will depend on the prior class-ability joint distribution for each race.

We now turn to deriving the steady-state with discrimination to generate the priors to use in (43). With a given unconditional probability of a worker being high ability, p_H, and given that for each race the probability of each of the four possible combinations must sum to one, the class-ability distribution is uniquely determined by $p_{h,h,R}$ and $p_{h,l,R}$. One generates the steady state by setting the right hand side of (12) equal to $p_{h,h,R}$ and setting the analogous transition expression for high-class and low-ability workers equal to $p_{h,l,R}$ for each race R and then solving these two equations for $p_{h,h,R}$ and $p_{h,l,R}$. Substituting for P_S and P_{JP} in (12) with their explicit formulas gives the following steady state equations:

$$p_{h,h,R} = p_{h,h,R}\left(q_{0,R} + q\frac{r_h^2 p_{h,h,R}}{r_h p_{h,h,R} + (\alpha r_l + (1-\alpha)r_h)p_{h,l,R}}\right) \qquad (14A.28)$$

$$+ (p_H - p_{h,h,R})\left(q_{0,R} + q\frac{(\alpha r_h + (1-\alpha)r_l)^2(p_H - p_{h,h,R})}{(\alpha r_h + (1-\alpha)r_l)(p_H - p_{h,h,R}) + r_l(1 - p_H - p_{h,h,R})}\right)$$

$$p_{h,l,R} = p_{h,l,R}\left(q_{0,R} + q\frac{r_h(\alpha r_l + (1-\alpha)r_h)p_{h,h,R}}{r_h p_{h,h,R} + (\alpha r_l + (1-\alpha)r_h)p_{h,l,R}}\right) \qquad (14A.29)$$

$$+ (1 - p_H - p_{h,l,R})\left(q_{0,R} + q\frac{r_l(\alpha r_h + (1-\alpha)r_l)(p_H - p_{h,h,R})}{(\alpha r_h + (1-\alpha)r_l)(p_H - p_{h,h,R}) + r_l(1 - p_H - p_{h,h,R})}\right)$$

In the special case of $r_l = 0$ there are analytic formulas for the roots. The steady state values for $p_{h,h,R}$ and $p_{h,l,R}$ in this case are given by:

$$p_{h,h,R} = \{\alpha(2\alpha - 1)p_H qr_h(1 - (1-\alpha)qr_h) + q_{0,R}[p_H((1-\alpha)^2 qr_h + \alpha) - (1-\alpha)(1 + \alpha qr_h)]$$

$$+ \sqrt{\genfrac{}{}{0pt}{}{-4\alpha(1-p_H)q_{0,R}(1-(1-\alpha)qr_h)(q_{0,R} + \alpha p_H qr_h) + \{q_{0,R}[1 + \alpha(1-(1-\alpha)qr_h - p_H((1-\alpha)^2 qr_h + \alpha)]}{+ \alpha p_H qr_h(1 - (1-\alpha)qr_h)\}^2}} \}/$$

$$2\alpha(1 - (1-\alpha)qr_h)^2 \qquad (14A.30)$$

$$p_{h,l,R} = \{\alpha p_H qr_h(1 - (1-\alpha)qr_h) + q_{0,R}[1 + \alpha(1-(1-\alpha)qr_h) + p_H((1-\alpha)^2 qr_h + \alpha)] -$$

$$\sqrt{\genfrac{}{}{0pt}{}{-4\alpha(1-p_H)q_{0,R}(1-(1-\alpha)qr_h)(q_{0,R} + \alpha p_H qr_h) + \{q_{0,R}[1 + \alpha(1-(1-\alpha)qr_h - p_H((1-\alpha)^2 qr_h + \alpha)]}{+ \alpha p_H qr_h(1-(1-\alpha)qr_h)\}^2}} \}/$$

$$2\alpha(1 - (1-\alpha)qr_h)^2 \qquad (14A.31)$$

When $r_l = 0$, the welfare externality (43) becomes:

$$(1-\alpha)r_h\{(1-\alpha)p_{h,h,B}p_{h,h,W}(p_{h,h,B}p_{h,l,W} - p_{h,h,W}p_{h,l,B})$$

$$+\frac{\alpha p_H[(1-\alpha)p_{h,l,B}p_{h,l,W}(p_{h,h,W} - p_{h,h,B}) + p_{h,h,B}p_{h,h,W}(p_{h,l,W} - p_{h,l,B})]\}}{(\alpha p_H + (1-\alpha)p_{h,h,W})(p_{h,h,W} + (1-\alpha)p_{h,l,W})(p_{h,h,B} + (1-\alpha)p_{h,l,B})}$$

$$(14A.32)$$

The denominator of (48) is clearly positive. The second line of the numerator is also positive since past discrimination guarantees that, conditional on ability, Ws are more likely to be high class than Bs. Thus, (48) is positive if $p_{h,h,B}p_{h,l,W} - p_{h,h,W}p_{h,l,B} > 0$. Using (46) and (47), one can set $p_{h,h,B}p_{h,l,W} - p_{h,h,W}p_{h,l,B}$ equal to zero and solve for $\dot{D}$. Doing so produces the following roots:

$$D = 1; D = -\frac{\alpha p_H q r_h}{q_0} < 0; D = \frac{q_0 + \alpha(1 - \lambda)p_H q r_h}{\lambda q_0} > 1$$

(14A.33)

This means that for $D \in (0, 1)$ that $p_{h,h,B}p_{h,l,W} - p_{h,h,W}p_{h,l,B}$ is either always positive or always negative. At $\alpha = 1$, it is

$$\frac{4(1-D)(1-p_H)p_H q_0 q r_h}{1-\lambda} > 0$$

(14A.34)

Q.E.D.

NOTES

1. The fifth circuit decision which upheld the university's use of affirmative action is at 631 F.3d 213 (5th Cir. 2011).
2. See Roland G. Fryer et al. (2008) for a model of why class-based affirmative action is less efficient than race-based affirmative action if the employer or university is trying to acheive racial diversity.
3. There has been a recent empirical debate about whether affirmative action actually hurts minorities creating a mismatch between their capabilities and the schools they are admitted to. Richard Sander (2004) claimed that affirmative action in law schools caused black students to be admitted to law schools that they had difficultly succeeding in and, as a result, led to lower rates of bar passage and fewer black lawyers. This claim has been convincingly challenged by numerous others (see, e.g, Ayres and Brooks 2005; Ho 2005; Rothstein and Yoon 2008; among others).
4. See Wickelgren (2005) for a detailed but informal exposition of this argument.
5. 539 U.S. 306 (2003).
6. Of course, an unconstrained governmental organization may not choose the efficient level of affirmative action (they may have other goals not included in the model, such as diversity or providing role models). But when affirmative action is prohibited, this chapter indicates inefficiency is guaranteed.
7. Since I also assume that offspring have the same race as their parent, the model is not applicable to gender-based affirmative action.
8. While I talk in terms of pay, the same reasoning applies if one thinks of workers as competing for different jobs rather than getting paid their expected job performance at a single job.
9. Because the model in this chapter has a one period employment stage, there is no role for direct employer learning about ability. If there were, then, as suggested by Joseph G. Altonji and Charles R. Pierret's (2001) results, the degree of voluntary affirmative action should also decline with a worker's experience. I thank Harry Holzer for pointing this out.

10. A steady state distribution is one that is constant over time. For example, a steady state distribution for class in this model is one where when one generation has this distribution when it is young, realizes its school success, then begins to earn its wages from employment, and passes this wealth to its children (the next generation) in the form of class, the next generation will have the same class distribution as the prior one.

11. University applications typically require a great deal of information about the wealth of the applicant's parents. Employers can ask about an applicant's family background in an interview and there are many other sources of information about a person's wealth. Changing this assumption, however, will not change the qualitative results that past discrimination makes race a valuable signal of ability when schooling success is known.

12. Of course, universities may not be following such a policy now.

13. To derive these results, one must write h_A as a function of h_S and the unconditional precision of ability to allow for the fact that improving the precision of schooling success will improve the precision of ability given class.

14. It is important to allow for discrimination in q_0 but not q. This ensures that all minorities are equally disadvantaged by discrimination. If only more able minorities were disadvantaged, then class would provide less information about ability for minorities than non-minorities. This might provide an efficiency benefit to favoring non-minorities even after discrimination ends since high class non-minorities would be more likely to be high ability than high class minorities.

15. Increasing q_0 for minorities would help all minorities equally, regardless of ability. Thus, it would not increase the speed of convergence in the conditional ability distribution.

16. Of course, affirmative action is not the only policy that can increase the correlation between ability and schooling success. If other policies are costly, however, then it is not optimal to use them to achieve perfect correlation between ability and schooling success. Thus, the existence of other policies that achieve the same goal does not eliminate the benefits of externally-induced affirmative action. Moreover, affirmative action may be the only policy that can simultaneously increase equity and the correlation between ability and schooling success. Thus, if the government values equity, affirmative action may be more appealing than these other policies.

17. Similar results were obtained from a simulation that computed the welfare externality for all combinations of the following parameter values:

$$r_h = .1,.3,.5,.7,.9; \; r_l = .1r_h,.3r_h,.5r_h,.7r_h,.9r_h; \; p_H = .01,.11,.21,.31,.41,.51$$

$$\alpha = .01,.11,.21,.31,.41,.51,.59,.69,.79,.89,.99; \; \lambda = .01,.11,.21,.31,.41,.51$$

$$q_0 = .05,.15,.25,.35,.45,.55; \; q = .04,.14,\ldots,1 - q_0 - .01; \; D = .49,.59,.69,.79,.89,.99$$

18. By a monotonic effect on the sign of the welfare externality, I mean that if the welfare externality is positive for some set of parameter values, then it is positive for any smaller value of α or $q_0 + q$ when the other parameters are held constant.

19. These follow from the fact that if $X \sim N(\mu, \sigma_x^2)$, $Y \sim N(\gamma X + \delta, \sigma_y^2)$ and $Z \sim N(a + bX + cY, \sigma_z^2)$ then $(X, Y | Z)$ is normal with mean:

$$\{\mu - \frac{(b + c\gamma)(a + c\delta + (b + c\gamma)\mu - Z)\sigma_x^2}{(b + c\gamma)^2 \sigma_x^2 + c^2 \sigma_y^2 + \sigma_z^2}, \tag{*}$$

$$\gamma\mu + \delta - \frac{(a + c\delta + (b + c\gamma)\mu - Z)(\gamma(b + c\gamma)\sigma_x^2 + c^2\sigma_y^2)}{(b + c\gamma)^2 \sigma_x^2 + c^2 \sigma_y^2 + \sigma_z^2}\}$$

and variance-covariance matrix:

$$\frac{\sigma_x^2(c^2\sigma_y^2 + \sigma_z^2)}{(b + c\gamma)^2\sigma_x^2 + c^2\sigma_y^2 + \sigma_z^2} \qquad \frac{\sigma_x^2(\gamma\sigma_z^2 - bc\sigma_y^2)}{(b + c\gamma)^2\sigma_x^2 + c^2\sigma_y^2 + \sigma_z^2}$$

$$\frac{b^2\sigma_x^2\sigma_y^2 + (\gamma^2\sigma_x^2 + \sigma_y^2)\sigma_z^2}{(b + c\gamma)^2\sigma_x^2 + c^2\sigma_y^2 + \sigma_z^2} \qquad \frac{\sigma_x^2(c^2\sigma_y^2 + \sigma_z^2)}{(b + c\gamma)^2\sigma_x^2 + c^2\sigma_y^2 + \sigma_z^2} \qquad (**)$$

20. One can use the relationship between h_A and the unconditional precision to determine the constraints on the relationship between the unconditional precision of ability and the precision for schooling success that are necessary to ensure that $\gamma < 1$, so that a steady state exists. Again, these constraints are not particularly illuminating.

REFERENCES

Altonji, Joseph G. and Charles R. Pierret. "Employer learning and statistical discrimination," 116 *Quarterly Journal of Economics* 313–50 (2001).

Athey, Susan, Christopher Avery and Peter Zemsky. "Mentoring and diversity," 90 *American Economic Review* 765–86 (2000).

Ayres, Ian and Richard Brooks. "Does affirmative action reduce the number of black lawyers," 57 *Stanford Law Review* 1807–1854 (2005).

Becker, Gary S. *The Economics of Discrimination* (2nd Edition), Chicago: University of Chicago Press (1971).

Bobo, Lawrence and Ryan Smith. "Antipoverty, affirmative action, and racial attitudes." In S. Dansizer, G. Sandefur, and D. Weinberg, eds, *Confronting Poverty: Prescriptions for Change*, Cambridge, MA: Harvard University Press (1994).

Chung, Kim-Sau. "Role models and arguments for affirmative action," 90 *American Economic Review* 640–48 (2000).

Coate, Stephen and Glenn C. Loury. "Will affirmative action policies eliminate negative stereotypes," 83 *American Economic Review* 1220–40 (1993).

Fang, Hanming and Andrea Moro. "Theories of statistical discrimination and affirmative action: a survey," In Jess Benabib, Matthew O. Jackson, and Alberto Bisin, eds, *Handbook of Social Economics*, Amsterdam: North-Holland (2011).

Fryer, Roland G., Glenn C. Loury and Tolga Yuret, "An economic analysis of color-blind affirmative action," 22 *Journal of Law, Economics, and Organization* 319–55 (2008).

Ho, Daniel E. "Affirmative action does not cause black students to fail the bar," 114 *Yale Law Journal* 1997–2004 (2005).

Holzer, Harry and David Neumark. "Are affirmative action hires less qualified: evidence from employer-employee data," 17 *Journal of Labor Economics* 534–69 (1999).

Holzer, Harry and David Neumark. "Assessing affirmative action," 38 *Journal of Economic Literature* 483–568 (2000).

Kahn, Lawrence M. "Customer discrimination and affirmative action," 29 *Economic Inquiry* 555–71 (1991).

Loury, Glenn C. "A dynamic theory of racial income differences." In Phyllis A. Wallace and Annette M. LaMond, eds, *Women, Minorities, and Employment Discrimination*, Lexington, MA: Lexington Books (1977).

Loury, Glenn C. "Intergenerational transfers and the distribution of earnings," 49 *Econometrica* 843–67 (1981a).

Loury, Glenn C. "Is equal opportunity enough," 71 *American Economic Review Papers and Proceedings* 122–26 (1981b).

Lundberg, Shelly J. "The enforcement of equal opportunity laws under imperfect information: affirmative action and alternatives," 106 *Quarterly Journal of Economics* 309–26 (1991).

Moro, Andrea and Peter Norman. "Affirmative action in a competitive economy," 87 *Journal of Public Economics* 567–94 (2003).

Rothstein, Jesse and Albert H. Yoon. "Affirmative action in law school admissions: what do racial preferences do?," 75 *University of Chicago Law Review* 649–714 (2008).

Ryoo, Jaewoo. "Statistical discrimination, affirmative action, and mismatch," 95-06 *CARESS Working Paper* 1-30 (1995).

Sander, Richard. "A systematic analysis of affirmative action in American law schools," 57 *Stanford Law Review* 367–434 (2004).

Washington Post. "Misperceptions cloud whites view of blacks," July 11, 2001, p.A1.

Wickelgren, Abraham L. "Affirmative Action: More Efficient than Color Blindness, 10 *Texas Journal on Civil Liberties and Civil Rights* 183 (2005).

15. The multi-layered action of trademark: meaning, law and market
Giovanni B. Ramello

1. INTRODUCTION

'*What's in a name?*' Juliet wonders, thinking of the abhorrence her beloved Romeo's family name arouses among her own relations (Shakespeare, *Romeo and Juliet*, act 2, scene 2). Centuries later, the same question is being asked, with less tragic overtones, by the academics who study the relationship between names, signs and economic behaviour.

Now as in Juliet's time, the answer to this query is a matter of some import. In fact it holds the key to understanding the economy of the third millennium where signs – the category of social tools that scholars call 'semiotic devices' – dominate even global markets and trade dynamics, sometimes acquiring a cult-like status and following among consumers, firms and policymakers. Today, trademarks have become so ubiquitous and important to business that they are deemed to be – rightly or wrongly – not just a basic tool for competition and trade, but also a fully fledged (though intangible) part of a company's assets (Heberden and Haigh, 2006).

Protecting the trademarks and designations by which names are deployed in markets is therefore a matter of current policymaking interest and debate. In Europe, a number of legislative schemes have sought to protect EU producers from global competition through identification of provenance.[1] The thinking behind these regulations is not just to help consumers make better-informed decisions, but also and especially to put in place competitive levers that give certain national and EU products a commercial advantage. Today, the sign has come even further, transcending its 'distinctive' function to become a production input, a quality certification mark, a capital good, and even a consumer good, through a set of strategies referred to as 'branding' (Ramello and Silva, 2006; Ramello, 2008).

For law and economics scholars, it is interesting to explore the mechanisms that lie behind branding, and whether the traditional rational choice hypothesis still holds in this new world where consumers and firms shift away from reality to exchange not just tangible goods, but also dreams and meaning.

To understand this new world, one important question we can ask (whose answer may partly subvert the conventional view of markets and trade) is: What is so special about signs that makes them a focus for producers and an engine of trade, and what is it that consumers actually see and buy?

This chapter will chart how trademark has progressed from its original function of providing auxiliary information to buyers in order to reinstate a competitive market. Today, branding has transformed it into a tool for capturing market power, that shifts consumption from the concrete reality of goods to the more subtle and elusive realm of meaning.

The discussion is organized as follows. Section 2 uses semiotics to explore the link between signs and behaviour. In Section 3 we present the information economics view according to which trademark is a tool for averting a market failure, and so inherently beneficial to efficiency. Section 4 then describes trademark's metamorphosis into a brand, and how this has altered the relationship between the market and signs. Section 5 explores the final frontier, in which the sign completely breaks away from tangible goods to acquire a separate identity in the eyes of markets and consumers. Section 6 sets out the conclusions and suggests some avenues for further study.

2. SIGNS AND BEHAVIOUR: ELEMENTS OF SEMIOTICS

The question asked by the unlucky Juliet gives us a starting point for unraveling the role of signs. To answer it we can turn to semiotics, the science that studies signs, of which names are a particular case.[2] A sign, to put it briefly, is a device for denoting something else. Words, for example, are signs used to represent particular objects, experiences, states of mind, and much more.

Human communities are naturally densely populated with signs, and so are relationships between individuals. Signs are essential instruments for social living that perform a variety of functions. First of all, signs minimize the cost of social expression/communication and, insofar as they are socially shared, produce information economies of scale. In this sense, economics has always underpinned the social life of signs, which are devices that 'economically' encapsulate a broader concept.[3]

However the relation is not univocal, and the same sign can convey different meanings depending on the context. For example, 'diesel' can denote a type of engine fuel, or a maker of casual clothing and accessories.

So what we find is a complex process of association between signs and meanings, which must be fully understood to grasp how the role of signs in the market has changed. In the terminology of modern semiotics, the system can be described as follows: a 'sign' defines a system of relations between a 'signifier' (i.e., the perceptible form of the sign), a 'signified' (i.e., the meaning or particular mental idea for which the perceptible form stands) and a 'referent' (the tangible object to which both the signifier and its meaning refer) (Beebe, 2004). In the preceding example, the word 'diesel' is the signifier and casual clothing is the referent, while the signi-fied is whatever meaning this sign evokes in the minds of consumers. Yet all this will be altered in the context of engines, precisely because there is no univocal relation between signs and meanings. The associations are created case by case, so that a single signifier can embrace an elaborate web of meanings that fluctuate depending on the context. We gener-ally speak of a complex system of signification with multiple meaning-generating paths that can be adapted to fit the needs and/or roles of the individuals who perceive them. This dynamic is crucial for comprehending the economic life of trademark.

Sometimes, the effect of this process is to 'reify' the signified, so that the meaning associated with a sign, rather than the tangible object to which it refers, becomes the focus of attention. In such cases, as we will argue below, the sign becomes a sort of good in its own right, subject to its own economic valuation and separate consumption.

3. SIGNS, MARKETS AND EFFICIENCY: THE TRADITIONAL ECONOMIC ANALYSIS OF TRADEMARKS

The conscious and instrumental use of signs in markets began with trade-mark.[4] In particular, trademarks acquired a key economic role as road building and the expansion of commerce created more distance between producers and consumers. Though these developments favoured spe-cialization of production, division of labour and the ability to exploit economies of scale, they also broke off the direct relationship that had existed between buyers and sellers, to the point of triggering a market failure (Wilkins, 1992; Blackett, 1998; Ramello, 2006.) The new, long-distance trade severed the links and bonds of trust between producers and consumers, because buyers could no longer determine the provenance and expected quality of goods from different suppliers. Meanwhile anonym-ity gave producers an incentive to cut costs by lowering the quality of goods, making them fall short of consumer expectations. Trademark rem-edied this information gap by labelling goods with their origin, and thus attesting to their authenticity. Even when goods can no longer be traced to a known local source (e.g., a shop or craftsman), trademark provides a virtual substitute: a name denoting a particular location and producer. The signifier (that is, the trademark) carries a meaning that gives extra information (essentially, the producer's identity) to consumers who purchase its associated referent. In this guise, trademark becomes a distinctive sign that helps consumers identify and choose between different products.

This economic utility of trademarks was seized upon early on by various human societies, who used them widely in a variety of settings as organized trade began to emerge (Blackett, 1998). Forebears of the modern trademark can be found, for example, in the Etruscan civilisation, in ancient Rome, in the Greek city-states, and in imperial China, applied to a vast assortment of goods, from vases to textiles, to wine, etc. (Ramello and Silva, 2006).

More recently, modern economic theory has made solid arguments in favour of trademark as a necessary signal for producing efficiency in the presence of asymmetric information. At issue here is what is called the 'adverse selection' problem. Consumers without adequate information do not know what they are buying, and so make choices that are bad for the market overall. The result is a supply of products whose quantity and quality are both lower than the efficient level.[5]

In such circumstances, creating an informational signal will benefit consumers, producers of good-quality goods, and the market as a whole. Hence 'the brand-name good' is an 'example of an institution which counteracts the effects of quality uncertainty' (Akerlof, 1970, p. 499).

As regarded here, trademark is clearly an informational vehicle whose ability to foster trade and efficiency transcends the effect on individual consumers. According to the literature on the economic effects of liability systems, the ability to identify producers through trademark gives consumers a criterion for making an optimal choice, while at the same time producing the public good of deterrence, which as we shall see serves to internalize the externalities. The insight here is again from Akerlof (1970, pp. 499–500), who points out that 'brand names not only indicate quality but also give the consumer a means of retaliation if the quality [of the purchased good] does not meet expectations.' If this happens the consumer can respond by no longer buying the good and negatively influencing other prospective purchasers, thus harming the manufacturer's future profits.

In more serious and generalized cases such as fraud, misleading advertising, or recalls of defective goods, the above repercussions may be amplified by the financial markets, causing the incriminated company's shares to lose value (Jarrell and Peltzman, 1985). All these consequences, taken together, act as a sort of financial penalty that encourages good behaviour on the part of firms (De Alessi and Staaf, 1994). This deterrence works alongside the conventional regulation of markets, enforced by public authorities that rigidly define what is permitted and police any infringements.[6]

Other arguments for the efficiency of trademark hinge on the opportunities it offers for organizing production. According to the theory of the firm developed by Williamson (1985) and further refined by the 'firm capabilities' (Teece, 1988) and 'new property rights' (Hart, 1995) approaches, controlling residual rights over production through trademark becomes a way to determine the boundaries of the firm, and so identify the most efficient production hierarchy (say, a large vertically integrated corporation, or a small stand-alone firm specialized in a specific area).[7] By securely anchoring a large part of the production's value in the owner's hands, trademark frees firms to benefit from vertical disintegration or delocalization through extensive use of outsourcing and licensing.[8]

4. THE ECONOMIC METAMORPHOSIS OF THE SIGN: FROM TRADEMARK TO BRAND

As noted earlier, the capabilities of semiotic devices extend well beyond just identifying provenance. Their sphere of meaning can in fact be expanded and dilated at will for a variety of ends. From an economic standpoint, alongside its informational utility, trademark offers firms another way to gain competitive advantage through 'differentiation', whose extensive use opens a new chapter in the economic trajectory of trademark: its transformation into a 'brand'.

The previous section illustrated trademark's ancillary role in the market, as a sign that 'labels' goods with their history and provenance. However, signs may also cause consumers (and investors) to differentiate between equivalent goods, almost as if they possessed distinct intangible attributes.

Signs, therefore, can embed two levels of meaning: straightforward information about provenance, that helps buyers distinguish between goods under the *unus inter pares* assumption that all the goods belong to a competitive market; but also a 'differential distinctiveness' that sets the trademark (and product) apart from others, making it less substitutable (Beebe, 2004). Differentiation makes the sign more visible than its competitors, and so reduces homogeneity.

In legal practice, this is what is generally meant by 'trademark strength', which essentially describes the ability of the mark to acquire uniqueness in the eyes of economic actors. When this happens, the sign and its referent become more visible than those of competitors, producing what is known in marketing as brand 'awareness' or 'salience' (Ehrenberg and Barnard, 1997; Aaker, 1991).

Naturally, a small degree of differentiation is inevitably present in markets.[9] Goods are rarely perfectly homogeneous because, even in a competitive market, minor factors can still slightly reduce substitutability (for example, how likeable the seller is, or other psychological aspects that, in a barely perceptible way, diminish the effect of price competition).

However it comes about, the effect of differentiation on the market is to make the signifier and its associated good less substitutable than competing ones, allowing the seller to charge a premium over the competitive price. In other words, the producer gains market power and, in competitive terms, can shift toward a monopoly price.[10] Though this is generally good for sellers' profits, it also introduces more inefficiency into the market as more market power is gained. As a result, the overall social welfare outcome of trademark is difficult to assess, as reflected by conflicting views in the scholarly debate.[11]

In any case, differentiation is the first stage in the sign's metamorphosis from a trademark, with a static semiotic value that serves to remedy an information gap, to a brand that shifts the balance from signifier to signified, so that the latter becomes part of the good being sold and is sometimes confused with the referent.[12] The semantic value of trademark, transformed into brand, thus becomes the focus of firms' strategies for attracting and building relationships with consumers, ultimately turning the brand into a product in its own right. Branding is inherently about creating market power (i.e., reducing product substitutability) and, as widely established in the marketing literature, increasing the consumer's willingness to pay for a particular good and brand (Yoo and Donthu, 1999).[13]

Naturally, long before scholars, firms had already grasped the possibilities of brands and devised strategies to capitalize on consumers' susceptibility to signs. An example of this is the practice of capturing brand loyalty and repeat purchases by creating psychological switching costs that generate endogenous inertia, but whose social welfare outcomes are open to question (Aaker, 1991; Klemperer, 1995).

The shift in focus from products to brands, on the part of both consumers and firms, and the resultant choice inertia, can be further exploited through practices that transfer a brand's effect to a different market. This is called 'brand extension' if the brand is transferred to a similar product, or 'brand stretching' if it is applied to a completely different one.[14]

Such practices can create informational economies of scale that, at a stroke, remedy multiple information asymmetries in disparate markets by creating a single signal (Choi, 1998; Cabral, 2000). Yet they also enable firms to transfer their market power gains, via the brand, to enjoy supernormal profits in distant markets (Pepall and Richards, 2002). Insofar as the brand becomes a vehicle for creating and transferring market power, we enter the domain of 'brand equity', which denotes the incremental utility for the consumer or the added value for firms of the brand (Aaker, 1991; Yoo and Donthu, 1999).

The sign itself is thus invested with a specific value that can be independently transferred from one product to another, and therefore also counted as a balance-sheet asset in its own right.

5. THE PROCESS OF UNBUNDLING: THE SIGN AS AN ASSET AND OBJECT OF CONSUMPTION

The emergence of brand loyalty and brand equity underscore a new, more complex and multifaceted relationship between consumers and distinctive signs. Brands go well beyond the original, purely informational function of trademark to touch the emotional and psychological spheres, opening up enticing profit opportunities for firms. The underlying economic theory has yet to be fully worked out, but offers interesting scope for further research.

Some authors have begun to notice a form of 'unbundling' in various contexts, whereby the sign detaches itself from the product or good to acquire its own character and identity that can be exploited in markets in various ways.

For example, considering a supply-side perspective and with reference to the literature on the firm as a carrier of reputation, Tadelis (1999) shows how brands allow firms to convert their accumulated reputation inertia into a tradable asset that can be exchanged just like any other resource. What emerges, then, is a market for intangible assets which, just like tangible assets, have a standalone financial and productive value.

Many authors go so far as to say that intangible assets today make up most of the value of firms, with the lion's share going to brands, which have effects on production and profit (Heberden and Haigh, 2006).[15]

This claim is confirmed by Clifton, Simmons and Ahmad (2004), who studied the market value of certain brands and their contribution to the capitalization of firms. They found that in some cases brands can account for half of a company's capitalization (e.g., Mercedes-Benz, Coca-Cola, Nokia), or even 70% (e.g., Disney, McDonald's). These cases illustrate the vast importance taken on by intangible assets, compared to physical assets, in a variety of market sectors. Obviously, none of this has come about by chance. It is a result of specific business policies targeting strong investment in branding. For some firms, the emphasis on branding is relatively recent, while in other cases it has a venerable history. Coca-Cola, for example, obsessively curated its intangible and semantic sphere practically from the outset (Reymond, 2006). In any case, branding has today become central to nearly every industry sector, including those that once seemed more tied to the 'concrete' side of manufacturing, such as carmakers. The Ford Motor Company, for example, has increasingly discovered the value of intangible assets, prompting it to spend over 12 billion dollars to purchase famous brands such as Jaguar, Aston Martin, Volvo and Land Rover (Clifton, Simmons and Ahmad, 2004).

In general, the transfer of value from the concrete to the semantic sphere leads to exploitation of licensing, so that firms largely shift from producing goods and services to producing meaning, from which they extract profits directly through production of associated goods, or indirectly through transfer of licenses.

The balance sheet value of the brand merely confirms that firms today ascribe to brands an independent worth, which must of course have its counterpart on the demand side. In effect, we observe a similar shift in consumption, as brands increasingly appear to become consumer goods in their own right (Beebe, 2004). The sign and the signified, both by nature intangible, are now exchanged alongside other goods, not so much to remedy information asymmetry as to satisfy deeper needs of individuals in the psychological and social spheres. This creates a 'value of the sign', sometimes equated with the final price commanded by the trademark (or rather, the differential over an unbranded product), but which can actually have a much broader import not fully captured by a monetary value. People consume certain goods and signs to demonstrate status, to signal their membership of (or distance themselves from) a social group, and to perform complex social and individual functions (Beebe, 2004).

This was the insight set forth by Veblen (1899) in his celebrated book *The Theory of the Leisure Class*, which introduced the idea of vicarious consumption. Sometimes consuming a good involves producing a message – i.e., a meaning – that is not strictly tied to the function of the 'vehicle' good. The brand, as a sign and hence a vehicle of meaning, amplifies this mechanism and makes explicit its operation on two levels. One is the ordinary and tangible domain of economic value, while the other is the more intangible sphere of communication, meaning and relations between individuals.

This dichotomy has prompted certain criticisms of the neoclassical tradition on the part of heterodox approaches and other social sciences (see Babe, 1995; Baudrillard, 1972), but also stimulated orthodox economists to produce original contributions that seek to better understand consumer behaviour (Bagwell and Bernheim, 1996; Corneo and Jeanne, 1997).

What emerges overall is a progressive 'individualization' of the sign as it becomes detached from goods and production. The semiotic device ancillary to the market acquires its own economic valuation, independently of the associated referent, which is often only a pretext for selling a new symbolic good tied to the sphere of meaning (Beebe, 2004). Some scholars speak of a decline of referents and a 'divorce' of the brand from the goods it was supposed to accompany, culminating in a commoditization of signs and the advent of an 'experience economy', where consumption happens in the sphere of feelings and goods are merely a pretext for entering this realm (Lemley, 1999; Pine and Gilmore, 1999; Beebe, 2004).

Even law appears to have acknowledged this shift, with legal sentences that are clearly grounded in the above interpretation. Judge Alex Kozinsky (in Beebe, 2004, p. 657), for example, has noted that trademarks have 'begun to leap out of their role as source-identifiers and, in certain instances, have effectively become goods in their own right'.

Legislation has followed suit, shifting from its original goal of protecting consumers to instead safeguarding firms' investments in creating meaning and brands. For example, the often-discussed antidilution measures enshrine the metamorphosis of trademark into a tool for creating property rights over a signifier/signified relationship.[16]

The goal is no longer to protect the informational value of the trademark and avoid consumer confusion, for which the existing regulations were sufficient, but rather to punish behaviours that, though legitimate, may indirectly encroach upon this newly forged semantic sphere and its economic exploitation. The dilution claim is generally raised for well-known or famous trademarks whose informational impact on consumers is very widespread. It can therefore be regarded as a form of indirect infringement. Essentially, dilution is claimed whenever a trademark – even if it does not confuse consumers – produces 'detriment to the distinctive character' of another famous mark[17] according to European law, or results in 'lessening of the capacity of a famous mark to identify goods and services' according to US law.[18] The main idea is that, even if there is no infringement or confusion – which previous laws could already remedy – the use of a sign similar to a famous one in a non-competing market can still be forbidden because it *lato sensu* weakens the distinctiveness (and most importantly the differentiation effect) of the famous mark. This can happen by 'tarnishment' if applied to inferior-quality goods that might lower consumers' opinion of the famous mark,[19] or by 'blurring' when there is a sort of semantic free-riding, so that the new sign does not confuse the consumer but still indirectly exploits, and thereby impoverishes, the distinctiveness of the famous mark (Lunney, 1999).[20]

The general legislative principle that emerges is to preserve the semantic value of trademarks, in the market and the minds of consumers, by the difficult route of defining property boundaries in the semantic sphere. Such a solution requires directly protecting the signified through a new intellectual property right that extends beyond the tangible market to cover the market for meanings. By so doing, the law protects firms' investments in creating new semiotic products and confirms the altered function of the mark, which now assigns a legal and economic monopoly over a broad relation between signifier and signified.

6.   CRITICAL ISSUES IN THE MEANING ECONOMY

Overall, the discussion so far has highlighted the special relationship between markets and signs, that goes beyond the purely informational sphere to penetrate the emotional and psychological realms. Signs can inform, but they also stir up associations and feelings, to the point that they become a sort of product that contains meaning. Trademark offers a way to bring into the immaterial economy even apparently extraneous sectors. Just as books and records make it possible to exchange information fixed in a tangible medium,[21] trademark sells meaning through a referent that accompanies the sign. This completes the construction of an information and knowledge society, where tangible objects are largely overshadowed by their intangible connotations.

However, much about this new economy has yet to be studied, and in-depth work is needed to avoid drawing hasty or inaccurate conclusions. On the whole, the multiple effects of trademark, arising from its fluid character and adaptability to serve various ends, prefigure a certain ambiguity in its social welfare outcomes that should invite more caution on the part of policy makers and operators.

The first and most obvious caveat, from an economic analysis perspective, is the perplexity of tackling inefficiency with further inefficiency. As we said before, trademark was originally created as a signal to reinstate competitiveness and thus pursue efficiency. Yet the strong differentiation generated by branding moves the market away from a competitive equilibrium, and tends to create monopolies. The original market failure is thus averted only at the cost of falling into another one, tied to market power. Whether the final balance is worthwhile depends on the magnitude of these two effects. If the informational benefit outweighs the harm of the monopoly, a mild amount of market power can be regarded as the price premium commanded by quality. Conversely, if the inefficiency introduced by market power outweighs the positive effect of the informational signal, social welfare is diminished even though firms might secure higher profits.

Differentiation can also be strategically exploited to build barriers to entry, leading to actions for excluding competitors that may also harm broad swathes of firms, and in some cases entire national industries. Where there is asymmetric access to financial resources and/or information inertia that benefits brand owners, branding will give them a chance to erect strong barriers to entry even against competitors that are equally or more efficient in producing goods. In fact, a brand's likelihood of dominance is in proportion to its communicative power. Thus, a strong brand entering a new market can overwhelm and displace even locally well-established firms, that may struggle to attract or retain consumers' attention and loyalty once powerful outside brands enter the market. This process has already harmed the national industries of certain developing countries (Baroncelli, Fink and Javorcik, 2005), and is generally a key feature of 'global branding', which aims to establish itself internationally by displacing less visible local products. A similar practice, in international trade, is the 'leverage of tying' encountered in antitrust, whereby a producer with sufficient market power in one area exploits it to restrict competition in the 'tied' market (Whinston, 1990). Interestingly, the above mechanism could be described as exploiting a monopoly over attention, with exclusionary effects on firms that have production capacity but cannot compete with the meaning.

In other situations, there is a sort of 'competition for the attention' of consumers that can be used to weaken the visibility of weak signs and boost the market power of more visible signs. Such a situation has been noted by some authors in the pharmaceutical market, where the introduction of 'pseudo-generics' (generic drugs produced by the same firms that make the branded products) has the aim of increasing competition in the segment of non-differentiated (and more substitutable) goods, to make the branded product's signal more visible (and attractive) to consumers (Kong and Seldon, 2004). In such a circumstance there is overproduction of information, beyond what is actually needed, with part of the excess serving to make the buyer's choice more confusing.

This is an outcome that runs counter to the original purpose for which trademark was established. The signal is used to distort the competitive structure of the market and create pockets of monopoly. What emerges is a 'paradox of information that misinforms'. The brand can become a vehicle for distracting consumers from the reality of the market, in order to gain market power or extract incumbent rents. This has also been observed in blind tastings of cola drinks. Though Coca-Cola is preferred by a large majority on the market, when tasting unbranded products people alter their preference, and in fact express a greater liking for the competitor Pepsi-Cola (Reymond, 2006). These findings suggest that the beverage brand has the counter-informational role of misdirecting the preferences and choices of consumers, who are to a certain degree being 'fooled'. Correcting the information asymmetry and restoring efficiency here would require curtailing investments in branding, which in practice appears to confuse consumers and impair the transparency of the market.

In the light of these phenomena, some commentators argue that the role of branding today is simply to 'squeeze every last drop of value out of the system' to counteract the 'profits crisis' of capitalist society. With the inexorable rise in productivity and production capacity in the post-war era, firms have gradually lost their ability to extract large profit margins from traditional manufacturing and services, forcing them to invent new strategies (Thrift, 2006, p. 281). However this debate has as yet been only roughly sketched out, and will need to be developed further.

7.   CONCLUSIONS

In the history of markets, the Shakespearean question 'what's in a name?' has repeatedly arisen. However the answer is not straightforward, and varies depending on the economic conditions and opportunities for profit. Its discussion also requires understanding the different perspectives of semiotics, economics and law. In spite of this complexity, markets have swiftly and successfully adapted to exploit names and signs in whatever ways best maintain their vitality and create profit opportunities.

In this work we have broadly discussed the various economic roles of trademark, a 'semiotic device' that remedies information asymmetry by identifying producers and the quality of their goods or services, but which also instigates branding strategies that boost firms' market power through differentiation, to ultimately create an intangible economy of meanings.

The origins of trademark as a sign used in exchanges can be traced to the geographical separation between makers and buyers of goods. At that juncture, trademark remedied the market failure arising from information asymmetry, giving owners an incentive to invest in quality, which they could internalize as reputation. Trademark protection thus became an economic instrument that, opportunely designed, could produce incentives for maximizing the efficiency of the market. However, trademark's ability to extensively leverage meaning also opened the door to differentiation strategies, whose benefits from an overall efficiency perspective are less clear. Often, they amount merely to rent-seeking activities aimed at erecting barriers to entry, that have little to do with signalling mechanisms. This can happen more and more as meaning takes prevalence over the tangible goods that it accompanies.

Taken to its logical conclusion, such a process creates a new market for signs and meanings whose economic outlines remain largely to be understood, and whose social welfare outcomes require a careful analysis that is to a good extent still incomplete.

NOTES

1. We refer in particular to the designations of origin in the agri-food and manufacturing sectors. From a legal perspective, these are not the same thing as trademarks. However their economic rationale is comparable to that of a collective brand, and so they can be dealt with similarly (see Silva and Peralta, 2011; Moreschini et al., 2012). On the proposed legislations, see for example the European regulation proposal on country of origin marking COM (2005).
2. Recent findings of neuroscience, in particular on the functioning of neural networks and the way in which perception takes place, and how it is organized and consolidated over time, throw new light on the meaning and value of symbols. See for example Dennett (1997).
3. Communication theory would call this 'maximum efficiency' of information transfer (Shannon and Weaver, 1962).
4. There are many economic interactions based on signs, and the analysis could be extended in various directions which are not, however, relevant to this work. One example is money, either in its current form or embodied in objects such as seashells, which is likewise a sign that conveys a meaning in terms of value.
5. The well-known outcome of such a situation is a reduction in both the size of the market and the average quality of goods; in the extreme case of Akerlof's 'The Market for Lemons' (1970) all trade is eliminated, to the detriment of economic welfare.
6. On responsibility as a complement to regulation, see for example Shavell (1987).
7. See, recently, also Burk and McDonnell (2009).
8. The franchising contract is the simplest solution of this type. See Ramello and Silva (2006).
9. This view is shared, for example, by Tirole (1988). Semiology seems to agree since it detects (see Barthes, 1964, Elements of Semiology in Beebe, 2004, p. 662) an inescapable process of 'semantization' whereby any object becomes 'pervaded with meaning. [. . .] [A]s soon as there is a society, every usage is converted into a sign itself'. Communications studies likewise converge on this position (Babe, 1995).
10. Differentiation causes a shift from a horizontal demand curve (the case of perfect competition) to one that is negatively sloped (imperfect competition). As we know, the unit profit margin increases with diminishing price elasticity of demand according to the usual equation $(p - MC)/p = 1/\eta$, where p is the market price, MC is the marginal cost and η is the price elasticity of demand. It is thus easy to see that in perfect competition, when the demand curve is horizontal and $\eta = \infty$ the market power is zero, while it becomes positive with increasing elasticity, that is, when the demand curve becomes sloped and η diminishes.
11. For an in-depth discussion of this question see Ramello (2006; 2012) and Ramello and Silva (2006).
12. The literature in fact notes that 'a brand is a trademark, or combination of trademarks,

which through promotion and use has acquired significance over and above its functional role of distinguishing the goods or services concerned' (Blackett, 1998, p. 8).

13. See also Orbach (2008).
14. An example of brand extension is the production of iPod and iPhone by Apple. An example of brand stretching is the production of soft drinks by Virgin, an airline operator (and, before that, a record label).
15. It is interesting to note that, viewed in this light, brand has a similar function to money (another sign), with both acting as a 'store of value'. See note 7.
16. We refer to the implementation of Directive 89/104/EC, art. 4(4)(a) and 5(2) in Europe, and to the Federal Trademark Dilution Act of 1995 in the US. For a fuller discussion of this question the reader is referred to McCarthy (2004) and Ramello and Silva (2006).
17. Adidas-Salomon AG v. Fitnessworld Trading Ltd., 2003, 1 C.M.L.R. 14.
18. Lanham Act, Section 43c, 15 USC Section 112.
19. For example, if a producer of land mines were to use Armani as its trade name, this could by an indirect psychological association taint the reputation of the famous Armani brand in consumers' minds, and the quality they associate with it.
20. The semantic value of the famous brand is essentially 'dispersed' by indirect association with the similar brand. For example, a garment manufacturer that used the name Martini for its clothes would be appropriating some of the informational value of the Martini trademark through a form of indirect free riding, and so weakening its distinctive character.
21. Thomas Edison, the inventor of the phonograph, spoke of 'canned sound' (Ramello and Silva, 1999). Similarly, we can think of trademark as 'canned meaning'.

REFERENCES

Aaker, D.A. (1991). *Managing Brand Equity*. New York: Free Press.
Akerlof, G.A. (1970). The Market for Lemons: Quality Uncertainty and the Market Mechanism. *Quarterly Journal of Economics* 84: 488–500.
Babe, R.E. (1995). *Communication and the Transformation of Economics*. Boulder, CO and Oxford: Westview Press.
Bagwell, L. and Bernheim, B.D. (1996). 'Veblen Effects in a Theory of Conspicuous Consumption'. *American Economic Review* 86: 349–73.
Baroncelli, E., Fink, C. and Javorcik, B.S. (2005), 'The Global Distribution of Trademarks: Some Stylised Facts'. *World Economy* 28: 765–81.
Baudrillard, J. (1972). *Pour une Critique de l'Economie Politique du Signe*. Paris, Gallimard.
Beebe, B. (2004). 'The Semiotics of Trademark Law'. *UCLA Law Review* 51: 621–704.
Blackett, T. (1998). *Trademarks*. MacMillan, London.
Burk, D.L. and McDonnell, B.H. (2009). 'Trademarks and the Boundaries of the Firm'. *William & Mary Law Review* 51: 345–94.
Cabral, L.M.B. (2000). 'Stretching Firm and Brand Reputation'. *Rand Journal of Economics* 31: 658–73.
Choi, J.P. (1998). 'Brand Extension and Informational Leverage'. *Review of Economic Studies* 65: 655–69.
Clifton, R., Simmons J. and Ahmad S. (2004). *Brands and Branding*. The Economist-Bloomberg, Princeton, NJ.
Corneo, G. and Jeanne, O. (1997). 'Conspicuous Consumption, Snobbism and Conformism'. *Journal of Public Economics* 66: 55–71.
Da Silva, E.F. and Pereiera Peralta, P. (2011). 'Collective Marks and Geographical Indications – Competitive Strategy of Differentiation and Appropriation of Intangible Heritage'. *Journal of Intellectual Property Rights* 16: 246–57.
De Alessi, L. and R.J. Staaf (1994). 'What Does Reputation Really Assure? The Relationship of Trademarks to Expectations and Legal Remedies'. *Economic Inquiry*, 32: 477–85.

Dennett, D.C. (1997). *La mente e le menti. Verso una comprensione della conoscenza*, Sansoni, Milano.

Ehrenberg, A. and Barnard, N. (1997). 'Differentiation or Salience'. *Journal of Advertising Research* 37: 7–14.

Hart, O. (1995). *Firms, Contracts, and Financial Structure*. Oxford: Oxford University Press.

Heberden, T. and Haigh, D. (2006). 'The Role of Trademarks in M&A'. *Intellectual Asset Management Magazine* June/July: 37–41.

Jarrell, G. and Peltzman, S. (1985). 'The Impact of Product Recalls on the Wealth of Sellers'. *Journal of Political Economy* 93: 512–36.

Klemperer, P. (1995). 'Competition When Consumers Have Switching Costs: An Overview with Applications to Industrial Organization, Macroeconomics and International Trade'. *Review of Economics Studies* 62: 515–39.

Kong, Y. and Seldon, J.R. (2004). 'Pseudo-generic Products and Barriers to Entry in Pharmaceutical Markets'. *Review of Industrial Organization* 25: 71–86.

Lemley, M.A. (1999). 'The Modern Lanham Act and the Death of Common Sense'. *Yale Law Journal* 108: 1687–715.

Lunney, G. (1999). 'Trademark Monopolies'. *Emory Law Journal* 48: 367–487.

McCarthy, J.T. (2004). 'Dilution of a Trademark: European and United States Law Compared'. *Trademark Reporter* 94: 1163–81.

Moreschini L., Ramello G.B. and Santagata, W. (2012). *Un marchio per la valorizzazione dei territori di eccellenza: dai siti UNESCO ai luoghi italiani della cultura, dell'arte e del paesaggio*. Rubbettino, Roma.

Orbach, B.Y. (2008). 'Antitrust Vertical Myopia: The Allure of High Prices'. *Arizona Law Review* 50: 261–87.

Pepall, L.M. and Richards, D.J. (2002). 'The Simple Economics of Brand Stretching'. *Journal of Business* 75: 535–52.

Pine, B.J. and Gilmore, J.H. (1999). *The Experience Economy. Work is Theatre and Every Business a Stage*. Boston: Harvard Business School Press.

Ramello, G.B. (2006). 'What's in a Sign? Trademark Law and Economic Theory'. *Journal of Economic Surveys* 20: 547–65.

Ramello G.B. (2012). 'Economia del marchio Origine, trasformazioni e implicazioni per la gestione della produzione locale,' in Moreschini L., Ramello G.B. and Santagata W. (eds), *Un marchio per la valorizzazione dei territori di eccellenza: dai siti UNESCO ai luoghi italiani della cultura, dell'arte e del paesaggio*, Rubbettino, Roma.

Ramello, G.B. and Silva, F. (1999). *Dal Vinile a Internet. Economia della Musica tra Tecnologia e Diritto*, Edizioni della Fondazione Giovanni Agnelli, Torino.

Ramello, G.B. and Silva, F. (2006). 'Appropriating Signs and Meaning: the Elusive Economics of Trademark'. *Industrial and Corporate Change* 15: 937–63

Reymond, W. (2006). *Coca-Cola. L'enquête interdite*. Flammarion, Paris.

Shannon, C.E. and Weaver, W. (1962). *The Mathematical Theory of Communication*. Urbana: University of Illinois Press.

Shavell, S. (1987). *Economic Analysis of Accident Law*. Cambridge, MA: Harvard University Press.

Tadelis, S. (1999). 'What's in a name ? Reputation as a tradable asset'. *American Economic Review* 89: 548–63.

Teece, D.J. (1988). 'Technological Change and the Nature of the Firm', in G. Dosi, C. Freeman, R. Nelson, G. Silvergberg and L. Soete (eds). *Technological Change and Economic Theory*, Pinter: London.

Thrift, N. (2006). 'Re-inventing the Invention: New Tendencies in Capitalist Commodification'. *Economy and Society* 35: 270–306.

Tirole, J. (1988). *The Theory of Industrial Organization*. Cambridge, MA: MIT Press.

Veblen, T. (1899). *The Theory of the Leisure Class. An Economic Study of Institutions*. London, Macmillan.

Whinston, M.D. (1990). 'Tying, Foreclosure and Exclusion'. *American Economic Review* 80: 837–59.

Wilkins, M. (1992). 'The Neglected Intangible Asset: the Influence of the Trade Mark on the Rise of the Modern Corporation'. *Business History* 34: 66–95.

Williamson, O. (1985). *The Economic Institutions of Capitalism*. New York: Free Press.

Yoo, B. and Donthu, N. (1999). Developing and Validating a Multidimensional Consumer-based Brand Equity Scale. *Journal of Business Research* 52: 1–14.

Index

Aaker, D. 346, 347
Abraham, K. 50
accident risk reduction, and
  behavioural economics *see*
  behavioural economics perspective
  of regulation versus liability, and
  accident risk reduction
accident-insurance premiums, taxation
  of 36
accidents-between-strangers model,
  product-related risks 54, 55
active courts and menu contracts
  281–307
  active courts equilibria 285–6, 287,
    288, 290–3, 294, 295, 296–7,
    300–6
  active courts model 284–5
  asymmetric information 281, 282,
    283, 284, 289
  bundle contracts 287, 298–9, 304,
    305
  contractibility at ex-ante stage 283–7
  equilibria with no menu contracts
    285–6
  ex-ante welfare 281, 285–6, 288, 289
  hold-up problem 286, 296, 297–8,
    305
  menu contracts 286–8
  menu contracts, definition 287
  menu contracts, and non-
    contractibility 287
  menu contracts, simple and bundle
    contracts 287
  model 282–5
  passive courts equilibria 285, 287,
    288, 289–93, 294–5, 296–7,
    300–6
  passive courts model 282–4
  pooling equilibria 281, 285, 286,
    287
  separation of buyer types and
    increased welfare 285–6, 289–90
  simple contracts 287, 297, 301–2,
    303–4, 305, 306

take-it-or-leave-it offers 282, 284,
    285
truth-telling constraint 295–6,
    299–300, 301, 304, 305
activity levels, and tort liability *see* tort
    liability and regulation, economics
    of activity levels
Adams, M. 170
adjudication, and evidence *see*
    evidence
administrative costs
  and average harm, strict liability
    when victims choose value of
    asset at risk 89
  tort liability and regulation activity
    levels 42, 46–7
  tort standards and legal expenditures
    156
adversarial versus inquisitorial
    systems 168–70, 176, 177,
    178
adverse selection problem and quality
    uncertainty, trademark, multi-
    layered action of 344
affirmative action, efficiency with
    purely historical discrimination
    308–40
  conditional ability distribution after
    discrimination ends 311
  constitutionality in higher education
    310
  convergence, schooling success and
    future productivity 311
  minority preferences, importance
    of, and voluntary affirmative
    action 310–11
  minority's expected ability greater
    than a non-minority's of the
    same class 310–11
  parents' success, impact on children's
    success 311–12
  voluntary affirmative action,
    criticism and limited use of
    309–10